THE WEDDING
OF THE DEAD

Studies on the History of Society and Culture
Victoria E. Bonnell and Lynn Hunt, Editors

THE WEDDING
OF THE DEAD

*Ritual, Poetics, and Popular Culture
in Transylvania*

GAIL KLIGMAN

UNIVERSITY OF CALIFORNIA PRESS
BERKELEY   LOS ANGELES   LONDON

University of California Press
Berkeley and Los Angeles, California

University of California Press, Ltd.
London, England

Library of Congress Cataloging-in-Publication Data

Kligman, Gail.
   The wedding of the dead: ritual, poetics, and popular culture in
Transylvania / Gail Kligman.
      p. cm.—(Studies on the history of society and culture)
   Bibliography: p.
   Includes index.
   ISBN 0-520-06001-6 (alk. paper)
    1. Maramureş (Romania: Judeţ)—Social life and customs. 2. Rites
and ceremonies—Romania—Maramureş (Judeţ) 3. Folk poetry—
Romania— Maramureş (Judeţ) I. Title. II. Series.
DR281.M3K55   1988
949.8′4—dc19   87-25638
                                                    CIP

Printed in the United States of America

1 2 3 4 5 6 7 8 9

A cassette of recordings illustrating the primary ritual
sequences of weddings, funerals, and death-weddings may be
obtained from the author.

lui MIHAI POP

> *Străină, străinătate*
> *Mult mni-ai fo soră şî frate*
> *Şî mni si pînă la moarte.*

Contents

Acknowledgments

My greatest debt is to the people of Ieud who, over the years, have welcomed me into their lives with interest, warmth, and friendship. To them, I offer this book—my interpretation of vital aspects of their lives—as an expression of my respect and affection. Mulţam fain!

I am also indebted to many persons whose encouragement was indispensable to the completion of this project, including friends and colleagues here and abroad and the members of my family. To all of you, too numerous to cite, my deepest gratitude. I especially wish to acknowledge the extended Balea family (particularly Mătuşă Juji and Şandri), Dan Chirot, Harvey Goldman, Eric and Margo Hamp, Keith Hitchins, Vlada Ilić, Ken Jowitt, Claude Karnoouh, Albert and Lori Kligman, Michael Kligman, Ben Lee, Kiki Munshi, Jason Parker, Mihai and Irina Pop, Moishe Postone, Brigitte and Martin Riesebrodt, Marshall and Barbara Sahlins, Nancy Scheper-Hughes and family, Michael Silverstein, Beth Shephard, Theda Skocpol, Mira Stevanović, Betsy Traube, Ruth Tringham, Beatrice Troyan, Katherine Verdery, Susan Woodward, and Jack Zipes, as well as Nicu, Ioană and Mihai, and Toderău.

I wish to thank the following institutions for their generous support throughout the various phases of this project: the American Council of Learned Societies, the Center for European Studies at Harvard University, the Center for Slavic and East European Studies at the University of California-Berkeley, the International Federation of University Women, the International Research and Exchanges Board, the Mellon Foundation, the National Endowment for the Humanities, and the University of Chicago Social Science Divisional Research Fund. I am also grateful for the cooperation of these institutions in Romania: the Academy of Social and Political Sciences, the National Council for Science and Technology, the Institute for Ethnographic and Dialectologic Research, the American Embassy, and, notably, the Ethnographic Museum of Maramureş.

I am also grateful to Eugene Hammel and Greg Urban for their computer assistance. Their efforts resulted in the Romanian font used in manuscript form. In like fashion, I wish to thank Sanda Golopenţia for her generosity in scrutinizing the final draft of the Maramureş ritual texts, and Donna Buchanan for her good-natured assistance with proofreading and related tedious tasks. Last, but surely not least, I wish to express my appreciation for the tolerance and good will extended by the University of California Press, especially by Sheila Levine, Mary Renaud, and Barbara Armentrout. Thank you all!

Notes on the Maramureş Dialect

An exact phonetic transcription of the spoken dialect would be overladen with diacritic marks that, for typographical reasons, have had to be omitted. Translation of the dialect into literary Romanian, however, would result in a significant distortion of the "texts," altering the rhymes, rhythms, nuances, and oral compositional subtleties. For the sake of clarity for the general reader, as well as representativeness of the oral tradition, I have chosen a mode of transcription that may be considered an adequate compromise: it retains basic features of the spoken dialect while simplifying the representational form. To this end, I wish to thank Dr. Prof. Mihai Pop, Magdalena Vulpe, and Ioană and Mihai Dăncuş for their generous assistance, as well as acknowledging Iuliana Balea of Ieud and Professor Ronelle Alexander of Berkeley for their contributions.

There is considerable variation from one village to another; hence, the transcription adheres to the *grai,* or speech, of Ieud. Pronunciation also differs within the village; this difference tends to be accentuated between the generations. The following points should be noted in reading the texts:

1. In Maramureş, there is a tendency to eliminate the final syllable of verb forms, of vocative forms of proper names (e.g., *Ştefan* = *Şte*), of the preposition *fără* (without), which becomes *făr.* As is general in spoken Romanian, the consonants *l* and *n* in final position are frequently dropped: *drumul* = *drumu; nimen* = *nime.*

2. All pronouns have been written with *i* preceding *e* because of the colloquial pronunciation; this is not specific to Maramureş but is a general phenomenon: *el* = *iel*.

3. In Maramureş, the phonetic distinction between the reflexive particle *se* and the future particle *să* has been lost. As a rule, *se* is pronounced as *să*. Similarly, the preposition *pe* is pronounced as *pă*; *de pe* = *di pă*; *dece* = *diptce*. Also, *aşa* is pronounced as *aşă* or *ăşe*, depending on the rhyme.

4. The consonants *m, n, l, t* are palatalized in position before *i* or *e*: *n'e* as in *bin'e*; in the case of *m + i = mn'i*, for example, *mire = mnire*. Also, *t* and *d* followed by *e* or *i* are pronounced as soft sounds.

5. The final *i* of the plural forms of names and of second person verb forms is not pronounced after *s, z, ş, ţ*.

6. *Şi* becomes *şî* except when followed by *i*, for example, *şî m-am dus, şi ieu*.

7. The following correspondences are relatively constant:

Standard Romanian	Dialect	Examples
v	*z*	*vin = zin*
f	*s*	*fin = sin*
ch/e	*t*	*chemat = temat*
gh/e	*d*	*gheaţa = deaţa*
j/o,u	*gi*	*joc = gioc*
p/i	*pti*	*picior = pticior*
b/i	*bdi*	*bietu = bdietu*

8. Regarding pronunciation of vowels:
   All accented *es* are more open than the normal Romanian *e*, as is the accented diphthong *ea* in final position, for example, *mea = me*.
   The diphthong *oa* is pronounced as an open *o*, for example, *doarme = dorme*.

For further detail on the Maramureş dialect, see Vulpe 1984.

Notes on the Ritual Poetry

Punctuation of the Romanian rhymed couplets has been kept to an absolute minimum. Capitals indicate lines. Periods are the major linguistic unit and set off the couplets, or triplets when expanded. In the latter case, two-line phrases that are not couplets can usually substitute for the second line of a couplet; also, the first line of the couplet may be introduced by a formulaic. No transcription conventions for performative analysis (such as pause, intonation, prosody) are used. In keeping with performative style, however, vocatives are not highlighted by commas. (The substitution of names and terms of address is determined by context and the performer.) In the wedding shouts, optional formulaic nonreferential phrases have generally been deleted. For example, *hai hai dorule hai* or *e hai și iară hai* can introduce or close a couplet, thereby bracketing it. This occurs infrequently for individual lines. In funeral laments, lamenters customarily repeat each line in the construction of the couplet.

The Romanian and English lines correspond, although their punctuation differs. In the interest of conveying meaning and feeling, the translation is not literal, nor have I attempted to produce the poetry in rhyme. Here, I borrow from J. Massey, who translated Feuerbach's *Thoughts on Death and Immortality* (1980). Feuerbach, like his romantic predecessors, believed poetry to be the "language of the heart." In his translation, Massey noted that he did not "reproduce the heavy beat or the rhymes of the doggerel," arguing that the poetry is more significantly "a didactic attempt to clothe philosophical ideas in aesthetic form" (1980, xlii).

Introduction: Beyond Dracula

Having some time at my disposal when in London, I had visited the British Museum, and made search among books and maps in the library regarding Transylvania; it had struck me that some foreknowledge of the country could hardly fail to have some importance in dealing with a noble of that country. I find that the district he names is . . . in the midst of the Carpathian mountains; one of the wildest and least known portions of Europe.

Jonathan Harker's journal,
Chapter 1, *Dracula*

We are in Transylvania; and Transylvania is not England. Our ways are not your ways, and there shall be to you many strange things . . .

Count Dracula to Jonathan Harker

I must confess that Dracula was not the compelling force that lured me to Transylvania. To be sure, the count of Western popular and literary fame is not of Transylvania's nobility. Their Dracula was a fifteenth-century prince, Vlad Ţepeş, otherwise known as Vlad the Impaler, son of Vlad Dracul.[1] Our Dracula is a Gothic man, son of an English imagination that gave life to a man and a place whose symbolic significance has deeply penetrated Western thought. Dracula is a popular figure, a man (notably not a superman or a monster) through whom the horrors of death and the frustration of mortality may be confronted. Culture over nature, body and soul reunited: Dracula embodies and struggles with the treacherous intermingling of fundamental dilemmas of human existence—death, love, sexuality, desire, domination, control over nature. By defying death, Dracula defies nature. He is neither alive nor dead, but rather thrives betwixt and between the living and the dead. As

1

Craft stylishly notes (1984, 117), Dracula "is *nosferatu*, neither dead nor alive but somehow both, mobile frequenter of the grave and the boudoir." But this Dracula is a cultural construct. He is a figure through whom the paradoxical relationship between sexuality and mortality may be probed. Because ultimately he is human, he must succumb to the natural order of our cultural process. Immortality is left to the gods. Nonetheless, given his nature and complexities, Dracula's very essence ensures his production and reproduction throughout time. After all, death is a universal phenomenon.

Dracula, in contrast, is not. He is culturally constituted, just as our image of his Transylvania is. That Transylvania is conceived of as a rather uncivilized boundary of European civilization. (It was to magical Transylvania that the Pied Piper led the children of Hamelin.)[2] Only in the chaos of "one of the wildest and least known portions of Europe" could Dracula thrive. Only in the "horseshoe" of the Carpathian Mountains where "every known superstition in the world is gathered" (Wolf 1975, 4) could the objectivity of scientific rationalism be suspended and death be denied by Western thought. There, in the imagined wilds of that outermost border of familiarity, it was acceptable, even desirable, for the imagination to reflect freely on flagrant transgressions of social norms unthinkable in late Victorian culture. Closer to home, propriety had to prevail, desire had to be checked against wanton expression; science and religion conspired to bring sexuality and death firmly under their reins.[3] When Count Dracula arrived in the "civilized" world of England, his secret was destined to be discovered by the learned man of science, A. Van Helsing, M.D., D.Phil., D.Lit. Eventually, employing the wisdom of science informed by the tenets of Christian morality, the good doctor and his Crew of Light put an end to the ravages of this bedeviled being. Together, as well as apart, science and religion triumphed, in reality and fiction, as the arbiters of the social contract of society.[4]

Dracula is an enduring personality in Western culture; his natal territory, "Transylvania," has also attained mythical stature.[5] This is not, however, a book about Dracula, nor is it my intention to demystify his significance in the West. Contrary to popular belief among many Americans, Transylvania does exist.[6] Although vampire lore is not restricted to this locale, it is more than coincidence that vampire beliefs are most commonly associated with this area.[7] Historically, Transylvania and the Balkans were the meeting place of Eastern and Western trade and religion. In these lands the Catholic church encountered considerable resistance to its eastward expansion in the seventeenth century. To influence those who subscribed to the teachings of Islam and Orthodox Christianity, the Catholic church seems to have employed vampire lore to considerable advantage. According to Twitchell (1981, 15), its emissaries proclaimed that "all who were buried in unconsecrated ground would be denied eternal rest, instead becoming vampires." Moreover, "if the church fostered the threatening parts of the vampire superstition, it also provided solace for the true believer, for it took upon itself the defense of the local populace. It was a closed system, with the institution that was providing the monsters also providing the protection" in the form of the Bible, crosses, and rosaries.[8]

Today, the meeting place of East and West is Eastern Europe in general. Politics has superseded trade and religion as a defining characteristic. And it is in Eastern Europe that Transylvania is located—in the Socialist Republic of Romania at present, a location all the more interesting in view of the mythical status often attributed to communism and communists. In any case, the popular assumptions (negative and positive) about "Transylvania" and "communism" surely underscore the potency of symbols. This book *is* about particular inhabitants of Transylvania and the beliefs and ritual practices that contribute to shaping their lives in a contemporary socialist state. Therefore, it *is* my intention, in part, to go "beyond Dracula" and demystify the mythical Transylvania, thus bringing the venerable count's alleged homeland to life. Indeed, he was correct to observe that "our ways are not your ways." What about the ways of Transylvania, the "land beyond the forest"?

Transylvania's history is long and tumultuous, and it continues to be contested as states rewrite history and vie for rights to a "formalized social past."[9] Transylvania bridges Hungary and Romania, and therein lies the source of the current Transylvanian debate: once part of the Austro-Hungarian empire, Transylvania is now one of the three provinces forming the Socialist Republic of Romania. It is the most ethnically heterogeneous of the three, populated predominantly by Romanians, Hungarians, and Saxon Germans.

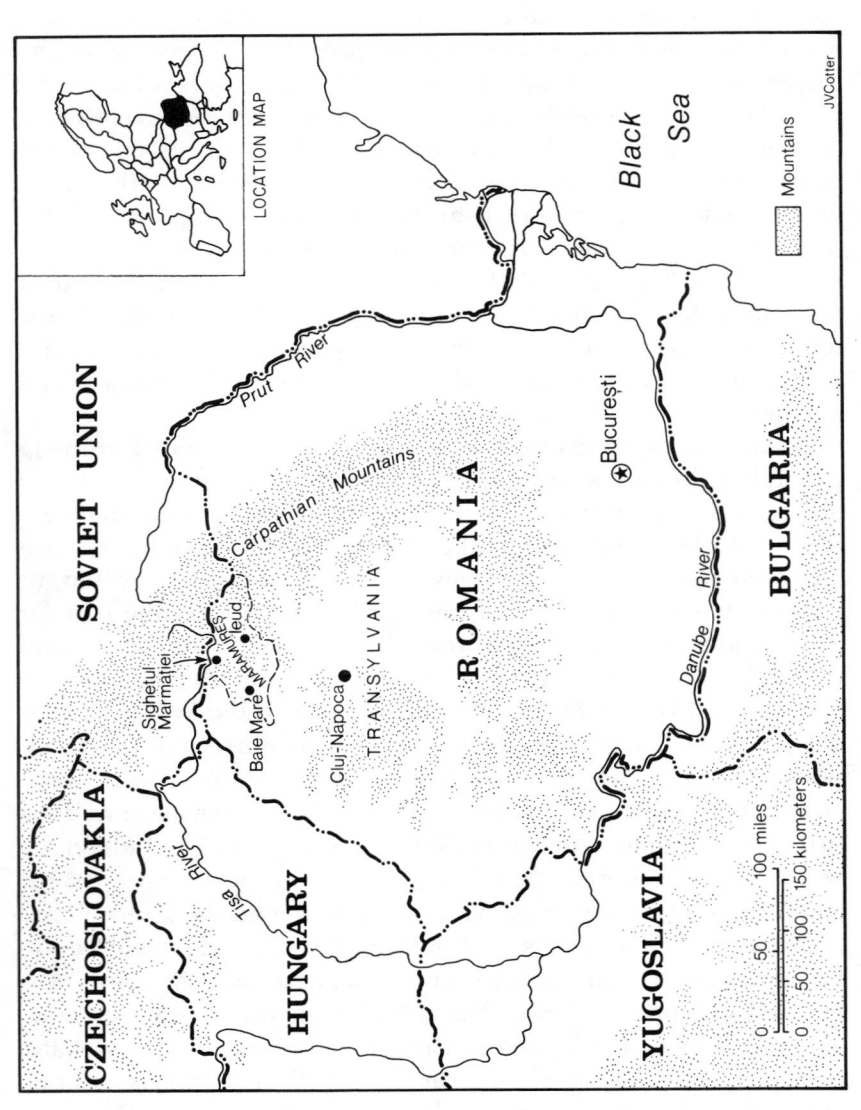

The Carpathian Mountains, whose primary branches run north-south and east-west respectively, form a natural chain demarcating the eastern and southern boundaries of Transylvania. MacArthur (1981, 21) notes that "inhabitants of Romania jokingly remark that their country is inside-out, with its mountains in the middle and its plains exposed on the borders."

It was Maramureş, an isolated northern region of this Transylvania, that seduced my curiosity. The area known as "historical Maramureş" is surrounded by mountains except to its northwest.[10] The Maramureş Mountains (1,500–2,000 m) mark the northeastern border with Bukovina and the Ukraine; the Rodnei Mountains (2,000 m) serve as the southeastern boundary; the Ţibleş Mountains (1,400–1,800 m), the southern; and the Gutîi Mountains, the western. The Gutîi Mountains diminish into rolling hills that separate Maramureş from the neighboring western region of Oaş. The Tiza River constitutes a northern border abutting the Soviet Union. I was fascinated by the lyrical beauty of the land and the colorful, textured apparel and weathered faces of many of its inhabitants, which lend human tones to the natural richness of the landscape. Wooden houses and intricately carved churches are testaments to history and a particular way of life, mode of production, and relationship with the environment.

Yet tangible signs of modernization cannot be ignored. Building codes demand that new houses conform to a two-story minimum, and villa-type homes, of cement and wood, are increasingly found along primary roads and dotting village interiors. Electricity, refrigerators, televisions, cars—all are sought and acquired as soon as possible, reflecting in part a desire to be "modern," to make life easier and more comfortable, or, in other words, to redefine oneself through possessions. The meaning of private property has been radically altered, no longer referring particularly to land, but rather to objects.[11] The boundaries of self, family, village, and region have all changed, expanded to articulate with the state. History is in the process of being revised. But from whose standpoint?

Enchanted tourists and social scientists, mostly from Western Europe and the United States, find solace in the idyllic beauty and traditional way of life that superficially characterize Maramureş. Meanwhile, progress-oriented officials in Bucureşti (Bucharest), Romania's capital, speak disdainfully of Maramureş's "backward-

ness" and seemingly resistant "uncivilized peasant way of life."
How to reconcile obvious emblems of the past—peasants and their
way of life—with the dynamic "modernity" of the socialist present?
From center to periphery, Moroşeni, as inhabitants of this region
call themselves, are now cast as living guardians of a creative Romanian cultural heritage (see also Marrant 1977). The present of
peasants may have been rationalized, but as Verdery (1983a, 428)
has pointed out about other Transylvanian villagers,

the long-term trend . . . is not precisely toward an ever more antagonistic
relationship between peasant and state but toward dialectical simplification of the social field within which both parties operate, a simplification
that has worked to the state's advantage and left peasants relatively more
powerless. In the present, the stage is set for further simplification of the
field by eliminating the peasants themselves.

Recognition of the dynamic relationship between center and periphery, individuals and states, local systems and their broader
contexts—these are topics of contemporary inquiries and are crucial to an understanding of human thought and action.[12] Throughout history, centers of power have eagerly defined the "other" in
an attempt to legitimate the self. To varying degrees, social relations, identities, and interactions have been predicated upon constructed hierarchies of domination and subordination. Although an
encompassing definition of "peasants" as a category does not exist,
it is generally agreed that "structural subordination of the peasantry to external forces is an essential aspect of its definition" (Mintz
1973, 74) and thereby ensures continual expropriation of surpluses
and limited access to positions of power.[13] For the peasants of Maramureş, history has repeatedly proven officially determined categories transient; until 1918, Moroşeni were peasants in Hungary
(although not necessarily Hungarian peasants); today, they may be
peasant-workers (not necessarily Romanian) in Romania or Romanians in "open-air ethnographic museums" (*Romanian News*, June
1981, 15), depending on the frame of reference. Their structural
subordination is such that some suggest peasants will cease to
exist.[14]

Peasants, the primary subjects of this book, have always been
objects. They have been exploited by lords and nations, as well as
by scholars. Although the world's population has a peasant major-

ity, peasants have rarely been regarded as responsible actors; generally, they have been acted upon and silenced. As we shall see, this does not mean that they have nothing to say (Karnoouh 1982, 105; Verdery 1983a, 371). The historical experience of Moroşeni, partially determined by their relative isolation and poverty, has given rise to a strong regional identity (Marrant 1977) that today confronts the nationalist interests of the Romanian state.

Since 1948, the Communist Party of Romania has pursued the building of its socialist state, in part through centralization, mass education, the establishment of modern bureaucracies, and the fostering of a Romanian national identity. Property and social relations have been rapidly transformed. Centralization of the means of production with emphasis on forced industrialization initially led to dramatic economic development (Jowitt 1971; Turnock 1974; Cole 1976; Chirot 1978; Graham 1982; Shafir 1985), but it is now recognized that this growth was at the expense of the agricultural sector. Moreover, because the priorities of state planners have reflected "production mentalities" focused on rapid transformation in the economic, political, and social realms, cultural transformation has been considered an essentially derivative phenomenon. This raises the dilemma of what Jowitt (1974, 1176) terms the "paradoxical character of system-building regimes":

In their attempt to critically redefine society, Marxist-Leninist regimes simultaneously achieve basic, far-reaching, and decisive change in certain areas, allow for the maintenance of pre-revolutionary behavioral and attitudinal political postures in others, and unintentionally strengthen many traditional postures in what for the regime are often priority areas.

In short, rapid planned change is a complex and often confounding process.[15]

Implicit in the building of the socialist state is the construction of the "new man" (Ceauşescu 1976).[16] Who that new man is and how he shall be fashioned remain ambiguous. What is known is that this individual should embody the values of socialism, cleansed of bourgeois tendencies.[17] To achieve this end, ideologues must educate the masses and scrutinize political, social, and cultural products (e.g., music, art, literature, speeches) to determine their acceptability. (Thus censorship is rationalized as not only legitimate but also critical.) This process of creating a "new socialist

man" is obviously not a simple task. Lenin cautioned that "the transformation of all customs and practices . . . is a work of de-
. cades." Nicolae Ceauşescu, president of Romania, has acknowledged the wisdom of that observation: "As you can see, we have had an easy time constructing factories. But it is incumbent on us to transform man at the same rate so that he will be capable of mastering new techniques . . . and new ways of thinking." As Karnoouh has noted, the much-desired new man has not yet emerged. Rather, the "ideal citizen of the post-Stalin Communist state is once again a bastard compromise between worker and peasant, in which the first would carry the promises of an ever-awaited future affluent society, legitimated by the historical fidelity of the second" (1982, 105).[18]

To be sure, socioeconomic transformation under the dictates of the Communist Party has greatly altered the rhythms of village life. In part, this study is an attempt to examine ideology as lived, rather than as posited from center to periphery, recognizing that both frames of reference interact with and influence each other. Within the overarching system of social and production relations promulgated by the state, the necessities of everyday life incorporate the intricacies of family and community, social and productive relations. As E. P. Thompson notes: "What changes, as the mode of production and productive relations change, is the experience of living men and women" (1979, 21). How do the Moroşeni conceptualize and perceive themselves and their "lived-in" world, as others design the alteration of their more familiar identities? In this book, I analyze the beliefs and practices associated with particular life-cycle rituals—weddings, funerals, and death-weddings— as a means of providing insights into the lives of these people. For the Moroşeni, their traditions have always been integral features of their identity. Through these familiar structures of experience, they have made sense of and interpreted their "lived-in" world.

Thus, this book is about fundamental aspects of contemporary life in a Maramureş village: how certain significant events—life-cycle rites—are constituted, managed, understood, and made meaningful. I wish neither to reify nor to decontextualize a local community, nor to deny it an identity other than that determined by external forces. Instead, I hope to remain sensitive to the complexities of life in this village, and to life in the Socialist Republic of

Romania, therein highlighting the relationship between structural and historical necessity.

The Dynamics of Ritual

Why focus on life-cycle rituals in a modernizing, socialist state? Peasants, rituals—they are reminders of a propertied past and are often associated with resistance to change, mystified thinking, and the like. Although these rites are elaborate, visible components of everyday life in Maramureş, they are no longer characteristic of most of Romania.[19] By any measure of modernity, Maramureş is relatively backward. Such a statement, however, requires more thorough consideration. How is this evaluation of backwardness revealing or misleading? Throughout this period of rapid change, these ritual traditions have increasingly become the organizing structures through which communities in this region reconstitute themselves as communities. That, in and of itself, indicates the depth of socioeconomic transformation. Moroşeni respect their "traditions," yet they too are avid conspicuous consumers, as eager as anyone else to acquire the commodities that lessen daily burdens.

The Romanian state has sanctioned the Orthodox church to represent its religious heritage; the Orthodox church, in turn, has tacitly sanctioned popular ritual practices—in an area that until recently was of Uniate (Greek Catholic) persuasion. What is the relationship between religion and ritual? And, of greater interest to me, what is the relationship between ritual traditions and the state? Resistance to change, in certain circumstances, may suggest or belie counterhegemonic undertones. Why does the state tolerate, indeed value, these traditions—the "folklore" of this peripheral area? Peripherality provides an obvious, but inadequate, answer (Marrant 1977; Karnoouh 1982). It must be recognized that the particularities of geographic location, an "archaic" dialect, and "ancient" traditions all in this northern corner of Transylvania serve the interests of the state in its claims for political and territorial legitimacy. And the state, inventing its own traditions (Hobsbawm and Ranger 1983), requires the participation of its historical tradition bearers—the peasants. Clearly, to focus on ritual is not simply to romanticize the past, a presocialist past at that. Instead, the focus on life-cycle rituals offers a means to explore the extant beliefs and practices that constitute contemporary communities and that locate persons within these communities as well as within the Romanian state.

About Ritual

Ritual may be seen as a dramatic form of symbolic action that articulates the relationship between a symbolically constructed order of meanings and a system of interpersonal and institutional relationships.[20] The rituals to be explored in this book comprise a system of beliefs and practices that address existential anxieties as well as the practical complexities of everyday social experience. Hence, they refer to transcendent and material concerns. Life-cycle rituals encode the norms, values, and rules of the social world they represent. In so doing, they reflect the past and constitute the present—hence the jargon of ritual simultaneously reflects and constitutes social reality. Rituals, through the representation of rules, norms, and values, provide prescriptive and proscriptive codes that inform (but do not determine) consciousness and action. Thus, rituals are both exemplary and constraining. Within this framework, they also incorporate that which is within the realm of normative possibility. Although rituals, deeply embedded in local life, invite the crystallization of existing norms and values in every symbolic mode, it needs to be stressed that existing norms and values are themselves responsive to sociohistorical circumstances. They do change (although, as increasing materialism in ritual display demonstrates, not as readily as commodities). Hence, rituals do not present a synchronic, static vision of culture in history, but rather produce a structure of relations in time and space sensitive to historical transformation. As T. Turner points out: "Ritual, as a symbolic model of the social order that also attempts to be an effective means of regulating that order, is grounded upon the same fundamental structural and *dynamic* principles as society itself" (1977, 61, emphasis added). Rituals impose a hegemonic view upon what are actually paradoxical realities, thereby ordering and controlling the transitions and the potential disorder associated with them.[21] Karnoouh, emphasizing this, notes that rituals are able to transform events into an intelligible reality "due to the charismatic force of [their] representation" (1983a, 33). In this manner, rituals control both desire and danger while introducing them into the conceptual, and affective, orders of experience.

As I will discuss more fully in the final chapter of this book, however, experience is not as consistent as the ideals extolled in ritual would have it be. Consequently, a direct correspondence between ritual and daily practice does not exist.[22] There is, rather, a dynamic interaction between ritual representation and everyday experience. This is significant both for individuals as actors in a social system and for emotional-affective states. As the Durkheimian legacy teaches, ritual "works upon" both conceptual and affective dimensions of action. Its power lies in an ability to articulate the nature of social consciousness while appropriating individual experience to it (Mauss 1950; Munn 1974; Bourdieu 1977). Again, ritual (re)presents the ideals of social organization. It does not—nor can it—dictate individual behavior or affect. The "life cycle" treated by these rites is that of individuals in social contexts, as social selves. These rites address the cultural shaping of consciousness, emotion, and action. They treat collective, as opposed to individual, subjectivity. (Therefore, individuals attempting to control their fates resort to magic practices performed privately or with a specialist.)[23] The focus of these collective representations is on conventionalized behavior, on the sociocentric rather than on the egocentric (or on social identities rather than individual identities). Consequently, as Tambiah (among others) has underlined: "Rituals as conventionalized behavior are not designed or meant to express the intentions, emotions and states of mind of individuals in a direct, spontaneous and 'natural' way. Cultural elaboration of codes consists in the 'distancing' from such spontaneous and intentional expressions because spontaneity and intentionality are, or can be, contingent, labile, circumstantial, even incoherent and disordered" (1979, 124).[24] As noted in the preceding discussion, lack of control is not the "function" of these rites. It is important to keep this in mind throughout the reading of this book. What is said and what is actually done day to day, or individually felt, may differ considerably. These rituals do not necessarily represent everyday interactions. Instead, they pose the premises of the social contract on which everyday interactions are based.

The specific rituals to be analyzed in this text—weddings and funerals—are the most marked occasions of the life cycle because they produce as well as reproduce the social order itself, conjoining individual and social-structural developmental cycles. Life-cycle rituals, in particular, may be viewed as condensed, symbolic expressions of the nature and dimensions of social relations and exchange. Weddings and funerals realign social relations and, hence, affect economic institutions. And they require collective participation, thereby representing the ritual transformation of the individual as a transformation of the collectivity. During these events, categories that order beliefs, values, and codes for action are brought together and reorganized. Even though the primary concern of these occasions may appear to be the "texturing of social and domestic relationships" (Thompson 1971, 7; and M. Pop 1976, 172), the "field" of such relationships is not confined to the local. These rites of passage help social actors redefine their social selves within the changing context of their lives. Currently, that context is the Socialist Republic of Romania.

In essence, these life-cycle rites express a system of thought and action that structures fundamental relations between the sexes, life and death, and nature and culture. This system makes it possible for disorder—such as illness, untimely death, or upheaval—to be meaningfully incorporated into experience and made comprehensible. The most poignant case occurs in the death-wedding—a symbolic marriage that takes place during the funeral of an unmarried person of nubile age. Via the cyclical movement of individuals through time and space, this ritual complex of weddings, funerals, and death-weddings constitutes a symbolic microcosm of the processes of cultural continuity and change.

But what about birth? Why not discuss it in like detail? To be sure, birth is a fundamental feature of the life cycle. In the cultural sense of the life cycle of these people, however, birth is not as publicly ritualized as marriage and death, which are the events of the cultural cycle that give meaning to social and biological change. Birth provokes the incorporation of a child into the social world of the living and the dead (see Karnoouh 1986). But within the framework of Christian cosmology as understood in this community, children are not fully acting persons until their first communion. Prior to World War I, gender was not differentiated through clothing styles until first communion or until the child was able to unknot his or her preserved umbilical cord. (The "presentation of the body" will be elaborated throughout this analysis. See, for example, Hebdige 1979; T. Turner n.d.) Moreover, the relationship between birth and social life was, until recently, a precarious one. During the interwar period, both the birthrate and the infant mortality rate in this region were the highest in Europe (Marrant 1977, 89). The death of an infant was, and is, understood as a manifestation of God's will. If a child died, then God might give another.[25] Men and women are meant to reproduce. One consequence of this strong belief in God's will is that these Romanians do not experience in the same way the hardships felt by urban residents or members of the younger generation in today's pronatalist state (see Nydon 1984).[26] Life and death are ultimately expressions of God's will, and birth is therefore not accorded the same social significance it receives where the "individual" is celebrated from the moment of birth (as in American culture). Because this book represents an attempt to reveal an other's beliefs and practices, birth will not be treated explicitly. Nonetheless, throughout this exploration, birth should be considered the absent presence that it is.

Ritual Poetry

Ritual in Maramureş features elaborate ritual action and ritual language. These will be explored throughout Chapters 2, 3, and 4; at this point, however, a few words on ritual language are in order. A rich oral poetic tradition flourishes. Generally speaking, poetry holds a privileged position in Romania (as it does elsewhere in Eastern Europe).[27] It is also used by the state for educational, ideological purposes (Pop and Ruxăndoiu 1976; Kligman 1983). Cultural ideologues use these poetic forms to inculcate progressive values. Pro-communist poetry highlights the merits of socialist work in transforming society and culture, as well as commitment to the Party and to progress through scientific rationalism and technological advance.[28] Poetry, popular and literary, is considered to be the "chosen music" of words. Rhymed couplets, traditional and improvised, constitute the primary mode of oral communication during ritual occasions (when they are sung, shouted, or wailed, depending on the event), but they are also used during informal social interactions as well as in correspondence (for example, love letters, letters sent from the front).[29] Karnoouh notes that in Maramureş, people "sing when they drink, sing for the hen during a wedding, lament the dead, sing Christmas carols, dance and sing for the bride . . . but never do they think they are creating poetry" (1983a, 43). Rather, poetry is an integral mode of conceptualizing the world in which these people live; it is not recognized as a unique genre of communication. Romanian poetry is usually characterized by a seven- or eight-syllable line, the latter being most common, with five and six syllables occasionally encountered. Couplet-rhyme formation, end rhyme, internal text redundancy, inversion, and parallelisms are also typical (Brăiloiu 1967; I. Bîrlea 1968, 2:28–74; Bartók 1975, 5–43; Pop and Ruxăndoiu 1976, 79–87).

Ritual poetry, which is the focus of this inquiry, falls within the broader category of lyric poetry. According to Romanian specialists, "the vitality (of lyric songs and shouts) is determined by their greater capacity to adapt to contemporary life" (Pop and Ruxăndoiu 1976, 339). Poetry is considered the child of experience and is a vehicle to make sense of it. "He who experiences much, he is the one who makes songs" is the claim of a couplet that was constantly cited during discussions about poetic discourse. "Poetry is a good comrade in joy and in sorrow," suggested a seventh-grade pupil in 1979. Poetry in ritual or written form or transmitted over the radio in modern songs is part of a living tradition. In Maramureş, the weddings feature *strigături* (shouted couplets) and songs; the funerals feature laments.[30] (These will be discussed in the chapters on weddings, funerals, and death-weddings.) Everyone, male and female, shares a facility with and understanding of the codes and conventions of this poetic tradition. Aesthetic judgments are based on whether the creative process yields couplets that *a să văji*, or go together, or harmonize in the broadest sense. As Karnoouh has pointed out, harmonization "by means of comparison between two or more terms is not a matter of a simple formal agreement between a series of verses and distiches, but beyond that, establishes a complex correspondence (semantic, metaphoric, and symbolic) between a concrete situation . . . and the exigencies of a Law" (1983a, 43).[31] The ritual poetry that will be discussed throughout this book primarily, although not exclusively, represents the voices of women, because women are central ritual participants in life-cycle rites. Women are predominantly featured during the ceremonial sequences, with the exception of the bargaining for the bride. And during funerals, only women lament. Poetic discourse, however, is not a domain only for women. Women do not customarily "shout" while dancing. Men and women are both highly proficient at the poetic discourse of celebration (throughout the wedding and at other celebratory events).[32] That women are highlighted during the life-cycle rites, and therefore in this book, is a consequence of cultural premises, which will become clearer as presentation of this rich material unfolds. Both men and women are the bearers of tradition. There is an immanent complementarity even though one or the other sex may appear to be a more active participant. In such cases (as is true of birth), the other is a vital absent presence. These rituals pertain to communities, to social selves.

The rhymed couplets of ritual language are collective representations par excellence. They are also understood to be objectified forms (Jakobson 1960; Silverstein 1979). Hence, they are generally accepted as unsigned or unauthored texts, that is, as external to individual intentions. Content ranges from the expression of fundamental attitudes about life, norms, and values to specific problems of dispute, personal trauma, and social change. Thus, these couplets provide a versified discourse about matters such as morality, sexuality, drinking, love, kinship, aging, and death, as well as socio-economic-political change. The content of these couplets is intimately linked to the circumstances in which they are invoked, but it may also point to transcendent social concerns, thereby offering a forum for social and political critique. (This is historically the case.) It must be pointed out, however, that the ritual context for voicing these concerns creates only a quasi-public sphere in which opinion may be presented but not posited with conviction. The formal features of ritual and oral poetry create a certain anonymity, but individuals live within the state, and the state's inhabitants are ever aware of its presence. Hence, local discourse exists in relation to dominant discourses. Villagers may talk about poetry and protest in terms of counter-hegemonic potential, but this function is circumscribed by the nature of power relations and the possible consequences. I did not hear forthright political criticism during ritual occasions. At this level of interpretation, intimate knowledge of context is crucial for the translation of intent and meaning.[33]

The dynamic relationship between text and context is fundamental to the comprehension of symbolic language (both speech and action as well as ritual poetry and ritual acts). Regarding oral poetry, figurative language colors the "poetic imagination" (see especially Friedrich 1979a). Language, by and large, communicates through metaphoric processes that include metaphor and metonym. These reflect primary conceptual processes involved in thought, action, and expression;[34] they are central to an analysis of ritual language and action. Metaphor, briefly described, is usually associated with similarity; it is "a way of conceiving of one thing in terms of another, and its primary function is understanding" (Lakoff and Johnson 1980, 46). Metonym, intrinsically related to metaphor, is based on contiguity; "metonymic concepts allow us to conceptualize one thing by means of its relation to something else" (ibid., 39; metonym is generally discussed in terms of part-whole relations). Metonym is grounded in empirical experience and is, therefore, highly referential in its function. Together, metaphors and metonyms "form coherent systems in terms of which we conceptualize our experience" (ibid., 41).

The life-cycle rituals analyzed in this book form a coherent system through which life—and death—is made comprehensible and meaningful. The "effectiveness" of these rituals depends on their cultural contextualization—the dynamic text-context relation noted above. The language (in speech and act) of the wedding rite borrows extensively from the cultural vocabulary of bargaining; marriage generates exchange between families, and exchange relations entail bargaining. Thus it is said in Maramureş that a "bride is like a hen." The language of death, however, cannot borrow from the vocabulary of bargaining. Death does not entertain bargaining. Instead, death's vocabulary is one of the transformation of physical and emotional states (such as loss, putrefaction). And so death is characterized as an insatiable belly. Yet, the language of "love" (marriage) also draws on metaphors of separation and demise. But then, as we will see in Chapter 4, marriage and death are inextricably related. An exploration of this rich, highly condensed symbolic language offers a privileged understanding of the Moroşeni's conceptualization of their world. As Sahlins points out, "Symbols are symptoms, direct or mystified, of the true force of things" (1981, 7).

The analysis of these particular rituals concentrates on the cultural semantics of life and death: the relations between the living and the dead, men and women, nature, culture, and, more recently, civilization. (The colloquial distinction between culture and civilization assumes culture to be a regional or local practice; there is an implicit sense of limited possibility.[35] Civilization is associated with developed technologies and knowledge. The latter is not confined to historical progression: it is used to refer to Roman as well as to contemporary Western and Ceauşescu's promised Romanian civilization.) I will not engage in a formal analysis of the ritual poetry itself, but rather will focus on the general interpretation of cultural meanings.[36]

This study begins with a chapter about contemporary village life in Maramureş and emphasizes the basic features of social relations and social organization, past and present. The second, third, and fourth chapters are detailed analyses of the life-cycle rituals themselves: weddings, funerals, and death-weddings, respectively. The concluding chapter situates the analysis of ritual in the broader context of the state.

Fieldwork in Romania

The relationship between text and context, as well as the interpretation of cultural meanings, is relevant to an understanding of research in Romania. This study is based on seventeen months of fieldwork in a Maramureş village, the primary research having been done during thirteen months in 1978–79.[37] For foreigners, research in Romania is an academic privilege, not a right. Bilateral exchange agreements between the United States and Romania facilitate research arrangements for Americans,[38] but the tensions generated by the international debate about communism and capitalism strongly influence the climate for research in Romania.[39] In 1978–79, international as well as internal conditions were more favorable than they are today, and scholarly exchanges still functioned reasonably well. The 1980s have brought ideological intensification on both sides and a sharp deterioration of relations. Research has become increasingly more difficult; at present, it is virtually impossible.

This project was begun during a period of mutual tolerance tempered by growing skepticism. In 1978, the regional official who accompanied me for the requisite introduction to local authorities informally advised me to take stock of a complicated reality. He intimated that cooperativization had been "problematic" in this particular village and that the scars from that episode had healed slowly.[40] Requests for access to local statistics would probably be futile. Moreover, people were likely to be apprehensive about possible repercussions of talking with me, a foreigner from a capitalist country. After all, I was an American, and a single woman, doing research alone in an area close to the Soviet border. By local custom, single women do not travel unaccompanied. My behavior was different, and perhaps worthy of concern. What was I actually doing there?

In Romania association with foreigners is openly discouraged. This prohibition is most exacerbated in Bucureşti and other urban areas, but it is enforced throughout all levels of Romanian society. Citizens are required to report the content of their discussions with foreigners to the appropriate persons at work, in their community, or in their apartment complex.[41] Also, in 1980, State Decree #225 prohibiting the residence of foreigners, except first-degree relatives, in the homes of Romanians was modified to also forbid the pitching of tents in courtyards. Infractions of this law may be costly to well-intentioned Romanians, and the price is not always restricted to monetary reprisal. For researchers who need to reside in villages, exceptions to this law are usually approved through a complicated bureaucratic procedure involving national and local authorities.[42]

Everyone who lives in or visits Romania is subject to bureaucratic encumbrances to a greater or lesser degree. The difficulties I encountered during my fieldwork are not necessarily representative of the experiences of others;[43] certain of my problems were atypical. For example, I was unable to gain access to local records that are consulted regularly by foreign researchers working in other communities. This was *not* the fault of government officials who, to the contrary, extended their assistance on my behalf. Unfortunately, certain village authorities chose to interpret local history and center-periphery relations according to their own interests, and I became the innocent victim of others' wounds. Thus I do not have adequate data on residence patterns, production (cooperative or private), land tenure, property and kin relations. Although I, and national officials, eventually learned of this deception, it was by then impossible to make use of these materials.[44]

In addition to the forewarning I had received from the regional official, the then village priest soon clarified his position and volunteered words of caution about my questioning. He pointedly noted that I had a long "shadow," something others also noticed.[45] Many gracious people forthrightly declined to discuss certain topics with me (such as land, cooperative organization, economic matters, inheritance, post–World War II local history); they understood that they were not at liberty to do so, at least not directly. Over the thirteen months, I nonetheless learned about many of these matters as my ideologized "capitalist" identity faded into the bonds of familiarity and friendship. But these gifts of knowledge were given only after thoughtful consideration and were mostly in the form of veiled speech—poetic creations. To be sure, reciprocal discretion was implicitly demanded. Hence, the limits of inquiry were ultimately defined by the burden of responsibility to those who welcomed me, shared their experiences with me, assisted me, and who might unintentionally be held accountable for my cultural curiosity.

Recognition of this responsibility, at the very least an ethical one, partially explains the focus on ritual (as collective, representative action) rather than on individual lives. As already noted, ritual practice is widespread and elaborate in Maramureş; furthermore, Maramureş is famous for its rich traditions. The Moroşeni are proud of them especially because of their roots in the past and their dynamic meanings in the present. Although folklore is by no means politically neutral, it has nevertheless been construed as a legitimate domain for research. (Recall that folklore is now meant to represent a legacy of the creative vitality of the Romanian people. Rituals are classed in the category of folklore.)[46] Thus, ritual offered a reasonable emphasis, satisfying my interest in the significance of symbolic expression in contemporary socialist society, while minimizing overt dangers for others.[47]

Having been granted permission to do research and to live in a village, suitable accommodations had to be arranged.[48] In my case, local ethnographers negotiated a residence on my behalf as I waited anxiously elsewhere. The woman who was eventually to be my *gazdă* (hostess) later told me that she had initially been reluctant to take me in. She had to attend to her then bedridden, semi-paralyzed mother-in-law and felt she did not have the time or energy to devote herself to two dependents. Her image of me, as yet unseen, was that of a woman raised in an American city who would therefore require attentive mothering or nursing. Surely I would have pretensions to that life style to which I was accustomed, a life style I would not find in her home. They could offer a bed with a straw mattress, an oil-burning lamp, an outhouse, and water heated on a wood-burning stove that also supplied warmth during the cold winters. And didn't I need more privacy? "My" room connected the kitchen and the family bedroom where everyone else slept; it was the room used to receive guests. The best icons and woven cloths were displayed there.[49] As she insisted that first week, "We don't have 'conditions' for *domni*" (the urban intelligentsia, in her parlance), a dilemma further compounded by my being an American. She would then present her rather luxurious image of my world.

"Conditions" were also of concern to the local authorities, who were not entirely pleased by this choice of residence, claiming that I would be more comfortable in a house with electricity (such as theirs). That may have been true, but it would also have been impossible to establish relations with anyone had I lived in the home of a local authority. The hidden motives for their concern were rooted in past events, combined with the desire for an easily earned income supplement. (My rent was determined and paid by the National Council for Science and Technology, or the Academy of Social and Political Sciences, depending on the year.) I remained adamant about my refusal to change residence. My hostess and I hit it off the moment I arrived and the much talked-about American became a reality. When those local and regional representatives who had accompanied me left, she presented me to her ailing mother-in-law. By evening, they had decided to welcome me fully.

We talked late into the night during those first days. I had no desire to move unless the family requested it. Perhaps most important, the immediacy of our rapport contributed to my feeling comfortable and less alone in an otherwise utterly unfamiliar environment. (It has always impressed me that the researcher-researched relationship is inverted during the initial period of "assimilation" into a community, and, at all times, there is a mutual curiosity.)[50] Furthermore, the choice of this household was clearly fortuitous for my research. The mother-in-law was an esteemed godmother in the village; my hostess was known for her agility with ritual language, and her own mother was formerly a midwife. Because of the mother-in-law's physical condition, her godchildren came to visit regularly. Women frequently consulted my hostess about ritual preparations (food and ideas about ritual expression). The husband was highly regarded also, so men would inquire of him about me. For me as an outsider, the process of meeting people was made easier by my place of residence. (This was part of the local ethnographers' intent in arranging for me to stay there. Despite my concern about imposing, I was indeed grateful for their insistence.) To be sure, I would have preferred "conditions," especially a private room. But the advantages (personal and research-oriented) far outweighed the disadvantages.[51] I did not change residence.

There is a historical basis for the concern about conditions for domni. The hierarchical social organization characteristic of this region is still evident today. That I was educated, as well as a foreigner, evoked all the class and status connotations associated with the category of domn and informed my host family's assumptions about proper treatment of me.[52] Deference and respect were foremost. In that first week or two I was to be served separately in my room (where all guests with status are served). That I was also a woman complicated matters. For them, I was a cultural curiosity contradicting all their familiar categories. I was a single woman in an unknown corner of the world who should have been married by then, but I was a scholar and obviously had other concerns in life. I was not permitted to perform household chores, even though these are customarily the responsibilities of women. My hostess or one of her two daughters would make my bed. I was to be waited on. I understood the cultural motivation of this behavior toward me, but I was extremely uncomfortable with it. (Nor did I ever become comfortable with a general expectation that the mother should wait on everyone, especially her sons.) Commensality—the sharing of food and drink—establishes social relations. The manner in which food and drink are offered also differentiates guests from family and friends. I was going to be there a long time, and deference meant lonely meals.

Clearly, my status as respected guest had to be transformed, and as far as I was concerned, the sooner the better. And so our negotiations began; reasonable compromises were reached. Shortly thereafter, I joined the family at all meals, although my place had

to be marked: an embroidered cloth was always put under my set-
ing. (I was not allowed to eat from communal bowls or with wooden
utensils.) I made my own bed and suggested that the daughters
might do the same with theirs, as they were young women, and
their mother had more than enough to do. I also tired quickly of
the predictable arguments about which daughter would do this
task. The sons were simply not expected to assist; they chopped
wood instead. There were only a few occasions when I participated
in household chores, and then my hostess suffered the (undeserved)
verbal abuse of others. To illustrate, Easter is preceded by spring-
cleaning. The extended family was to be present, as well as foreign
colleagues of mine. There was much to do and little time. Hence, I
pulled on my rubber boots and took the pots and metal bowls to the
stream to scrub them. There I joined many other women engaged
in the same activity. My hostess and I were by then like family with
each other and did not think about the public breach of propriety.
(The incorporation of outside women into the family is a critical
feature of patrilineal systems and will be discussed throughout this
book.) In a sense, it was normal that my hostess would allow me to
help with household chores. But from the community's point of
view, I was neither fictive daughter nor bride, but a foreign guest.
By that evening, the area was flooded with torrents of gossip deni-
grating my hostess for having taken advantage of me. From that
time on, I refrained from assisting; the social consequences for her
were too great. Throughout this process of incorporating me, an
unusual outsider, into the family, the various extended family members and I engaged in extensive discussions about gender and generational relations. It was an experience of mutual learning. This
was true for the community at large, but the learning was most intensive in the family context where the details of daily living were
constantly explored together.

My gendered "identity" fluctuated between that of a symbolic
male and a courageous, warm, and considerate woman. The ambiguities of my identity had ramifications in other domains. I was not
perceived to be as pretentious as domni are expected to be. But
my status as a foreign intellectual required formal recognition. How
was I to be addressed? My relative youth and openness tended to
contradict the formality of most terms of address. (It is assumed
that professors are much older.) I found the formal "Miss Kligman"

awkward in everyday interactions. Most people settled on addressing me simply as *domnişoară*, miss. This diminished the hierarchical, formal aspect that my last name added, yet was not as informal or familiar as the use of my first name would have implied. Although "miss" gnaws at my feminist sensibilities, it was a reasonable compromise in their culture, and in their language.[53] But finding a term of address for me was problematic for my hosts' children, who ranged in age from fourteen to over thirty. These young adults were expected, by tradition, to address me formally and were chastised if they called me by my name. Our discussions about this pointed to cross-cultural boundaries of communication and the tensions between formality and familiarity. In a changing social environment, my presence was a dilemma for the youthful who grasped the experience of "modernity" through our acquaintance. I, of course, would have preferred my familiar identity in all of its dimensions, because it would have lessened the distance of "otherness" that I necessarily experienced. The most basic lesson to be learned is that identity is indeed socially constructed in time and space.

Representations and Meaning

This brings me to one last point about fieldwork, namely, its analysis and presentation in book form. This study is based on extended participant-observation of daily and ritual life in a northern Transylvanian community. My notes come from over sixty hours of in situ recordings of life-cycle rituals, as well as intensive interviews, fieldnotes about my impressions, attention to the mundanities of gossip (often tiresome but always revealing), review of the literatures, and so on. The account that follows is the result of *my* interpretation of this very "rich data"; it represents my understanding of the lives of others. To be sure, my understanding is both privileged and informed, but it is, nonetheless, mine. I have chosen to tell their stories through the medium of life-cycle rituals. Life-cycle rites may be viewed as narratives about peoples, their social ideals and identities, their comprehension of the relationship between the sexes, between life and death. Indeed, in this Transylvanian village, their traditions—rituals, oral poetic discourse, and the like—have always been integral features of their lives. It is

through these structures that they have made sense of and interpreted significant aspects of their experience. Ritual and its language have also enabled them to comment on broader practices,
even if these practices have been understood in terms of a local
centrism that casts the community as the center of the universe.
Since the institutionalization of Romanian socialism (such as it is),
that focus has been blurred. In the last four decades, every aspect
of Romanian society has been fundamentally transformed, affecting
every citizen in essential ways. As E. P. Thompson reminds us, however, " historical change eventuates, not because a given 'basis' must
give rise to a correspondent 'superstructure,' but because changes in
productive relationships are experienced in social and cultural life,
refracted in men's ideas and their values, and argued through in their
actions, their choices and their beliefs" (1979, 22). Because life-
cycle rites highlight continuities and changes that are experienced
by individuals, families, and communities throughout the life cycle, they may also serve as a dynamic context for analyzing cultural
continuity and change. These rituals are deeply embedded in the
community life of this Transylvanian village (just as other rituals
are embedded in other communities throughout the world). Thus,
they offer us a powerful lens through which to gain insights into the
practical and meaningful concerns of these people's experiences—
their beliefs, values, and practices—in the Socialist Republic of
Romania.

But life and mortality, desire and death are universal phenomena, familiar to us all. Throughout time, different voices have given
the life cycle meaning in different ways. This book seeks to represent the voices of Transylvanian villagers. As Count Dracula noted,
Transylvania's ways are not our ways, and "there shall be to you
many strange things." Yet, I would add, there will be many familiar
things that resonate deeply with our own concerns. And perhaps
the analysis of these rites will offer us insights into our own cultural
practices.

Chapter One

Social Organization

Oamenii întâi cântă, pe urmă scriu.
People first sing, later they write.
Bălcescu 1953, 60

The Village: Past and Present

During a dry summer, three men got lost in a forest. Being thirsty, they went in search of water. One of them came to the top of a hill—where the Church on the Hill is . . . and heard the sound of running water. He shouted: Eu aud! (I hear) and put the name Ieud to this place where he then settled.

Collected by the author, 1978

When the Romanians first came here, they lived in huts, from Bîrsana up along the Iza. First there were only five who settled in these parts. They were called Vlad, Balc, Mariş, Pleş, Chindriş. They had received rights to the land and mountains. . . . Three of them settled right there at the place we call "the monastery" by the spring (toward sunrise from Ieud) and first they made a large wooden cross and put it in the ground. One night, the cross disappeared from there . . . and was settled right where the Church on the Hill is. The men searched for the cross in the forest until they found it and then they moved there. In that area (known as that of Băleşti) there's very little water, so the three men went to find a better source of water so they could graze their animals and make themselves a mill. One climbed to the top of a tree and heard the sound of running water towards sunset and he shouted to the others: "Hey come because I hear (Ieu aud) . . . that is, water." One of them down below heard but didn't understand well what the one at the top had said and he yelled to the other: "Come, back to the east from the top because there it is wet (i ud)." When they convened, they laughed at this misunderstanding and later, back in the valley, they said in jest the name "Ieud."

Collected in 1893
by P. Bilţiu-Dăncuş [1]

25

*   *   *

According to the legend, such were the origins of Ieud, one of the oldest and most picturesque villages in Maramureş.[2] The Church on the Hill, the Biserica din Deal, dates from 1364. Written documents further attest to the existence of Ieud in the fourteenth century, title having been granted in 1365 to Balc, son of Prince Sas, son of Prince Dragoş Voda (Mihaly 1900, 57; Filipaşcu 1940, 98; Popa 1970, 87–89). Founding families of Ieud lay claim to *diplome,* or diplomas granting titles and land, received from the Hungarian King Ludwig I in 1419 and 1427 (Mihaly 1900). Like most villages in Maramureş, Ieud had a rural aristocracy, known as *nemeşi* (nobles), whose traditional and hereditary rights to land, prestige, and local political power were reinforced by these royal grants.[3] Thus, from Ieud's beginnings, social relations were hierarchically ordered (Pop 1976, 17).

Other status distinctions have historically pertained to Ieud as well. Locally it is touted as the "intellectual" village, having contributed generals, lawyers, and, previously, many priests and nuns. What is allegedly the oldest Romanian written document—*Manuscrisul de la Ieud* (Lives of the Saints)—was found in the Biserica din Deal; moreover, some claim that the first personal letters in Romanian (regarding a business transaction) were sent by a Ieudan in 1595. Tourist literature today contributes to this reputation, suggesting that it is "here that the first Romanian-language school functioned" and that "historians consider the place the cradle of Romanian writing" (*Romanian News* 14, 1981, 159).

Ieud is also generally regarded as a religious village. From 1701 until 1948 Ieud adhered to the Greek-Catholic church; since then, the priest has followed the Orthodox rites sanctioned by the state.[4] Religion has had profound influence in Maramureş, and particularly in Ieud: witness not only the two wooden churches dating from the 1300s and 1700s, respectively, but also a third large cement church recently consecrated in the center of the village. Ieudeni attribute their high natality and absence of divorce to the tenacity of religious and secular tradition.

Ieud used to be one of the wealthiest villages in Maramureş. Its inhabitants were engaged primarily in agricultural and pastoral labor. Forced cooperativization in 1950 and 1962, as well as nationalization of the forests, radically altered its status; Ieud is now one of the poorer villages.[5] The primary motive for cooperativization in Ieud was not based on economic or production potential. Rather, it was aimed at undermining the authority of the Uniate church and destroying the richer class of peasant landowners, or *chiaburi*, then accused by the state of being rural exploiters, an accusation that was not implicitly accurate because it did not always reflect actual exploitation (Chirot 1978; Verdery 1983a, 36–39). Although the historical record is not conclusively documented, it is generally held that Maramureş was a region of free peasants; feudal serfdom was not customary. Fellow villagers generally considered these "class enemies of the state" hard-working; they also accorded an idealized historical respect to the chiaburi because they were descendents of nemeşi. The chiaburi were godparents to numerous families of poor peasants. Hence, during the period of cooperativization, many villagers supported the landed peasantry in their resistance to relinquishing their private property. But threats, arrests, and exorbitant or impossible quotas eventually resulted in acquiescence. In 1962 the chiaburi were successfully enrolled in the cooperative farm. Further cooperativization was not actively pursued, however, leaving Ieud a semi-cooperativized village.

Ieud is in the Iza Valley, one of four valleys (the others are Mara, Cosău, and Vişeu) that constitute "Old Maramureş," with its major city of Sighetu Marmaţiei approximately 45 km to the northwest of Ieud. Ieud, with a population of approximately 5,000 in 1985,[6] consists of the village proper and four small hamlets marking outer boundaries of habitable land. The larger two of these hamlets, Gura Ieudului and Plopşor, begin and end the main road through Ieud. Gura Ieudului links Ieud with the primary route running through the Iza Valley. Buses on this route stop at the "mouth of Ieud," where other vehicles enter Ieud. Since 1979 the road has been paved into the center of the village, where it again becomes a dirt road running through and beyond Plopşor into the forests. All other roads and paths in the village are dirt.

Upon entering Ieud proper, one soon notices the cooperative farm. Nearby is the veterinarian's building. Continuing along the main road, one then arrives in the central area of the village where diverse state-owned buildings are in evidence: the council building and adjoining post office, telephone and telegraph, two apartment buildings occupied by local bureaucrats and teachers, a general school through the tenth grade, a *cofetărie* (sweet shop), a book store with necessary paper and related supplies, a communal library, and a tailor's shop. A bit further on, one encounters a "universal" store (essentially a general store) and the *bufet*, or local bar, that, ironically, is diagonally across the road from the priest's residence. Moving on, there is a cultural clubhouse; a medical dispensary with birthing rooms; a small mixed-goods store with limited food, yard goods, and household supplies; an industrial store; and, finally, a nursery school. The new church and the wooden Church in the Flatlands are centrally situated on opposite sides of the main road. The Church on the Hill is just on the other side of the stream that descends from the surrounding hills and runs the entire length of the village, joining the Iza River. The majority of houses cluster along both sides of this stream and the main road that parallels it. Most of these houses are wooden, but cement structures are competing with the more familiar traditional ones. New houses use wood only for embellishment in the Maramureş style. (Nationalization of the forests—thereby curtailing access to their lumber—as much as modernization has contributed to the decreased use of wood for houses.) Many houses along the main road have installed electricity; although its installation in more remote areas of the village appears haphazard, most houses in Ieud proper will eventually have this convenience. Presumably, more and more television antennas will appear: in 1985, there were 250 families with televisions compared with 20 a decade ago. Running water is a venture for the future.

Traditionally, villages in Romania are divided into two halves: upper (*susani*) and lower (*giosani*), the designation indicating either altitude or proximity to the source of a river (Papahagi 1925, ix; H. Stahl 1980, 21). In Ieud, the latter dictates the method of reckoning. Space is divided into hills and valleys or flatlands. Formerly, this division defined social relations and activities. There used to be two priests in Ieud, one for each of the famous wooden churches (the Church on the Hill and the Church in the Flatlands). A priest and his primary assistants (deacons and sextons) were associated with and served the inhabitants of either susani or giosani during life-cycle and calendar rituals. Today there is only one priest in Ieud, but his assistants still divide their responsibilities in the traditional manner.[7]

The inhabited areas of the upper and lower parts of the village are separated from the village boundaries by fields that both divide and connect the four hamlets and the center of village life (Kligman 1981, 116). (The distance between Gura Ieudului and Ieud is diminishing as new houses are built along the main road; the other hamlets remain relatively unaffected.) Whereas the national road at Gura Ieudului and the forests beyond Plopşor designate north-south boundaries, east-west territory is defined by nine encircling hills linking Ieud with villages beyond them. These hills provide land for hay, pasturage for sheep and cattle, and wild berries. The hills and fields are obvious environmental indicators of pastoral and agricultural interests. (Primary agricultural products include corn, potatoes, hay, oats, and barley; corn and potatoes are the most important today. Production of apples and plums has declined. The number of privately owned sheep has been drastically reduced. Much of this is said to be a consequence of cooperativization. The cooperative owns half of Ieud's arable territory. Because much of this land belonged to the wealthy peasants, it is also among the best property.)

Each hill has a name. This is particularly important vis-à-vis pastoral concerns: a hill conveys not only place and direction but also use by a specific group of families. The names of hills are as significant as the names of persons: "If they didn't have names, how would you know how to go?" Hills locate action and discourse in temporal and spatial terms. Fields function in much the same way. Unlike hills, however, which are spatially distinct, fields are not broken up in any readily discernible fashion (by fences or rocks), and therefore are not assigned individual names. Instead, they are identified by who works them and what is cultivated: one goes by "X's place for potatoes" or "near the cooperative's part." In this manner, fields and hills acquire socially constituted identities; space is culturally personalized.

Because space is thus imbued with personality, these broader confines demarcating village boundaries in turn give shape and form to the fundamental social organization of the village. The basic social unit is the *gospodărie,* or household (P. Stahl 1979b).

A gospodărie consists of the domestic group—generally parents, children, and grandparents—as well as the courtyard and garden: in short, the people and property needed to make a relatively self-sufficient unit (Karnoouh 1980). It is important to emphasize the integral relationship between a particular territory and the group of people occupying and utilizing it (Musset 1981, 22).[8] Names are based on the gospodărie, not on the nuclear family per se. Like hills and fields, household space is associated with groups of people. The family unit accrues social identity not in terms of the individuals making up a household but rather in terms of the productive and reproductive group.

The gospodărie is a microcosm of village social organization.[9] Perhaps the easiest entree into its structure and activities is through the markers that visibly define it. Each gospodărie is bounded by a fence, usually made of straight posts and boards vertically or horizontally placed (*palant*) or braided tree limbs (*gard*). The primary entrance into the fenced-in area is a large, intricately carved wooden gate. The wooden gates of Maramureş are famous throughout the country (Nistor 1977). The traditional carving on the gateposts is now the basis of the Maramureş style; this carving can be seen adorning the entryways and balconies of new buildings, of both the old (wood) and the new style. The gates represent an ongoing reconstruction of value and identity, within both local and national contexts. Functionally, these large gates open into the courtyard. Through them, people, animals, wagons, and machines may enter. For convenience, people may also enter through a smaller gate or lower fence next to the large gate, and there is at least one other small gate or fence at the far end of the property.[10]

Within the courtyard can be found various storage structures: a shed for hay; a barn for cows, oxen, horses, and other animals, if the family still maintains them, and for corn feed; and pens for chickens and pigs. The location of these structures varies considerably, as does that of the house. Many houses have wells from which water is drawn for drinking, cooking, and light washing; heavy washing of clothes, pots, and flax, and watering of animals is done in the stream throughout the year. (In the winter women can be seen chopping holes in the frozen stream so that they may attend to their chores. Their husbands often admonish them about this practice because it is believed to increase suffering from rheumatism. They urge their wives to heat basins of water on the wood-burning stoves, but the women contend that the results are simply not as good.) Households without wells take advantage of the privileges of neighborly relations (Kideckel 1981, 41). Some houses also have apiaries in their courtyards.

Close by the house itself is the *grădina*, or garden. It is generally two or three hectares, enclosed by another fence to discourage destruction by animals or people. The grădina is central to the life of the household. Most important, products necessary for the family's basic subsistence are cultivated in it (Karnoouh 1980, 81). Corn, a staple for humans and animals,[11] is planted there, as are grains, beans, green beans, beets, and cabbage. Closest to the house, in the portion known as the *grădiniță*, or little garden, are vegetables such as lettuce, cucumbers, onions, carrots, tomatoes, garlic, eggplant, and herbs. The latter are used for rituals, medicine, and cooking. And, last but not least, flowers are planted in the garden. The significance of the garden and flowers as "key" symbols of the relation between life and death and between nature and culture will become apparent through the analysis of the ritual cycle.

The household consists of both the animate and the inanimate: the courtyard and its yield, the buildings, and the animals—all of which contribute to the well-being of the predominant component, the people in the family unit. A culturally constituted dynamic liaison exists between the components of the household; relations are "embodied," or personalized.[12] When a person dies, not only do the family members mourn the loss, but it is also lamented that "the house cries," "the table cries," "the courtyard cries." The household is a totality through which the family, as well as its individual members, derives social identity. Just as the village is spatially defined, so its constituents are spatially located. The fence surrounding the gospodărie symbolically defines the limits between corporate family relations and the rest of the community. Hence, one must examine the ordering of social relations within the family to understand the ordering of social relations in general.

Family Structure and Social Relations

The nuances of *neam*, or family, are critical for understanding Maramureș identity, an identity derived from their boasted descent from freeholders rather than from serf peasants. In Maramureş the hierarchical ordering of social relations stems from the fourteenth-century village organization based on nemeşie, which has persisted into the twentieth century (M. Pop 1976, 20; personal communication). Roots of this hierarchical organization may be traced to the medieval local headmen, the *cnezi*. Maramureş villages formed political unions led by these cnezi and, through hereditary right, their descendents. Later, the princes, or *voivode*, of Maramureş continued this hierarchical, hereditary form of rule. (Today, 57 of the 76 villages mentioned in fourteenth- and fifteenth-century documents boast of family links to these early leaders. See Popa 1970, 177, 180.) Generally, status, prestige, and authority are conferred on families through recognition of hierarchical relations. Family encompasses all persons, living and dead, who are related consanguinally, affinally, and ritually. (Ritual kinship is realized primarily through the institution of *năşie*, or godparenthood.)

A neam is classified as *bun* (good), *slab* (weak), or *rău* (bad, often used interchangeably with weak). These attributes are passed from generation to generation with or without contemporary justification. Because *bun*, *slab*, and *rău* also refer to types of blood, a biological factor is implied. Blood is linked with heredity and evolutionary transmission through generations. Goodness or weakness/badness of a neam refers to a certain inherited status, nemeş or not-nemeş. The acknowledged founding families of Ieud, for example, are known as "good families": among them, Balea, Gorzo, Pleş, and Ivaşcu. Families of nemeşi were usually *gazde* as well, that is, propertied and wealthy. While nemeş and gazdă were synonymous, and while "good family" was generally equated with higher social class (nemeş), these attributes alone were not enough to determine the reputation of a family. Other requisite components included honor, moral fortitude, religious commitment, hard work, wisdom, prudence, and *omenie* (good will, humanitarianism, and decency). As Musset points out, one inherits more than material interests; one also acquires the spiritual characteristics of one's ancestors, both their virtues and their vices (1981, 59). The past resonates deeply (although not necessarily accurately). Thus, coming from good or bad roots is a matter of pride or shame;[13] one's family may be something to celebrate or to bear quietly and counteract by sterling comportment. The following strigătură, heard commonly at weddings before cooperativization, underscores the posi-

tive correlation between social class (nemeş, gazdă) and a good
family (neam bun):

Trăia neamurile mele	Long life to my family,
Şi ieu să trăiesc cu iele.	And may I live long with them.
Să trăiască mult şî bine	May they live long and well.
Că mni-i cinste nu ruşine.	For me, it is an honor, not a shame.
Tăte neamurile mele	All of my family (relatives),
Tăte-s gazde cu avere.	All are wealthy proprietors!
Nici ieu nu le fac scădere.	Nor will I lower their standard—
Tăte-s gazde şî stau bine	They are all wealthy and well-off—
Nici ieu nu le fac ruşine.	Nor shall I cause them shame.

Maramureş is one of the few regions where the dictates of social
hierarchy remain tenacious. Those families that claim hereditary
relationships to a prestigious past reap the benefits of pride and
respect. Every family in Maramureş is conscious of its identity and
how that is interwoven into the web of local social relations, which
are distinguished by designations of "we" and "they." Whether one
comes from a good or bad family still figures significantly in the formation of alliances. Today, although most of the once wealthy and
propertied families are now members of the cooperative, they re-
tain their status as descendents of peasant nobles, as members of a
neam bun.[14] Post-cooperativization, people still marry *după neam,
nu după avere* (after family, not after wealth). (Note the dissocia-
tion between family and wealth, which formerly were coincidental.) The traditional hierarchy prevails, deeply embedded in local
culture, despite the obvious modification of material conditions.[15]
This hierarchy is reflected in other spheres as well, most notably
in the church. In earlier times, nemeşi were accorded the privilege
of sitting in the chairs lining the side walls of the old wooden
churches (Eretescu, personal communication). Today, men still
take their places in church *pe neamuri* (by family) in status order.
These places, which are not visibly marked, are known as *locul lui
X* (the place of X) and are passed on from one generation to the
next. They have been transferred to the new church also. Family
prestige tends to prevail over actual wealth, although the latter can
enhance the position of someone from a "weaker" lineage.
   Generally, marriage choices are influenced by status distinc-

tions: marriage is most often contracted between families of the same rank; marrying up or down occurs, but it is not the norm.[16] The following traditional verse indicates that marriage between individuals from families of different ranks is not only discouraged but in fact can never be:

Că noi nu ni-om mesteca	For we will never be mixed,
Şohan cît a si lumea.	Never as long as humanity exists,
C-a ta ziţă-i de harbuz	For your [family] roots are from gourds
P-îng-a me de grîuţ tuns.	Alongside mine of special wheat.
A ta ziţă-i de ovăz	Your roots are from oats
P-îng-a me de grîu ales.	Alongside mine of choice wheat.
. . . .	. . . .
Ziţa me cu ziţa ta	Your family and my family
Şohan nu-i deasemenea.	May never be allied.

(I. Bîrlea 1968, 55)

In this verse, the tenacity of status differentiation based on lineage and blood is legitimized on natural grounds by invoking a culturally valued hierarchy between nature's products. *Harbuz* is a variety of squash that everyone has; it is common, as are oats. *Grîu*, or wheat, especially the finest, is not available to commoners and is a symbol for a good family, prosperity, and pride. The roots are so different that they cannot naturally combine. The human species is similarly distinguished.

Marriage is exogamous (from third-degree relations on) within the confines of a preferred local endogamy (M. Pop 1976, 16). The constraints of lineage as well as degree of relation are recognized and generally respected. Another verse suggests that the cultural construction of these constraints, thereby differentiating between the naturally and the culturally acceptable, is consciously understood:

Hai mîndrule să giurăm	Hey, sweetheart, let's take the oath
Pă cruce verde de lemn.	On a green wooden cross,
Că la popă nu putem	For we can't at the priest's
Că veri al doilea sîntem.	Because we're second cousins.
De n-aş si cu mîndra neam	If I was not related to my sweetheart,

Ne-am si cununat de-un an.	We would have been married a year ago.
Da cu mîndra sîntem neam	But with my sweetheart we are related;
Nu ni-om cununa şohan.	We will never marry.

The green wooden cross is a metaphor that indicates a natural union sanctioned by nature's church, the forest, but not by culture's. One Moroşan pointed out that, limitations notwithstanding, "the communities in Maramureş, especially in the Iza Valley, are all interrelated through alliances." M. Pop suggests (1976, 17) that families of inferior status (which are the most numerous) marry within the village; those of intermediary position may go beyond the village, but usually not much farther than villages in the surrounding vicinity. Families of highest status have fewer possibilities and extend the bounds of village endogamy to the region. Given the size of Ieud, adherence to village endogamy for all statuses has been more feasible than in other villages and is still considered most desirable. The changes in family organization wrought by socioeconomic transformation during the last decades, however, have affected the choice of marriage partners to some degree, with regional endogamy gaining popularity. For example, young men living or working in the nearby city of Sighetu Marmaţiei can meet eligible *fete* (young women) from other villages. Proximity makes it possible for the families to use their networks to check out each other's status. (This sleuthing has destroyed many a potential marriage.) In any case, although maintaining status levels through marriage is still the norm (a factory worker might marry a school teacher, but not a doctor, even if they are from the same village), there is also room for adjustment to the exigencies of daily life, especially in the cities.

The most readily apparent changes in categories of relations and status considerations have occurred in the institution of godparenthood.[17] It used to be that the most prominent families were godparents for the majority of families in Ieud; hence, only three or four persons were godparents for the entire village. This is no longer true. Status has been reconstructed and manipulated. In part, this is structurally predictable. Godparenthood, or *năşie*, institutionalizes between two families a ritual-spiritual relationship predicated primarily on social and economic obligations (see Marian

1892, 161–73). Godparents officiate at the significant rites of passage: birth and marriage. Generally, the ritual sponsor at a marriage is also the ritual sponsor for the children born to the couple. The relationship between godparents and godchildren is both enduring and corporate in nature and establishes ritual kin bonds between the two families. (It should be mentioned that the godfather's wife is the godmother.) In the event that a godparent dies, this position is supposed to pass on to the godparent's eldest son or to another child (M. Pop 1976, 15; Hammel 1968, 41–50). Marriage between the two families is precluded on the grounds of ritual kinship.

Here it is necessary to distinguish between Orthodox canon law and folk practice. Canon law requires that a child have baptismal godparents and marriage sponsors.

Canon law neither prescribes nor proscribes patterns of kinship between sponsors, the methods by which they are selected, or the social relationships which are to obtain between them and the sponsored child and its relatives, except that baptismal (but not marriage) sponsorship creates an impediment to marriage between sponsor and sponsored, and their kinsmen, to the third degree. In canon law, the marriage witnesses are not spiritual kin of the bride and groom—that is, they are not sponsors in a religious sense at all, and so no impediment to marriage is created. (Hammel 1968, 8)

In the lay interpretation, however, sponsorship at marriage as well as at birth is sacralized.

Traditionally, godparents play a mediatory role. For a married couple, they arbitrate marital disputes (parents being biased by blood relation). Equally important, godparents facilitate economic exchanges. Because of this function, there is a degree of structural predictability in the current changes in the institution of năşie. Godparents manage the redistribution of resources and underwrite costs, particularly for weddings. Beck properly notes that they are sought out as wedding sponsors "because of their capital and their social networks" and describes the socioeconomic mechanisms operative in the *naş-sin* (godparent-godchild) relationship (1976, 368):

On one level, it equalizes by transferring capital from wealthy to less wealthy; on another level, it conserves by emphasizing the asymmetrical patron-client relationship; and on still another level, social mobility may be involved as the status of the naş improves with greater investments in more fin(s) [sin] and the fin's status improves reciprocally.

Thus, this relationship entails both honor and obligation. The efforts and expenditures of godparents are compensated ritually. Godchildren are expected to pay visits of respect to their godparents on important holidays such as Christmas, New Year, Easter, and name days. Female godchildren lament for a deceased godparent. Also, godparents may periodically (but not more than once annually) invite all of their godchildren to honor them collectively in a ritual known as the "gathering of the godchildren." On the designated day, all the godchildren come to their godparents' house for a meal and a general celebration. Upon arrival, each couple offers the godparents the contents of a woven sack (*traistă*): flour, grain, corn, plum brandy. During the evening, each godchild will purchase two shot glasses of brandy for his or her spouse (four glasses per couple); payment is given to the godparents. In this way, godparents recover some of their costs.

Today, as before, one's choice of godparent is based on utility, financial and otherwise. The criteria for determining utility have been altered, however. One village elder sadly commented, "It doesn't matter if the godparent is morally corrupt nowadays" (interview 1978). The rules governing godparenthood are changing. There is a growing tendency for couples to select naşi for their wedding, rather than to continue the tradition of inherited, corporate relationships (see also Musset 1981, 95). Until recently only the groom chose godparents, but now the bride may invite her own as well, although they are honorary; the groom's godparents baptize their children. In keeping with ascribed status distinctions between the bride's and the groom's families, the bride's godparents are referred to as *nănaşi mnici*—little godparents. The groom may decide to follow the traditional custom vis-à-vis his godparents but to also invite another couple to be naşi, more or less honorarily. This is an effective, if somewhat blatant, means to maximize economic and social benefits.

As a rule, if people who are asked to serve as godparents are not "first families," they have cultural capital (wealth or status) of some sort. Couples often choose a relative from the city, an official, an intellectual, or even a foreigner—someone who can bestow prestige on the couple; status differentiation persists. Position is recognized and ritually honored; the village mayor and the president of the cooperative are frequently asked to be nași. Their choice reflects, in part, the manipulative adaptive posturing noted by Jowitt (1974, 1179) that preserves and protects one's private interests. Both the mayor and the cooperative president have mediatory roles within and beyond the village. Acceptance of godparenthood establishes a ritual kin relationship, which creates a double bind for the godparent, who is both constrained by obligation to political authority and compelled by the force of the ritual kin tie (see also Cernea 1976, 273). In Maramureș, there are still echoes of former ways: "Services are not rendered on the basis of impersonal rules, but on the basis of personal recognition" (Jowitt 1974, 1184).

Having looked at the family in broad social terms, it is now appropriate to turn to a more detailed examination of the family's structure. Most social relations within the family are hierarchically ordered and stratified according to age and sex. Generational solidarity supersedes sexual solidarity. The hierarchy of relations is reflected in the terms of address between family members. Children address parents and elders throughout their lives as *dumăta* (informal you) or *voi* (formal or plural you). Women also use *dumăta* when addressing their husbands, at least in public. Men, in contrast, use *tu* (familiar you) with both children and wives.

Patriarchy, patrilineality, and patrilocality are dominant; the system is male-biased. Inheritance is bilateral, however, meaning that both sons and daughters receive equal shares of land—as *zestre* (dowry) for daughters at marriage and as inheritance upon the parents' death or old age for sons (Beck 1976, 368; interviews 1978; see also Friedl 1963). Cooperativization has affected land distribution, and the only property that many families have to divide is the courtyard. To avoid complications, sisters will often sell their shares of the yard to a brother for a reasonable price. Following the rule of ultimogeniture, the youngest son remains in the family house and inherits it and its contents, including farm equipment. He usually marries last, since it is customary for siblings to marry in birth order. This order tends to be applied more strictly to sisters than to brothers (Musset 1981, 54). In essence, the youngest son receives future title to the gospodărie. He and his wife, in exchange, are expected to care for his elderly parents. There are exceptions to this rule, not the least of which is incompatibility, in which case another son may choose or be requested to remain in the natal home. Or there may be no sons, or the youngest son may have sought a career in a city. As an institutionalized form, like godparenthood, ultimogeniture is changing in response to rapid socioeconomic transformations.

In villages, because the youngest son stays in his parental house, it is the father's duty to provide other sons with houses when they marry. Daughters are provided with necessities for the household.[18] Houses for sons are built on family property if feasible; otherwise, a plot is purchased. These houses are financed collectively, with the members of the household contributing funds and labor reciprocally over time. In formal terms, the formation of new nuclear families does not necessarily divide the unity of the household. If a son and his wife live in the parental home or in a separate house (or several separate houses, depending on the number of sons and the amount of available resources) but share the yard with the rest of the family for productive purposes, they still are part of the gospodărie under the authority of the father until he is incapable of exerting this authority. This hierarchy of family relations is symbolically demarcated in spatial terms by a fence. When a son moves to separate property with a separate courtyard, then he has formed a new gospodărie.[19] Each head of a nuclear family "manages a household" (*a gospodări*), regardless of living and productive arrangements. This verb form encompasses the establishment of individual nuclear families through conjugal relations. The noun *gospodărie* classifies nuclear families spatially and temporally in relation to extended family ties and production relations.

The patrifocus, or patrilineal tendency, reverberates throughout the system of social relations. This is best illustrated with names and the construction of identities. From the time of birth, every individual has an official name that is a link to the family; this name consists of a baptismal or given name and a patronym. (There are approximately seventy-one patronyms in Ieud.)[20] Official names are known as "written" (*scris*) names because individuals are recognized by them within a system of jural relations at local, regional, and national levels. A written name is one's link to the state. Because of the large population, there is considerable redundancy of written names. Therefore, everyone also has a spoken (*zis*) name,

and it is by this name that people are really known.[21] This spoken
name identifies a person more precisely than his or her official
name. "Names derive from the necessity to differentiate" (interview 1979). Most spoken names are determined by one of two
major systems. One involves *porecle*, or nicknames, which evolve
either from inherited family surnames or from a particular character or social activity of an ancestor, for example, *ştiop* (lame), *deacu*
(deacon). If too many people still have the same name, then additional nicknames will be taken on, usually referring to family traits
(see also Salzmann 1981, 11–26).

The other major naming system is based on the hierarchical association of given names or first names, again underscoring age and
sexual stratification.[22] A person is generally identified through the
patriline by using the genitive form of the father's first name. This
extends as far as memory of descent permits (four to six generations). For example, Gheorghe is recognized as Gheorghe a lui
Ştefan a lui Văsîle, that is, Gheorghe son of Ştefan who is son of
Văsîle; or Marie is recognized as Marie lui Ştefan lui Văsîle, that
is, Marie daughter of Ştefan son of Văsîle. The genitive of the
mother's first name is used only if her husband dies at an early age,
leaving her a young widowed parent. Then, her children are usually known as Gheorghe lui Nuţa lui Ştefan (lui Văsîle, and so on),
that is, Gheorghe son of Nuţa wife of Ştefan.

Girls and women are recognized as persons only in relation to
men. Until a girl marries, she is known as "daughter of . . . ," for
example, Marie lui Ştefan. When she marries, she changes her
name and her social identity, taking on the name of her husband
and his family; Marie lui Ştefan becomes Marie lui Petre and Marie
lui Petre Pleşului (Marie daughter of Ştefan becomes Marie wife of
Petre and Marie wife of Petre son of Pleş). The patrilineal, patrilocal focus of relations is evident in the terms used to indicate that
someone will marry (or has married). A young man *se însoară*
(takes a sister; see Lévi-Strauss 1969; de Heusch 1981, 29–81), or
marries, and either stays in his father's home or moves into his own; a
young woman *se mărită* (takes a husband), or gets married, and becomes the wife of someone, taking his name. It is the exception to
virilocality that illuminates the bias of the system of relations. If a
family has only one child, a daughter, or has many children but the
age difference between the youngest son and youngest daughter is
considerable, then the daughter will not marry out but will remain

in her parental home. The rule of male ultimogeniture is modified to accommodate this situation; the daughter's husband marries in, coming to live with her family. This is noted by saying that he married in (*s-a măritat*), using the feminine version (M. Pop 1976, 18). The son-in-law then adopts the surname of his father-in-law, at least until the elder dies. Even though the son-in-law's surname is linked to his wife's family, she is nonetheless identified in relation to her husband: Gheorghe lui Chindriş after marrying Ioană Deacului is known as Gheorghe Deacului, while his wife becomes Ioană lui Gheorghe Deacului.

The establishment of a married couple is remarked by saying that two people *se cununa* or *se căsătoresc* (the terms are used interchangeably). The first term means to be crowned and refers to the Orthodox Christian practice of placing crowns on the heads of the betrothed during the church service. The crowns are exchanged on the heads of the bride and groom three times, after which the couple is "married." *A se căsători* essentially means to marry, the result being the formation of a *casă*, or home. Marriage entails not only the union of two individuals but also the alliance of their families, who are said to *a se încuscri*. The parents become *cuscri* to each other (the couple's siblings becoming *cumnaţi*; the wives of male siblings are recognized through the feminization of the male form: *cumnat-cumnată*, feminization being the rule). The bride is the daughter-in-law, or *noră*, to her husband's family; the groom, the son-in-law, or *ginere*, to his wife's parents. An acknowledged hierarchical relation between the two families reemphasizes the patrilineal, patrilocal bias: the parents of the groom are known as *socri mari*, or great (big, superior) in-laws; those of the bride as *socri mnici*, or little (inferior) in-laws (M. Pop 1976, 20; Masson 1982, 48). This status distinction favoring the male's family also applies to godparents, his being *nănaşi mari* and hers *nănaşi mnici*.

Because of the preference for patrilocal residence, when a young woman marries, she, not her husband, is most often the one who leaves home to live *între străini*, or among strangers or foreigners. Alienation is central to the meaning of *străin*, which is used to describe the experiences of brides, soldiers, and foreigners—and in Romanian, the experiences of all three evoke images of thorns, martyrdom, and death. Marriage alienates the bride from her natal family and incorporates her into the family of her husband. (As will be seen, the wedding ritual publicly dramatizes the changes that occur within corporate households.) The observation of Lévi-Strauss (1967, 45) applies throughout southeastern Europe: "It is the men who exchange the women and not vice versa," and their exchange leads to the establishment of male-dominated households. A bride joins her husband's family and contributes her share by working and bearing children. Although the introduction of a bride, an outsider, into established family routine poses a threat to household organization, the continuity and growth of the household depends on the successful incorporation of outside women (Denitch 1974; Rheubottom 1980, 233). Denitch refers to this as the "'patrilineal paradox' in the sense that the structure denies the formal existence of women, while at the same time group survival depends upon them" (1974, 260).

Women are *in* but not *of* the patriline. The new bride enters her husband's family with little status. Her identity is that of wife of "X," and noră, or daughter-in-law, with all that connotes. Although it is not an envied position, it is nonetheless aspired to; the major concern of girls between ages sixteen and twenty is getting married. To be unmarried at twenty-one is to be an "old maid" (*fată mare*). The following verse describes the transition from daughter to daughter-in-law:

De-acasă cind am plecat	When I left home,
A mnei părinți m-o-nvățat.	My parents instructed me
Să mă uit unde-oi păși	To pay attention where I step,
Să nu-ntorn vorbă soacrii.	Not to talk back to my mother-in-law,
Unde păşesc să mă uit	To pay attention where I'm going,
Şî de-a mnei socri s-ascult.	And to listen to my in-laws
Că Dumnezău aş-o lăsat	Because God left it that way:
Pă pămînt să crească flori	Flowers to grow on earth,
Noi să merem de nurori.	We to go as daughters-in-law;
Pă pămînt să crească stini	Thorns to grow on earth,
Noi să merem la străini.	We to go to strangers;
Pă pămînt să crească iarbă	Grass to grow on earth,
Ieu să siu noră de treabă.	I to be a well-behaved daughter-in-law.

Legitimacy is lent to the circumstance of girls by their juxtaposition with natural phenomena. Hopeful and full of life, girls are associated with flowers until they "go as daughters-in-law"; then, life among strangers is thorny, difficult. Regardless, the comportment of daughters-in-law is as common as is grass.

After the bride takes leave of her mother, her interaction will be primarily with her mother-in-law. This is signaled in the wedding ritual when the bride is brought to the groom's house for the first time. Members of the wedding party call out to her mother-in-law to welcome her:

Ieşi afară soacră mare	Come out, great mother-in-law
Că-ţi aduc o noră tare.	Because I bring you a strong daughter-in-law,
Nici pre mnică, nici pre mare	Not too little, not too big,
Făr pă voiă dumnitale.	Just to your wishes;
Nici la iarnă friguroasă	She isn't cold in the winter
Nici la vară calduroasă.	Nor hot in the summer.

It is most important for the bride to negotiate a workable relationship with her *soacră*. According to tradition and ideology, mothers-in-law are naturally rotten, and the bride is usually perceived as victim.

Soacră soacră poamă acră	Mother-in-law, mother-in-law, sour apple,
De te-ai coace-o un an şî-o vară	If you were to ripen her a year and a summer,
Tăt îi si acră şi-amară.	She'd be sour and bitter all the same.
Că din străin pînă faci frate	Until you make a brother out of a stranger,
Nu-ţi rămîne sănătate.	Your health deteriorates;
Pînă o faci mamă dulce	Until you make her like a real mother,
Sănătatea ţi să duce.	You lose your health.

Clearly, the relationship between mother-in-law and daughter-in-law is an exceedingly troublesome one.[23] As Lamphere points out (1974), in patricentered, patrilineal households, conflict rather than cooperation among women is structurally encouraged. Trouble is always blamed on women (Hammel 1968, 15; Benedict 1972, 24). As noted earlier, while assuring the continuation of the family, a bride threatens household solidarity and, significantly, the authority of the mother-in-law in terms of the developmental cycle of the domestic group. (As indicated in the above verse, by the time conflict is reasonably resolved, the women are too old to benefit.) All women are participating members in a household, but they are not simultaneously (and inherently) *of* it.

Only with the birth of children, preferably male, does a woman accrue status and, consequently, power and authority. The birth of a girl is met with disappointment.

Măicuţă cînd m-ai făcut	When you bore me, mother,
Cît de bine ţi-o părut.	How happy you were.
C-ai gîndit că-i fă fecior	You thought you'd make a son,
Şî-ai făcut jele şî dor.	But you had only sorrow and longing;
Dacă m-ai văzut că-s fată	When you saw I was a girl
Ti-o durut tăte deodată.	Your whole body ached.

Girls do not solidify the positions of their mothers; they cause them pain.

. . . .	. . . .
Că mama care face fată.	For the mother who has a girl,
Că străinu-i ca şî stinu	A stranger is like a thorn,
Mai amar decît pelinu.	More bitter than wormwood.

Because all females share the predicament of structural alienation, the bond between mother and daughter is said to be highly valued. Marriage of a daughter socially ruptures that bond. This dichotomous relationship elicits frequent comments from mothers about the problem with daughters: "A girl is a worry; after all, she may become pregnant out of wedlock, God forbid. Boys drink and all, but that's different," said one village woman. There is an implicit acceptance of women's subordination to men, and through them, to mothers-in-law. The daughter's compassionate mother does not recognize that she is at the same time the tyrannical mother-in-law of her son's wife. Because the birth rate in this village is high, most women have at least one daughter, whom they can pity, and one daughter-in-law, who can be a scapegoat. One mother-in-law toasted her new daughter-in-law with the following verse:

Săraca mamă cu fete	Poor mother with daughters:
Mult le ţine pă scumpete	She keeps them dearly,

Şî le dă şî nu le vede.	Then she gives them away and doesn't see them.
Şi ieu spun că le-am ţinut	And I assure you I have kept them;
Le-am dat şî nu le-am avut.	I gave them and didn't have them any longer.
Am rămas cu cinci feciori	I was left with five sons,
Şî cu tăţi mni-oi lua nurori.	And for each I will take daughters-in-law.
Ţine-mni Doamne ce-am luat	Dear Lord, take care of what I've got
Să nu siu de rîs în sat.	So I won't be the laughingstock of the village.

Implicit in this text is the exchange of women. Moreover, in "taking a daughter-in-law" the mother-in-law exercises her rights over the new bride; however, the mother-in-law also realizes that her own position is hierarchically relative. The community at large acknowledges a mother-in-law's rights, but if the daughter-in-law does not obey her mother-in-law, does not work arduously, and is not sexually honorable, the mother-in-law, as well as the daughter-in-law, will be publicly ridiculed.

It is often difficult to know the exact tenor of interrelations within households. Mothers-in-law may resort to positive public posturing to mask the strain of tense relations. One mother-in-law was known to compliment her daughter-in-law during family gatherings (such as weddings)—perhaps to assuage her own guilt, for the daughter-in-law said that she and her mother-in-law had a very difficult time with each other. Here is the mother-in-law's toast:

Frunză verde frunzule	Green leaf, little leaf,
Să trăiască nora me.	Life to my daughter-in-law!
Să trăiesc şi ieu cu ie.	May I also live with her!
De ne sfădim cîteodată	If we argue from time to time,
Ieu o iert şi ie mă iartă	I forgive her and she forgives me:
Iară sîntem laolaltă.	Again we are together.

One elderly mother-in-law confessed that she hoped her husband would not die before she did; she feared being left to the mercy of her daughter-in-law, whom she had mistreated. The implication was that the daughter-in-law might take her revenge, and the old woman could do nothing about it.

It is necessary to assess the "ideology" about mothers-in-law against the actuality of living arrangements. Unlike the Balkan *zadruga* (Byrnes 1976), all but the youngest son are expected to move out. If two or more sons and their wives are living in the parental home, it is considered temporary. Hence, a mother-in-law lives in close quarters with only one daughter-in-law for an extended period. Because sons usually marry in birth order (if not by choice, then by the general custom of fulfilling military service prior to marriage), each son's wife must live as a member of her husband's family at least until the young couple has a house of their own. Very few girls will consent to marriage before their intended completes his military service. Folklore and daily discourse attest to the sad fate of brides abused by their mothers-in-law during the absence of recently acquired husbands (I. Bîrlea 1968, 54–58). Some girls resist marriage to someone they like because of his mother's reputation. While a girl's family still may force her to marry, today most parents respect the wishes of their children (although children are also expected to take heed of their parents' objections).

Mothers-in-law are not so much the butt of jokes as they are the objects of fear and contempt:

Mîndruluț cu patru boi	Little sweetheart with four oxen,
Nu mă-mbdi noră la voi.	Don't invite me to be a daughter-in-law in your house.
Casa voastră-i sus pă ptiatră	Your house is raised upon stone;
Şî-ai o mamă blăstămată.	You have a mother that is cursed (evil).

Even though the young woman's suitor is evidently well-off, having four oxen and a wooden house raised above the ground against the cold, the material advantages do not outweigh the emotional disadvantages. In the verse (collected from an elder and referring to the period before cooperativization), the young woman addresses her sweetheart familiarly but acknowledges that marrying him means joining his family—*casa voastră*. It is important to emphasize the lack of direct correspondence between ideology and practice. Cultural "texts"—in this case ritual verses—reify the norms of patrilineality. They do not represent the particularities of daily, individual experience.

A young woman escapes the harshness of leaving her mother and gaining a mother-in-law if she is an only child or the youngest, in which case her husband is expected to marry in.[24] His position as son-in-law is viewed in the same negative light as that of the daughter-in-law who lives with her husband's family. Both involve a loss of social self and a change of identity; the son-in-law who marries in takes the surname of his wife's household. In certain ways, his condition is considered to be worse than a daughter-in-law's because it violates the accepted norm of patrilocality. Hence, during the wedding festivities, it is not unusual to hear a woman admonish the bride who remains at home:

Taci mnireasă nu zdera	Be quiet, bride, don't cry;
Nu te duci din casa ta.	You're not going from your home.
Da las să zdere mnirele	But let the groom cry,
Că zine de ginere.	Because he's coming as son-in-law,
Şî pune clopu-ntr-un cui	And he'll put his hat on a hook
Şî nimnică nu-i a lui.	And nothing is his.

This bride is spared the fate of most. Although, traditionally, brides cry intensely during their weddings, it is not as warranted for the bride who is not moving from her natal home. Putting a hat on a hook conjures up the image of the man returning home after a day's work; but because he is ginere, it is not his home. His authority is symbolically lessened. Young men are therefore cautioned:

Măi bădiţă bădiţel	Hey, sweetheart, dear one,
Fă-ţi căsuţă din nuiele	Make a little house out of branches.
Numai ginere nu mere.	Only don't go as son-in-law;
Fă-ţi casa lîngă părău	Make your house along the stream,
Că ginere-i tare rău.	For it's very hard to be a son-in-law.

In a world of male priority, almost anything is better than going as ginere.[25] It is suggested that the young man make himself a house out of the branches used for making the braided fences that enclose a household. Moreover, it can be a "little house" (*casuţă*), or one

that does not have a garden (Karnoouh 1980, 80). He should even
build this house in an undesirable location if that means he will
avoid going as ginere and compromising his symbolic male authority (Simić 1969).

Whereas going as ginere is highly discouraged, it is nonetheless
better than remaining single (*că ginere încă i bine, că să aibă orişi-
cine*, or as a son-in-law it also is good just to have someone). Marriage rationalizes life and death. Its purposes are manifold:

> to have a consort [with whom] to . . . divide the good and bad, joys and
> sorrows; to have legitimate offspring who will continue the family name,
> so their blood and seed will never be extinguished . . . to have someone
> to take care of them, to support them in old age, and after death to mourn
> them, remember them and pray for the forgiveness of their sins; and not
> have it said that one was born and lived in this world for nothing, which is
> too often the case for those who remain unmarried. (Marian 1890, 1–2)

Marriage forms the ideological basis of and for social and sexual
relations by restructuring identity and social action, that is, by
transforming social and sexual relations. Because marriage involves
the productive and reproductive cycles of the cultural order, it is
perceived to be of the essence of this order (being dialectically related to death), and so it is highly stressed (see also MacCormack
1980, 11). Attempts to ensure marriage begin at birth. The first
bath water of a baby boy is thrown over "one patch of flowers so
that he will not have to go to more than one place to ask for the
hand of someone; the bath water of a baby girl is thrown over many
flowers so she will have many suitors."

Social relations are not only hierarchically ordered according to
age and sex, but they are also further differentiated by marital
status. (Marriage is so highly valued that if persons of marriageable
age die prematurely without being married in this world, then they
are married in the next. This is the topic of Chapter 4.) Those of
marriageable age who choose to remain single or who have no suitors (a distinct minority)[26] are ritually ridiculed on New Year's Eve.
The figure of an old *babă* (grandmother) is placed near a young
single man's house; in her woven sack, she carries an obscene note.
The figure of an old man (*moş;* also ancestor) is left near a young
single woman's home; he too bears an obscene and insulting note,
and an erect phallus protrudes from his baggy pants (Dăncuş 1973).
These figures are not greatly appreciated by their recipients be-

cause they are publicly as well as privately embarrassing.[27] New
Year's Eve is a time of annual regeneration, reminding the community of their own reproductive generativity. The masked figures ac-
cent the failure of those who have not fulfilled their roles; ritual
inversions enable the ancestors to mock those who digress from
the normal developmental cycle (Kligman 1981; Karnoouh 1986,
80–81). The notes, such as the following one, generally blame the
single status on antisocial, unacceptable behavior that is an inversion of that which is expected.

Io-s fecior de la Vişeu	I'm a young man from Vişeu.
Cu liceu ieu stau căm greu.	I'm not well-educated,
Şî la Unitate am plecat	And I went to the Unitate—
Pă trei oameni am întrebat	I asked three people,
Unde sînt fete de măritat?	"Where are there girls to marry?"
Şi iel la ——— m-o mînat	And he sent me to ———
Că-i fată de măritat.	Because there's a girl ready for marriage.
Că nu-i fată cu avere	She's not a girl with holdings;
Da îi fată cu plăcere.	She's a girl of pleasure,
Şî la lucru cînd i de lucrat	And when there is work to be done,
Să pune în pat	She puts herself in bed—
Dar nu sîngură	But not alone—
Şi ieu de acolo am plecat.	And (so) I left there.

. . . .

(Collected in Breb,
Maramureş, 1978)

This note contains an additional forty-five lines. The *Unitate* in line
three is a factory in Sighetu Marmaţiei where young women work.
Eligible young ladies are supposed to be industrious workers and,
most certainly, virgins. The note implicitly denies the possibility of
an individual choosing to remain unmarried. This custom reveals
that ritual behavior generally represents the normative system but
may also tolerate reasonable alternatives. Deviation, depending on
the degree, may or may not be considered acceptable social-sexual
practice.

Gender and Social Relations

Relations between the sexes have been structured by generalized
sex-bound delineations of public and private domains of activity
that reflect separately organized spheres of productive relations
(Kligman 1981, 123–35). Although the sexual division of labor appears to stress sexual separateness, it also underscores the complementarity of productive and reproductive activities (see also Friedl
1967). Men tend to deal with the public sector; women, the private. In keeping with patrilineal, patrilocal biases, men have been,
until recently, the formal representatives of households, the public
arbiters of interfamilial relations. Women are the informal mana-
gers of domestic affairs, the private mediators of intrafamilial relations. As T. Turner notes, men are primarily concerned with the
"relationship of the group as a whole to the external environment,"
whereas women focus on the "internal stability of the group" (1976,
434). This division of social action is dramatically reiterated in the
ritual cycle: men are most prominent in calendar customs; women,
in life-cycle rites (Kligman 1981, 136). Calendar customs are associated with specific periods of the annual religious and productive
cycles: Christmas, Easter, the shepherd's rites in mid-spring. Because these events tend to be celebrated by communities, men
usually serve as the primary ritual representatives. Life-cycle rites,
as we have seen, focus on individual and familial occasions.

Spatial differentiation is associated with the sexual division of labor. Men are more mobile, working away from home in the fields,
forests, mines, mountains, and, now, cities. (Commuters are disproportionately male; Chirot 1978; Moskoff 1978.) Men go to the
monthly local animal markets and are generally the ones who purchase larger animals such as pigs, sheep, horses, and cattle. (Today,
most people buy pigs and sheep, no longer having the means to
maintain cattle and horses. Also, especially today, women do buy
pigs, as shall be seen in the last chapter.) The experience of men is
both socially and geographically broader than women's (see Ardener
1975, 6). Women work primarily in the domestic sphere. They are
responsible for the functioning of the household. Daily tasks include the feeding of household members (humans and animals),
washing, cleaning, and caring for the yard and garden. Women may
go to local markets to sell and purchase foodstuffs, including eggs,

cabbages, chickens, and other household necessities. The movement of women is relatively constrained, however. They are meant to perform their tasks efficiently and return home. This pertains to activities within the village as well: going on an errand does not sanction stopping to chat with a friend for twenty minutes. Women are called to account for prolonged absences by their husbands, mothers-in-law, or mothers.

Although there is a sexual division of labor, categories of productive activities are not necessarily exclusive. Women work in the fields planting potatoes, making haystacks, and so on, but they do not typically wield scythes. Because they are responsible for the nourishment of family members, women also bring food daily or weekly to their male kin working in the fields. Men will help plant the larger yard, although they do not plant the flower garden. An example of the complementarity of tasks involves the killing and preparing of pigs, an event that occurs before Christmas (and, if the family is rich enough, during the rest of the year as well). Slaughtering is done by men. Usually, a specialist is hired and aided by male members of the household. The pig is butchered in the cold, early morning hours (dawn is announced by the pained squealing of pigs as they meet their demise). When the animal is carved, its pieces are delivered to the women of the household, who then spend as much time as necessary to prepare all of the pig without waste or spoilage. This generally requires working until the early morning hours of the next day. From the pig, staples and specialties are prepared: *slănină* (pork fat) is immediately placed in salt brine where it remains several days; cutlets are cut and packed; hams, sausages, and the like are made. Slănină is the basic animal meat in the diet; it is plentiful. Everything else is considered a special treat because of its scarcity.

Although it is dangerous to generalize too broadly, it may nonetheless be suggested that men produce or acquire goods for their families (including women) and that women transform the goods for consumption, culinary or otherwise. Until recently, women were solely responsible for the production of clothing for all seasons, and they processed cloth and wool from start to finish. Certain tasks were performed socially: women spun, wove, knit, and embroidered together (and still do). Today, however, it is no longer profitable to produce clothing as a domestic enterprise; the cost of unpaid time and labor is too great. But girls are still expected to produce the requisite items for their dowry: blankets, rugs, towels, and so forth (see note 18). Families that have the means, however, may engage someone else to make some or all of it.

People buy ready-made clothes, particularly shirts, for daily wear. In the village, however, "traditional" dress continues to be favored. Elders and children wear this type of attire every day; women may wear traditional dress or a variation. Almost everyone regularly uses certain elements of this mode of dress, especially the woolen vests and jackets. Women wear aprons, although these are now usually made with synthetic material instead of wool, which is more costly. During the winter months, men put on their heavy, warm woolen pants. For ritual occasions and Sundays, almost everyone "dresses," meaning that they go out in their best "village" clothes, even those who do not live in the village. Urban workers who return on weekends don their village dress, as do local teens returning home from high school in Sighetu Marmaţiei. This is an important marker of identity in a time of rapid change. Those who never dress in this fashion are either outsiders or "intellectuals" (or consider themselves to be). The status distinction is intentional. Teenagers and those of marriageable age avidly engage in the politics of self-presentation. Gossip is quick to relate who has purchased what, where, and for how much. Local aesthetic standards are mercilessly applied, as they simultaneously are transformed. Women constantly seek new, intricate patterns for the socks and sweaters they knit, which will then be scrutinized by the curious and envious eyes of others.

Some women operate as individual entrepreneurs, acquiring knitting machines and private business. Others travel far and wide to return with scarves and material for sale. The supplementary income gained from such endeavors may be minimal or significant; in any event, it enables women to contribute financially to family economies. Personal necessities (such as clothing) can be paid for by these funds, or, in the case of a successful seamstress or knitter, her income may go toward the construction of a new house or the purchase of a car. Access to the wage-labor market offers women a degree of autonomy. In relative terms, however, the number of women in such positions is small. What is salient is that women are participating in family strategies to maximize resources during a period of fundamental socioeconomic change.

To be sure, externally imposed changes, in accordance with the goals of Party five-year plans, have transformed the economic and occupational structure of the village, making basic subsistence economy inadequate (Cernea 1969 and 1976; Dragăn 1973). This has necessarily resulted in the diversification of the family, with one or more persons entering the wage-labor force to supplement income (Beck 1976; Cernea 1976; see also Friedl 1959; Simić 1973). In Romania, rapid industrialization has occurred simultaneously with planned urbanization through the transformation of select villages into towns or urban centers (Sampson 1980). Industrial centers are dispersed throughout the country rather than concentrated in a few areas. One result of this strategy has been the increase of commuters to and from factories, mines, and building projects. Rural-urban contact is daily (20 percent of the labor force commutes every day). This commuter strategy alleviated problems that would have been engendered by lack of infrastructural resources in the burgeoning urban areas (see Konrad and Szelenyi 1976) but contributed to difficulties in the rural sector. Commuters are disproportionately male, however, meaning that agriculture has been steadily feminized; women now account for approximately 70 percent of the agricultural work force (see also Fedorova 1982; Chirot 1978; Moskoff 1978). Today, poor agricultural productivity is attributed in part to the predominantly female composition of agricultural workers (*New York Times*, March 9, 1981, A4). Ceauşescu himself conceded that his government has neglected the development of agriculture in favor of industry to the detriment of the nation (see Jowitt 1978). Plans to reverse this condition involve making agriculture attractive to men. The implicit sexism in these views is a poor—although convenient—excuse for planning, development, and implementation failures.

The feminization of agriculture in Maramureş has unintentionally reinforced traditional norms and roles. Men used to commute to the forest; now they go to the city. Women, constrained by household and childcare obligations, have become the nurturers for the state as well as for the family. This mode of integrating women into the national economy has accentuated many of the traditional patterns of relations and intensified tensions in them. Women remain economically subordinate, although, as intended, the structure of family relations is slowly changing (Cernea 1969; Jowitt 1978, 63–73). A female core occupies the village more or

less continuously. As men lose touch with the daily affairs of the
village as a result of commuting or seasonal labor, their authority in
the community and even in the family diminishes. Because men
may no longer claim to be the primary organizers and contributors
to family economy, fathers are losing some of their power over their
sons, in particular. The lessening of patriarchal authority does not
imply a generalized increase of status and authority for women,
however. Women may have responsibility for household finances
and management, but village matters continue to be directed by
men from the village or elsewhere.

All members of a family contribute to its well-being, whether or
not everyone lives in the village. The reciprocity inherent in village social relations is extended to urban-rural relations (Simić
1973; Konrad and Szelenyi 1976). Family ties are manipulated as a
means to counter formal organizational demands and to maximize
personal and familial advantage. Most Ieudeni are still primarily
engaged in agricultural or pastoral labor. Fifty percent of the population are members of the cooperative, which concentrates on the
production of grain, corn, oats, beets, and potatoes. Zootechnology
is used in the raising of sheep and cattle. The cooperative farm
work force is primarily female; most positions of authority are
staffed by men. Local officials estimate that less than seven hundred individuals work in other occupations. Among these are workers in forestry (approximately 100); in factories producing parts or
larger, total-production factories, light industry, or construction
(450); in mining (80); and in transport (40). The significant feature
of Ieud's work force is that 90 percent of healthy inhabitants participate in seasonal labor. Since World War II families have come to
depend on added income from seasonal migrant work such as haying and harvesting. These hard-laboring peasants have discovered
that, although this work is brutally demanding, it can be extremely
lucrative, if contracted and performed in kin-composed teams.
Moreover, the controlling presence of kin ensures the propriety of
adding unmarried but able daughters to the migrant labor force.
Girls often beg their parents to let them go to work so that they can
pay for new clothes (of course, a certain portion of their earnings
will be turned over to the collective family till). It is not uncommon
to see girls who have gone on to high school in the city spending
several weeks of the summer working in the fields of a collective

farm elsewhere in Romania. (The attractiveness of seasonal labor
for capital gain has not been consistently beneficial for local education. Only 25–30 percent of students go on beyond the mandatory
ten grades to finish high school. Also, with many potential laborers
earning wages elsewhere, mothers frequently call on the assistance
of their school-age children. Absenteeism is, therefore, a continual
problem.)

Increased wealth, which is significant in terms of both money
and staples (grain, corn, hay), is used for ritual display. The socialist ownership of land and enterprises precludes investment of
funds into these endeavors; hence, cash incomes are directed to increased conspicuous consumption. People seek material goods and
comforts. They hope to acquire televisions, radios, cassette record-
ers, refrigerators, stoves, freezers, knitting machines. They save
for bicycles and cars. Young people are desperate for *blugi* (blue
jeans) and Western cigarettes and music. At the same time, they
want the fanciest material for their traditional set of clothes. Embroidered vests for men and women have become more elaborate
and gaudy; a new one is an item of great admiration. Houses are
also more elaborate and larger (partially dictated by building codes).
New, shiny furniture is purchased gradually and fills at least the
room reserved for entertaining guests and for special occasions.
(This room is a "show" room. It is not used except to honor or im-
press others.) Wall rugs hug the walls, revealing the newest patterns—*la modă*, the mode. The colors have changed from subtle,
natural hues to bright, shocking tones. All of this reflects an ongoing reconstruction of status values and presentation of self. It is as if
everyone must announce their modernity. Increasingly, identity
seems to be defined dramatically through objects.

Increased conspicuous consumption is evident at ritual occasions, especially weddings. Wedding guests are expected to contribute cash (100–500 lei, or approximately $8–$40); the once customary gifts of decorated, fancy breads or a bottle of *horincă* (plum
brandy) no longer suffice. Those that cannot afford the cash gift frequently do not attend the wedding. (Kin relations mean one may
have multiple obligations during the wedding season.) The cost for
close relatives as well as for the godparents, not to mention that for
the parents, is considerable. The expense of a wedding or a funeral
may amount to more than 10,000 lei per family per occasion. (At

weddings, not only must sufficient quantities of food and drink be obtained and prepared, but musicians must also be engaged.)[28] Certain features of weddings in other villages are not practiced in Ieud, except among the Gypsies. Notably, the bride is not danced with for money, that is, in other villages guests get to dance with the bride if they pay for the privilege—which can result in a significant sum of money for the newlyweds. Ieudeni look upon this custom with disdain and consider it *ţigănesc*, or Gypsy behavior; it is thought to be an insult to women. Although the extraordinary sums collected at weddings elsewhere are not typical of Ieud, funds nonetheless are gathered and defray some, if not all, of the expense. Donors eventually recoup their output through future reciprocal exchange.

Reciprocal exchanges occur not only within families but also within other domains of social organization: neighbor relations, and age or gender-defined groups. With regard to the former, extended families often used to live in the same area of a village. These families together formed *vecinătăţile* (neighborhoods; Cernea 1974b, 52–53; Chirot 1976b, 139). According to Chirot (idem), these families had "certain limited economic, political and social functions. . . . They organized some types of work, particularly those relating to cleaning their section of the village, collecting wastes for fertilizer and maintaining streets." Such a configuration of families does not exist in Ieud; however, neighbors are important both socially and economically.[29] Neighbors participate in major rites of passage; in addition, they contribute their labor to preparations for these events. They also assist in the planting and harvesting of fields (for which they are reimbursed in kind or goods). They participate in voluntary collective work (historically stemming from imposed corvée). Work bees are organized to help build a house or to transport fertilizer to the fields—in short, to carry out tasks that are better performed ensemble. The person who has organized the collective effort provides a hearty meal at the end of the day's work (Lenghel-Izanu 1973, 68; also Károly 1969, 231–34).

Neighbor relations are especially important for women because their mobility is constrained. Interaction with people other than members of the household and those who come to visit occurs primarily with neighbors (Musset 1981, 25; see also Flandrin 1976, 41). Women bake bread together, sew, spin, knit or weave, and generally lend assistance to one another. Reciprocity is implicit in these activities, and, if not honored, a quarrel or feud ensues. During the long, cold winter nights, girls and women used to organize *şezătoare* (a sitting, or a work bee). These still take place but are not as important as they once were. It was during the şezătoare that women made significant progress on their task of clothing their family. Girls learned the necessary skills for spinning, weaving, embroidering, sewing, and preparing dowry items. Sisters contributed labor for each other's dowry; eventually, the effort would be reciprocated in kind. (This is similar to brothers' contributions of labor and capital to the building of houses.)

Social activities are also organized by age or sex. The Sunday *horă*, or dance, and the şezătoare are of special significance to adolescents and, in turn, to the community in general.[30] These events are ritualized occasions not only for work and play, but also for courtship. The hierarchical ordering of social relations is displayed in them. The horă used to take place each Sunday (except during Lenten periods). Arranged by the young men, the dance was a public event that took place in the *ciupercă* (mushroom), an open wooden dance floor covered by a roof, located in a central area of the village. Following the church service and family meal on Sunday, a group of young men would invite the musicians to accompany them to the dance. En route, the musicians played melodies to which the young men sang or shouted rhymed couplets. This signaled the community that it was time to gather for the dance. The dance was of interest to everyone. Children came to watch, to play, and to learn the dances by practicing unobtrusively; adolescents came for entertainment and with the hope of courting or being courted; women of all ages stood on the sidelines attentive to the nuances of every glance. Gestures were considered highly meaningful; the ability to read them filled gossip networks with hot information. Men were not as interested in the goings-on of the elementary forms of courtship; rather, they took advantage of the opportunity to talk with friends and relatives and to play cards undisturbed.

The major action, however, was on the dance floor. Chaperoned by older women, the Sunday dance was controlled by the young men. This was appropriate in view of the public authority of men. One's entrance into the dance was fraught with anxiety; this occa-

sion meant joining the pool of potential spouses. A boy or girl had
to be invited by an "initiate" to enter the dance for the first time.
(This applied to "strangers" as well, that is, persons visiting from
other locales.) Girls additionally needed to receive permission
from their mothers. Ideally, as for the order of marriage, siblings
entered the dance by order of birth. Entrance into the dance was a
type of initiation, or puberty, rite. The dance enabled the young
men to exercise their sense of machismo to the fullest. Often their
"shouted" and improvised couplets could be instruments of ridicule
and insult quite damaging to young women. On occasion, romantic
rivalries were voiced in verse. Or young men would express their
romantic sentiments through this mode of metaphoric communication permissible in public. Young women were at the mercy of the
young men, and they were expected to be passive and obedient. A
girl was invited to dance either by having her name called or by
simply a nod or glance. She then moved to join her partner where
he was positioned. A young man never invited the same girl to
dance two consecutive dances. If he did not wish to be associated
with anyone in particular (considered the wisest choice), he attempted to dance with as many girls as possible. A girl did not have
the right to refuse to dance with someone unless she had already
promised to dance with another; if she refused without justification, she was ostracized from the dance and could not join it until
invited to do so (which might never again happen). The dance
event emphasized men's public solidarity in contrast to the individuality of the girls who were placed in direct competition with
each other—another example of the dynamic of the patrilineal
paradox.

Such were the rules of public courtship—*were*, because the
Sunday dance in Ieud is becoming an event of the past. Changed
economic conditions have decreased the number of adolescent
males in the village, making it impossible to organize the dance.
(In uncollectivized villages, the dance continues, if sporadically.)
The dance is held on specific occasions, however, most notably on
the second day of Christmas and the second day of Easter. (Each
holiday is celebrated for three days—three being a ritually significant number linked with the Holy Trinity: day one for the church
and family, day two for the dance, day three for communal relations.) Then, the dance publicly marks the end of the period of

fasting that precedes Christmas and Easter (Advent and Lent) and the commencement of active courtship. Furthermore, everyone returns home on these holidays, so there are enough people to hold the event.

Whereas the dance is in the public domain and is male-associated, the work bee (sewing, weaving) is in the private domain and is female-associated.[31] Şezătoare are organized by women and girls. One family will agree to host the work bee for a certain period of time (one week or more) during which female relatives and friends are invited to attend at night. There may be many şezătoare in the village at the same time. The women and girls gather to spin, sew, and embroider. They discuss social matters, local gossip, and new patterns; tales are told, songs sung. The hours and tedious work pass congenially. Like the Sunday dance, these work bees also provide occasions for courtship, again in a ritualized manner: later in the evening, young men *umblă pă la fete* (go to the girls). The young men are not in control, however, as they are at the dance. In the domestic sphere, women are accorded authority and take responsibility for household activities. At şezătoare, girls and young women direct social interaction. Their control is manifested in several ways. Girls used to collectively perform ritual love charms to attract the young men.[32] The following verse is common:

—Ce torci?	"What are you spinning?"
—Nu torc, că-ntorc:	"I'm not spinning but unspinning:
Feciorii, de prin tăte şezătorile	Bachelors from all work bees
Di pă tăte uliţăle	From all of the little paths,
De la tăte căsele.	From all of the houses
Cîţi-s cu optinci	How many are with peasant sandals
Tăţi să zie aici.	All of them to come here
Să aibă:	To have:
Şoareci în cioareci	Mice in their woven woolen pants,
Furnici în optinci	Ants in their peasant sandals,
Şî fuga să zie aici!	And quickly to come here!
Că de n-or zini—	Because if they don't come,
Boala i-a stropşi.	Illness will strike.
. . . . . .	. . . . . .

| Nime şi nimnic să nu-i poată opri | No one and nothing will be able to stop them |
| Pînă la Anuţa or sosî. | Until they arrive at Anuţa's." |

(Lenghel-Izanu 1971, 70)

The young woman acting as charmer directs the question to each unmarried girl until all have been asked. *Descîntece*, or charms, always proceed in the above manner, that is, through inversions (Rosetti 1975). A curse is included should the signified (the boy) not perform as expected. Again, the competition among women for men—unspinning the bachelors from other work bees—is evident. This competition is a structural consequence of the patrilineal paradox.

The arrival of the young men encourages conversation, joking, and singing. Not too late in the evening, the young men begin to leave. The nature of leave-taking is left to the discretion of the young women. Several conventions operate to attract the attention of a particular girl. Generally, a subtle glance serves to indicate that the young man wishes her to escort him out. He will depart, leaving the door slightly ajar. If the young woman wishes to acknowledge his request, she will quietly go outside through the open door, it being his invitation to do so. Or the young man may leave the door open and go around the house to the window (if the desired young woman is sitting near it). He will tap on it, and then if she wants to, she will go out. The couple will spend a few minutes talking privately (or perhaps kissing). In this instance young women are able to control social interaction and, furthermore, are able to refuse the advances of young men—as they may not do at the dance. A refusal must be made carefully; otherwise, the girl risks retaliation at the dance when she may become the victim of insulting strigături. Today, that is less likely because the dances occur infrequently. Şezătoare, however, persist, even though their courtship function has lessened.

The dance and the work bee are ritualized, highly controlled occasions for courtship. The former occurs in public male space; the latter, in domestic female space. Relative authority within these domains is exercised respectively. Women may refuse men within the privacy of the domestic sphere; but they may not do so publicly in front of the entire community without serious consequence. (For married couples, offenses may result in beatings; wife-beating is fairly common.) Both occasions, the dance and the şezătoare, produce and reproduce the hierarchical ordering of social relations and the division of labor in condensed symbolic form.

Religion and Social Organization

The structure of social organization is symbolically reiterated in religious belief and practice. Ieudeni, by decree of state, are formally Orthodox; however, several centuries of Uniate hegemony have left a strong presence in Ieud. This is especially noticeable in practices related to the cult of Mary (which is not as elaborated in Orthodoxy), during Lent when women pray at the fourteen stations of the cross, and in the learning of catechisms (foreign to Orthodoxy). Otherwise, the rites of the Orthodox and Greek Catholic faiths are reasonably similar, with certain doctrinal differences.

In the Orthodox as well as the Uniate church, men and women are spatially separated: the men occupy the larger front section of the church; the women stand in the back. In the small, older wooden churches, which are now primarily historical monuments, there are more spacious forechambers for the men; women remained in the smaller spaces in the back, which also served as entrances to the churches. On the most important holidays—Christmas, Easter, Rusalii (Pentecost), St. Mary's Day—women crowd around the outside of the wooden church where services are held, ears pressed against the wood so they can hear the priest. (It is not uncommon to see their bundled-up figures huddled together outdoors in the freezing winter weather.) The older churches are too small to enable all the women to enter; the irony is that women are the most religious in terms of daily practice. In the new church, which now serves the community, there are no formal dividers except two small tables behind the men's section, which are used for collecting funds and placing candles from the women.

In essence, men represent their families before God, just as they represent their households in the village. Women are on the fringes of the sacred and the public. Religion plays an important role in fostering and shaping the order of relations. God and ordinary people are related through sacred and secular practices. (Icons adorn household rooms and form part of everyday signifying practices about the cosmological order.) Hierarchical relations between animals, humans, supernatural beings, and God are implicit in the structure of the cosmos. These relations are further differentiated by gender. Men receive the word of God before women do (spatially in church and metaphorically and literally in its teachings): if gender equality was meant to be sacredly sanctioned, the original sin of Eve negated the possibility.

Clearly, religious belief is fundamental to the indigenous folk ideology of gender. Central to the conception of men and women are notions of purity and pollution. The human body experiences carnal desire; periodically, corporeal pleasure must be tempered. The body requires cleansing so that a balance between physical and spiritual well-being can be maintained. Religion regulates this balance through food prohibitions and days of fasting. Each week consists of *zile de post* (days of fasting) and *zile de dulce* (days of sweetness). Wednesday and Friday are days of fasting, during which people are not supposed to eat meat, milk, eggs, butter, olive oil, or fish. (Many people also fast on Mondays.) Instead, people eat corn bread, *coleşă* (mush), onions, potatoes, beans, sour pickles, cabbage (see Lenghel-Izanu 1939, 271–75). People young and old still adhere to these restrictions. Since zile de post are days of abstinence, weddings and other occasions for celebration and excess do not begin on these days.

From a broader perspective, the annual cycle is punctuated with periods of fasting. (Including the weekly fast days, there are a total of two hundred fast days; see Benedict 1972, 37; Kligman 1981, 108–12; Musset 1981, 87.) The major fasts are for Easter (forty days before and one week after), Christmas (forty days, from November 15 to January 6), St. Peter and Paul (June 25–28), and St. Mary (August 1–15). During these periods, people are expected to follow the regime for zile de post. Today, however, only the elderly strictly maintain this custom. Marriages, the dance, and other celebrations do not take place during these times. Spiritual reproduction is favored, whereas social reproduction is temporarily restrained. By alternating periods of excess and restraint, feasting and fasting, religious ideology legitimizes itself. Body and soul are thus believed to be spiritually cleansed, an important factor in the conception and presentation of self.

A primal component in the religious tale about life and death, and purity and pollution, is blood. Blood is life's force (a factor significant to the power attributed the menses, discussed below); excessive letting of this substance weakens or kills. Blood is sustenance and, as such, is a critical feature of Christianity. "The sacrament of communion is based on the transfer of energy through blood" (Twitchell 1981, 13), and believers partake of Christ's power by imbibing his life's force—the blood of communion: "Whoso eateth my flesh, and drinketh my blood, hath eternal life; and I will raise him up at the last day" (John 6:53–57). But just as excessive loss of blood is perilous, so is excessive intake. The Bible cautions against addiction to this powerful force; lust in and of itself is sinful, and lusting after another's blood leads to the commitment of mortal sin.[33]

With regard to purity and pollution, the bodies of women are more problematic than men's are. Women are considered constitutionally *becişnice* (weak; in the vernacular, polluted) and *spurcate* (polluted, defiled). According to church teachings, it was Eve who sinned, the ultimate proof that the innate nature of the female sex was associated with temptation and lust.[34] From the patriarchal, Christian perspective that has permeated the worldview of these Transylvanian villagers, the Devil presides over self-indulgence and finds a susceptible audience among women, who are thought to be "by nature" prone to traffic with him. This ideology of gender, emerging from a religious tale of sexuality, guilt, sin, and evil, therefore links women with devilish appetites. Because women have been, and are, considered the weaker sex (a characterization with which many women still concur),[35] they have been assigned to the domain of the diabolical, aligned with the Devil in action. Desire is an integral feature of the Devil's purview, and, among mortals, it is women who manipulate desire's potentialities or are readily manipulated by it. In Ieud, men and women alike state emphatically that *tăte femeile sînt a dracului* (all women are the Devil's), meaning that women have qualities similar to the Devil's and are, similarly, difficult to deal with.[36] (This is an allusion to the Fall—woman as acceding to temptation and being temptress herself. The Devil and women are symbolic media through whom deviation from norms may be explored.) Ieudeni invoke the authoritative voice of religion to lend credence to this "truism." It is

said that women, left to their own desires, will not respect the
norms of social, much less sexual, intercourse. (This will be discussed further in the third chapter's section on the association
between women and death.) The "Devil, his active principle, femi-
ninity, and his incarnations, women, represent the wish for a liberty, that of desire which leads to social disintegration" (Karnoouh
1983a, 110).[37] Desire run amok creates monstrous beings of one
sort or another that arouse trouble for the living. "Civilization" is
society's recourse.[38]

In popular belief, through transformations of symbolic logic,
menacing fairies and spirits are thought to be women (Kligman
1981, 48–58). Moroşeni are warned not to be fooled by the seduc-
tive entreaties of the *fată pădurii* (girl of the forest). Illnesses enter
a house in the form of a female being who then "weakens" others,
for example, *ciumă*, or plague (see Vulpesco 1927, 36). Tradition
dictates that on New Year's Day and on Easter, everything possible
must be done to prevent a woman from being the first person to
enter a household from outside. Otherwise, the family will suffer
from illness and bad luck. In a similar vein, death is thought to be a
woman who comes to people and cuts them down with a scythe.
(This represents an interesting inversion, as women do not customarily wield scythes.) Not surprisingly, women, the symbolic kin of
dangerous beings, are the primary customers for magic practices
(such as the love charms associated with courtship, mentioned earlier); sorcery is also, by and large, a female profession (Kligman
1981; Karnoouh 1983a). In light of all these beliefs, women's characters are always questionable and frequently denounced. It is not
accidental that a bride's virginity is scrutinized during the wedding
ritual, but no one inquires after the groom's. The burden of purity
is placed on women, who are expected to uphold the norms of
society and, therefore, of patrilineality. Ultimately, the Devil and
desire are subdued by the powers of patriarchal will exhibited
through God and men.

The belief in the pollution of women stems partially from their
menses and from the natural endowment of female generativity.
Scholars argue that women have the innate potential to threaten
the social order (Lévi-Strauss 1966, 82–94; Ortner 1974; MacCormack and Strathern 1980). The act of giving birth, the sacred obligation of women, is colored by natural, profane blood. Although

blood is positively valued because it is the essence of health, kinship, and certain holy sacraments, it is also negatively valued because it is associated with natural processes perceived to be threatening and polluting: menstruation, birth, and death. Many believe
that "a woman is not clean when she gives birth." At the same time,
women are encouraged to have many children because it is believed that with each child the mother's blood is changed, making
her healthier (although perhaps physically weaker). Birth is coupled
with sexual sin. After a birth, neither mother, child, nor midwife
may enter the church for forty days. During this period, the mother
and child are expected to stay near their house so as not to *a se
spurca tot satul* (pollute the entire village). The forty days constitute an imposed time of purification after which prayers are read
that reinstate the mother and midwife, as well as welcome the
child into the social milieu of the village.

The blood of birth and its link with sin create a ritual kin tie
between the mother and the midwife, or *moaşă*. Interestingly,
moaşă is also the word used to designate a grandmother, the woman
who has given birth to the mother of the child. (In similar fashion
a grandmother may be addressed as *mama dulce* by her grandchildren.) A midwife is recognized as a symbolic grandmother, or
godmother. The ritual kin bonds are, again, corporately extended.
She and her husband thereafter are respectively addressed as
moaşă and *moş* by the women (and their families) she has helped to
give birth. The mothers are the midwife's *nepoate*, meaning both
goddaughters and nieces. The children born with her assistance,
her *nepoţi*, are simultaneously her godchildren and her nieces or
nephews. After her death, the midwife will be lamented by her respective "goddaughters" and mourned by all of her godchildren.
(See Chapter 3.) The terms *moaşă* and *moş* also mean "ancestor."
Birth introduces the newborn into the world—of the living as well
as the dead—thereby assuring the reproduction of the patriline.
(See Karnoouh 1986.)

Because of the nature of the midwife's tasks, she is said to *umblă
cu păcatele*, or be involved with sins. (Elsewhere in Romania this
phrase has the additional connotation of performing an abortion.)
If a woman goes into labor at night, her husband must go to fetch
the midwife. In view of the symbolic syncretism between darkness,
evil, and sin, the husband is obliged to call the moaşă three times.

Otherwise, it is feared that the midwife is being tricked or tempted by the Devil, the greatest sinner of all. (Three is considered "sacred"; hence, certain acts of sorcery require that the person resist responding until called three times.) The midwife works with sins; therefore, she herself is in a precarious position.

To dispel potential danger, in addition to the church purification prayers her goddaughters ritually purify her. Once a year, on the second or third day of Easter or Pentecost, the moaşă's goddaughters honor her (in the same way that godchildren ritually, but sporadically, honor their naşi). The *sărbătoarea nepoatelor* (celebration of the goddaughters) is a holiday that celebrates female solidarity in terms of the shared ability to give life; at the same time, it purifies that aspect of femaleness considered to be polluted and polluting. The goddaughters go to their midwife's house late in the afternoon. On entering, each woman ritually purifies the midwife; after dipping her hands in a bowl of blessed water, the goddaughter runs her hands over the midwife from head to toe three times, saying: *"Ierte-ţi Dumnezău păcatele dumnitale şî a cui ti-o făcut pă dumăta"* (God forgive your sins and who has sinned against you). Each goddaughter brings a gift of grain, meat, sugar, or flour for the midwife. In return, the midwife provides food and drink. The women celebrate together. There is a great deal of singing, strigături, and gossip. Husbands arrive later in the evening to take their wives home because some of the women have overindulged in drink and require assistance. The men relish this opportunity to escort their wives home; usually, it is the wife who must retrieve her husband from the local bar.[39]

The sărbătoarea nepoatelor continues, in spite of the changes wrought by the communist regime. Although unlicensed midwives are no longer permitted to practice, formally trained midwives assist in the village birthing room. Because they help bring children into the world, they are accorded the ritual honor that is their due. On the appropriate day, all of the living moaşe in the village are acknowledged by their goddaughters.

But women are not seen only as polluted beings; they are "deemed both good and bad, and both evaluations may be represented as stemming from their naturalness" (Jordanova 1980, 66). This is significant because the tendency to locate "femaleness in biology" (MacCormack 1980, 18) and in the natural order leads to

overgeneralized (if appealing) analyses of nature-culture-gender relations. Women are naturally polluted because of their menses, but
they also are naturally pure because of their milk (see Harrell
1981). Whereas menstruation is associated with sexuality and pollution, lactation is associated with motherhood and nurturance.[40]
Lactation is considered purifying, especially because it often temporarily prevents the flow of blood. Hence, in Ieud (and much of
the Catholic-related world) the female temptress gives way to the
virgin bride. The sacred dimension of life-giving is encapsulated in
the icon of the suckling child nourished by the generosity of his
pure mother. This is an image that graces the walls of every home.
(Again, the veneration of Mary is a Catholic phenomenon and is
not typical of Orthodoxy. The continuing allegiance to Mary in
Maramureş, particularly the pilgrimage on her saint's day, August 15, celebrates the historical religious roots of belief and ignores the contradictions posed by the present Orthodox practice.)
Virginity and purity are fetishized and sacralized. As will be seen in
later chapters, complex beliefs about pollution, honor, virginity,
and shame have been constructed in cultural self-defense against
the physical manifestation of female maturity (see Campbell 1964;
Douglas 1966; Herzfeld 1980; Kligman 1981, 123–38). The patrilineal paradox is a case in point. Family honor and prestige rest on
the virtue of the female sex, those who are in but not of the family.
Birth is shrouded in pollution and purity through blood and milk.

Concepts of the sacred and profane and of purity and pollution
are used to "explain" and to interrelate categories of relations such
as gender (male, female), species (animal, human), order (nature,
culture) and activity (domestic, agricultural/pastoral). The milking
of sheep provides an interesting example of cultural logic illuminating the ambivalence in the hierarchy of relations thus formulated.
In most parts of Maramureş, women are not permitted to milk
sheep, although they do milk cows. Sheep, but not cows, are sacred (see Campbell 1964, 26). Because sheep are God's animals,
lamb is sacrificed and consumed on Easter. Pollution via sexuality
or blood cannot be risked. One shepherd explained in explicitly
sexual terms why women should not milk sheep. His argument was
based on practical considerations. Cows are milked from the side,
but sheep must be held between one's legs. If women were to milk
sheep in the presence of shepherds (which is done collectively at

the sheepfold), how could the shepherds resist the temptation? (Only recently have most women begun to wear panties under their peasant skirts.) Most people, however, attribute the taboo on women to menses. Accordingly, menstruating women in particular are discouraged from approaching the sheepfold. It is believed their blood will curdle the sheep's milk. Women and sheep are placed in opposition: menstruation, women, pollution versus lactation, sheep, purity. Men are caught in the middle. Tales of the rivalry between sheep and women abound. In a secularized variant of the Adam and Eve theme, a shepherd succumbs to the sexuality of a woman and loses the prescient assistance of a miraculous lamb ("Siu Oii," collected 1978, Ieud). Women are also blamed for "stealing" the milk of sheep; that is, by sorcery they cause sheep to be "dry," or unable to give milk. (Shepherds must be attentive to the condition of their sheep; they also have recourse to counter-magic to rectify such situations.) The economic motivation for these "attacks" must be noted. How much milk sheep give on the day the shepherds depart for high pastures determines the amount of milk and cheese received later in the summer. Sheepfolds are composed of several families, friends, or relatives. Competition may arise among them or between different sheepfolds. But any problems with sheep's milk are attributed to the evil workings of women. Thus women, again, are responsible for dissension, trouble, and disease in and between households.

In addition to providing a framework for the genesis of an ideology of gender, religion also influences the general organization of daily activity and the division of labor. This is not a deterministic relationship, but, rather, a culturally pervasive power that provides central symbols and metaphors by which people orient their lives and derive meaning. Daily activity is oriented around several "supra-cycles," all of which involve ongoing change: the seasonal cycle controls agricultural and pastoral activities; the alternation between day and night regulates hours for work and non-work; and the life of Christ structures periods of work and non-work, celebration and restraint. While these cycles are interrelated (see also Kligman 1981, 110–13), the life of Christ is the most overarching, permeating daily, as well as ritual and religious, discourse and action.

At the most basic level, the life of Christ constitutes the most general social liaison among Ieudeni (and Moroşeni); through Christ, there exists a common spiritual kinship and enterprise. Strangers, acquaintances, and relatives, regardless of class or status distinctions, share this bond, which is established and reestablished with every encounter, be it in passing or on entering a room. Because people are considered to be most fundamentally linked through Christ, the life of Christ structures greeting and interaction.[41] Throughout most of the year, people use the following greeting and response:

Laude-se Isus (*or* Laudăm   Praise Jesus (*or* We praise the
    pe Isus).   Lord, Jesus).
—În veci, amin.   —Forever, amen.

At Easter, the greeting changes:

Hristos o-nviat.   Christ has risen.
—Adevărat c-o-nviat.   —Truly he has risen.

On Ascension Day, forty days later, the greeting becomes the following:

Hristos s-o înalţat.   Christ has ascended.
—Adevărat s-o înalţat.   —Truly he has ascended.

This is used for three days only. Thereafter, until the following Easter, the standard greeting of *laude-se Isus* is used.

These formulaic greetings are important in the construction of self (and communal "self") and otherness. They simultaneously relate and segregate. Failure to extend this form of greeting distinguishes "others," or outsiders. A villager who does not utilize this greeting is viewed as highly antisocial; however, I never heard any person from Ieud, including Party members, "intellectuals," and those who now live in cities, use any other form of greeting among themselves (whether they met in the village or elsewhere). The "segregating" feature of this greeting with respect to class, status, and religion is worthy of note. Before World War II, there were approximately one hundred Jewish families in Ieud. That they could not share this greeting obviously differentiated them from the predominant Christian population and functioned as a cultural form of anti-Semitism.[42] Gypsies, who are considered "others" but not religious outcasts, were spared this affront (although they were and are subjected to others). Today, as before, the religiously based greeting immediately marks non-Moroşeni or unrelated city dwellers. To them, villagers use the forms of greeting common elsewhere, which are based on the time of day: *bună dimineaţă* (good morning); *bună ziuă* (good day); *bună seară* (good evening). (Until I was known in the village, people greeted me in this manner; afterward, I was accepted as an honorary Ieudeancă.) Also, when Ieudeni go to cities (other than Sighetu Marmaţiei), they use the standard forms of greeting. They (peasants as well as workers) know that others regard this village greeting as uncultivated. But in Ieud, the religious greeting is a marker of identity, a sign that one eternally belongs to the village and the church. This form of greeting was introduced by the Greek Catholic or Uniate church (see note 4) in the eighteenth century; it is not an Orthodox practice. Suggesting that its persistence under the communist regime and Orthodoxy represents a form of symbolic protest would be to exaggerate; however, the relevance of this practice to symbolic statements of identity has been noticed by those interested in the doctrinal differences between the Orthodox and Uniate churches. [43]

There is a link between the life cycle of Christ and the seasonal cycle. Easter, the time of Christ's resurrection, roughly corresponds with the arrival of spring. Both Christ and nature are reborn. When Christ ascends, crops begin to grow. If the seasons determine certain aspects of the human relationship with nature (see Marx 1957, 88), the church nonetheless proclaims its relationship with the human order by curtailing work (regardless of season) on major holidays, especially Christmas, Easter, Rusalii, and St. Mary's. (The Party attempts to deny church influence by refusing to recognize these days as official holidays, but people manipulate the system to their advantage. Christian holidays do not go unobserved by the majority of the people.) These Christian holidays form part of the cycle of calendar customs, which, in turn, are associated with the seasonal cycle.

The relationship between calendar and life-cycle customs is complex, recapitulating the general structure of social organization. Men are the primary facilitators in calendar customs. They are the ones who publicly represent their families before God and the community. Calendar customs tend to be concerned with the general well-being of the community. "Often, too, they [calendar

customs] are performed at well-delineated points in the annual
productive cycle, and attest to the passage from scarcity to plenty
and from plenty to scarcity" (V. Turner 1969, 169). Calendar customs enable men to fulfill their roles as social protectors and ensure
"the public good by metaphorically giving life to the community:
they cure the sick, bless the fields with abundance, and the women
with children" (Kligman 1981, 138). Women are the principals for
life-cycle rituals. They are responsible for the well-being of the
family and domestic life. Life-cycle rites address the private domain of familial life within the context of the community. Women
bring children into this world; the alienation of young women from
their natural families upon marriage continues this process; and
women care for and lament the dead in this world and the next.

Calendar and life-cycle rituals involve both the spiritual and the
social reproduction of the community as a whole and of the individuals it comprises. The mission of religious rites is much the
same, and a tension exists between these interrelated cycles. There
are customs and holidays that are restricted specifically to the
church-cycle, however, whereas there are no calendar or life-cycle
rites that are not sanctioned by the church in some manner, if only
in terms of signing the cross or a spoken blessing. (The exception is
sorcery, but many of its forms require a religious blessing or the
power of the Devil.) From the priest's point of view, there are many
pagan elements bound by centuries of practice to religious customs.[44] The predominance of religion is recognized in the hierarchical distinction between the sacred and secular. Religious beliefs
and practices magnify the sacred dimensions of calendar and life-
cycle rites, that is, that which is ordained. By so doing, the glory
and will of God are honored. Life and death are sacralized; moreover, human frailty is exonerated ideologically.

This is especially significant for life-cycle rituals. In secular reality, pollution and sin are believed to be inherent components of
life. The human developmental cycle naturally entails "pollution":
birth, sexual maturity, and death. Appropriately, nature's processes
provide "natural" symbols and metaphors by which the human biological life cycle is rendered comprehensible (see Weiner 1980). To
illustrate, for females, flowers are the symbols of vitality, hope, and
virginity. A girl is said to "blossom forth" (to attain puberty). The
euphemism for menstruation is having *flori pe poale,* or flowers on

one's skirt. Virginal girls wear brightly colored, floral-patterned skirts. A bride is always a "flower" in her "mother's garden" until she "blossoms forth." Then her mother "sells" her (marries her off; the exchange metaphors will be discussed in the next chapter). Girls, like flowers, are at the height of their vitality when they are "picked" by their husbands-to-be. For young women, marriage represents a symbolic death. Similarly, "man's life" is described in a lament verse as "that of a wildflower: today you exist; tomorrow, gone." Marriage and death both effect changes in status and identity. In a male-biased system, man's life formally describes the human condition in terms of the broader cosmological order. (Recall that women are dependent on men—fathers and husbands—for their identities.) At this level of organization, people (represented by men), like flowers, live and die. Natural processes conquer cultural constructs.

Religion, however, resurrects hope. Through its teachings, it offers cultural symbols and metaphors by which human physical, social, and spiritual processes are made meaningful. The separation of body and soul rationalizes the vulgarity of the material conditions of the natural processes of living and dying. The dynamic relationships between the living and the dead, the sacred and the profane resolve the dilemmas of biology, pollution, and sin. Conjoined, the religious and secular ritual cycles symbolically make sense of the contradictions in human experience. They provide a means to negotiate relations between self and society in a rapidly changing environment. This is particularly salient in contemporary Maramureş. The state has become more present in the lives of everyone (Verdery 1983a, 1983b; Shafir 1985). Socialist transformation of property and of the means and modes of production has required redefinition of the relations of individuals to the state. The exigencies of rapid industrialization and modernization have disrupted family structure, the division of labor, gender relations, and, in many cases, residence patterns. As a result of employment in the wage-labor force or pursuit of higher education or specialized training (which generally do not occur in the village), family members are increasingly dispersed. Throughout the year, Ieud is populated mostly by women, children, and the elderly.

To be sure, the rhythms of daily life have been radically affected. Strikingly, in Ieud, the ritual system has emerged as the stable organizational factor in a much-altered village life. Seasonal laborers leave the village at the beginning of Lent to return for Easter. This is repeated for Pentecost (Rusalii), St. Mary's in August, and Christmas. The villagers remain in residence through the cold winters, when most weddings take place. Death of a family member supersedes all other obligations at any time. On these ritual occasions, identities and social bonds are constructed as well as reaffirmed. People are rooted within the social organization of family and community. Of these rites, weddings and funerals in particular facilitate the process of commentary about the lived-in world as experienced in personal, local, and national terms. Hence, they constitute powerful media through which to gain insight into the practical and meaningful concerns of daily existence in contemporary, socialist Romania.

Chapter Two

Weddings

Să trăiască mnireasa   Long life to the bride!
Pentru ie i vesălie.   The celebration is for her.

A marriage is a type of negotiated exchange like that in the market; if you bargain with closed eyes, you'll pay dearly.

Interview, Ieud, 1978

Symbols are symptoms, direct or mystified, of the true force of things.

M. Sahlins 1981, 7

Marriage constitutes the ideological basis of social and sexual relations, transforming them by restructuring identity and social action. Because of the cultural significance of marriage (Van Gennep 1960, 116), weddings—the occasions through which marriages are publicly realized—are highly marked. Weddings celebrate the reproductive (biologic) and productive (social) cycles of the cultural order; they are social events that reify social norms and values. Customarily, weddings are three-day events that dramatically demarcate as well as facilitate the complex status and role changes that occur among the participants; weddings exemplify the "iconic relationship between the structure of rituals and that of the social transitions they mediate" (T. Turner 1977, 54). The wedding rite orders and controls these transitions by providing a means to reorganize the economic, political, and social aspects of social relations and to articulate the nature of social consciousness while incorporating the individual's experience into it (Mauss 1950; Munn 1974; Bourdieu 1977, 104; T. Turner 1977). "Ritual, in short, typically collapses sociocentric (i.e., relatively 'objective') and egocentric (i.e., 'subjective') levels of iconic representation within the same condensed symbolic vehicle. It thus provides a means of imbuing the objective, sociocentric order with the subjective meanings it encodes, and of manipulating both dimensions of meaning as a function of one another" (T. Turner 1977, 63). Hence, rituals as metaforms of social organization symbolically affect the subjective orientations of the participants; in this case, of the *neamuri* (extended families) of the bride and groom, close neighbors, guests of honor, and the peers of the bride and groom.

Because of the patriarchal social organization (including preferential patrilocal residence), the life of the bride is perceived to be the most disrupted by marriage. Accordingly, the wedding rite focuses on the bride and the public reconstruction of her social persona within a male-biased sociocultural milieu. The wedding emphasizes normative behavior. As Munn has suggested, "Ritual should be viewed as a . . . generalized medium of social interaction, linking the individual to a community of significant others through symbolic mobilization of *shared* life meanings" (1974, 605; emphasis added). Hence, the wedding is hardly ordered by concern for the bride's personal feelings. Rather, it has everything to do with the collective identity of women. It provides an occasion for women to reflect publicly on being women while the bride is introduced to her new subordinate status and role. Bourdieu's remark is apposite: "Social categories disadvantaged by the symbolic order, such as women and the young, cannot but recognize the legitimacy of the dominant classification [here, of social relations in a patriarchal order] in the very fact that their only chance of neutralizing those of its effects most contrary to their own interests lies in submitting to them in order to make use of them" (1977, 105). In Maramureş, the private domestic world is primarily the women's realm, and because in the extended family household women interact mostly with each other, they dominate each other. The wedding promotes the reproduction of this structure of relations. The rite is simultaneously a vehicle for the legitimization of the position of women and for their collective cathartic expression about this position.

Throughout the wedding, the various transitions prompted by marriage are stressed, bringing to the fore the primary concerns and the central cultural values of the community and the tensions inherent in them. These themes and values are reiterated during different ceremonial segments of the ritual, with the emphasis depending on the aim of the particular sequence. This reiteration gives rise to the oft-mentioned redundant character of rituals (Bloch 1974, 76; Tambiah 1979, 134–42). Because marriage, like death, involves radical changes in the individual and collective self, in both biological and social terms, the most elaborated cultural concerns in the wedding are the multilayered dimensions of alienation, separation, and death, as well as honor and shame. The bride is the locus for their symbolic coalescence. Because of the patriarchal social organization, the bride is usually the one who is alienated from her natal family; she is "sold" by her mother and "bought" or "bargained for" by the groom. Moreover, her change from unmarried girl to married woman incurs a culturally marked physical alteration: the loss of her virginity. The groom's loss of virginity is not culturally recognized or ritually validated. The bride, in effect, gives her blood to his patriline. Hence, the symbolic death of one phase of the life cycle is most pronounced in the person of the bride. Upon her honor—as virtuous daughter, virgin bride, wife, and daughter-in-law—rests that of others (see discussion of the patrilineal paradox in Chapter 1). Indeed, what is transferred through the wedding rite is mainly the rights to the bride's reproductive power (see Rheubottom 1980, 242). The implicit preoccupation during the wedding is sexuality and, more specifically, the bride's virginity, for it symbolizes the potential to create sacred life, thereby guaranteeing the continuation over time of the family and its honor.[1]

Entrance into the world of culturally sanctioned sexuality via marriage signifies entrance into the world of adults. Gone are the carefree days of youth. Marriage begins the process of aging, the result of life's tribulations, which are considered to begin in earnest after marriage. Marriage means responsibility. Life acquires a new seriousness of purpose. As one woman said, echoing many, "After you've married, you're no longer free. You have a husband. Where are you going? Where are you coming from? You have to make dinner, children; troubles, worries, and problems come." The following verses contrast the carefree youth with the married adult in a more joking way:

Bine-i tînăr şi holtei	It's good to be young and a bachelor,
Că meri sara unde vrei.	For in the evenings you go where you want.

După ce te-ai însurat	After you've married
Stai cu nevasta în pat.	You stay in bed with your wife.
Nu te însura măi vere	Don't marry, hey, cousin,
Că nevasta mult îți cere.	Because a wife asks for a lot:
Și ciorapi și izmene	Socks and long underwear
Și la noapte p-îngă ptele.	And at night to be next to your skin.

In short, marriage leads to children, old age, and death. Marriage is understood to be a symbolic death, and the various losses thereby incurred (such as virginity and youth) are vocally mourned throughout the wedding.

In this chapter, I will present a general overview of the three-day village wedding (*nuntă țărănească*). Most couples, even those who live in the city, still choose to celebrate their marriage in this way. (Because of work schedules, however, a growing number of couples opt for a one-day wedding. This form has already become standardized and will also be treated briefly.) Even though the ceremony has changed over time and varies performatively from wedding to wedding, what will be depicted here in detail are the primary ceremonial episodes of an "ideal typical" wedding.[2] Because of the formalized structure of the major ceremonial segments, ritual actions are consistent enough to be readily generalized; the ritual texts presented here are, however, an amalgamation from several weddings. (Unless otherwise stated, all texts were recorded at weddings in the winters of 1978 and 1979 in the village of Ieud.)[3] The risk of presenting an idealized description of a village wedding seems justified not only because of the transformative character of ritual, but also because ritual defines a normative relationship between the individual and the collectivity.

A further word about the texts is necessary. Most are examples of *strigături,* or shouted rhymed couplets. These shouts form the primary mode of communication and celebration during weddings (as well as during events celebrating the godparents, the midwife, a son leaving for the army, and so forth). At weddings, couplets are sometimes sung instead of shouted, depending on the inclinations of the participants, but shouts seem to be preferred. Although certain strigături are specifically associated with wedding orations such as the *horea găinii* (the Song of the Hen) or Toasting the Bride, most verses are not restricted to this occasion.[4] These couplets can be "traditional" (that is, more formalized) or improvised. Their content generally addresses central cultural concerns—drinking, aging, morality, love, socialization—but they may also be about current disputes or personal problems. (Illustrative, but by no means comprehensive, texts will be presented.)[5] Underlying themes of alienation, death, honor, and shame are reiterated throughout the wedding. For example, strigături about transformation of the bride's status from unmarried girl into married woman occur in almost every ritual sequence, varying according to the function of each sequence and who is shouting. To avoid inordinate redundancy in an account of a ritual event that is structurally repetitive, verses that may be typical of more than one ritual segment will be cited only once. Other verses will be used in the chapter on death-weddings to exemplify a metaphorical relationship between marriage and death.

The phases of the wedding ritual symbolically alienate the bride from her natal family and incorporate her into her husband's family. The ritual dramatizes this complex process entailing not only the creation of a new family unit but also the establishment of relations between families (as well as the implicit negation of certain kinds of relations between others; see also Belmont 1982). Weddings celebrate the reconstitution of social relations delineated by Van Gennep (1960). The first phase involves rites of separation and includes preparations; the dance of the groom's flag and that of the bride's crown; the first of a series of symbolic bride bargainings; the dressing of the bride; and the asking of forgiveness from the parents of the bride and groom. The liminal or transitional phase consists of the church ceremony; the post-ceremony meals at the homes of the bride and groom; the ritual exchanges between wife-takers and wife-givers; the asking for the bride; and the selling of the hen. The final phase of incorporation entails bringing the bride to the groom's house; the bride's entourage coming after the bride; and the undressing of the bride. An integral component of each sequence is commensality (Cohen 1981; Kideckel 1981). Food and drink foster and maintain social relationships; they provide sustenance for the sociopolitical body as well as for the physical body. Weddings are about social relations; hence, food and drink are of their essence.

Every wedding is bounded by events that initiate and conclude the realignment of social relations. Thus, all weddings are preceded by betrothal and succeeded by a postnuptial celebration between the principal families. Betrothal formally announces the proposed relations between the bride- and groom-to-be; the post-nuptial party formally recognizes the consequent relations between in-laws (*cuscri*). Since betrothal is the prerequisite to marriage, it is also prerequisite to a discussion of the wedding rite. When a young man wishes to ask to marry, a sponsor (usually his godfather or an uncle) goes *a peți* (to ask in marriage). (In Ieud, the mode of asking is not formalized as it is in other villages. See, for example, Meițoiu 1969, 133–35; Şeuleanu 1985.) The suitor's representative must propose the union to the bride's father and ascertain if he is likely to agree to it.

Honor and shame are central to the tensions inherent in this proposal. Negotiations are as private as possible in case approval is not forthcoming. (The reasons for refusal are many and do not necessarily reflect economic interests, because the deeply entrenched hierarchy of social relations tends to minimize gross discrepancies of means. Refusals are more likely the result of past quarrels between the families or the bride's being too young or an only child.) One man recounted his experience of going a peți. When he arrived at the girl's house, there were people who were not family members present. To defuse curiosity as to why he had come, he claimed he had heard there was a pig for sale, and he wanted to take a look at it. The father accompanied him outside to the shed, and there they discussed the potential match (positively). The bride's father purportedly concluded the conversation by remarking that the man was after a sow, rather than a pig. Masks in the form of metaphors save face. In the service of honor, practical matters often function as pretexts to draw someone outside for the sake of privacy. Today, many young men ask for their intended on their own. This does not mean that honor is any less important.

Once the wedding has been agreed to, at least three weeks must ensue between the agreement and the wedding. During this time the priest reads the banns (*hirditişiu*) in church.[6] This ostensibly provides ample opportunity for objections to the marriage to be raised or for cancellation to occur. Both parties repeatedly express concern that things will proceed without difficulties: "to be to the end (the wedding); not today this way, tomorrow another." This is a liminal period fraught with anxiety.

The reading of the banns informs the community about prospective marriages and is usually a reliable public index of their probable realization. Privately between the families of the bride and groom, however, it is never wholly certain that a wedding will take place until a symbolic agreement between the bride and her future mother-in-law is "signed." This occurs when the two women shake hands through their woolen aprons worn over their chemises. Fathers, the economic heads of households and their public representatives, can agree, but there is no binding symbolic conviction in that. Traditionally, men conclude business transactions with a handshake and toast (P. Stahl 1979a, 38; see also Kideckel 1981). This lends social authority to the exchange. (See Burguière [1982, 10] on *fides manualis* mentioned in Roman law.) Because a bride's dealings will be primarily with her mother-in-law rather than with her husband and father-in-law, the seemingly innocent gesture of a handshake overtly symbolizes cooperation between these two women; at the same time, it signifies the bride's submission to the authority of her future mother-in-law. The aprons must be woolen, because wool symbolizes prosperity.[7] That the women must shake hands through their aprons is also symbolic. Sheep are tended by men, and women use the products of sheep—milk, meat, wool— secondarily. In like manner, the link between mother-in-law and daughter-in-law is secondary; women are not directly connected to each other, but, rather, are related through men. The handshake is a gesture of solidarity and competition. Today, some mothers-in-law also give their future daughters-in-law money so that the marriage will be prosperous. Afterward, they drink plum brandy and eat cakes.

Following this exchange, a betrothal party takes place. This is known as a *credinţă* (celebration in good faith) or a *tomală* (engagement party). This party is the popular, secular counterpart to the reading of the banns. Engagements cannot be celebrated during periods of fasting. Hence, for the winter wedding season engagement parties may begin on the second day of Epiphany.[8] The party is held at the bride-to-be's house. The groom arranges for musicians to attend, although some young couples now rely on radios, cassettes, or records. (Most people complain, however, that a party is not really a party without live musicians; the sense of active participation is lessened by listening to recorded music as opposed to producing one's own.) Friends and relatives are invited. Each young man arrives with a half liter of plum brandy; a couple (husband and wife) bring one full liter. The bride provides stuffed cabbage, cakes, and other food. The party continues throughout the night. Previously most engagement parties were held on Saturday nights (or Tuesdays or Thursdays—non-fasting days). Today they occur on Sunday evenings so that the celebrants, in accordance with the wishes of the priest, do not attend the Sunday service in a state of inebriation. The conclusion of the engagement party signals the start of detailed wedding preparations.

Wedding Preparations

Parallel wedding preparations take place in the homes of the bride and the groom.[9] The most critical activities are the engaging of musicians, preparation of food, and inviting of guests. The couple invites the guests themselves, perhaps with the assistance of their principal wedding assistants or siblings (see Meiţoiu 1969, 135). Each family hires four musicians: two play violins, one plays guitar, and one, accordion or bass. A head cook, known as the *socăciţa*, is employed by each family to supervise the preparation of the generous supplies of food and drink (refer to note 28, Chapter 1, for examples of quantities and costs). (The services of women in the village who are known as skilled cooks may be requested for smaller celebrations, but this is less typical.) The socăciţa is paid for her efforts, which adds to the income of her family. (Not all women take on this responsibility for financial motives, however; some are simply talented cooks who have a penchant for organizing large affairs.) The cook's staff consists of female relatives and friends of the bride's or the groom's family. On the Tuesday before the wedding (if it begins on Saturday evening, for example), all of these women gather at the bride's or groom's home. Over the next days, they will prepare, under the direction of the socăciţa, quantities of the following foods to suffice for three days: *hăluşte* or *curechi umpluţi* (stuffed cabbage), *tăieţăi* or *laşte în zamă* (noodle soup; the noodles are hand-made), *carne* (meat—mostly pork in the form of schnitzel, although stews may be made as well), *găină* (chicken), *pită* (bread, white and corn), and *prăjituri* (cakes, large and small). These foods are eaten on other festive occasions as well as on Sunday, the day of rest and recreation. In addition to food, beer and horincă must be obtained. The plum brandy must be *tare*, or strong, for the men, and *îndulcită*, or sweetened with sugar and cinnamon, for the women, who claim to prefer it because it is not as strong as *horincă tare*. (Wine is offered when available, but that is infrequently.)

The week before a wedding is filled with household tasks. Upon their completion, the head cook toasts each of the women who have assisted her (and who will continue to do so during the wedding). She thanks them, wishing them well and wishing the bride and groom *noroc* (good luck), *să fie într-un ceas bun* (to be in a good hour—an idiom that indicates having good luck). Two shot glasses per woman are given mandatorily; their content need not be emptied but rather acknowledged, if only symbolically. Two glasses are necessary, because "for a wedding—it should be with a mate!"

Dances of the Groom's Flag and the Bride's Crown: Jocul Steagului *and* Jocul Cununii

The wedding formally begins with the *cusutul* and *jocul steagului*, the Sewing and Dance of the Groom's Flag. This takes place on the evening before the church ceremony or, most often, on Saturday evening. Friends of the groom especially gather at his house to "sew" the flag. The *steag*, or flag, is a dominant symbol of marriage; it is a masculine symbol of colorful vitality and power in which relations between men and women, life and death, and the values of patriarchy are symbolically encoded (see also Kligman 1981, 8; Musset 1981, 11). The flag is the responsibility of the groom's "best man," or *stegar* (flagbearer), his closest unmarried cousin from his father's side of the family. The militaristic aspect of the flag and flagbearer is persistently evident in language and in deed. The groom is referred to as "our king," "our prince." The flagbearer accompanies him throughout the wedding, proudly displaying their "strength and vitality": it is the flagbearer who gains entrance into the home of the bride when the groom's entourage goes to claim her; he brandishes the flag as the groom's party marches through the village; he stands solemnly behind the groom as the latter takes his vows in church. Effectively, the stegar represents masculine virility. The flag that he bears is, in the words of one Ieudan, a "sign that the groom (whom he serves) is an honest boy," that is, to express his virility, he has taken a woman in marriage, harnessing sexual desire to social responsibility.

On the designated evening, the flagbearer sees to it that the groom's peers assemble to sew the flag, which is attached to a pole approximately two meters in length. It is said that formerly, while tending sheep in the mountains, young men used to delicately carve poles for their sweethearts' spinning forks, which were later used for their wedding flag. Today a plain pole is used, which is layered with *baticuri* (scarves) provided by female friends, as are the embroidered handkerchiefs and necklaces that are placed over the scarves. The scarves must be black, white, green, and red. Black is the color of the groom's hat and also invokes the presence of the dead; white is the color of the bride's crown and symbolizes her virginity and the sacredness of the sexual union; green represents growth and the freshness of nature; and red, burning love. The scarves are sewn together with only red thread, because *dragoste înfocată* (inflamed love) creates the binding power of marriage. On either side of the pole, handkerchiefs and necklaces add to the "richness" of the flag. A mirror may be discreetly positioned to keep away evil spirits. A length of fresh greenery is sewn along the side of the pole covering the place where the scarves are attached. This greenery (which is also sewn into the bride's braids) forms the flag's "crown." (The crown is kept until the arrival of the couple's first-born; then the crown is boiled and placed in the first bath water so that the child will be *norocos,* or have good luck.) Small bells that jingle as the flagbearer "dances" the flag or a strand of lights that twinkle may also be secured to the flag's crown. The flag is ready when it is thought to be lavish enough. Nowadays, a "basic" flag may be rented from the church. This is becoming an increasingly popular custom, and the Sewing of the Flag is more accurately the adorning of the flag. With the scarves already in place, the groom's peers embellish it with handkerchiefs, jewelry, and ribbons.

After the flag is "sewn," the jocul steagului begins in the evening. The groom's flag is danced by the stegar, who chooses a girl to dance it with him. The groom's male peers form a circle around them. The flagbearer shakes the flag in rhythm to the music as he and his partner move with small steps in clockwise direction, "as the sun goes." The music is that played for the young men's dance at the Sunday hora, although at weddings, older men may join in the dance. Women, however, never dance this dance. The Sewing and Dancing of the Flag constitute the ritual separation of the groom from his bachelor friends, from courtship (the Sunday dance), and from the prerogatives of youth. It underscores the death of that phase of his life cycle.[10]

The young men shout strigături continuously during the Dance of the Flag, emphasizing the gravity of the transition that is about to occur. One may have many sweethearts, but only one wife. (Divorce is as yet unknown in this village, although it is common in neighboring villages.) Marriage, like death, is a final transaction. Marriage, unlike death, however, is considered to be a type of "negotiated exchange," and wedding discourse is replete with the cultural vocabulary associated with bargaining. It is the one bargain in life that *must* be skillfully executed; the "goods" are not exchangeable, at least not in theory. Hence, the young men will shout:

Hop tri şi iară tri	Hop three and again three.
La cusutu steagului	At the Sewing of the Flag,
Gioacă ruja macului.	The flower of the field poppy dances,
Gioacă ruja să scutoară	The flower dances to shake—
Mîndru fecioraş să-nsoară.	A handsome young man is marrying—
Gioacă ruja să clăte	The flower dances to shimmer—
Mîndră mnireasă să ie.	Take a beautiful bride.
La luat şi la ibdit	At taking [a bride] and at love,
Nu trebe omu silit	A man should not be forced
Să să afle celuit.	To find himself tricked.
La ibdit şî la luat	At love and at taking,
Nu trebe omu mînat	A man should not be sent (directed)
Să să afle înşelat.	To find himself deceived (cheated).
Aiesta nu-i tîrg de ţară	This is not a country fair
Să dăi şî să cumperi iară.	To give and buy again.
Aiesta nu-i tîrg de boi	This is not a sale of oxen
Să iei şî să dăi-napoi.	To take and give back.
Ochişori mîndri-nvărgaţi	Beautiful eyes of two colors,
Luaţi samă ce luaţi	Pay attention to what you choose
Ca să nu vă înşelaţi.	So that you don't fool yourself.

Hop tri şi iară tri is a formula used to mark the rhythm or to establish it if shouts are not produced in time with the music. The formula introduces and follows each line. Moreover, each young man uses it to signal that he is about to shout. Whereas at the Sunday dance shouting may be simultaneous, the strigături in the Dancing of the Flag unfold consecutively. One person may shout several lines, or another may finish a couplet antiphonally. The text is relatively standardized; other verses may be added or substituted. There is no attempt at improvisation. The purpose of this text is to acknowledge that a young man among friends is about to get married. It also registers the necessity for caution; there is no room for the follies of youth or careless judgment. The structural inversions in the text mirror the qualitative inversions existing between types of bargaining situations. In a customary *tîrg*, a term connoting both the marketplace and the bargaining that occurs within it, there is always the risk of being cheated or misjudging quality. In most cases, any loss incurred can be recouped through clever management and resale. This, however, is not an option in the "taking" of a spouse.

When the Dance of the Flag is ended by mutual consent of the musicians and the dancers, the flagbearer lifts the flag horizontally over his head and slowly twirls it around three times. He good-naturedly recites the following saying, directing its message to the groom:

Pă cînd să pline anu	When the year is over
Să sie gata Danu.	Dan should be ready (born).
Pă cînd s-o plini doi ai	At the end of two years
Să sie un Mihai şî un Nicolai.	May there be a Michael and a Nicholas.

The joys of marriage in a patriarchal society are most easily assured (from an ideological point of view) by the birth of male children, a cultural fact about which the couple is amply reminded during the wedding ritual.

Following the jocul steagului, the groom, accompanied by his flagbearer and male friends, departs for the bride's house to attend the *jocul cununii*, the Dance of the Crown.[11] En route, the young men sing songs, many of which mourn the loss of their friend, the groom. They arrive at the bride's house late in the evening (10 P.M. or later). Upon entering, the groom and the flagbearer are seated behind the table. The stegar places the flag prominently above them, straddling a corner. Food and drink are served. In the meantime, friends, neighbors, and relatives of the bride continue dancing until the Dance of the Crown begins.

The crown is white. It may be handmade out of nylon flowers, paper ones, or a mixture of synthetic and real ones, or it may be store-bought in Sighetu Marmaţiei, and flowers added to it. The bride's crown is usually danced by her *druşcă*, her bridesmaid or maid of honor. She is a close unmarried cousin from the bride's side of the family (as the flagbearer is a cousin from the groom's father's side of the family). The druşcă places the crown on a plate covered by a white cloth with embroidered or crocheted edges. She and a partner of her choosing hold the crown over their heads and lead a circle of young men and women in the Dance of the Crown. The groom and the flagbearer watch. The dance is performed to a couple-dance melody (unlike the dancing of the flag done by young men to a melody for the young men's dance). The white crown is the symbol of the bride's virginity, and it is displayed for her peers— and future husband—to appreciate. The bride's virginity is being handed to the groom on a platter, an act that will be repeated later in the wedding during the Song of the Hen, a ceremonial act much more explicit in intent. It is fitting that the bride's crown is danced by both men and women: the bride's virginity is the critical element upon which male and female honor and shame rest. Not surprisingly, the groom's honor is taken for granted; his flag proclaims his "honest" virility. The bride's virginity, however, must be publicly scrutinized, especially by her husband-to-be. Thus he and his aide watch the Dance of the Crown. As is customary in dancing, only men shout. They form the "legitimate" core of patriarchy and public social relations. Moreover, men appropriate the sexuality of women (and not vice versa). The shouts are practically identical to those of the Dance of the Flag; functionally, they are interchangeable, and the message is the same. The following couplets were recorded at the same wedding as the strigături for the Dance of the Flag:

Hop tri şi iară tri   Hop three and again three.
Cine-o făcut aici gioc   Who is responsible for the
                                            dance,

Dăie-i Dumnezău noroc	God give [them] luck
Ca sămînţa-n busuioc.	Like the seeds of basil.
Dăie-i Dumnezău tihneală	God give [them] bliss
Ca sămînţa-n astă vară.	Like this summer's seeds.

Additional couplets wish that God bless the couple with luck so that their marriage will be a good one (that it be blessed like the seeds of basil, a holy plant) and that they continue to have the understanding and good will that led to their union. Other verses allege that "this summer at the harvest" the couple's love was ignited and that mutual understanding culminated in this marriage. The seeds of summer are the ones that flourish and are harvested. Again, natural phenomena provide the model for social process.

The conclusion of the Dance of the Crown ends the evening's activities for most of the participants. Friends, relatives, and neighbors go home to sleep, since they may have no opportunity to rest on the following day when the festivities are in full force. At the bride's house, only the musicians, her immediate family, the bridesmaid, the flagbearer, the groom, and the bride remain. Then the first of three symbolic bride bargainings commences. This is the only ceremonial interaction that occurs directly between the principals, the bride (*mnireasă*) and the groom (*mnire*) themselves. The groom may be aided by his flagbearer, whereas the bride must initiate the exchange. The content is not formalized, although again discourse borrows from market bargaining. The style may be accented by friendly teasing. This event results in the groom giving the bride white ribbons that he has purchased, to link her braids together. The stegar presents the druşcă with similar ribbons. In return, the bride places a small bouquet (*struţ*) of greens or flowers in the groom's hat; the bridesmaid decorates the flagbearer's hat. This is the last time that the bride will place a bouquet in a young man's hat, because to *instruţa feciori* (to place flowers in the hats of young men) is the privilege of *fete* (young women); it is a gift of hope and vital affection, and it may also indicate that a young man is "going steady." In addition to the bouquet, the bride gives the groom woolen wristbands that she has woven for him to wear under his billowing shirt sleeves. Until recently, the bride's mother presented these cuffs to her son-in-law when she welcomed him before the ceremonial Asking for the Bride (an event that occurs later in the wedding). The exchange of ribbons and bouquets concludes the evening's activities. The groom, the flagbearer, and the bridesmaid go home to sleep. The flagbearer has the responsibility to escort the bridesmaid to her home because young women never go alone in the dark, and it may be well after 1 A.M. when the first night of the wedding ends.

Within the broader scope of rites of separation, the Dances of the Flag and Crown and the symbolic bargaining form a ritual complex that may be seen as a condensation of the process of marriage for the bride and groom themselves. The focus of these acts is egocentric, that is, about the immediate transitions that the bride and groom have committed themselves to. The Dance of the Flag highlights separation from one's peers and former social activities: the Sunday dance, the sewing bees. The bride is absent from the Sewing of the Flag, and the groom does not take part actively in the Dance of the Flag. But both dances are for and about them. Strigături "discuss" the seriousness of marriage. Marriage concerns the formation of a new family unit; it requires the acquisition of rights to the bride's reproductive capacity. The Dance of the Crown publicly declares the bride's virginity to her fiancé, thereby joining her virtuous honor to his. Finally, the reciprocal giving of symbolic tokens of love—the ribbons, bouquets, and cuffs—constitute a personal exchange of vows or commitment between the bride and groom.

But marriage, the union of a man and a woman, is not a private matter; it is fundamentally social, celebrating the union of families and the reproduction of the sociocultural order. The flagbearer and the bridesmaid are the symbolic successors of the bride and groom; marriage is generative over time. Hence, as the wedding progresses, it moves from the egocentric to the sociocentric. On the first evening of the wedding, during the symbolic bargaining, the bride and groom actively negotiate their marriage. Thereafter in the ceremonial bargainings, they become participant observers in a live cultural drama about their marriage and about marriage in general.

The Wedding

No church weddings may be consecrated until the regular church service has been performed and the priest has eaten his midday repast. For a Sunday wedding, most people attend the morning service before beginning wedding activities. The only exceptions are the people at the home of the bride if she lives a considerable distance from the church. The Dressing of the Bride requires several hours, and if it is deemed that church attendance will delay the wedding too much, then the service is missed.

Gătata Mniresii: *Readying of the Bride*

Following the morning church service, the musicians and the bride's girlfriends as well as close female relatives and neighbors, young and old, gather at the bride's home. The *gătata mniresii* (Readying of the Bride)—also called the *îmbrăcarea mniresii* (Dressing of the Bride)—is about to begin. This requires a minimum of two hours, most of which is spent braiding the bride's hair and sewing fresh greenery into her plaits, which will be tied together with the groom's gift of white ribbons.[12] Older women do the honors, just as they later will wind the new bride's bound braids around her head, indicating her status as a married woman.[13] The groom's ribbons link the bride's braids together as a symbol of his claim to her soon-to-be-lost maidenhood.

Before the bride's hair is braided, she is dressed. She wears a richly embroidered white shirt and an underskirt over which is placed the white bridal skirt and a white apron. The latter have layers of appliquéd ruffles. It is the duty of the bridesmaid to make or borrow the bridal skirt. The bride's outfit is finished with a new white, fancily worked sweater (since most weddings are in winter) under a new woven or embroidered vest. A scarf may be draped around her neck. She wears the *zgărdan*, or beaded choker that she wears every day, around her throat, as well as costume-jewelry beads on her chest. (These have replaced the *zgardă scumpă*, or coral necklace, that formerly was a dowry necklace; the number of rows indicated her family's wealth.) When the bride is dressed, the braiding begins. Fresh leaves of *pospan* (a hearty type of greenery) and, sometimes, small white flowers are sewn into her braids. Again, as with the groom's flag, only red thread, the symbol of burning love, is used.

Throughout the Readying of the Bride, the musicians play melodies specific to the occasion. The girlfriends and unmarried female relatives accompany the music with songs of separation or with shouts. Most of these are about the bride's leaving home to live among strangers and her not being a maiden anymore. Just as the Dance of the Flag marked the groom's separation from his bachelor peers, so the Dressing of the Bride formally marks the separation of the bride from the cadre of girls. It is appropriate that only girls sing (or shout) at this time; the married women remain silent. The girls "mourn" about, as well as for, the bride. They represent the collective voice of unmarried girls. Through them, the painful emotions of parting are objectified (see M. Pop 1976, 189). It is an emotional time; there is poignant crying. The bride, in fact, is obliged to cry; ritual crying (*plînsul mniresii*—the Crying of the Bride) is prescribed (see Graur 1976, 286–88; M. Pop 1976, 189; and p. 47, above). The elder women are prepared to induce weeping with the aid of onions or pins if tears are not naturally forthcoming; however, such measures are rarely required.[14] Usually, the words of the shouts or songs suffice, as may be gleaned from the following examples. The first texts deal with the change of status from unmarried girl to married woman. These are similar to the strigături for the jocul steagului in that they contrast the responsibility of marriage to the carefree existence of unmarried life.

Mniresucă ce-ai făcut?	Sweet bride, what have you done?
Ce-ai făcut n-ai făcut bine	What you did, you didn't do well;
Nu mai ieşti fată ca mine.	You are no longer a girl like me.
Mnireasă din doi părinţi	Bride from two parents,
Ce gîndeşti că te măriţi?	What are you thinking that you are marrying?
Măritată nu-i p-o sară	To be married isn't for a night
Să grăieşti cu feciori iară.	[And then] to flirt with young men again.
Cununiţa ta ce verde	Your green crown,
Cum te scoate dintre fete	How it removes you from among girls
Şî te bagă-ntre neveste.	And puts you among married women.
Bine-i fată cu drăguţi	It's nice being a girl with a sweetheart;
Rău îi cu coconi mnicuţi.	It's rough with young babies.
Bine-i fată a feti	It's nice being a girl;

| Rău a sta şi-a ciupăi. | It's awful to stay and bathe babies. |

The green crown refers to the white wedding crown embellished with green leaves. It is used to create the end rhyme for the couplet: verde-fete; the word for white is *alb(a)*. Also, the green crown recalls that of Christ and is symbolic of the bride's martyred existence. Each of these shouts juxtaposes unmarried status with marriage. Marriage is different from flirting with boys; marriage requires the responsibilities of fidelity and raising a family.

The next texts emphasize the bride's *înstrăinare* (alienation) from her family and unmarried friends:

Mniresucă cu ciurcei	Sweet bride with earrings,
Sărută-ţi părinţii tăi	Kiss your parents,
C-amu te duci de la iei.	For now you are leaving them.
Mniresucă cu mărgele	Sweet bride with beads,
Şî p-a tale surorele	[Kiss] your sisters, too,
C-amu te duci de la iele.	For now you are leaving them.

This verse relies on parallel construction to stress the simultaneous separations the bride must endure. The bride's special attire is noted; the price of her lavish appearance is the change in her life that it presages. To fulfill the joys of love and marriage, she must suffer a rupture from those who have been most dear to her.[15] Joy and sorrow are the paradoxical ingredients of love. The bride's presumed trepidations about leaving home are expressed for her by her unmarried friends in the following couplets:

Rămas bun mamă şi tată	Good-bye mama and tata,
Hai să vă sărut odată.	Here, let me kiss you once.
Să vă sărut p-amîndoi	Let me kiss both of you,
C-apoi mă duc de la voi.	For afterward I am leaving you.
Vă mulţămesc de crescut	Thank you for raising me
Şî de tăt ce mni-aţi făcut.	And for all that you have done for me.
Îi vide pă mîni p-alaltă	You'll see by tomorrow or the next day
Cum ţi-a si fără de fată.	How it will be for you without a daughter.
Îi vide pă mîni pă gioi	You'll see by tomorrow or Thursday
Cumpăra-m-ai înapoi.	You'll want to buy me back again.

These couplets are about leave-taking and lead into the next ceremonial event before the church ceremony: the *rămas bun* (see first
line of the verse above) when the bride and groom formally *ia
rămas bun* (take leave) of their respective families. In the couplet,
the bride's imminent departure from her natal family is emphasized, as is her absence, which will be felt, if not immediately, then
soon enough thereafter. "She" (through the voices of her friends)
suggests that her parents may want to buy her back.

Many verses are directed to the mother who has "sold" her
daughter (as discussed in Chapter 1). There is a disguised under-
tone of anger and an explicit one of sadness. These sentiments, evident in the following verses, are collectively presented by the unmarried young women and are part of an ideologically normative
ritual that legitimates a male-biased order. They are not necessarily
the personal feelings of the bride herself—which she does not have
the opportunity to express during the wedding.[16] Indeed, she is a
relatively passive performer in a dramatic spectacle about marriage. A bride's sentiments are structurally engendered.

Mămucă dacă m-ai dat	Dear mother, since you have given me away
Mni-a si rău şî mni-a si banat.	It will be hard and painful for me.
Mă duc mamă de la tine	I am leaving you, mama
Şî dorul mneu îţi rămîne	But longing memory of me remains for you.
Ie-l mamă şî-l pune bine.	Take it, mama, and put it away carefully,
Şî-l pune deasupra-n ladă	And put it on the top in the chest
Şî-l mai cată cîteodată.	And look for it from time to time.
. . . .	. . . .
Nu-i bai mamă că mă dai	It's no big problem, mama, that you give me away;
Ştiu că nu mai mei în rai.	I know you won't go to heaven any more.

In the following verse, which often accompanies couplets about the
Leave-Taking, or *rămas bun*, separation is prominent.

Rămîne drumu cu flori	The path with flowers remains
Plin cu fete şî feciori.	Full of young men and women.

| Ieu mă duc p-un drum cu stini | I am setting out on a path with thorns |
| Şî-oi trăi între străini. | And I will live among strangers. |

The bride laments her fate. She will part from her unmarried peers and family, and she will lose her virginity. The path with flowers, symbols for virginity, signifies the vitality of youth and blossoming sexuality (see Brătulescu 1981, 91). The path will remain the same, but she is embarking on a different path, a path with thorns. She must lose her maidenhood and live among unfamiliar people. This verse, as will be seen in the next chapter, parallels couplets common to funeral laments.

The Dressing of the Bride culminates with the placing of her crown. A young boy positions it on her head, a gesture to ensure a male first-born. It is a symbolic equivalent of the culminating episode of the jocul steagului when the flagbearer turns the flag above his head wishing male heirs. (Lampland [1977, 79] notes that in the Hungarian peasant wedding just before the couple retires, "a small boy is thrown into the wedding bed to assure that their first born [will] be a boy.") By the time the bride is readied, a messenger from the groom's house has usually arrived to announce that the groom has left for the church. This means that the bride must take her leave from her family and proceed to the church.

Belciug, Iertăciunea, *or* Rămas Bun: *Leave-Taking*

The bride and groom must formally take leave from their families. This is known as the *iertăciunea* (forgiveness) because the departing member begs forgiveness from the family for having erred in any way; or the *belciug* (*belşug* means bounty, wealth) because the son or daughter receives his or her parents' blessing; or the *rămas bun* (leave-taking, exhortations to remain well). While the particular content may vary from house to house, the form of the Leave-Taking is standard. It is a very solemn occasion, punctuated only by brief melodies from the violin. Only the wedding principals participate directly in this event: the bride or groom, the immediate family, the bridesmaid (at the bride's), the flagbearer (at the groom's), the godparents, and the cook. The wedding guests witness this moving event, joining in the crying. An esteemed friend of the family, frequently the deacon, delivers a sermon-like speech about holy matrimony. He talks about the secret gifts of marriage and warns that marriage is not all bliss—they will encounter both joy and sorrow, happiness and hardship. When he finishes, he toasts the groom (or the bride; both take their leave from their families, but for simplicity's sake, this description will refer to the groom). Then the groom faces his father. Holding the shot glass, he asks his father to forgive him. This may be done in a direct statement: "I beg you to forgive me"; or it may be more eloquent, begging forgiveness and wishing the family health, luck, and good will. The degree of emotional control seems to dictate how lengthy the toast can be; it is not unusual for men to shed tears. The father replies with his blessing, "God give you luck, a good mind, and understanding throughout your life. Heed the words you have just heard [from the sermon]. God give you life." The groom then turns to his mother and toasts her. He may ask her forgiveness as well, although that of the father, the head of the family, is sufficient. The mother toasts her son in return. The toasts continue until all of the primary actors have clinked glasses. Each toast is acknowledged by the sound of the violins calling brief attention to the moment.

The Asking for Forgiveness generally takes place first at the home of the groom since it does not take several hours for the groom to be readied.[17] His wedding attire consists of a black hat, a richly embroidered and appliquéd white shirt, heavy white woolen pants (winter dress pants), and a new woven or embroidered vest. After the groom is dressed, the belciug occurs, and someone goes to alert the bride that her fiancé will soon set out for the church ceremony. She must gauge her time accordingly; if the distance to the church is considerable, her leave-taking cannot be too drawn out.

After the iertăciunea, the groom (and the bride, at her house) is given something to eat in order *să nu jure flămînd, să nu sie viață goală* (not to take the vows on an empty stomach so that life will not be empty); it is believed that eating beforehand will enable the couple to ingest the richness of the marriage service. Then the groom and his cortège go to the church to await the bride. If the groom is from another village, he goes on horseback to the bride's village, where the wedding will take place. He is accompanied by male friends and the flagbearer. Each horse is adorned with flowers and ribbons. On a sunny day against a snow-laden background, the arrival of the groom is a brilliantly colored spectacle. Usually, he proceeds directly to the church to await his bride, or he may go to her house and then they go together. After the church ceremony, the wedding is celebrated in her home until it is time for her to be taken to his house.

The march to the church is a momentous happening: within a short while, the groom's life will be radically transformed. The flag is proudly but quietly displayed as they proceed along the main road. En route, the groom's male friends sing a dirge-like song. Marriage is a type of symbolic death; hence, it is not surprising that the following song sung *pă drum* (on the road) resembles the funeral laments also sung pă drum. The association of ideas creates the seeming similarity.

Pă drumu care mărg ieu	On the road that I am taking
Nu-i fîntînă nici părău	There is neither a well nor a stream
Să-mni stîmpere doru mneu.	To temper my longing.
Nu-i fîntînă nici vîlce	There is neither a well nor a spring
Să-mni stîmpere jalea me.	To temper my sorrow.
Lung i drumu Clujului	The road to Cluj is long
Da mai lung a dorului.	But that of yearning is longer.
Drumul Clujului să gată	The road to Cluj ends;
A dorului niciodată.	That of yearning, never.

The couplets play on the symbolic equivalence of actions and themes common in funerals. As the casket is being carried to the cemetery (following the Leave-Taking from the house), the dead are said to embark upon a road. Similarly, the groom is going on an unknown path characterized by the lack of certain elements (in funerals, it is said that "there is not . . . a window, a door, wind") and by endless yearning. The living mourn the dead; they long for him or her. The groom mourns the loss of his bachelorhood, family, and youth. But his yearning is more ambiguous; it is as much for what he has lost as for the acquisition of sexual prerogatives.

On arrival at the church, the groom's entourage assembles in the women's section of the church while waiting for the bride. Presumably, the bride has already begun her procession to the church. Again, the dirge-like atmosphere emphasizes the symbolic equivalence with death. Tradition allows the bride to walk as slowly as she desires; it is said that this is the last time in her younger years that she will determine when things are done. It is a last gesture of independence before she becomes a wife and daughter-in-law. Tradition also cautions the bride not to walk too slowly, however, and thereby aggravate her waiting groom and his mother. When her cortège arrives at the church, both parties take their places inside, with the exception of the couple's unmarried friends. They remain outside dancing, while the couple takes the vows that remove them from the ranks of the unmarried. Life goes on. The courtship that is a part of dancing will eventually lead to another marriage. The system reproduces itself in time and in space.

The Church Ceremony:
The Cununie, *or Crowning*

The ceremony takes place in the front, or male, section of the church. *Cinstea* (honor), in keeping with the hierarchy of relations, is spatially indicated. The groom, or the *împărat* (king), stands slightly ahead of his bride, who is at his left side. Her bridesmaid stays to her left. The nănași mari (the "great" godparents, or those of the groom) stand behind the couple, because it is the responsibility of the godparents to usher their godchildren through marriage. If the bride has also invited godparents (nănași mnici), they stand behind her, while the groom's godparents stand behind him. Because the godparents are central figures in the lives of their godchildren, they receive honor and respect in the form of ritual kinship, ritual toasting, and courtesies. The flagbearer remains behind all of them, giving "honor to the godparents." Everyone else gathers on the sides and in the back of the church.

During the ceremony, the bride and groom hold on to a long white banner. They, as well as the godparents, hold tall white candles given to them by the sexton. It is said that if the godfather's candle goes out, the groom will die; if the godmother's is extinguished, the bride will die. Because the godparents are supposed to be the guardians of their godchildren, they are especially careful that the candles remain lit.

Before the service for holy matrimony, the priest places the church's wedding crowns on the heads of the bride and groom. The service draws its name from these crowns: it is known as the *cunu-*

nie (the Crowning).[18] The crowns are worn throughout the service. It is considered a fatal omen should either crown fall. During the service, the priest exchanges the crowns on the heads of the bride and groom three times, each time blessing them. Then the couple exchange rings. The groom, the bride, the bridesmaid, the godparents, and the flagbearer follow the priest in a circle three times around the altar, all the while holding on to the white banner that the couple has held throughout the service. When everyone is back in place, the priest gives a short sermon and issues the marriage vows, first to the groom. Kneeling, the groom swears on the cross and the Bible that he will live with his wife in peace and good understanding, that he will love her and not leave her, neither in good times nor in bad, until the end of his life. He pledges his "fidelity, support, and protection" (Musset 1981, 120). He kisses the Bible and the cross to seal his promise. This scenario is repeated by the bride. She pledges "fidelity, assistance, and obedience" (Musset ibid.). The couple is then considered married before God. (In the Orthodox church, the exchange of the crowns seals the holy marriage; the swearing of vows is specific to the Uniate ceremony. This oath cannot be undone, because the Catholic church, to which the Uniate church belongs, forbids divorce. Today, there is a compromise: couples may choose not to take these vows—but everyone does.)

The flagbearer is the first to emerge from the church. Joy and exuberance fill the churchyard, as the crowd outside waits with great anticipation for the newlyweds to come out. Women gather near the church threshold to scrutinize the manner in which the couple leaves: if the bride steps before her husband, she will rule the household. Long ago, a circular ritual bread (*colac*) was held by the godparents in front of the couple at the entrance to the church. The couple gazed at the sun through the center hole; then they broke the bread in half. Whoever had the larger half supposedly would have the greater authority in the marriage. Many magic acts are used to influence the future: the number of children, the sex of the firstborn, and so forth (see Musset 1981, 120).

Following the wedding, the groom and his party return to his house; the bride, to hers. The wedding continues to unfold in parallel. The groom's march home is triumphant; the excited flagbearer throws the wedding flag into the air or shakes it vigorously in time to the music. In marked contrast to the solemn procession to the church, the return from it is electric. The mood is celebratory; the air is filled with lively songs and shouts in both the groom's and the bride's returns. On arrival each wedding party (at the bride's and at the groom's houses) is greeted by the cook, who is standing on the entry steps. From there, she throws grains of wheat over the groom (or bride, as the case may be) and anyone else in the vicinity. This is the *ţipatul grîului*—the Throwing of the Grain —which is also referred to as belciug, or bounty. This ritual is the blessing from the hearth, the symbol of family, prosperity, and warmth; the cook, temporary matron of it, welcomes the newly-wed. While throwing the grains, she shouts a verse like the following one, which is from the ţipatul grîului at the groom's; as in the Dances of the Flag or the Crown, the verses are used interchangeably for both bride and groom:

Ieu ţîp grîu din tălgerel	I throw wheat from this plate:
Mnirele îi frumuşel	The groom is quite handsome
Şî mnireasă ca şi iel.	And the bride is also beautiful.
Ieu ţîp grîu din farfurie	I throw wheat from this plate:
Mnirele-i de omenie	The groom is a decent person
Şî mnireasa aşă să sie.	And the bride should be like him.
Ieu ţîp grîu roşu ca focu	I throw wheat red as fire:
Mîndru le sie norocu.	Beautiful may their luck be.
Ieu ţîp floarea grîului	I throw flowers of wheat:
Bun îi neamu mnirelui.	The groom's family is good.
Ieu ţîp grîu nu ţîp săcară	I throw wheat, I don't throw rye:
Mnirele-i un cap de ţară.	The groom is the leader of the land.
Ieu ţîp grîu pîngă colaci	I throw wheat beside the breads,
Păste mniri păste nuntaşi	Over the groom, over the wedding guests,
Şî păste scumpii nănaşi.	And over the dear godparents.
Noroc să dăie Dumnezău!	God bless them with luck!

The text is similar in structure to *descîntece*, or charms, of which this is one type. The cook declares first what she is doing and then, through positive association, its significance. (The Throwing of the Grain is similar to charms in discourse but not in sense.) *Grîu*, or wheat, is a symbol of abundance, fertility, and fecundity. In comparing him to grîu, the cook attributes to the groom the most highly valued qualities: he is physically attractive (as is the bride), from a good family, a leader, and a decent individual. The couplet contrasting wheat and rye is an interesting reference to hierarchy; the cook's clarification that she is throwing wheat, the best grain, provides a metaphor for leadership. (It is important to recognize that these formalized couplets may bear little relation to the couple's qualities and background, but all grooms and brides are royalty for a day.) At the bride's, it is said in jest that the number of kernels caught in her outstretched apron indicates the number of children to be born to the couple (see also Meiţoiu 1969, 143). The separate performance of the Throwing of the Grain is a more recent variation. In other villages and in one-day celebrations here, the bride's mother-in-law throws the grain. Formerly, in Ieud, this event took place at the groom's house after the bride's virginity had been verified through the ritual play of the Song of the Hen. The logic of the wedding rite has been distorted to emphasize the dramatic.

Upon completion of the Throwing of the Grain, the wedding party enters the house. The musicians situate themselves on a corner platform that has been made for them or on side benches; the other members of the party find places around the tables, which are long boards on sawhorses, placed in a U-shaped formation. Because the wedding guests sit on both sides of the table, many people can be accommodated. If it is an especially large wedding, additional tables are extended from the table at the bottom of the "U." Also, if possible, two rooms are used. (Most houses have a kitchen, a guest or a show room, and a sleeping room; the latter two are transformed for weddings and funerals.) On each table, there are grains of wheat, a spindle of wool, and the ritual bread, colac, with basil in its center. These are symbolic magic tokens embodying abundance and fertility (the wheat), prosperity (the wool), and holiness (the ritual bread with basil, a holy plant). Through symbolic appropriation, these tokens are meant to yield positive results for the newlyweds (particularly the bride) and their guests. The significance of these items being placed on the tables is that ingestion is the most fundamental means of appropriation. And indeed, once everyone is settled, the first meal is served.

Before people begin to eat, the *păharnici* (glass-tenders) begin

their rounds. Several people usually are given the responsibility to
see that everyone has enough to drink. In the meantime, the musicians have started to play. Except for occasional meal breaks, they
play continually. Because strigături are the primary mode of communication, constant music is necessary. Music establishes meter
and inspires creativity: "When you go to a wedding, well, you
know, everything enters your head," a woman noted. "You hear the
violin and then you can shout." The following strigături describes
the role of music:

Ceterucă glas cu dor	Violin, voice with longing,
Soţiă gîndurilor.	Wife of my thoughts.
Ceterucă glas cu jăle	Violin, voice with sadness,
Soaţă a gîndurilor mele.	Wife of my thoughts.

While waiting for the meal to be served, people drink and shout
individually, antiphonally, and collectively. This is the way Ieudeni
celebrate.

The meal lasts several hours. During the clearing of plates, the
cook and her helpers are careful not to pass in front of the bride or
the groom with empty plates or bowls. Bounty is negated by emptiness; it is a sign that "things will not work out well." (Recall that
the couple cannot take their vows on an empty stomach. Generally,
an empty container is considered to be unlucky. In similar fashion,
if someone carrying an empty bucket meets another person, he or
she will put it on the ground, which is thought to neutralize the ill
effect.) During most of the festivities, the bride and groom (individually or united—later, they will eat a meal together) sit between
the godparents. Spatial arrangements are similar to that in the
church service: the godfather sits next to the groom, the godmother next to the bride. If there are two sets of godparents, the
groom's sit on his side; hers, next to her. The godparents and the
couple are usually seated at the far right corner of the connecting
table. From that vantage point, they can fully enjoy the celebration. Wedding guests intermittently come forward with bottle or
glass in hand to toast them.

While the meals are in progress, emissaries from the groom's
party go the bride's house, bearing symbolic gifts of food and drink,
the sustenance of sociality. A close male relative of the groom carries two liters of plum brandy; a close female relative holds two rit-

ual breads. (Burgière [1982, 10] relates the sharing of bread and wine to Roman custom, arguing that the popular rite has juridical value: "it legitimized a relationship by celebrating it through forms of behavior that reinforced its public character . . . or through symbolic gestures and formulas that attested to its irrevocable character.") When they arrive at the bride's, the groom's emissaries go directly to the storage room to present their gifts. Gift-giving is an expression of social interaction and a means to recover some of the resources depleted through the enormous expense incurred. All wedding guests offer a present—be it brandy, flour, eggs—and an additional 200 lei or more (approximately $17). No one attends a wedding empty-handed. Gifts are not simply expected; they are mandatory. The obligation is mutual, thus creating a system of cyclical reciprocity (and reproduction of the system).[19]

Having made the ritual offering from the groom's household to that of the bride's, the emissaries join the bride's party. They toast her and then form a circle among themselves and shout strigături. Shortly thereafter, they return to the groom's to await the appearance of members of the bride's family, who reciprocate in kind. In the interim, the celebrations continue in full force. The emissaries more often than not report about their journey by shouting the following standard verse:

Bine-am mărs bine-am zinit	I traveled well, I returned well
Dragu mni-i ce-ai tîrguit.	And was pleased by what you bargained for.
Bine-am mărs bine-am întrat	Well I went, well I entered
Dragu mni-i ce-ai cumpărat.	And I was pleased by what you bought.
Drumu-i lung şi tăt cu tină	The road is long and muddy
L-am făcut de la inimă.	I did it for love.

The representatives, members of the groom's family, state their approval of the bride. They compliment the groom on his bargaining skill—on his acquisition of a good wife. The verse is related to another, which refers to the shouter's neam:

Dragu mni-i la vesălie	I like to celebrate
Cu oameni de omenie.	With decent [good] people.

There are many variants to this basic theme; they are self-adulatory because the person shouting is related to the host of the event.

The ritual exchange of bread and brandy is known as the giving of *pominoc* (which is structurally related to the giving of alms, or *pomenile*, during funeral rites). The order in which these obligatory prestations occurs is unequivocal, reflecting the idealized power relations between the wife-takers and the wife-givers. Status differentiation according to the hierarchical ordering of relations by gender is formally noted in the terms of address used to refer to the heads, actual and symbolic, of the two households: socrii mari (great in-laws; parents of the groom) and nănaşi mari (groom's godparents), and socrii mnici (little in-laws; bride's parents) and nănaşi mnici (bride's godparents). The reciprocal and equivalent offerings establish ties of exchange between the two families (Lévi-Strauss 1969, 52–68).

Having constituted a basis for interaction—relations between households—it is appropriate for the groom to go after the bride, to bargain symbolically for her. Once again, it must be stressed that marriage entails an exchange resulting in the acquisition of the bride's reproductive power. (In status terms, regardless of equivalent symbolic prestations, the exchange is asymmetric.) In an idealized situation such as the wedding, that which is normative is presumed to exist; the bride's virginity is an expected reality upon which honor and shame are staked. At this juncture in the wedding, two ritual plays highlight this cultural preoccupation with sexuality and virginity through a symbolic lexicon articulated primarily through verbal dueling. Whereas the bride's virginity was symbolically displayed to the groom in the Dance of the Crown, it will now be publicly proclaimed.

Cererea Mniresii: *Asking for the Bride*

The ceremonial sequence known as Asking for the Bride (*cererea mniresii*) is one of the most dramatic episodes in the wedding ritual. It dramatizes in highly condensed form the groom's acquisition of the bride. The ritual play begins when the groom's party arrives at the bride's house around 1 A.M. As they near, the sounds of their music and mirth alert the bride's family. The bride's mother (the soacră mnica) goes out to greet her son-in-law. She presents him with two liter bottles of horincă, one in each hand, and kisses each cheek. This is another giving of pominoc—like the one that symbolically established relations between the two families—this time between members of the bride's and groom's families, or more precisely, between the mother who is "selling" her daughter and the groom, her son-in-law. While this is happening, the flagbearer and two male assistants attempt to enter the bride's house. In past times, a ritual fight, reminiscent of bride capture (see M. Pop 1976, 150; and also Konstantinović 1973; Lockwood 1974), occurred between male members of the bride's and the groom's groups, as the former resisted the latter's efforts to advance. Although the fight was meant to be a ritual battle (only symbolic resistance was to be offered), serious brawls often resulted. Eventually, "the groom's family established their control in the [bride's] house" (account from the nineteenth century in Dăncuş and Katz 1973, 123). The power symbolism of patriarchal social and sexual relations was readily apparent. Today, the entrance of the stegar and his assistants peacefully signals the bride's guests that they must exit and make room for the groom's party. In the interest of hospitality, the bride's guests honor them, if reluctantly, by leaving, but they then crowd around the doorway and the windows to witness the ritual asking.

The cererea is a complex verbal duel. In many parts of Romania, lengthy formalized poetic orations are recited (see Marian 1890, 452–97); fixed poetic verses are not common in weddings in Ieud, however—although one Ieudan recently composed such a text to accompany a film made in Ieud about weddings. The bride's father and the groom's godfather (his ritual sponsor or symbolic father) are the principal actors. This is as it should be, for in public dealings men represent corporate households; they officiate over interfamilial matters. The initial pretext for the verbal exchange is that the groom's party is lost in the night. They were en route to the market or the forest (depending on the location of the bride's house). If en route to the forest, indicating that the bride lives in the upper part of the village—susani—then the weary travelers say they are hunting for the first flowers of spring (since most weddings take place in winter).[20] If the party was off to the market, they say they hope to acquire a fine white lamb.

Both flowers and lambs are symbols of purity and vitality. An implicit ambivalence is associated with these symbols. Lambs and sheep are sacred animals; as discussed in the first chapter, women, because of their natural condition of pollution, are not permitted to

milk sheep for fear that the milk will curdle. Regarding flowers, recall that the euphemism for having one's menses is "having flowers
on one's skirt." Virginal young women wear brightly colored, floral-
patterned skirts; married women customarily do not (unless the
background is a subdued color, preferably black). In this wedding
sequence, the groom's party attributes the lateness of their intrusion to their eagerness to be the first to find the flower or the lamb.
This points to competition over eligible women as well as to matters of honor (virginity). (Recall that water from a boy's first bath is
thrown over one flower patch so that he will acquire the first girl
he seeks.)

The tone of the opening exchanges is polite. The host offers customary hospitality: bread, drink, and shelter. He repeatedly inquires, however, about the true nature of his visitors' intentions;
strangers in the night are highly suspect, especially as the neighboring village is reputed to be one of thieves. The godfather may
insist that they are going to the forest to search for the first flowers
of spring. (For the sake of simplicity, this account will refer only to
the flower, which is the most popular, even when the bride is from
the lower part of the village.) If they are unsuccessful, they will at
least return with fir wood—and not brush wood. The honor and
prestige of the groom's neam are metaphorically invoked through
the opposition of these two types of wood. The fir tree is considered to be a hearty, noble tree that further signifies continuity of
the life cycle. Brush wood, however, is thin and burns too quickly.
The groom's honor and prestige clearly must be matched by the
bride's virginity.[21] Anything else is unacceptable (leading to an unsuccessful hunt).

Once the groom and his party are settled inside the house, the
groom's godfather implores the host to search for a flower there in
his home. It is the first indication of what he is really after. It is well
known through the strigături that a "bride is like a flower."

Fost-ai rujă de Rusalii	In the late spring, you were a rose
În grădina maicii tale.	In your mother's garden.
Cînd ai înflorit mai tare	When you blossomed the most
Mă-ta ti-o făcut vînzare.	Your mother sold you.

The flower is grown in her mother's garden, creating a bond between mother and daughter that can never be replaced but that

must be broken when the time comes. (Pentecost, or Rusalii, is in late spring.) The versified versions of the asking hint at the processes of alienation and appropriation, the latter distinguished by the change in sexual status. The expedition is "explained" in the following way:

O mîndră garofă	A beautiful carnation
Care de crescut creşte	Which to grow, grows,
Şi de-nflorit înflore	And to blossom, blossoms,
Da de rodit nu rode.	But to produce, does not.

The purpose is to find this ripe flower; the verse goes on to say:

Şî s-o răsădească	And plant it
În grădina împărătească.	In the king's garden.
	(Marian 1890, 458–59,
	also see 591)

The godfather points to the white scarf on the groom's flag, thereby defining the flower's purity of color. The host obliges and returns with a young girl of four or five years. She is dressed in white bridal attire, with the exception of a floral-patterned skirt. The integrity of the symbolic system is evident, as is the ambivalence. The girl is displayed before the groom and his party. (In any bargaining situation, the customer must examine the merchandise.) The girl recites the following verse, the only fixed-phrase text in this ritual play:

De vă plac, vă plac	If I please you, I please you;
De nu, silă nu vă fac.	If not, I won't force you.
C-oi pune cununa-n ladă	I'll put my bridal crown in the hope chest
Ş-oi feti o vară întreagă.	And remain a maiden yet another summer.

The text is fixed, just as is the ideal unfolding of any girl's life. This episode reflects every girl's hope to become a bride one day. The godfather looks her over, but politely refuses: "She's lovely—to her health; may she too be a bride someday."

He then asks again that the bride's father search for something whiter. Skillful bargaining requires subtle manipulation. The intensity of the verbal exchange heightens with the host accusing the guests of unwarranted pretensions. "It's great for a man when he receives you in his home, puts you at his table, and then you tell him what to do in his home," the host says sarcastically. He has given them food and lodging, yet they are unsatisfied. "As in any duel," notes M. Pop, "the adversaries try to intimidate each other through taunting words; they insult each other in the popular style" (1976, 150). "Once a Gypsy, always a Gypsy," the bride's father challenges. This is a stab at the legitimacy of the groom's claims to honor and prestige. "Ah, but effort never meets death," the god-father responds to his host's retort (meaning that in that case he would not bother to ask; he would simply steal—a reminder that the groom need not resort to the former practice of bride theft) and again comments on the unfortunate reputation of the neighboring villagers as well as of Gypsies. Simultaneously, the nănaş suggests the bride's father will be rewarded for his efforts. It should be noted that the conflict that arises during ritual bargaining is re-solved by proverbs that encapsulate behavioral norms. These prov-erbs function to constrain threats to the transformative progression of the ritual structure and to the goal of the ritual (Silverstein 1979, 207–16).[22]

His temper calmed, the host is again persuaded to look for a whiter flower and returns with the bridesmaid. She, like the little girl, wears a floral-patterned skirt. She is not, however, quite what they want, although she is designated the future property of the groom's flagbearer. (The exchange of ribbons and bouquet between the flagbearer and bridesmaid on the first evening was a symbolic equivalent of this.) In this manner, a symbolic betrothal takes place, ensuring reproduction of the social order.

The scene repeats, and on the third try, the father enters with his daughter, the bride. She is dressed entirely in white save her underskirt, which may be floral-patterned; she is still a virgin. The variegated flowers of youthful skirts have given way to pure white; the bride is purest and is thus sacralized for "sacrifice." (Note again the relationship between marriage and death.) The white flower has blossomed forth. The father's social graces are vocally applauded. Having reached an agreement, the father and the godfather shake hands, whereupon the godfather proposes a toast to the flower that has been picked by the groom. The "flower" is now the groom's party's to "plant" (*răsadi*). The bride joins the groom at the table. They have finally been united.

A deal between households has been concluded. Because bar-gaining is dependent on successful manipulation, the text is not formalized, thereby allowing each participant to exercise his skill and wit. The progression of events is developed via metaphoric discourse. While the verbal duel continues on the level of metaphor, metonymic acts narrow the ambiguity of the symbolic content. Of course the object of the bargaining is substantive, not symbolic.

The conclusion of the first ritual play satisfies the wedding guests' curiosity; their stated purpose in attending the wedding is "to see what the groom bought," "to see how he bargained." It is the groom's ritual sponsor, however, who bargains for the bride in this public scenario. The groom interacts directly with the bride only on the first evening when they bargain with each other for ribbons and the struţ in the privacy of the bride's immediate family. As the ritual unfolds, it becomes increasingly more symbolic; the discussion moves from one about the marriage of the particular bride and groom to one about marriage in general.

Hence, in the ritual play cererea mniresii, the groom as represented by his godfather seeks to acquire purity, a virgin bride. After considerable negotiation, the host produces his daughter. As in any bargaining situation, the buyer looks for the best; the burden lies on the seller to convince the prospective customer that what he has to offer *is* the best. Bargaining is an age-old verbal art, however, and the "best" often has less to do with the real quality than with verbal agility. All brides must be virgins, even if it takes a chicken's blood to prove it.[23]

Horea Găinii: *Song of the Hen*

Because honor demands it, the bride's virginity must be publicly certified. This is accomplished in the second ritual play, the *horea găinii*, the Song of the Hen,[24] which follows the meal and general toasting accompanying the cererea. The horea găinii usually begins around 4 A.M. at the bride's house. The bride's symbolic mother, in this instance the woman who prepares the wedding meals (and who feeds the wife-takers literally and metaphorically), attests to her "daughter's" virginity through a versified dialogue with the symbolic mother-in-law, the groom's godmother. As in the Asking for the Bride, the bargaining has shifted from the interpersonal exchange between the bride and groom to a socially symbolic exchange between the cook and the groom's godmother. Through the room filled with the groom's party (seated at tables) the cook, in the symbolic role of the bride's mother, carries a cooked hen bedecked in greenery and necklaces of bread. Just as the bride's braids are adorned with fresh greenery and her neck with jewelry, so the hen is fashioned into an icon of the bride. As the cook progresses through the crowded room, she bargains in strigături with the "mother-in-law" to sell her the hen. After extended banter, the godmother buys the hen, which is then eaten. In part, this play again dramatizes the process of appropriation: the cooking of food may be seen as a metaphor for the process of social reproduction. The cook, just like an unmarried girl's mother, transforms raw meat into cooked meat (Lévi-Strauss 1970, 336–37). The hen is cooked in the kitchen and then carried to the point of consumption. When appropriated, it is consumed. (Marian [1890, 649] reported that in Bukovina a roasted chicken or hen was placed before the groom, who cut it and divided the pieces among the guests, godmother first. The bride was the only person who did not taste even a morsel. Symbolically, the bride is being eaten.)

In the first play, the principal actors were the bride's father and groom's godfather, who, in the public realm, are the heads of households. It was through them that the marriage was originally broached, and it is through them that approval of the exchange in the play is publicly granted. But in the private realm, that is, in the home, women dominate. First symbolized by the handshake through woolen aprons, the bride's subjugation to her mother-in-law is again stressed. Once the bride takes leave of her mother, her interaction will be primarily with her mother-in-law, and that relationship is reputed to be exceedingly troublesome. While assuring the continuation of the family, the presence of the bride simultaneously threatens the solidarity of the household and the authority of the mother-in-law. Because marriage signals the termination of the mother-daughter bond and the commencement of the mother-in-law/daughter-in-law relationship, it is appropriate that the bargaining over the "hen" occurs between the bride's symbolic mother (the cook) and the groom's symbolic mother (his godmother). Moreover, while hunting is typical of the male-dominated Asking for the Bride, cooking is the focus of the Song of the Hen.

The horea găinii, like the cererea mniresii, is awaited with great anticipation. They are both highly entertaining and are judged by the performances offered. Whereas the Asking for the Bride emphasized marriage's transformation of social relations, the Song of the Hen stresses its transformation of sexual relations. Social norms do not permit forthright public discussion of sexual matters; hence, the discussion is carried on via metaphoric discourse. The specific content of the conversation between these women gives rise to pointed satire and joking. Of all the ceremonial sequences, this one encourages the greatest use of poetic improvisation (the bargaining in the Song of the Hen is done in verse, while the Asking for the Bride requires conversational improvisation). If the cook (the seller) is not especially *bună de gură* (good of mouth, or clever-tongued and quick-witted),[25] then another women who is may follow closely behind her telling her what to say (or there may simply be a substitute cook). The horea găinii is considered to be the most fun (*are haz*), and the wedding guests expect it to be. They want a good show, and a "shadow" is a means to guarantee one, although this may leave the cook at the mercy of the godmother, who may choose to take advantage of the situation. The following was one godmother's way to make fun of the socăciţa:

Frunză verde şî una	Green leaf and one [an opening formula]—
Să strîge socăciţa.	Let the cook shout.
Frunză verde de acaţi	Green acacia leaves—
Mnie nu-mni trebe avocaţi.	I don't need a lawyer.
Că avocaţi-s la Vişeu	For lawyers are in Vişeu;
Nu-s aici pă capul mneu.	They're not here on my back.
Iei stau şî să sfătuiesc	They stay and advise,
Şi ieu găină tîrguiesc.	But I am bargaining for a hen.

The godmother draws attention to the cook's being advised what to say, just as lawyers advise their clients. She derides the cook for adopting a city practice (lawyers are in Vişeu, a city east of Ieud). Legal transactions require the assistance of lawyers, and the process is a "headache." All the godmother is doing is trying to bargain for a hen. The image of a lawyer helping in the marketplace to bargain for a hen is amusing; it also downplays the jural aspects of marriage. But, of course, women—who purchase poultry in the market—do not attend to legal matters (at least in theory).

When the musicians play the first few bars of the music associ-

ated with the horea găinii, the guests crowd into the room. The
cook may be preceded by the glass-tender, who announces his and
the cook's arrival in verse and clears a path so that the cook can
move toward the godmother seated at the table at the opposite end
of the room. In the following text the glass-tender introduces the
cook by encoding a series of events leading to the wedding:

Zî-mni ceteraş un ptic mnie	Play a little for me, violinist.
Am un leac de vesălie	I feel a little like celebrating,
La oameni de omenie.	For people of goodness
Faceţi-mni un drum de ţară	Make me a country road.
. . . .	. . . .
Că noi zinim de az-vară.	For we have been coming since the summer;
Noi de az-vară am plecat	We left in the summer.
Că zinim de la Arad.	For we came from Arad
Dac-am gătat de lucrat	When we finished working
Şî grîu de săcerat	And the wheat was reaped.
C-am ştiut că-i nuntă-n sat.	We knew there was a wedding in the village.
Faceţi-ne drumul bun	Make us a good road,
Că zinim de la Crăciun.	For we have been coming since Christmas,
Că noi am plecat de atunci	For we left then.
Pă vineri am fost în Cluj.	By Friday we were in Cluj.
Şî-am zinit cîtilin tare	And we came very slowly;
Sîmbăt-am fo în Baie Mare.	Saturday, we were in Baia Mare.
Şî-am zinit cîtilinaş	And we came slowly;
Duminică am fo în oraş	Sunday, we were in the city [Sighetu Marmaţiei].
Vrem să merem la nănaş.	We want to go to the godfather
Cu un ptic de băutură	With a bit to drink
Şî cu o leacă de friptură.	And with a little roasted meat.
Uitaţi-vă nănaşi bine	Take a good look, godparents,
Că şî socăciţa vine.	For the cook is also coming,
Cu zadie sufolcată	With her apron pulled up on the side
Şî cu găina-nstruţată.	And with a decorated hen.
Nănaşu şî mnirele	Godfather and groom,
Scoateţi portofelele	Take out your wallets!
Şî plătiţi găinile.	And pay for the hen.

The glass-tender asks the *ceteraş*, or the head violin player, to play
for him because he is happy. He asks that a country road be made
for him and his companions, that is, that the people in the crowded
room make way for them. There is also a wordplay on the construction of national roads (*ţară* is the word for nation and the word for
countryside). That they have been traveling since the summer refers to the clichéd notion that romance blossoms in the summer
especially while working in the fresh air, and the path of burgeoning romance ideally leads to marriage. While he only alludes to romance, he describes contemporary conditions that have altered
the rhythm of village life. The path of love parallels the road back
to Ieud. He claims that they are coming from Arad, a city in the
southwest of Romania where many Ieudeni contract in teams to
work at collective farms, a highly lucrative, although demanding,
endeavor. After fulfilling their obligations (such as reaping), they
are paid and return to the village; this usually coincides with a ritual occasion. The glass-tender asks for a good road because they
have been traveling since Christmas, and country roads are treacherous in the winter. Christmas marks the beginning of the winter
wedding season; after the holidays, betrothals occur. Hence, the
bride and groom supposedly fell in love in the summer, got engaged after Christmas, and will soon finish their journey toward
wedded life. The glass-tender explains the route from Arad—
through Cluj in central Transylvania, Baia Mare, the administra-
tive capital of Maramureş, and then Sighetu Marmaţiei. People arrive home from work stints bearing supplies, money, and gifts; the
glass-tender states they want to give the godparents liquor and
roasted meat. The alcohol signifies the celebration of a concluded
deal; the roasted meat refers to the bride (roasted hen). His oration
then becomes abstract. He indicates that the cook is coming with
the hen. Her tucked-up apron is a common symbol for sexual temptation. It is the bride's sexuality that the groom, through his godfather, is purchasing. And that is what the horea găinii is about.

The cook announces her entrance from the kitchen to the musicians:

Zî măi ceteraş cu drag	Play, you violinist, with love
Să mă pot sui pă prag.	So that I can climb onto the threshold.

Zî mǎi ceteraş cu dor	Play, you violinist, with feeling
Di pǎ prag sǎ mǎ cobor.	So that I can descend from the threshold.

Love and desire make it possible for a woman to cross the threshold—to leave her mother and join her mother-in-law; love and desire temper reluctance. The cook advances slowly with the hen on a platter held high above her head for all to see. The hen as a ritual icon for the bride is not arbitrarily determined; there is a metonymic connection in the economic realm. Poultry—their care, preparation and sale—are the responsibility of women. Hens are particularly valuable to a household because their eggs provide both nourishment and additional income. (Today, to receive rationed goods, villagers are expected to exchange supplements of eggs.) So it is with the bride. The symbolic similarity is readily acknowledged: "a bride is like a hen." It is noteworthy that the bride's crown and the hen are danced and sung about in related fashion. The bride's virginity is displayed.

The cook extols the virtues of her "hen," incorporating into her sales pitch those virtues most desired in a bride:

Gǎina i bunǎ tare	The hen is very good;
I-am dat bine de mîncare.	I fed her well.
Gǎina i grasǎ tare	My hen is very fat,
Cu slǎninǎ pǎ stinare.	With fat on her backbone.

In other words, the bride is a good woman, well-raised and healthy. In Maramureş there is a preference for women who are *grase şi frumoase,* fat and beautiful. Bigger is better, healthier and more capable of childbearing and hard work. A girl's constitution is always carefully scrutinized before marriage. The cook's verse continues:

Gǎina i bine gǎtatǎ	The hen is well prepared
Şî de nuntǎ înstruţatǎ.	And decorated for a wedding.
Gǎina i bine tomnitǎ	The hen is well turned out
Şî de nuntǎ-i pregǎtitǎ.	And readied for a wedding.

This verse can be compared with the following one that is sung or shouted during the Dressing of the Bride:

Mniresucǎ mîndrǎ ieşti	Dear bride, you are beautiful.
N-ai oglinda sǎ te vezi.	You don't have a mirror to see yourself.

Să te vezi cum ieşti	If you could see how you're
gătată	readied,
Nu îi mai si supărată.	You would no longer be upset.

or:

Ai mai sta la mă-tă fată	You'd stay a girl at your mother's
Şi ai si nemăritată.	And you'd be unmarried.

The hen and bride are symbolically equated: virgins readied for sexual sacrifice and the responsibilities of marriage, both of which are positively or negatively valued, depending on the cook.

At this point, the godmother may interject:

Nu ştiu găină-i ori raţă	But I don't know if it's a hen or duck;
Nu să vede din verdeaţă.	You can't tell through the greenery.

The godmother is suggesting that the hen's virtues are not to be taken at face value. The bride-qua-hen's virginity is crucial to the upholding of social norms and to the well-being of the community (see Musset 1981, 64–67). Sexual decorum assures the maintenance of peaceful relations between women. Although men are known to be more promiscuous, women believe that they themselves are the perpetrators of sexual corruption, which fosters social disharmony. The godparent continues:

Nu ştiu cum i găina	I don't know how this hen is:
Nici-i siartă nici-i friptă	Neither boiled nor roasted,
Numa' o leacă cîrcălită.	Only a little browned.

Other strigături about roasting claim that women can't go to the forest because that is male space and women are sexually attacked by the foresters. The "discussion" is, after all, about sexuality. Thus, in defense of her family's honor, the cook may respond:

Da nu-i friptă găina	But the hen's not roasted,
Că pădurile-s departe	Because the forest's far,
N-am avut lemne uscate.	I didn't have dry wood.
Păduraru-i tare rău	The forester is very bad
Şi ne spune la bdirău.	And he informs on us to the mayor.
Şi fă bine şi-i-ierta	So be kind and forgive

De nu-i friptă găina.	That the hen isn't roasted.
C-am fript-o cum am putut	I roasted her as I could,
Că unsoare n-am avut.	For I didn't have grease
Amu-i lume de năcaz	Now the world is troubled.
Pune unsoarea pă obraz.	[We] put grease on our cheeks,
Și ieu am pus-o pă obraz	And I put it on my cheeks
Că să siu la drăguți drag.	To be pleasing to my sweetheart.

This string of couplets uses the preparation of the hen as a pretext to discuss changes that have taken place since the advent of modernization under the communist state. The motivating taunt is that it is difficult to ascertain the quality of the hen. With urbanization and commuting, social networks have been extended beyond familiar boundaries; it is not easy to discover a potential mate's background. The cook expands on this comment; the hen is not as well roasted as she might be because the cook didn't have proper resources to prepare her. Nationalization of the forests has curtailed access to vital supplies of wood for building, heating, and cooking. Now, wood can only be purchased on designated days. If one is caught by the forester taking wood, the offense is immediately reported. Things are not as free as they used to be. The cook also lacked grease (oil for cooking); it is not readily obtainable either. She adds that women now use grease (creams) to paint their faces; this refers to the earlier reputation of the Moroșencele (women from Maramureș) for their healthy complexions. Today's fashions are frowned on; made-up women are accused by elders of being loose women. The last line removes the double intent of this exchange. Superficially, it is only about pleasing one's sweetheart.

The cook then directly suggests that the two women get on with the bargaining:

Hai nănașă de gînde	Hey, godmother, if you like,
Și cu mine tîrguie.	Bargain with me,
Și m-ascultă ce ți-oi spune	And listen to what I tell you.
Ieu mai las dumneată pune.	I'll give a little, you add,
Că tîrgu n-are mînie	For bargaining has no anger [hard feelings].
Ieu mai las dumneată-mbdie.	I'll give a little, you add more.

The godmother may offer:

Ieu ți-oi da vreo zăce lei	I'll give you approximately ten lei,

Şî ţi cumpăra ciurcei.	And you buy yourself earrings.
Ieu ţi-oi da vreo zăce zloţi	I'll give you approximately ten zlotys,
Şî ţi cumpăra chiloţi.	And you buy yourself underpants.

The earrings are for self-adornment; the underpants bring in the sexual element, implying that sex should be concealed. Through innuendo, the godmother questions the cook's behavior. A girl can be discredited by her mother's comportment (and vice versa). A clever cook will not let such an insinuation go unnoticed:

| Chiloţi mni-o luat bărbatu | My husband got me underpants; |
| Nu trebe să-mni ieie satu. | The village doesn't need to get them for me. |

Her husband has exclusive claim to her sexuality; this is a basic tenet of marriage.

Until recently, women did not wear underpants except for woolen bloomers during the winter months. Older women still shun their use: "They're only in the way, especially in the summer while working in the fields. How do you pee inconspicuously? Before you could just stand with your legs apart." The need to purposefully cover sexual organs is said to reflect decreasing morality or lack of attention to propriety, particularly with ever-shorter hems. Panties act as a deterrent to temptation. One godmother exploited her opportunity to tease the cook, who had not paid proper attention to herself in public. Stating that she would give the cook money for panties, she explained why:

Socăciţa de la oale	Cook by the pots,
Cînd te duci în ptiaţă mare	When you go to the big market,
Trage-ţi sumna pă pticioare	Keep your skirts around your legs,
Să nu iei amendă mare.	So you won't get a big fine.
Că tu în ptiaţa cînd te-ai dus	When you went to the market,
Ţ-ai lăsat sumna în sus	You let your skirt up.
Miliţianu cînd s-o dus.	The policeman, when he went by,
Iel la tine s-o uitat	He looked at you
Şî ti-o văzut cum ai stat	And he saw how you were standing,
Şî-atuncea ti-o amendat.	And then he fined you.
Ieu găina oi cumpăra	I will buy the hen,

Mulţi bani pă ie nu ţi-oi da.	But I won't give you much money for her.
Ţi-aş da numa de chiloţi	I'll give you only enough for underpants—
Chiloţii să-i iei pă tine	Underpants to put on yourself,
Să nu faci poftă la nime.	So as not to arouse anyone.

The cook had been in the market in Sighetu Marmaţiei and had bent over, legs apart, so that her genitals were exposed. The policeman had indeed fined her. The godmother profited from this embarrassing event, making fun of the cook among friends and relatives. As mentioned above, a mother's actions affect the assessment of a daughter; this incident was sufficient to justify a lesser offer for the hen, and it was not contested. The "bargainers" frequently manipulate general themes in order to insult or criticize an individual. A goal of dueling is to leave the other speechless, or *cu gură cascată* (with mouth open). In the above instance, the godmother succeeded.

The haggling about price may continue for quite a while. The godmother may say:

Ieu ţi-oi da douăzăci şi cinci	I'll give you twenty-five lei
Şi ţi-i cumpara optinci.	And you can buy yourself leather peasant sandals.

And the cook responds:

Ieu optincă nu prea port	I don't wear peasant sandals,
Că nu cîntă cînd ieu gioc.	Because they don't sound when I dance.
Foie verde din cărare	Green leaves from the path—
Să-mni dăi bani să-mni ieu sandale	Give me money to get myself sandals
Cînd oi mere la plimbare.	When I go strolling,
Ca să vadă orişicare	So that anyone can see
Ce-o făcut nănaşa mare.	What the groom's godmother did.
Şi să-mni dai o sută două	And give me one hundred, or two
Că să-mni cumpăr cizme nouă.	To buy myself new boots.
Tare mîndru m-oi tomni	I'll fix myself up really beautifully;
Cu nănaşu m-oi ibdi.	I'll make love with the godfather.

The godmother offers the cook money to buy new sandals, but the cook immediately rejects that because the flat-soled sandals don't make noise during dancing. Wearing *optinci* is passé. The cook wants "city" sandals so she can be stylish when she is walking; unmarried persons flirt by strolling along the path and dancing. The cook, a married woman, introduces the basics of flirting to underscore the sexual flirting implicit in marriage. The parallel construction of the text hints that the godmother, in buying her daughter-in-law (and dominating her), is giving her husband to someone else (the cook). The price for this daughter-in-law is the godmother's husband. With money from the sale, the cook buys new boots and entices the godfather.

The cook may take the lead again:

Preţu la găina-i pus	The price on the hen is set
Tăt de la o sută-n sus.	From one hundred and above.
Că ieftină nu ţi-oi da	I won't give it to you cheaply,
C-amu s-o scumtit carnea.	For now meat has become more costly.

The cook plays upon the value of the bride as sexual "meat" to criticize the rising cost of meat and basic foodstuffs.

In keeping with the general strategy for market bargaining, the godmother tries to lessen the price by discovering defects:

Frunză verde a rugului	Green leaves of the wild rose,
Astă nu-i găină-i pui.	That's not a hen, it's a chick,
Găina i cît o cioară	For the hen is only as big as a crow
Şî-mni cere bani de o moară.	And you ask the price of a mill.

Yielding slightly, the cook concedes:

Nu ţi-oi cere mare plată	I won't ask a big price from you,
Numa pă nănaşu-odată.	Only with the godfather once.

Anticipation of the bride's loss of her virginity at the end of the wedding brings to the surface otherwise unmentioned sexual tensions. In the Song of the Hen, codes governing sex and sexuality are explored. Safeguarded within the frame of ritual, the strigături exchanged between the two women become increasingly suggestive. These verses are necessarily joking ones, jokes being a convenient vehicle to voice that which is normally at least suppressed, if not repressed. Woman, the temptress, here in the person of the cook, teases:

De-acasă cînd am plecat	Since I left home,
Doamne multe m-o mîncat.	My God, much has happened to me,
Şî m-am lozit la un pticior	And I bruised my thigh.
. . . .	. . . .
Nănaşule de nu crezi	Godfather, if you don't believe me,
Rădică sumnă şî vezi.	Raise my skirt and see.

But propriety prevails as she warns:

Nănaşule si cuminte	Godfather, behave yourself!
Nu rădică dinainte.	Don't raise it from in front!

Lifting her skirt from in front would reveal her genitals, which in the interest of propriety is not done.

The horea găinii is meant to validate publicly the bride's virginity. The groom's honor rests on her pristine condition. As in any bargaining situation, there is always an underlying fear of being cheated.[26] It is thus not surprising that in the strigături dealing with sex, infidelity is a constant concern. These strigături are often directed at the godfather:

Hai nănaşule-n grădină	Come on, godfather, to the garden,
Şî-om pune preţ la găină.	And we'll put a price on the hen.
Şî nuntaşii nu ni-or şti	And the wedding guests won't know
Că cu cît ni-om tîrgui.	For how much we've bargained.
Da nănaşule ce ni-om fa?	But, godfather, what will we do?
Că-i aicea nănaşa	The godmother is here,
Şî tare s-a supara.	And she'll get very angry.
Nănaşa i frumuşe	The godmother is pretty,
Da mai dulce-i gura me.	But my mouth is sweeter.
Nănaşu multe ibdeşte	The godfather loves many women,
Şî nănaşa nu priveşte.	Yet the godmother isn't aware.
Ieu găina ţi oi da	I'll give you the hen,
Da numa dacă mni-i săruta.	But only if you kiss me.

| Hai în şura cu iarba | Let's go into the barn with grass [hay] |
| Şî mni plăti găina. | And you pay me for the hen. |

The cook proposes to the godfather that they go outside and settle the bargain. (People generally discuss private business outside; recall the account of the man going to ask for the bride's hand.) The cook intends to be compensated sexually. To be sure, it is a woman who tempts; man simply cannot resist. The relationship between sex, women, sin, and evil is evident. Sex as the payment conjures up prostitution and the ambivalence of the mother-whore complex: the cook is both nurturing mother and unscrupulous woman; she is giver of food and sex, as well as mother and mother-in-law.

These strigături often become ribald or blatantly pornographic, much to the temporary enjoyment of all. Flowers are primarily the symbols for virginity; the hen is a multivocal symbol for the bride's virgin sexuality, and it is also a symbol for the female genitals:

Am găina huhuietă	I have a dressed hen;
Şi-i întisă subt lăcată.	It is locked with a lock.
Adă teia s-o descui	Bring the key to open the lock
Să o dau nănaşului.	To give her to the godfather.

Poultry must be plucked before it can be cooked and eaten. The cook announces that she has a hen to give to the godfather; it is ready, she only needs the key to get it for him. This superficially innocent strigătură addresses the bride's physical sexual readiness; she must lose her virginity. The lock brings to mind the chastity belt.

Că să puşte găina?	To shoot the hen?
S-o puşte-ntre pticioare	Shoot it in between the thighs
C-acolo-i carnea mai moale.	Because there is softer meat.

Ostensibly this hen must first be killed (again, the relationship between marriage and death). Shooting and stabbing are often used to express the act of thrusting the penis in and out; the site of that action leaves no ambiguity about the sexual nature of the discussion.

The following verse is a more explicit depiction of the hen as symbol for the female sexual organs:[27]

Socăciţă cu chiloţi	Cook with underpants,
Ţi-i găina tătă floci.	Your hen is all tufted.
În ţîpă chiloţii gios	Take down your underpants,

Şî o curăţă frumos.	And clean it nicely.
Rădîcă sus rotiţa	Lift your dress
Şî curăţe găina.	And clean your hen.

The godfather extends this offer to the cook. He is a gentleman and will "pluck" her hen for her. He will do a good job; that is, he will satisfy her needs.

The "hen," or sexually ready woman, is tantalizing to the godfather (and to any man), and many couplets play upon this natural condition:

Vai săracu nănaşu	My, the poor godfather,
Că i-am adus găina.	Because I've brought him a hen.
I-am adus-o-n ptele goală	I've brought [it] to him naked
La nănaş am făcut boală.	And given the godfather a hard-on.
Nănaşu i om cuminte	The godfather is a well-behaved man
Pune şurţ pă dinainte.	And pulls his shirttail down in front.

That is to say, he hides his erection. The teasing tone of such strigături induces much jocularity:

Găina-i cu nouă ouă	The hen with nine eggs;
Nănaşu-i numa cu două.	The godfather has only two—
Şî alea nu-s de găină	And those are not like the hen's
Că-s ouă cu rădăcină.	But are eggs with roots.
Cine şti bine-ai gîcit	Whoever knows, you've guessed well;
Gîndeşti că le-ai tipăit.	It seems you've felt them.

These couplets reveal practical knowledge about male and female sexual organs. The groom appropriates the bride's sexuality, which may then produce many "eggs" (children). The groom's "eggs" are rooted, fixed (testicles). Implicit in this text is an understanding of patrilineality and patriarchy: women produce children for the continuity of their husbands' families.

Sexual knowledge is acquired through experience. In the preceding text, the last couplet uses general anatomical information to embarrass the listener: one is not supposed to have sex on one's mind. Hence, sinful behavior is suggested. Similarly, in proposing that the godfather pay her outside, the cook cautions that they take care not to be heard, because they are engaging in adulterous behavior:

Hai nănaşule-n grădină	Come on, godfather, to the garden
Şî-om pune preţ la găină.	And we'll put a price on the hen.
Hai în şura cu iarba	Let's go into the barn with grass
Şî mni plăti găina.	And pay me [for] the hen.
Numa nu o tipăi	Only don't squeeze her:
Găina s-a cîrcăi	The hen will squawk
Şî or auzi oamenii.	And the people will hear.

The extent of haggling depends on the women's creative penchant, as well as on the general ambiance. If the cook in particular is bună de gură, then the crowd is usually very enthusiastic. The cook as seller must talk the most. Eventually, she will implore:

Placă nănaşă şi ie	Please, godmother, take
Găina din mîna me.	The hen from my hand.

The godmother obliges:

Ieu ţi-oi da vreo tri griţari	I'll give you a few coins—
Nănaşu-i cu sălar.	The godfather has a salary.
Noi găina vi-om lua	We will take your hen,
Şî pă ie plată v-om da.	And we'll pay you for her.

The godmother boasts of her ability to purchase the hen because her husband is a modern man; he has a steady salary. The cook may take advantage of that boast:

Hai nănaş nu te scumpti	Hey, godfather, don't be stingy;
Că n-ai ătîţa coptii.	You don't have so many children.
Că n-ai numa un fecior	You only have one son,
Şî li-i face profesor.	And you'll make him a professor.

Because the godparents have money (which is, in part, why they were asked to be ritual kin), the godfather should not be tight-fisted. Despite the rising cost of living, this "modern" man does not have the same financial obligations as most "peasants." The modern family only has one or two children; the "traditional" peasant family has many children to feed. This modern godfather has only one child, albeit a male (in keeping with tradition), and his child will be able to make a living on his own.

The godmother receives the hen and pays the cook. (Inflation has raised the ritual payment from 25 to 100 lei—about nine dollars. This payment is the cook's to keep; there is no bridewealth in Maramureş.)

When the cook is paid, she waves the bill for all to see. She proudly proclaims:

Uităţi-vă măi nuntaşi	Look, you, wedding guests:
Cîţi bani are un nănaş.	How much money a godfather has!
Cu banii di pă găină	With the money from a hen,
Poţi trăi o săptămînă.	You can live for a week.
Că nu-i lumea ca-nainte	For people aren't like [they were] before,
Pă bani să cumperi pemînte.	With money [they bought] land;
C-amu-n lume-i mai uşor	For now in the world it is easier:
Vreau să-mni ieu televisor.	I want to buy a television.

Conspicuous consumption encourages poetic innovation. The cook sarcastically jokes that she can manage for a whole week because of the increased price for "hens"; the cost-of-living increases have made poultry less common for ordinary meals. Before cooperativization, money went into the purchase of land, but with today's changed property rights, people no longer have land to be worked, so they have a little more leisure time—to watch television. (I recorded this at a wedding in 1979.) Before, a woman would boast she would buy new boots to wear to the Sunday dance, the traditional form of entertainment.

More recently, in 1985, a cook boasted about the item then highest on the list of consumer desires:

Cu bani di pă o găină	With money from a hen
Mni-oi cumpăra o măşînă.	I'll buy myself a car,
O măşînă Dacia	A Dacia.
Cu ie să mă pot căra.	I'll drive about with her
Cu mîndru alăturea	With my sweetheart next to me.
C-amu mni-i dragă lumea.	For now, life is pleasing to me
Că nu mni-i hie de nimnică	Because I don't need anything,
Numă o măşînă mnică.	Only a little car.

(In the last few years, the number of families owning cars has increased dramatically, especially in the city.)[28]

Once the hen is on the table in front of the godparents, the cook may "lament" the loss of her hen (a partial parody on funeral customs):

Săraca găina mea	My poor hen.
Rău îmi pare după ie.	I feel bad for her.
Ieri ierai pă după şură	Yesterday you were around the barn;
Azî ieşti cu ţîglare-n gură.	Today you're with a cigarette in your mouth.

In this verse, the cook parodies the style of funeral laments. Her sympathy is expressed to the "deceased." The day before the "hen" was wandering about freely, but no longer. The "hen" is now in the world of the sexually active. In fact, the decorated hen comes complete with a cigarette stuck in its mouth. It is meant to be a visual sexual joke, and everyone appreciates it. (Brides, however, talk about their extreme embarrassment; everyone knows that after the wedding, the bride will sleep with her husband, and shortly thereafter, her belly will protrude—if all goes well. Many women say it is only after the birth of their first child that they lose their self-consciousness.)

The cook continues her "lament":

Focu-o bată găina.	To hell with that hen.
Bine c-am scăpat de ie.	Good that I'm rid of her.
Asară pîngă vălcea	Last night around the spring
Trăge un căţel de ie.	A little dog "got" to her.

Having made her sale, the cook now boasts of her prowess as saleswoman. She reveals that the "hen" actually was not so innocent. Sexual cheating is a constant concern, underscored by the threat of cheating characteristic to bargaining. Honor seems to rest on verbal agility. The godmother denies the cook's disclosure:

Pentr-un păhar de la masă	For a glass of plum brandy from the table,
Mni-ai vîndut găină grasă.	You've sold me a fat hen.

The godmother toasts the cook for having provided her with a fat hen—as in "fat and beautiful," the preference of Moroşeni; being pregnant is implied. She then describes the place of this hen in her family:

Aripa-i a mnirelui	The wings are the groom's;
Clonţu-a ceteraşului.	The beak is for the violinist.
Da la mnireasă ce rămîne	What remains for the bride?
Şti-oa mnirele mai bine.	The groom knows best.

The "hen" is about to be consumed.[29]
Finally, the cook may inquire:

Unde i a mneu bărbat?	Where is my husband,
Să-i arăt ce-am ciştigat.	So I can show him what I earned.

The godfather may snidely retort:

Pă bărbat l-ai îmbătat	Your husband, you got him drunk,
Că să sie angajat	So he'd be engaged,
Să nu sie cu mine-n sat.	And not present with me in the village.

The godfather reintroduces the sexual theme and the cook's sexual duplicity. She deliberately made sure her husband was drunk so that she could enjoy the godfather, her lover, undisturbed. Women are evidently evil tricksters.

In almost all of the above verses, the bride's "mother" acts as ribald temptress; the groom's godmother makes order prevail. True to tradition, the woman's side (the bride's family) is unvirtuous; the man's, virtuous (even the women in it); this also underlines the idealized superior-inferior relations between wife-takers and wife-givers. Marriage is necessary to continue the moral order. And so it does. In the end, the "traditional" norms and values are hailed. Much to everyone's relief, religious and moral precepts are re-affirmed; the sociocultural order is celebrated.

The cook is usually accorded the last word:

Hai bărbate la bufet	Come on, man, to the bar.
C-amu-am bani să mă îmbăt.	Now I have money to get myself drunk.
N-am fo bată niciodată	I've never been drunk,
Nici fată nici măritată.	Neither as a girl nor married.

Da amu m-oi îmbăta	But now I'll get drunk,
Că mni-am vîndut găina.	Because I've sold the hen.

The cook ignores the godfather's insinuating remarks about her "honor." She counters by treating her husband to a good drunk. (It is a rare circumstance that prompts a wife to encourage her husband's drinking to inebriation; it is while in such states that men tend to beat their wives.) The woman declares she too will "celebrate" by getting drunk with him. She is going to drown in drink her guilt and sorrow for having "sold" her daughter.

The cererea mniresii and the horea găinii publicly dramatize the process of male appropriation. The Song of the Hen presents the sexual aspects of appropriation. Encapsulated within these plays is a normative overview of the nature and dimensions of social and sexual relations, that is, the division of labor (hunting and forest are male domains; the house and garden are female). The concluding transaction of the Song of the Hen publicly finalizes the bride's change of status and household allegiance. Womanhood clearly entails sex, a topic brazenly discussed through strigături to introduce the bride to it and incorporate the newlyweds into the realm of married couples. Changes within the structure of the households are symbolically indicated and demarcated.

Toasting

Following the meal honoring the selling of the hen, the groom and his party escort the bride to his house. It is the first time during the wedding rite that she goes to his house; this event marks the beginning of the incorporative sequence of the rite. When they enter the courtyard, one of the celebrants shouts to the groom's mother to come out:

Hai ăfară socră mare	Come out, grand mother-in-law,
Că v-aducem ajutoare.	Because we bring you a helper.
. . . .	. . . .
Bucură-te socră mare	Be joyous, grand mother-in-law,
Că ţi vine chieptenătore.	Because to you is coming a hairbrusher
Să-te chieptene pe capu	To brush the hair on your head—

Cu două lemne de fagu.	With two pieces of beech wood.
	(Marian 1890, 631)

The invitation to the groom's mother may be a polite announcement that her daughter-in-law has been brought and that she will, of course, serve as her mother-in-law's helper. Or the strigături may be more caustic, voicing the complexities of the relationship. The mother-in-law is told to rejoice at her fortune of receiving someone to assist her. Usually the couplets state that the daughter-in-law will help her care for her hair, a tedious task involving the removal of bugs and braiding. The bride's resentment of her subservient position is aired by joking that she will brush her mother-in-law's head with two sticks (some verses say clubs) rather than with combs. In other words, she will hit her mother-in-law over the head and be rid of her (and not only the bugs). Beech trees, mentioned above, are associated with the souls of the dead.

The mother-in-law comes outside and stands on the steps to the front door (as the cook did when she welcomed the guests after the church ceremony). The mother-in-law may offer a vocal welcome:

Să trăieşti că mîndră ieşti	Long life to you because you are beautiful.
Cu gura bine grăieşti.	You speak well with your mouth,
Ieşti mîndră şî de-omenie	You are lovely and decent:
Tumnai cum îmi place mnie.	Exactly what I like.
Frunză verde verdice	Green, green leaf—
Să trăia noruca me.	Long life to my darling daughter-in-law.
De-a si mîndră şî cuminte	If she'll be lovely and well behaved,
Cu tăte a si înainte.	Everything will go forward.

The mother-in-law honors her daughter-in-law with traditional accolades: she is attractive, knows her place (doesn't talk too much), and is a good person. She wishes her long life (green is the color of life and growth) and notes that as long as her darling daughter-in-law (diminutive form) acts as she wants her to, all will be fine. (If her expectations are impossible, her daughter-in-law may be provoked to hit her over the head as suggested in the preceding verse.)

The mother-in-law holds two ritual breads, one on each arm, and two bottles of horincă, which she gives to her daughter-in-law.

Everyone watches closely to see if the mother-in-law simultaneously kisses her daughter-in-law on the cheek. If she does not,
things do not augur well for the daughter-in-law.

The giving of bread and brandy is the final giving of ritual pominoc. The first established relations between the two families; the
second acknowledged affinity between the groom and the bride's
mother. The initial giving of pominoc consisted of reciprocal and
equivalent exchanges between wife-takers and wife-givers; the latter two are unidirectional, encapsulating that which is dramatized
in the ceremonial sequences following them. Thus, in the cererea
mniresii, the bride's mother (wife-giver) greets her son-in-law, who
has come to take her daughter. Subsequently, the groom's mother
(wife-taker) greets her daughter-in-law, who has been given to her.
The order of these exchanges exemplifies the structure of hierarchical relations stratified by sex and age (discussed in Chapter 1)
that result from marriage:

Wife-takers (higher status)	*Wife-givers* (lower status)
groom's family	bride's family
groom	bride's mother
groom's mother	bride

The bride, the groom, and his wedding party then enter the
house and settle themselves around the tables. There is yet another meal, this time in honor of the bride's arrival. (At many weddings, the Song of the Hen is repeated for the entertainment of
those who did not witness it at the bride's. In this case, the cook is
the groom's. The Song of the Hen is performed purely for amusement.) Throughout the meal, the wedding guests continue their
celebration of the marriage, shouting strigături and honoring the
bride with toasts.

Strigături tend to focus on old age (signaled by marriage and the
responsibilities it engenders), drinking, love, kin relations, and
honor (see Karnoouh 1983a). All of these facets of life are central to
celebrating a wedding. The following strigături address old age:

Cînd ieram mai tînerel	When I was younger,
Ieu mîncam carne de mniel	I ate the meat of lamb
Şî sărutam frumuşel.	And kissed nicely.
Şî-amu dac-am bătrînit	But now that I've aged,

| Ieu mînînc carne de capră | I eat goat's meat |
| Şî sărut gură de babă. | And kiss the mouth of my old lady. |

This verse laments the social and physical changes that occur as one ages. The parallel construction opposes youth and old age. Lamb is associated with young animals as well as virgin girls; the goat is a nanny goat, hence linked to old age and old women. The privileges of youth concede to the limitations of old age:

Bătrîneţe haine grele	Old age, heavy clothes—
Rău mă tem c-oi cădea-n iele.	I fear I will fall into them.
Cîtilin pă drum mă duc	I am slowly going on the road;
Bătrîneţele m-agiung.	Old age is catching up with me.
Bătrîneţe haine rele	Old age, bad clothes—
Rău mă tem c-oi căde-n iele.	I fear I will fall into them.
Aşă mă trec din viaţă	I am passing from life,
Ca roua de dimineaţă.	Like the morning dew.
Aşă mă trec din lumuţă	I am going from the world,
Ca şî roua di pă frunză.	Like water off a leaf.

Stages of the life cycle are visually marked by changes in the color and style of attire (see Bogatyrev 1971). Hence, old age may be conceived of as a set of clothing. Marriage results in altered fashion for women especially and locates everyone on the road to old age. While one goes slowly on the road (the road being the common way to express change of status: unmarried to married, young to old, life to death), old age nevertheless arrives. In the end, life, and youth, seems as fleeting as the dew that quickly evaporates. As is customary, the life cycle is compared to nature's cycle. Youth is a stage whose loss is mourned:

Săracă tinereţe	Poor youth,
Nu ştiu ce-am făcut cu ie.	I don't know what I did with it.
Că pă bani nu o-am vîndut	I didn't sell it for money
Nici în crîjmă n-o-am băut.	Nor did I drink it in the tavern.
Şî-aş da bani şî-aş teltui	I'd give money and spend it
Tînără de-aş putea si.	To be able to be young again.

People generally forego possession of something because they have sold it or, in the case of men, because they have "drunk it away." There is a certain element of personal control or responsibility involved in the liquidation of one's property. But the loss of youth is beyond human design; it is a natural process that cannot be manipulated even with money.

Drink is credited with easing the pains of life. Drink in moderation is the panacea for troubled affairs and the libation for love and friendship.

Uiăguţa şî păharu	The bottle and glass:
Stîmpără doru şî-amaru.	Quiet longing and bitterness.

One drinks for social reasons, not for self-destructive ones—at least in theory:

Nu beau pălincă să mor	I don't drink plum brandy to die,
Numa cu cine mni-i dor.	Only with someone I miss.
Nu beau pălincă să zac	I don't drink plum brandy to expire,
Numa cu cine mni-i drag.	Only with someone I love.

Drinking, however, is thought to make death less painful:

De-aş muri cînd oi si bat	If I should die when I'm drunk,
Nu m-aş tare supăra.	I wouldn't be very upset.
Da mă tem c-oi muri treaz	But I fear I will die sober
M-a mînca mare năcaz.	And I will be consumed by serious ills.

By nullifying consciousness and physical suffering, inebriation can be beneficial. But the deleterious effects of drinking are also recognized:

Şi ieu beau şî mîndru be	And I drink and my sweetheart drinks;
Cum om si noi gazde-aşe?	How will we be proprietors like that?
Ieu beau zin mîndra pălincă	I drink wine, [my] sweetheart, plum brandy,
Şî de noi n-a si nimnică.	And of us there will be nothing.
Ieu beau zin mîndru be bere	I drink wine, [my] sweetheart, beer;
Cum om strînge noi avere?	How will we accumulate holdings?

And so on. It is well beyond the scope of this study to give examples of the hundreds of general strigături collected during fieldwork.

Honor is a prominent theme during a wedding. One *da cinstea* (gives honor) to someone—the bride, the groom, a relative, the godparents—by toasting. The person toasting and the recipient of this honor stand facing each other, each holding a glass or a bottle. Following the toast, which may be a simple salutation for long life or a more complex text, they clink glasses (or bottles), take a sip, and exchange glasses. They utter the familiar *la mulți ani* (many years), clink glasses, take another drink, and then return the proffered glasses. (Toasts must be *cu soț*, or with a spouse, in a figurative sense.) A toast to the godmother who sees her children through marriage and baptism might be:

Să trăiască nănașa	Long life to the godmother
Că mni-i cinste cu dînsa.	Because I am honored with her.
Nănașucă să trăiești	Dear godmother, long life
Să cununi și î să botezi.	To marry and baptize.

Honor and shame are the central concerns of social relations and status, as was seen in the cererea mniresii and the horea găinii. In an impromptu exchange, a young woman chose to "discuss" differences of opinion about courtship with her mother through strigături, the ambiguity of the situation making this possible:

Lasă-mă mămucă lasă	Let me, mother, let . . .
Să grăiesc cu cine-mni place	Speak with who pleases me
Că rușine nu ți-oi face.	Because I will not shame you.
Lasă-mă mămuca me	Let me, mother,
Să grăiesc cu care-oi vre	Speak with whom I like
Că rușine nu-i ave.	Because you will not have shame.

The girl begs her mother to let her flirt with a young man, promising that her honor (virginity) and reputation will remain intact. The mother, however, did not trust the assurances (with all good intentions) of youth against desire:

Dragu mamii ti-oi lăsa	My dear one, I'll let you
Numa cînd ți-a si vremea.	Only when you are ready.

Dragu mamii is a formulaic expression essentially meaning dear one; there is a slight innuendo of admonishment.

The young man in question was also present, and he joined the "discussion":

Leagă mîndră cînele	Sweetheart, tie up the dog
Să nu saie pă mine	So it doesn't jump on me
Cînd oi mere la tine.	When I go to you.

Most families have dogs, and because they are often rather ferocious, one enters a courtyard with caution. He symbolically equates the biting dog with her mother. His sweetheart responded:

| Cînele ieu l-aş lega | I'd tie up the dog, |
| Da nu mă lasă mămuca. | But my mother won't let me. |

Her answer allows his insult to stand, by ambiguously stating that her mother won't allow her to see him. In this way, the daughter expresses her dissatisfaction but avoids reprisals for insulting her mother. The mother ended the conversation by speaking to the young man:

Cînele nu l-oi lega	I won't tie up the dog;
Pă tine l-oi amuţa	I'll sic him on you
Diptce îmi zii la mîndra.	Because you come to your sweetheart.

Parental authority is not to be disobeyed, and the honor of her daughter is not to be tampered with.

Strigături are a form of conversational speech during celebrations. They may be shouted for oneself and whoever listens, or as part of a dialogue with someone, or shouted ensemble as in singing a song. Many conversations may be carried on at the same time. Most people, however, will stop and listen to the toasts to the bride, especially if it is a close relative toasting her (and therefore likely to be poignant) or someone who is famed as bună de gură. Of course, not only is the bride honored by toasting, but also the majority of toasts are for her. It is her day. Men usually toast the bride or the couple with nonspecific strigături about enjoying the guests, wishing the couple, the godparents, or whomever good luck, long life, and good fortune. The concern of men is the well-being of the community. In public, men represent individual families as undifferentiated discrete units. But within the individual households, relations are differentiated, and women use the occasion of a wedding to vocalize the nature of this differentiation. Because a marriage transfers a woman from one household to another, the liminality experienced during the rite of passage temporarily breaches the boundaries between discrete household units. Accordingly, the constraints on internal privacy are also breached.

Hence, during the wedding, the primary toasts are those of women—married and unmarried—to the bride. Women elevate intrahousehold matters to the level of communal interest. Their toasts constitute a form of collective cathartic expression that both legitimates the position of women and protests it. Thus, unlike the toasts offered by men, women's toasts are specific: they tell the bride *exact cum o fost sau cum îi,* or exactly how it was or is. For all the celebrating, the bride dissolves into tears as she listens to her fate. This type of toasting may continue, uninterrupted, by any one woman for ten to fifteen minutes.

Unmarried sisters or girlfriends toast the bride in much the same manner that they "lamented" her leaving them during her dressing. They emphasize the advantages of maidenhood that the bride has chosen to abandon:

Cînd ai fo la mă-ta-acasă	When you were at your mother's house,
Tu ai mîncat numa mniere	You ate honey
Şî pă obraz puneai ruminele.	And put cream on your cheeks.
Şî amu mînînci căpşiuni	And now you eat strawberries,
Şî pă obraz pălmi şi pumni.	And on your cheeks, slaps and fists.

Life under the care of one's mother is sweet like honey and cream, whereas under the care of strangers, life is prickly and bitter. The bride is always warned that her husband is not her brother and her mother-in-law is not her mother, and both will beat her.[30]

Decît măritată rău	Instead of having married badly,
Mai bine în copîrşeu	Better in the coffin,
Ori fată pă traiul tău,	Or a girl on your own.
Că cum fac ieu aşă rămîne	For what I do, that's how it remains,
Şî nu-mi porunceşte nime.	And no one commands me.

It is better to be unmarried or dead than in a bad marriage (and it is assumed that most are so). Unmarried girls remain virgins, that is, they remain fete. Sexuality requires submission to the demands of one's husband and mother-in-law. A girl is not subjected to such constraints; she is free to do as she pleases. This is, however, an idealized perception. Girls are freer, but they are certainly not at liberty to go where they please with whomever and whenever. (Unmarried women in their thirties are pitied; it is a difficult position. But one such woman confided in me because I was a "cohort." She admitted that she never wanted to marry, precisely because she did not have to answer to anyone and she had nieces and nephews who would care for her in her old age.)

The strigături of married women to the bride are considered to possess the greatest didactic value. The woman shouting may join the bride's crying as she bares her heart and that of married women in general:

Săracile fetele	Poor girls,
De ar muri cu tătele	If they would die, all of them,
Să le-ngroape mamele.	And their mothers bury them,
Să le-ngroape dîntre flori	Bury them among the flowers—
Să nu margă de nurori.	Not to go as daughters-in-law.
Să le-ngroape-ntre mălini	Bury them among the cherry trees—
Să nu margă la străini.	Not to go to strangers.

The married woman laments the fate of girls who most frequently end up as she herself did and as the bride she is toasting has. Girls get married and must suffer the position of daughter-in-law; they must live among strangers and not among those to whom they are closest, their natal families. An unmarried girl who dies remains with her natal kin in the world of the dead; hence, a girl is better off dead among them than alive among strangers.

Another woman may describe the elementary rules of a married woman's comportment:

Mniresucă draga me	Little bride, my dear,
Ascultă-mă dacă-i vre.	Listen to me if you like.
Unde-i mere nu şede	Where you go, don't linger
Că bărbatul nu ibde.	Because [your] man doesn't like [that].
Că bărbatu-aşa ibde	For [your] man likes it so:
Din pticoare să păşeşti	To walk quickly,
Din gură să nu grăieşti.	Not to talk;
Din pticoare să mei tare	To go quickly,
Din gură să nu sii mare.	Not to be a big mouth.

The married woman tells her from experience that a wife should go about her business and not engage in inordinate gossip.

A lengthier "toast" tells the bride what being married signifies, what will happen to her from this day on. (Because the woman doing the toasting was admired for her creative facility with strigǎturi, everyone listened attentively.)

Mniresucă mnireasă	Little bride, bride,
Ascultă-mă dacă-i vre.	Listen to me if you'd like.
Ce ți-oi spune n-oi minți	What I'll tell you, I won't lie,
Da îi videa c-așa a si.	For you'll see that's how it will be.
Mnireasă cununa ta	Bride, your crown
Împletită mînînțel	Finely braided
Și purtată puținel.	And worn but little.
Cununița ta ce verde	Your green crown,
Cum te scoate dîntre fete	How it takes you from among the girls
Și te bagă-ntre neveste.	And puts you among married women.
Mîndru-i numele nevastă	It's nice to be called wife,
Da nu-i ca fată niciodată.	But it is never like being a maiden,
Oricît de bine ți-a si	No matter how good,
Nu-i mere și nu-i zini.	Because you won't go and come
Unde tu dragă-i dori	Where you wish, dear.
Că bărbatu ți-a porunci.	Because your husband will order you;
Că bărbatu nu ți-i frate	Your husband isn't your brother,
Să gîndești că nu te-a bate.	Don't think that he won't beat you.
Nu te-a bate cu bota	He won't beat you with a stick,
Da te arde cu vorba	But will sting you with harsh words.
De te-a dure inima.	That will break your heart,
Mnireasă de bună samă	Bride, rest assured.
Dai cununa pă năframă.	You give your crown for the scarf,
Și năframa-i tare gre	And this scarf is heavy;
Tăte grijele îs subt ie.	All the worries are beneath it.
N-ave grijă draga me	Don't fret, my dear,
Că cu tăte facem așe.	Because we all do it [wear the scarf].

Că mnirele-i din neamul mneu	The groom is from my family;
Ieu gîndesc că n-a si rău.	I think he won't be bad.
Mnireasă mnirele tău	Bride, your groom,
Sie ca bărbatul mneu	If he is like my husband,
Ș-apoi las să sie rău.	Then let it be bad.
Că ieu de cînd m-am măritat	Since I married,
Nici o palmă nu mni-o dat.	Not one palm has he given me.
Și de cînd îs măritată	Since I have been married,
Nu m-o bătut niciodată	He has never beaten me;
Bine-am trăit laolaltă.	We've lived happily together.

In all of the texts, personal appellations are never used; instead, the toasts are directed to the impersonal categories of "bride," "groom," "godparent," because the wedding ritual is not concerned with specific individuals; it is normative in scope. What happens to one bride will happen to the next; the system reproduces itself. Also, couplets in this toast are produced during the Dressing of the Bride as well. The difference between them is that during the latter, her unmarried peers sang these couplets to lament their friend's change of status and separation from them; in the toasts honoring the bride, married women shout these verses to verify from experience that which is happening to the bride and to welcome her among them.

A toast from the groom's sister to her brother laments his change of status and his "separation."

Să trăiești măi frate dulce	Long life, my sweet brother,
Înainte de-a te duce.	Before you go.
Să trăiești mîndră ți-i fața	Long life, handsome is your face;
Mîndră-ți sie și viața.	May your life also be beautiful.
Da un cuvînt te-aș ruga	But one word I beg of you:
Dacă de-aici îi pleca	If from here you go,
Nici de noi tu nu uita.	Don't forget us,
Că ni-o fost dragă lumea	Because life was dear to us
Pînă am fost la mama.	While we were at mother's.
Că îi ave nevasta ta	For you will have your wife,
Și de surori îi uita.	You will forget your sisters.
Că îi ave a ta soție	You will have your wife
Și cine să te mîngîie.	And someone to comfort you.

The sister asks her brother not to forget them—a request that is figurative rather than literal. In reality, the groom is not moving from his natal home; however, because he is marrying, he is establishing a new family unit that does not, in a strict sense, include his natal family.

Lengthy toasts are also directed to the groom by the married women after they have toasted the bride. The women speak to him from an empathetic position:

Măieran bociulios	Flourishing marjoram:
Să trăiești mnire frumos.	Long life, handsome groom.
Să trăiești să ai noroc	Long life with good luck.
Rălele să ardă-n foc.	May evil burn in fire.
Cîte tîrguri tîrguiești	How many bargains you bargain,
Șohan nu te celuiești	Never do you cheat yourself
Ca cînd te căsătorești.	As when you marry.
Că vinzi boi și cumperi cai	You sell oxen and buy horses;
Că meri-n tîrg i iară-i dai	You go to the market and give them again,
Cu de aiestă tăt să stai.	But with this, you always remain.
Măieran crescut în strat	Marjoram grown in rows:
Ține-ți bine ce-ai luat.	Take good care of what you've chosen.

The couplets are similar to those shouted during the Dances of the Flag and the Crown. The groom is admonished that marriage entails a final sale; it is distinct from any other bargaining situation. The groom is told to take care of his purchase:

Uită-te măi mnire bine	Look carefully, hey, groom,
Cine șede lîngă tine.	Who is sitting next to you.
Șede o violă-nflorită	A blossoming violet is sitting;
Să nu-o ții bănuită.	Don't keep her troubled.
Astă vară la cosît	This summer at the haymaking
Mîndră floare ți-ai găsît	You found a beautiful flower.
Astă vară la săpat	This summer at the digging
Mîndră floare ți-ai aflat.	You discovered a beautiful flower.
Ai rupt-o și-ai pus-o-n clop	You picked her and put her in your hat—
Dumnezău dăie-ți noroc.	God give you luck.
Dacă-i duci-o străine	If you take her as a stranger,
N-o ține supărățe.	Don't let her be troubled.
De ar curge apă zin	For if water would run wine,

Rău îi tînăr şî străin.	It's bad [to be] young and a stranger.
De ar curge apă lapte	If water would run milk,
Rău i tînăr şî departe.	It's bad [to be] young and far away.
Că sărăcuţa de ie	For the poor little dear,
La voi a si străine	At your [house] she will be a stranger.
N-a ave mamă cu ie.	She won't have [her] mother with her.
Ieu te rog mnire pă tine	I ask you, groom,
De asta ai grijă bine.	Take good care of her,
Că săraca-i tinere	For the poor [thing] is young,
Te rog ai bine grijă de ie.	So take good care of her.
De ţi-a greşi cîteodată	If she makes a mistake from time to time,
Sărută-o şî o iartă.	Kiss her and forgive her.
Da de nu îi şti-o cruţa	For if you don't know how to take care of her,
Floarea-ndată s-a usca.	A flower will dry up immediately.
Fetele-s ca florile	Girls are like flowers
Toamnă cînd cad brumele.	In the fall when the frost falls:
Astăzî îi mîndră înflorită	Today it is beautiful [and] blossoming;
Mîne vezi că-i veştejîtă.	Tomorrow you see that it is dead.

The groom is told by a woman who knows from experience what the bride's circumstances are. Her alienation is movingly depicted through the images of being a stranger and a potentially dying flower. No miracle (water turning to wine or to milk) can change the difficulty of being young and alone among strangers. Without the groom's support in working out a relationship with his mother in particular, the bride will lose her vitality and "die." Many toasts call his attention to the "flower" beside him, saying that in his home she will have no one but him.

By this time, the bride is often crying intensely as she listens to her fate. The woman who has been toasting the couple, having produced this hysterical state, may attempt to assuage the bride's distress:

Mniresucă nu zdera	Little bride, don't cry,
C-acoale-o fo zina ta	For there it was your mistake.
Că ţi-ai dat mîna cu badea.	For you gave your hand to your sweetheart,
Că ţi-ai dat mîna subt nuc	For you gave your hand under the walnut tree,
Şî ţi-ai luat ce ţi-o plăcut.	And you took what you pleased.

In this verse, the woman reminds the bride that she is the one who agreed to the marriage. No one told her to fall in love with him.

Or the married woman may command her:

Taci mnireasă nu zdera!	Shut up, bride, don't cry!
Las să zdere celelalte	Let the others cry,
C-o rămas nemăritate.	For they have remained unmarried.

Despite the negative sides of married life, unmarried girls aspire to it. Rationality is seemingly confounded by love in the guise of sexual attraction. Therefore, the bride should recognize her fortune; she is now married.

Or the married woman may tell her through implication that she has the opportunity to experience her sexuality freely:

Mniresucă nu si nebună	Little bride, don't be crazy.
Nu zdera după cunună.	Don't cry after your crown.
Pune cununa în cui	Put your crown on a nail,
Şî dă-i gură mîndrului	And give your mouth to your sweetheart
Că tătă huc îi a lui.	Because it all belongs to him.

The sexual symbolism is evident. Also, the placing of her crown on a nail should be contrasted to the young girl's putting her crown back in the hope chest during the Asking for the Bride.

Coming After the Bride

The feasting and general celebrating continue. By late Monday morning (the third day of the wedding), the lack of sleep combined with the excesses of food and drink have begun to take their toll on many guests. To survive the toasting, the bride and groom do not often imbibe the contents of the glass or bottle; instead, they politely clink glasses and touch them to their lips. Their wedding is an exhausting ordeal; there is little or no time to nap, and they are constantly on their feet to participate in the toasts honoring them. Nonetheless, it is a special occasion in their lives and it will be a long-cherished memory.

Around 11 A.M. or so, the news circulates that the bride's wedding party—her immediate family and the guests who remained at her home after she departed with the groom and his compatriots— is approaching the groom's house. They are purportedly coming after the bride *să-o fure* (to steal her). They want her back. This part of the wedding ritual and the Asking for the Bride (when the groom with his entourage initially "stole" the bride from her home) may be viewed as power struggles over property rights. In the Asking for the Bride, the groom's party arrived by surprise in the middle of the night and gained entrance into the bride's household and took control. Later, with banner held high proclaiming their strength, they triumphantly took the bride back to his house (*casă împăratului*, or the house of the king). But the bride's house does not readily accept her loss and makes a final attempt to recapture her. The groom and his guests are prepared to meet the challenge. (It is not after all a "surprise attack" in the middle of the night, but rather an attempt in broad daylight.) As the bride's group nears, the groom's entire wedding party goes out into the courtyard. There they dance a circle dance to the music of the groom's musicians. The bride and groom lead the dance. The bride's party enters the courtyard with little difficulty. They do so performing the identical dance, except the music is from their musicians. The circles are separate; the bride's relatives try to "steal" her into their circle— but in vain. Finally they admit defeat. The circles merge, as do the two bands. The power advantage of the wife-takers is again symbolically reiterated. Cooperation is possible as long as male dominance is acknowledged.

Following the dance, the merger of the two families is honored with a meal inside the groom's house. Several hours later, the bride's party returns home. They are accompanied by the young couple, the groom's *nănaşi*, his parents, and anyone else who wishes to make the journey. The wedding is almost over. The bride has been introduced to her new family and residence, and the two families have been joined. It remains only for the bride to be ritually undressed, that is, for her to don the married woman's scarf.[31]

Dezbrăcarea Mniresii: *The Undressing*
of the Bride

The Undressing of the Bride takes place at her parents' home. The *dezbrăcarea mniresii* is a parallel inversion of her dressing. The bride is seated on a stool in the middle of a room; she is encircled by married women, young and old, who dance around her, shouting strigături or singing while she is being "undressed." The groom's godmother performs this service while the bride's mother-in-law watches. (She must be present.) During her dressing, the bride's girlfriends sang songs or shouted strigături of separation. Now, the married women sing songs of incorporation:

Ie-ţi mnireasă cununa	Take off your crown, bride,
Şî o dă de-a rotiţa	And pass it around the circle of women.
Prin grădină la mă-ta.	In your mother's garden,
Unde-a sta cununa-n loc	Where your crown will stay in place,
Să răsară busuioc	[There] will grow basil,
Că nu-i si fată la gioc.	For you won't be a girl at the dance.
Să răsară tămîiţă	[There] will grow *tămîiţă* [an aromatic herb];
Nu-i mai si fată-n uliţă.	You will no longer be a girl on the path.
Nu-i mere şî nu-i zini	You won't go and come,
Că bărbatu te-ar ibdi.	For your husband will make love to you.
Şî bărbatu nu ţi-i frate	And your husband isn't your brother,
Să gîndeşti că nu te-a bate.	Don't think he won't beat you.
Nici soacra nu ţi-i mamă	And your mother-in-law isn't your mother,
Să gîndeşti că nu-l îndeamnă.	Don't think she won't urge him on.
Mnireasă de-amu-nainte	Bride, from now on
Drumurile ţi-s oprite	The paths are forbidden to you.
Numa tri ţi-s năpustite.	Only three are permitted you:
În grădină după ceapă	To the garden for onions,
La fîntînă după apă.	To the fountain for water,

Şî la mă-tă cîteodată

And occasionally to your
  mother's

Cînd îi si mai supărată.

When you're really upset.

The married women tell her to leave her crown at her mother's because she has joined them. Her mother will bury her daughter's
crown in her garden. Flowers will grow in memory of the virgin
that is no more: basil, a holy plant, and *tămîiţă*, a medicinal plant.
Once again the bride is reminded that she will no longer participate in the activities of her unmarried friends. Now, instead of flirting with young men on the path, she will stay home and make love
with her husband. The husband is blamed for limited freedom,
but, in reality, the mother-in-law (if she lives with them) is more
culpable. She dictates where the bride may go and when, and if
she is dissatisfied with her daughter-in-law's conduct, she may manipulate her son into punishing her. Mothers, in contrast, usually
protect their children from paternal punishment. Also, the paths
that the bride will frequent from now on are not marked by the
flowers and vitality from her maiden days, but rather are associated
with tears and submission. Onions produce tears; remember that
if a bride does not cry voluntarily, onions will be used to provoke
tears. Going after water is a task not relished by many, especially
in the winter, and it is a chore delegated to young brides and emphasizes their low status in the family. (This, however, is an idealized statement; if the young woman is otherwise occupied, a child
or a brother may go after water. But while they may complain
about being asked to fill the water bucket, the bride must simply
comply.)

The married women continue with their discouraging words
throughout the bride's undressing. They offer renditions of the
verses cited for the Dressing of the Bride and from toasts to the
bride: that she will exchange her bridal crown for the married
woman's scarf; that she must kiss her family goodbye; that her life
will be hard as a stranger. As in the preceding ceremonial sequences,
the bride cries intensely. While the bride's godmother attempts to
place the scarf on her head, the women may begin:

Mnireasă nu te lăsa

Bride, don't let

Ca să-ţi ieie cununa

[Her] take your crown

Şî să-ţi puie năframa.　　　　　And put the scarf on you,
Că năframa-i tare gre　　　　　Because the scarf is very heavy:
Tăte grijile-s subt ie.　　　　　All worries are beneath it.
Cununa-i haină uşoară　　　　　The crown is light clothing;
Zine mîndru şî-o doboară.　　　Your sweetheart comes and
　　　　　　　　　　　　　　　　knocks it off.

Mnireasă de bună samă　　　　　Bride, for sure
Dai cununa pă năframă.　　　　　You exchange your crown for the
　　　　　　　　　　　　　　　　scarf.

. . . .　　　　　　　　. . . . .

Afară ninge şî plouă　　　　　　Outside it is snowing and
　　　　　　　　　　　　　　　　raining;
Noi avem nevastă nouă.　　　　　We have a new bride.
Afară plouă şî tună　　　　　　　Outside it is raining and
　　　　　　　　　　　　　　　　thundering;
Noi avem nevastă bună.　　　　　We have a good bride.

The first couplets caution the bride not to give up her virginity so quickly. The crown, however, is light and not permanently fixed (recall the couplet from the Dressing of the Bride about the crown that is worn but little, which is true in relation to the life cycle); it is very easy for a man to remove it, and that is what is about to happen. The last couplets celebrate the incorporation of the bride into the fold of the married women. For the bride, the transition is "stormy" and nature seems to empathize with her state of turmoil. During this ceremonial sequence, the bride refuses the scarf twice, throwing it to the ground. But on the third attempt, her godmother successfully positions the married woman's scarf on her head. It is a momentous occasion. She has become a wedded woman just like those who surround her.

When the crown is loosened (the greenery from her braids having been undone), a girl three or four years of age is lifted up to take the crown from the bride's head. It is then placed on the child's head to ensure that she too will someday wear the crown. The removal of the bride's crown is an inversion of its placement. In the Dressing of the Bride, a young boy put the crown on her head; in the undressing, a young girl takes it off. The first "magic" act operates to produce a first-born male child; the second operates to produce another bride—who will then produce another male. In this way, the patrilineal paradox is perpetuated over time. The wedding succeeds in making the bride like all married women. This one is no different:

Cînd ai înflorit mai tare	When you blossomed the most
Mă-ta ti-o făcut vînzare.	Your mother sold you.
. . . .	. . . .
D-aşă-i rîndu la fete	But that's how it is for maidens,
Nu la una ca la tăte.	Not for one, but for all.

The young woman's position and status will improve as she begets children and progresses through the stages of the life cycle. Eventually she too will be not only a mother but also a mother-in-law. Reifying tautology, the system produces and reproduces itself.

Întîlnirea Cuscriilor: *Meeting of the In-Laws*

As stated in the beginning of this chapter, the wedding ritual is bounded by events that initiate and conclude the realignment of social relations. On the first Sunday after the wedding, the *întîlnirea cuscriilor* takes place; the parents of the bride and groom "meet." (The groom's parents are cuscri to the bride's parents and vice versa.) In keeping with the hierarchical ordering of social relations and the principles of patriarchy, the groom's family hosts the final celebration. That afternoon, the newlyweds, their immediate families, the bridesmaid, the flagbearer, and the godparents gather at the groom's parents' house. If possible, musicians are also invited. The afternoon and early evening are spent eating, drinking, and enjoying. Strigături and occasional dances fill the room. Whereas the marriage process began in the home of the bride, it ends in the home of the groom. The betrothal acknowledged the relations between the bride and groom; the întîlnirea cuscriilor acknowledges the relation between their parents, which is the result of the marriage between their children. The întîlnirea cuscriilor (also known as *ospăţ,* or feast) honors, or gives cinstea, to this bond.

The Wedding *Laolaltă*

While most people still celebrate their marriage in the traditional manner—the elaborate nuntă ţaranească (village wedding)—a truncated version of this wedding is gaining popularity in response to the work schedules of those in the state's wage-labor force, to the rising cost of living, and to diminishing access to resources. This less elaborate type of wedding has antecedents among the poorest families in the village who were unable to afford the customary wedding, as well as among the "intellectuals" (domni) who adopted foreign city habits to distinguish themselves from the peasants, whose habits they disdained.[32] (Nowadays, more and more brides are attaching veils to their crowns, although the rest of the wedding attire remains traditional. This innovation reflects an appreciation for the "cultured ways" of city dwellers.)

This type of wedding differs from the peasant one. The Dances of the Flag and the Crown are still done on the night before the church ceremony. After the cununie, however, the wedding parties of the bride and groom return together to the *căminul cultural* (community hall) rented for the occasion. Hence, the wedding unfolds *laolaltă*, or together—not in two simultaneous celebrations at the homes of the bride and groom, who are only gradually brought together. Upon arrival at the hall, the couple is welcomed by the cook, who performs the Throwing of the Grain. Once the guests are seated inside and the musicians have begun to play, a meal is served. Because the two families are already united, the giving of pominoc is omitted, although all guests contribute gifts at some point during the wedding. The Asking for the Bride is left out, because she has been at the groom's side since leaving the church. In a sense, the sacred church ceremony compensates for the omission of the secular union of the couple through the cererea in the traditional ceremony. But, without reservation, the Song of the Hen is done. (This may or may not be included in city weddings; when it is, it is for the benefit of relatives from *la țară* and for the entertainment of everyone.) The Song of the Hen is eagerly awaited; it is fun. In addition, it is the sequence that is most explicit about the sexual realities of marriage. Afterward, continuous toasting of the couple, and the bride in particular, ensues. The celebration lasts well into the night, if not continuing all night. The conclusion of the wedding is marked by the ritual Undressing of the Bride, which takes place in a clear area of the room where the bride is encircled by married women. The placement of the married woman's scarf ends the festivities. Those who are sober enough are then able to catch the workers' bus, which departs around 5 A.M.

The central concerns of this abbreviated wedding are still honor and shame, virginity, and alienation and incorporation—themes that are reiterated throughout the wedding celebration. The alterations and omissions of some ceremonial events reflect practical considerations. Exchanging pominoc, Asking for the Bride, attempting to recapture her—these ritual sequences lose their "performance potency" (Tambiah 1979, 162) when a wedding is laolaltă. While the wedding ritual is a dramatic spectacle and is appreciated as such, it is also creative and reflexive; thus, it is not only spectacle but also a result of the dynamic interplay between the constitutive representations and the experiences of Ieudeni (see Comaroff 1980, 42–44).

Summary

The nuntă, or wedding ritual, both constitutes and celebrates marriage. The three-day process defines and reorders social relations between individuals and groups who live in a sociocultural universe governed by the principles of patrilineality and patriarchy. In this world, social relations are hierarchically structured and stratified by age and gender. Marriage requires the transformation of categories and of relations, especially boy-girl, man-woman, and unmarried-married. Through the dramatic experience of ritual, boundaries are sequentially dissolved and established. (See T. Turner 1977, 67–68). The wedding manipulates and controls these transformations by enacting social process in terms the participants understand: a woman is alienated from her natal family and incorporated into the family of her husband. Ideologically, at least, these transformations—social and biological—are considered irreversible.

The structure of the ritual assures its effectiveness (T. Turner 1977, 62–63; Tambiah 1979, 124–30). The primary aim of the rite is to produce and reproduce the sociocultural order. At the most basic level, the wedding dramatizes the union of two individuals and the consequent relation between their families. Hence, from the broadest perspective, the betrothal preceding the wedding and the meeting of the couple's parents following it mark the limits of that which takes place in between; the engagement catalyzes the transformations that result in the establishment of relations between the couple's parents. The wedding mediates these two discrete events. The wedding proper begins with the construction and the Dance of the Groom's Flag by and among unmarried peers (a declaration of male virility) and ends with the ritual Undressing of the Bride by and among married women (an appropriation of female reproductivity). A complex series of transformations take place between these two episodes so that they may be meaningfully related. To do so, the ritual process moves the participants through various acts and levels of separation and incorporation, all the while emphasizing sexuality (which differentiates the end state from the beginning). Ritual reiteration compels and creates.

The themes of separation and incorporation are present in every ritual segment, although the degree of intensity varies. There are three levels of separation: (1) from one's unmarried peers, (2) from one's family, and (3) from one's familiar "self," which is composed of the roles and actions associated with being a member of the first and second groups. The third level of separation may be seen as an alienation of self without which the new social persona cannot be constructed via the process of transformation. Separation embodies a social death, hence the metaphorical relationship between the marriage and death. The theme of separation is most prominent during the Dance of the Flag and the Dressing of the Bride, and separation from family is most prominent in the Asking of Forgiveness. Separation is highlighted before the church ceremony.

The levels of incorporation are (1) into the ranks of married couples, (2) into the household and family of the groom (in most cases) as a married unit, (3) integration of the two families, and (4) into one's new social persona. Incorporation embodies a social rebirth, hence the metaphorical equation of death and marriage (to be further explored in Chapter 4). The theme of incorporation predominates when the bride is brought to the groom's house and when her wedding party comes to recapture her (incorporation into and of families) and during the ritual Undressing of the Bride (incorporation into the ranks of married women). The male bias of the system is underscored through the asymmetrical emphasis on the incorporative phases as well as through the focus on the bride's negation and reconstitution of self.

The wedding is primarily in the bride's honor; she is the object of alienation and appropriation. It is her physical, as well as spiritual, person that is directly acted upon, not the groom's (or anyone else's). She is dressed and undressed by others; she is socially prepared (in the Dressing of the Bride) to be transformed (in the Song of the Hen), to be reshaped (in the Undressing). The transformational process occurs in the "liminal phase," consisting of the Asking for the Bride and the Song of the Hen. During these sequences, the bride passively experiences her own metamorphosis through her symbolic self, the hen. The crucial element of the wedding underpinning the marriage is her virginity. In the Song of the Hen, the ritual sequence that publicly validates her virginity and presages its imminent sacrifice, the bride is acted upon physically in symbolic terms only.

It may be argued that the cererea mniresii and the horea găinii constitute incorporative phases vis-à-vis the scope of marriage: acquisition of the bride. From this perspective, the wedding rite may be viewed as a rite of separation for the wife-givers (who lose a family member) and one of incorporation for the wife-takers (who gain a member). The ritual progression is positive for the latter and negative (from this perspective) for the former (recall that the bride's family attempts to take her back, but their effort is unsuccessful). Clearly, the ritual structure encodes the structure of social organization. It is indeed a metaform of it. The parallel constructions and parallel inversions of ritual sequences facilitate and control the process of social and sexual transformation within the framework of the hierarchical ordering of relations.

The Dances of the Flag and the Crown and the exchange of ribbons and bouquets may be considered symbolic equivalents of the ritual prestations between families and the Asking for the Bride and the Song of the Hen. All these sequences are parallel constructions at different levels addressing the process of male appropriation and the certification of the bride's virginity and, consequently, the appropriation specifically of her sexuality. The exchange of ribbons and bouquets and the ritual prestations are symbolically parallel inversions. Establishment of relations between the bride and groom (note the similarity to betrothal) brings about relations between their families (similar to the Meeting of the In-Laws). All of the components of marriage are encapsulated and reiterated in these sequences.

The Dressing and the Undressing of the Bride are parallel (or structural) inversions of each other. The Dressing of the Bride separates her from the cadre of unmarried maidens, who lament her;

the Undressing of the Bride incorporates her into the ranks of married women, who welcome her. The content of the songs is similar, stressing the bride's multilevel alienation. Who performs them determines the performative force of these songs or strigături. The placing and removal of the bride's crown by a young boy and young girl, respectively, assures regeneration of the system. Both sequences are overseen or controlled by married women, who are the products and the producers (of children and brides) of these ritual events. (This may be compared to the emphasis on male dominance in the sequences about separation and incorporation.) The going after the bride by the groom's and the bride's families are also parallel inversions, with the former having a positive outcome and the latter, a negative one.

The temporal and spatial phasing of each sequence underscores its significance. To illustrate, the jocul steagului and jocul cununii explicitly introduce sexuality to the process of marriage, as that which distinguishes the nature of this interaction (and the bargaining for its "object") from that of any other; the Dances of the Flag and the Crown take place at night, the time associated with married sexual relations. The groom's flag, a symbol of virility and power, is always held high and proudly displayed. The unmarried are excluded from the church service and remain outdoors dancing, that is, participating in the activity associated with courtship; married couples witness the marriage within the church. Later, when the groom's party goes to ask for the bride, they do so at night (to stress the sexual element). Furthermore, they go after midnight so that their mission will be successful. They then occupy and control the bride's house. Because the bride's party goes to recapture her in broad daylight, they fail. The Song of the Hen takes place almost at the crack of dawn (when the cock calls), and the cook proceeds from the kitchen to the table with her hen. Finally, the bride's undressing occurs in the late afternoon or early evening so that she will be ready for bed that night.

In summary, an examination of the wedding ritual reveals how the rite moves from the directly personal or interpersonal to the sociocentric, simultaneously transforming the individual and reifying the social as the context for this transformation. The first sequences of the wedding (the Dance of the Flag through the Asking of Forgiveness) stress the interpersonal interaction between the bride and groom and their respective families and friends. The later sequences (from the ritual prestations through the end) emphasize the sociocentric "negotiation" of marriage. As the wedding progresses, the "discussion" about marriage between the bride and groom becomes a discussion about marriage in general. In the end, society generates marriage through the godparents, shifting interpersonal relations to the communal level. Bourdieu has commented, "It is practical kin who make marriages; it is official kin who celebrate them" (1977, 34). It was stated earlier in this chapter that marriage entails more than the sum of its individual constituents (the bride and groom). Marriage is fundamentally social, honoring in dramatic form the communal self. By objectifying experience, weddings celebrate the reconstitution of social relations; they "make sense" of experience. Hence, weddings are a powerful medium through which to understand—normatively—the lived-in world of the celebrants.

Chapter Three

Funeral Rites

Mult ieşti moarte blăstămată . . .
Very cursed are you, death . . .

Da viaţa omului	But the life of man
Îi ca floarea cîmpului.	Is like a wildflower:
Azî ieşti tînăr şî voinic	Today you are young and strong
Şî pă mîni nu ieşti nimic.	And by tomorrow you are nothing.

Recorded in Ieud and
Săliştea de Sus, Maramureş, 1980

Ieu sînt mai tare ca tine	I am stronger than you.
Uită-te bine creştine.	Look carefully, Christian,
Că ieu sînt urîta moarte	For I am ugly death.
Pă rînd voi duce pă toate.	I will take all of you one by one.

Cross inscription,
Merry Cemetery, Maramureş

Death, the eternal curse of the living, is a biological, sociological, cosmological, and existential reality. The physical demise of the human body—the corpse being the material manifestation of the destruction of the "self"—threatens the very foundation of society. Death interrupts the "dynamic equilibrium of social life" (Blauner 1966, 379). The person who existed no longer participates actively in the ongoing web of social interactions, no longer contributes physically to the production and reproduction of society. Hence, mortality is profoundly disruptive; it demands response. The stark individuality of the corpse focuses attention on the complex relationship between the individual and society, a relationship that must be dealt with in order to make sense of death. Unquestionably, death poses the ultimate challenge for rendering human experience meaningful.[1]

The contradictions in human understanding evoked by death, be they between mortality and the desire for immortality or between the social need to bury the dead yet keep them alive, have given rise the world over to culturally elaborated means of dealing with death and the dead. "Dramas of disposal" (funeral rites) and religions symbolically resolve the most vital dilemma of the human condition: the "spirit" tends to be one of culture's answers to physical mortality; monuments, tombstones, and oral or written testimonials are others (see Humphreys and King 1981). In the final analysis, ritual and religion honor the dead in order to celebrate life and the living (Huntington and Metcalf 1979, 1).

In Romania, the spirit that offers salvation from extinction is the "soul." Christianity has defined its essence as well as the framework within which the interplay between body and soul, action and thought, the living and the dead may be worked out. (The manipulation of the soul is to the understanding of death in Romania as that of the corpse is to an understanding of death in Borneo and Indonesia; see Hertz's classic study [1960].) Religion is central to the management of death; it offers an ideology of death that entails a prescription for life. Death and life are dialectically related. The dichotomization of these two phenomena, so characteristic of modern Western thought and practice, has not as yet occurred in Romania (Ariès 1981). Although death is distinctly antiprogressive in terms of the state's push toward modernization and scientific rationalism (see Kligman 1981, 150–51), its governance has been left to the Orthodox church, and not the Communist Party.[2] In this realm the church still maintains relative autonomy, as though its existence may be partially rationalized as an institution to deal with *ceia lume*, or "that world." The Communist Party has defined its territory as "this-worldly," and, for the time being, cannot afford to confront the philosophical and existential problems of death as a priority concern. (Theoretically, "that world" should lose credibility as modernization and education increase. See Lane 1981, 83.)

Although the powerful influence of Christianity must be recognized, it is equally important to note that "more than the other rites associated with important moments in man's life, in our [Romanian] folklore, the rituals associated with death have preserved ancient pre-Christian beliefs and practices" (M. Pop 1976, 157).[3] The village priest generally concurs with this scholarly appraisal; from his point of view, there are many "pagan" elements from

popular culture bound to religious customs by centuries of practice. Ceia lume represents an amalgamation of beliefs and practices
derived from religious ideology and the practical exigencies of
death. As will be seen, the fit between the two continuums is not
exact; there is considerable friction and contradiction. Christian
doctrine is perceived as the foundation on which the organizing
principles of life and death are based; hence, it is fundamental to
understanding indigenous conceptions about life and death. It is
beyond the scope of this book, however, to examine the content of
the formal Romanian Orthodox rites. For our purposes it is sufficient to note that the prayers and acts address the purification of
the soul, forgiveness of sins, and the church-sanctioned incorporation of the deceased into the other world.

In this as well as in the following chapter, the beliefs and practices associated with death will be analyzed as a means to explain
the basic relations of the cosmological order, most saliently the relationships between life and death and between culture and nature. (Tambiah defines *cosmological order* as "the body of conceptions that enumerate and classify the phenomena that compose the
universe as an ordered whole and the norms and processes that
govern it" [1979, 121].) The funeral ritual provides a general narrative framework through which a basic semantic code is structured. Tambiah notes that "cosmological constructs are embedded
(of course not exclusively) in rites, and [that] rites in turn enact and
incarnate cosmological conceptions" (ibid.). Moreover, the unfolding of the death ritual makes the affective process of grieving culturally "meaningful." It should be recalled from the preceding
chapter that rituals do not necessarily reveal the individual emotions of the participants; rather, they channel culturally articulated
feelings. The first section of this chapter will explore modes of
communication between this world and that world. Then the essential components of the funeral rite will be depicted and analyzed. Throughout, the primary emphasis will be on laments as expressions of cosmology and social relations.

Communication Between
the Living and the Dead

For the iiving, life and death must be made meaningful. Communication is required in this endeavor, as is the need, conscious or not,

for material self-awareness. Death, however, denies the physical existence of self and nonnegotiably prohibits communication between the living and the dead, thereby denying the living, who thrive on communication, empirical knowledge of death and the dead. That "that" world is believed to exist is, of itself, testimony to a projection of the living beyond themselves. To borrow Vernant's observation on the Greek epic, the world of the dead may be seen as a "heroic attempt [of the living] to push away as far as possible, beyond the uncrossable threshold, the horror of chaos, the horror of what has no form and no meaning, and to affirm in the face of and despite everything, the social permanence of . . . [the living who] must, by [their] very nature, be destroyed and disappear" (1981, 291). The dead are thought to live in their world, which is related to yet different from this world. The dead seem to communicate among themselves, but they do not communicate with the living. The rupture between this world and the other world completely severs direct communication between the living and the dead and highlights the radical disjunction between life and death.

Communication between the living and the dead is possible only in mediated forms: laments, the giving of *pomană* (alms), and dreams. These interactions underscore the dynamic and hierarchical relations between the living and the dead, in which the former must fulfill certain obligations to the latter. The performance of these prescribed deeds *da cinstea* (gives honor) to the souls of the dead. In this manner, pre-Christian practices are linked to Christian beliefs about death and the soul.

Immediately upon someone's death, female relatives (consanguines, affines, and ritual kin) must begin to mourn the dead (*mortul*) through lamenting. Lamenting is ritually obligatory (as is crying for the bride during the wedding ceremony) and is performed by women only. It is believed to be a sin not to lament the dead; anyone who is buried unlamented is anathema to God. One of the worst curses that may be directed at someone is *să dea Dumnezeu să n-ai pe nime să-te bocească!* (God grant it that you have no one to lament you!). Women present in the household of the deceased must lament following the ringing of the church bells for the deceased. This usually occurs thrice daily during the three-day funeral period (which begins at the time of death). Women, especially immediate kin, may also lament at will. On the day of the funeral, lamenting tends to continue until the burial is completed,

although this expression of grief is interrupted by periods of mandatory silence when the priest performs necessary rites and prayers.

Like other poetic forms in Romania, laments are composed of
rhymed couplets generally of seven- or eight-syllable lines. Although the common repertoire of laments is based on certain structural rules and thematic stereotypes, there is, nonetheless, considerable improvisation and individual elaboration (see Pop and
Ruxăndoiu 1976, 213–14).[4] In essence, the language of death concentrates on the transformation of physical and emotional states
evoked by death and on travel as the means of passage from the
world of the living into that of the dead. Laments recount the particular circumstances of death and the relationship of the deceased
to the lamenter and to the community; they portray the world of
the dead and the process of putrefaction, that of separation and incorporation from this world into that. Laments also facilitate fictive
communication between the living and the dead. The majority of
these lament themes are voiced interchangeably and repetitively
throughout the ritual sequences of a funeral. This contributes to
the general redundancy of ritual.[5] Certain verses, however, are
temporally and spatially associated with particular ritual acts, such
as when the coffin is about to be removed from the house or when
the cortège approaches the cemetery entrance. In short, some
couplets are invoked only in specific circumstances.

This raises an important point about the relationship between
ritual action and language, as well as about levels of meaning. It is a
point eloquently stated by Tambiah (1979, 153–60) in a discussion
on indexical symbols and icons; he notes that an indexical icon has
two dimensions of meaning: "symbolic or iconic" and "existential or
indexical." These distinctions are useful in that they

enable us to appreciate how important parts of a ritual enactment have
a symbolic or iconic meaning associated with the cosmological plane of
content, and at the same time how those same parts are existentially or
indexically related to participants in the ritual, creating, affirming, or
legitimating their social positions and powers. The duality thus points in
two directions at once—in the semantic direction of cultural presupposi-
tions and conventional understandings and in the pragmatic direction of
the social and interpersonal context of ritual action, the line-up of the
participants and the process by which they establish or infer meanings.
(ibid., 154)[6]

While in practice it is impossible to disaggregate ritual action and language, and Tambiah's insights encompass the totality, it is nonetheless helpful to look at these dual dimensions of the laments. Laments are used both referentially and indexically. The former address the semantic cosmological order (for example, the relationship between the living and the dead); the latter, "pragmatic" matters (such as the individual circumstances of death). Therefore, women use this collective form to simultaneously express existential concerns and ongoing social relationships. Because the living believe that the dead speak among themselves, they also think that the newly deceased, acting as messengers, are able to carry news from this world to the other. The implicit assumption that the dead will inquire after the living necessarily links the living and the dead and lessens the stark reality of mortality. Thus, through laments, women advise the individual about to be buried to tell X something on behalf of the lamenter or her family. Usually, a lamenter will caution the messenger to tell the "others" about their living kin, but in a manner that will not cause them consternation:

Dacă ———— te-a-ntreba | If ———— asks you
Cum îi rîndu p-aicea. | How things are around here:
Rîndu-i bun şi tăte-s bune | Things are good and all's well,
Doru lor ne duce-n lume. | But longing for them makes us crazy.

Spune cît îi socoti | Tell what you think appropriate
Să vă puteţi hodini. | So you [all] can rest.

This verse illustrates both aspects of indexicality, the existential and the pragmatic. The lamenter speaks familiarly (*tu*) to the messenger who is being sent (buried). In the last line, however, she acknowledges the unidirectionality of the messenger's journey by using the plural *you*, which incorporates the messenger among the dead.

Some women will attempt to deny the total break of relations, although this is less frequently heard:

Şi cu tăţi ti-or întreba | And everyone will ask you
Cum îi rîndu p-aicea. | How things are around here.

Nu spune tăte să creadă   Don't tell them everything;
Zie-acasă să le vadă.   Tell them to come home and see.

While the living long for the dead to return and suggest reasons for
them to do so, they also know that this will never occur. Women
will lament to soothe the pain of death, but they also will say that
that is the function of such pleas; to be sure, no one has ever responded to the invitation to return and never will do so. The living
must bear the frustration of eternal silence.[7]

Laments, as "privileged" language within "privileged" contexts
(ritual), may also be used to exploit the indexical, pragmatic aspect
of communication, thereby constituting a medium for social commentary and protest.[8] The funeral context facilitates the public
airing of village grievances because it is legitimated by the primary function of the ritual: communication with the dead. Hence,
"news," safely embedded in the customary structure of the lament,
may be sent to a deceased relative in "that world." (This will be
taken up in the final chapter.)

The dual capacity of laments also encompasses the cultural pat-
terning of grief. Death affects not only the deceased, but also his or
her family and the community as a whole. In Maramureş, there is
no noun for "lament." (Elsewhere in Romania, one speaks of *bocet*
[a lament], or *cîntec de jale* [a mourning song].) A woman laments,
a se cînta; she sings for herself—and others. She sings about death
in general and in the particular; the lament is meant to be both
iconic and indexical.

While mourning is both religiously and ritually dictated, the extent of overt expression is ideologically circumscribed. It is considered inappropriate to mourn too much and to show untempered
grief for young children and for the elderly (M. Pop 1976, 160).
Since children are angels without sins, the living should not be
overly saddened by their deaths. Moreover, if there is too much
crying, it is thought that the child's soul will drown during the journey to heaven because the lakes encountered en route will over-
flow from excess tears (see also Marian 1892, 400). The elderly, at
the opposite end of the life cycle, are believed to have lived a full
life; thus, their "time has come."[9] Death of the aged is considered
more routine. The most painful deaths are of those who die in the
prime of life: persons of marriageable age (the subject of the follow-

ing chapter) or who have growing children. For them, mourning is expected to be the most pronounced:

După tînăr şî-n putere I mai mult năcaz şî jele.	For the young and strong, There is more suffering and sorrow.

The period of active mourning generally lasts one year. This period is prescribed by Christian practices, but the elaboration of beliefs and actions is clearly subject to secular or pre-Christian influences. During this time, close kin of the deceased may not participate in celebratory events such as weddings or dances. (Marian [1892, 400] noted that dancing during this period was thought to be paid for in hell, where devils danced on the backs of those who did not respect the prohibition.) Also, women are expected to mourn longer than men. A widow who marries while in mourning is accused of not having loved her former husband; men, however, may remarry during the year's mourning and not be maligned. This is rationalized "under the pretext that they are not able to run the household and take care of children" (Marian 1892, 406; this rationale is still used today). In actuality, most village women do not remarry, but remain widows.

Mourning is the means by which the living honor the dead. During the funeral, the soul watches to see that nothing is omitted. Should this occur, it is believed that the soul will return and punish the living. Therein may be found the basis of many pre-Christian fears about ghosts, vampires, and related brethren. To avoid misfortune, the living are obliged to offer pomană to and for the dead, primarily in the form of commemorative meals and prayers, in addition to those acts that are ritually performed during the burial rites. These symbolic acts of communication satisfy the requirements of the dead as well as extend hospitality and reinforce social relations between the living and the dead. In return for this consideration, the dead inhabit their world quietly. It is believed that, until the final judgment, the dead need nourishment like all travelers (Kligman 1981, 166, n. 3). Thus, the living periodically replenish the resources of the dead. Pomană is given in the name of the deceased, and the phrase *sie de sufletu mortului* (to be for the dead's soul) accompanies every prayer or toast (the dead also require drink). Commemorative meals are given at the conclusion of

the funeral and then three days, nine days, six months, and one
year after it, as well as on communal memorial days, such as All
Souls' Day. (In Ieud, religious holidays from the Greek Catholic
faith, such as All Souls' Day, are still marked. Saint Mary's Day is
another not specific to Orthodoxy.) While a meal is in progress, any
passerby is invited to partake of it "for the soul of the dead." The
invitation must be accepted because it is said that otherwise the
soul will be offended. (Tourists frequently find themselves sitting at
a table, duly impressed by the "spontaneous" hospitality of the
local people.) Also, anyone who has attended a funeral may not
leave without a ritual bread as a token of the deceased's hospitality.
A special *pomană copiilor,* or alms for children, is offered at every
funeral: candies or pretzel-like breads are distributed to children,
many of whom appear expressly for this. Special breads are also
given to the officials presiding over the funeral.

Commensality is a key medium of sociality. In this way, social
relations between the living and the dead are established and maintained. Commensality mediates "religion and the social order"
(Ortner 1978), enabling the living to fulfill their obligations to the
dead and also to humanize the other world. It is thought that there,
the tables are full. If alms are not given as required, however, the
dead will find empty tables. Some people believe it is inauspicious
to die on a day of fast because this will eternally assure that the
deceased will have only meals appropriate for fast days. (The ambivalence is intriguing: fasting honors God and cleanses the soul,
which would seem to be auspicious under the circumstances.)

Whereas food is "food for the body," prayers are "food for the
soul." It is essential that the living pray for the dead. Prayers comfort the soul and fortify the soul's possibilities for mercy and as-
cendancy. Relatives light candles in church in honor of the dead,
giving them light in the darkness of death along with the gift of
prayers. Prayers are privately offered at will. The kin of the dead
may also pay for certain services to be read in honor of the dead, or
pay widows (believed to be "purer") to fast for the deceased to
cleanse the soul. The dead acknowledge their gratitude in kind
over time. When the living join the dead, the dead in heaven pray
for the souls of those who have prayed for them.

Symbolic communication of this type entails obligations of giving and receiving over extended cycles, thereby adding depth to

the process of exchange. According to the Maussian paradigm, the totality of exchange creates social relations and meaning.[10] Weiner's emphasis (1980) on a "reproductive perspective" as opposed to a reciprocity approach provides a useful framework within which to locate in time and space mutual obligations between the living and the dead. The living, collectively and individually, honor the deceased individually and the dead collectively. The death of an individual becomes an occasion to give alms to the many and to accrue future value for the givers. Because this is a continuous process, the dead, in turn, pray for the soul of an individual to help advance his or her journey and for the other souls who are believed to be already en route. Negligence by the living to any one funeral instigates different levels of retribution by the dead. In such cases, the recently deceased is believed to return soon after the burial and create havoc in some discernible form, illness being the most common. Unless the dead are properly recompensed (through extra alms, for example), the living lessen their future ease in the other world. In this sense, communication between the living and the dead, despite the necessity of mediation, is mandatory and incurs positive or negative consequences. (Mourning and fulfillment of obligations to the dead are of such significance that they are performed in the village for the deceased even if the individual has died away from the village and cannot be brought back for physical burial, as is the case for soldiers who perish at the front [M. Pop 1976, 160].) Thus the giving of alms manipulates the tenor of social relations, keeping the living at peace with the dead, and the dead in the grace of God. These acts are mutually beneficial, effecting the separation and integration of the living and the dead, while respecting the order of social relations.

The hope for communication with the dead reflects a need to keep them alive. A death heightens an immediate need to communicate. The ritual of prescribed mourning is the customary means of communication; dreams are another. During the official mourning period of one year, the living also express their desire to dream about the deceased. Dreaming about the dead is considered auspicious and serves as evidence of a soul after death. In a dream, the absence of communication between the living and the dead is breached. The shared context of "sleep" provides the channel through which the deceased is believed to come and speak with the living. The person who dreams about the deceased will then tell kin and friends about the dream; it is, for the dreamer, a deeply gratifying experience, satisfying the urge to remember and be remembered. Hence, one morning, the goddaughter of the recently deceased mother-in-law of the family with whom I lived arrived and excitedly recounted her dream: "Mătuşa Marie told me to come to you and tell you she is well and that I should help you plant the potatoes in the garden." This woman always helped Marie plant potatoes; Marie was her nănaşa, so she felt obligated to fulfill her debts to her. In fact, the potatoes had not yet been planted and it was indeed the time to do so. "So you see, it is exactly how she dreamed," commented my gazdă.[11] Dreams are thought to indicate that the dead cares enough to come. Also, doubts and fears about unfulfilled obligations are said to be alleviated by this privileged communication between these related worlds.

Ceia Lume: "Sacred" and "Secular" Conceptions of Death and the Dead

The Tripartite Model

Before proceeding to the funeral ritual itself, it is first necessary to describe the organization of "that world" as it is believed to be. The world of the dead comprises three levels: *rai* (heaven), *iad* (hell), and *purgatoriu* (purgatory). This model is appropriated from Christian dogma, specifically from Catholicism; purgatory is not a component of Orthodox belief. Although this region of Transylvania was for centuries (after 1701) associated with the Uniate, or Greek Catholic, church, at the official level, people today must adhere to Orthodox practices. Their belief system, however, is still derived from Uniate theology. (What will happen to this tradition after several generations of Orthodox teaching remains to be seen.) These beliefs are also conflated with folk beliefs, themselves derivative of theological teachings about life and death. According to folk beliefs, there are three "churches" on this earth: the *biserica luptătoare* (the church of struggle) for those who are in hell, the *biserica suferitoare* (the church of suffering) for those in purgatory, and the *biserica triumfătoare* (the church of triumph) for those in heaven.

Heaven is thought to be a beautiful garden adorned with flowers and angels; it offers eternal joy, reminiscent of a mother's garden, providing security and nourishment. In the midst of heaven, God sits on his splendrous throne of gold. Heaven is populated by those who have not sinned, at least not committed *pǎcate grele*, or hard sins. "Nothing tainted enters there," an elderly religious woman told me. Certain people ascend directly to heaven: children under seven, nuns, and those who die between Easter and Pentecost. It is believed that baptized children under seven years of age are pure angels who have not sinned "hard." (First confession usually occurs at the age of eight. It is pertinent to note that before World War I, boys and girls were dressed alike until they were seven, when they became capable of sin.) People who die between Easter and Pentecost benefit from the gates of heaven being open for the resurrection of Christ and his ascension. Those who do not go directly to heaven but who led a reasonably Christian life, and who are properly aided by their living kin, may eventually gain admittance to heaven from purgatory. The residents of heaven also pray for those who are not there, that God may forgive them and hasten their penance in purgatory.

Everyone else goes to hell or purgatory, depending on the kind of life lived. Hell is the domicile for those who don't "have God." It is the antithesis of heaven, characterized by eternal fire and suffering. Devils constantly strike their human cohabitants with sharp pitchforks. The punishments for offenses on God's earth are severe. Certain sins can never be absolved, and those who committed them are condemned to eternal damnation. Hard sins include illicit sexual unions (prostitution, bawdry, homosexuality), unredeemed or unconfessed theft, murder, suicide, and sorcery. The unbaptized are considered the unfortunate victims of their parents' negligence; hence it is possible for them to escape to purgatory if the living attend to their obligations. There is not, however, agreement on the matter of ascending from hell. Some believers are emphatic about the impossibility of ever escaping; certain sins can never be exonerated, and those who have committed them are condemned to eternal damnation.

Those who go directly neither to heaven nor to hell find themselves in purgatory. Among this lot are also individuals who have been spared the sentence of hell: for example, thieves and sexual offenders who have confessed and rectified their deviant behavior during their lifetime. Purgatory is thought to be an unpleasant environment in which fire burns continually (as it does in hell). From time to time, however, the souls in purgatory get a glimpse of the Virgin Mary; there is a glimmer of hope. For those in this liminal locale, the nature and degree of one's previous offenses determine the length of punishment—"which depends on what you've got in your sack" (*care cum are în trăistă*), referring to the totality of life's experiences. Being in purgatory is said to be "as if in jail. You go for a certain period of time." One may be pardoned from purgatory on fulfillment of one's sentence. This occurs after the soul has passed through the *vămi* (gates) that it encounters after it takes final leave of the body reposing in its grave. The gatekeepers must be appeased, as well as satisfied after their interrogations, before they allow the soul to proceed on its route to Judgment Day. To appease the gatekeepers, the living place coins in the coffin so that each toll may be paid. If the soul passes successfully through these, then it eventually arrives at a fork in the road. The path to the right is the road of flowers leading to heaven; that to the left is of thorns and goes to hell. The dichotomization of heaven and hell gives rise to confusion about the location of purgatory. Purgatory does not fit geographically, yet it is considered a place where those who have committed lesser sins are punished and in which they may reside after the final judgment, should they not go on to heaven. (It is thought that the Jews reside in purgatory—rather than hell—because they are "baptized.") Again, the fit between various conceptions of death and that world is often contradictory.

Secular Binary Structures:
This World and That World

The tripartite model of the world of the dead reflects a Christian-inspired vision of ceia lume in which heaven, purgatory, and hell represent a metastructure of good, bad, and evil, which together enable people to cope with the fundamental problems of life. The universe of the dead is not only perceived in terms of this morally differentiated model, however; it is also viewed as a distinct entity that is related to the world of the living yet essentially an inversion of it. The disjunction between the tripartite and binary "models" does not seem to be problematic for those who think and live them. The Christian version may be seen as dealing with the religious-existential aspects of death; the secular (for lack of better classificatory terms), with the material-cultural dimensions. (In other words, these two "models" also encompass the dual dimensions of indexical symbols; the relationship between beliefs and practices is well articulated.) In both, relations between this world and that world, and between the living and the dead, are dynamic.

Ceia lume is translated as "that world" (not "the other world") because of the semantic relation between *astă lume* (this world) and *ceia lume* (that world). While "the other world" is idiomatically correct in English, it implies a relationship based more on difference and opposition than on similarity and inversion. Also *this* and *that* maintain the conceptual structure of negative parallelisms characteristic of Romanian poetics.

The laments that color the funeral rite focus primarily on the secular cosmology of death and that world; thus the remainder of this discussion will be directed toward this interpretive frame. In that world, the hierarchical ordering of social relations obtains. Therefore, when people die, they go to their family in the world of the dead. This means that a widow joins her husband's family and not her natal family, which she left when she married; whereas an unmarried girl of marriageable age goes to her natal family. Social relations are continuous between the living and the dead.

What differs significantly in the world of the dead is the natural environment and the "life style" it encourages. The world of the dead is the paramount symbolic inversion of that of the living. Inversion is typically associated with systems of classification and negation (Babcock 1978, 13–36); systems of classification are cultural constructs that order human experience. From this perspective, Culture distinguishes human life from Nature. People, through purposive action, manipulate their environment. Culture is thus constituted of consumers—of Nature and of the products of human activity. But Nature metes out its ultimate revenge on the cultural centrism of the living: death negates life. That world is devoid of familiar cultural constructs; basic cultural amenities are lacking. The following verse notes that in the world of the dead

| Nici ară nici cară | One does not plow or cart things; |

Nici nu-l suflă vînt de vară.	Nor does the summer wind blow on him;
Nici îi pat de să culcă	Nor is there a bed on which to lie—
Numa pă lutu uscat.	Only on dry clay;
Nici îi scaun de şăzut	Nor is there a chair for sitting—
Numa pă glie şî lut.	Only earth and clay;
Nici îi foc nici îi lumnină	Nor is there fire nor light;
Nici nu fă nime de cină.	Nor does anyone make dinner.

That world is everything that the world of the living is not. Time and space remain naturally continuous, not ordered by human thought. This world and that world may be compared in terms of temporal and spatial contrasts that culturally structure the social organization of the living[12] (see the figure on p. 165). In the world of the living, the life cycle is marked by temporal progression. Social production and reproduction occur in this framework. Time is ordered cyclically, according to daily, seasonal, and annual schedules. By contrast, in the world of the dead there is stasis rather than growth or motion. Spiritual tranquility prevails. Time is eternal, unchanging, not divided into distinct modes of measurement. Spatial demarcations delineate the locales of this world and that world. Among the living, human beings are subjected to the elements. They live in villages or cities and reside in houses. The world of the dead, however, is hidden deep in the earth. The dead "live" in the cemetery in their coffins and graves.

Nature's life cycle is self-regenerative and provides the framework against which human endeavor is juxtaposed. Nature's changing times and temperaments shape human activity over the course of the life cycle. The human life cycle, however, terminates with death; there is no further development. No one ages in that world; nothing changes. It is death that most eloquently lends credence to Marx's trenchant observation that consciousness is determined by life.[13]

The world of the living is associated with life and productivity, both of which are viable under the sun. That which is in the earth is mysterious, dark like the concealing color of the earth's dirt and clay composition. There, in the darkness of the earth, is the location of death. Life has not only its time, but also its space, which is wholly unlike the space in the world of the dead. The space of the

	World of the Living	World of the Dead
Time:	Temporal progression (life cycle)	Stasis
	Cyclical: daily, seasonal, annual	Eternal
	Social production and reproduction	Spiritual tranquility
Space:	Under the sun	In the earth
	Village	Cemetery
	House	Grave, coffin

dead is unknown to the living. The living escort the dead to the entrance of this unknown world: they deposit the body in the earth. Physical decay of the body must occur naturally; cremation is shunned because it is believed to burn the soul as well as the body, thereby denying the possibility of immortality.[14]

The place of burial is the village cemetery encircling the church. The church is the moral and spiritual center of the world of the living; the cemetery is said to be the village of the dead. Its physical organization resembles the social organization of the village of the living. The cemetery in effect constitutes a primary genealogical referent; family members are buried on top of each other for generations, thereby constructing a spatial representation of family history. (See also Bernabé 1980, 69.) There is also a certain semblance of hierarchy: families of higher status or means are buried in the immediate area surrounding the church; those of lesser circumstance are situated toward the periphery.

Those who do not honor the Christian community of God are not permitted to be buried in the village cemetery. (No contradiction is seen regarding Party members who receive the last rites; most do, and they are buried in the cemetery.) In this category of outcasts fall unbaptized children, suicides, sorceresses, and, formerly, Jews, who were distinguished from the first three groups. Although not Christians, they were regarded as highly religious, and they had their own cemetery.[15] Although unbaptized children may not be buried in the cemetery, they are pitied, because they are not responsible for their plight. Thus, the living perform acts out of consideration for the innocent. For example, it is said that a falling star indicates that somewhere an unbaptized child is dying.

Infants and young children are thought to go directly to heaven. A falling star means the child's path is encumbered, and if something is not done, the child will fall from heaven. Hence, upon spotting a falling star, an individual should exercise the civil right to "baptize" the child by saying, "If it is a boy, let him be named Ion; if it is a girl, let her be Ioană." Similarly, if the midwife sees that a newborn is going to die before the priest can come, then she has the authority to baptize the child. She sprinkles drops of holy water on the infant while uttering, "In the name of our Father, I baptize your servant ———." (Every household has a bottle of holy water from Epiphany, which is kept throughout the year.) The midwife later registers the child with the priest.

Suicides and sorceresses are considered slaves of the Devil; for them, little can be done. They are deviants, or cultural marginals at best, and are abhorred. Accordingly, they are buried outside of culture in the wilds of nature—in a field designated for them. This area is left unattended. (In reality, it is acceptable practice to bury outcasts along the perimeter of the cemetery, but it is not seen as desirable.) When this practice is violated, the living fear unknown consequences. In one village, a priest allowed a sorceress to be buried at the periphery of the cemetery. Many villagers were horrified and legitimized their reaction by recounting how, as soon as her coffin was covered with dirt, a black snake (symbol of a demon) emerged from the earth and settled over the length of the gravesite, where it remained for weeks. (The veracity of this tale is not relevant; it is the explanatory power of the belief system that is significant.)

The cemetery has an identity of its own. It is a place to which one goes, but it is different from other destinations:

Cîtă lume mere-n ţară	How many people go into the country
De sărbători zine iară.	For holidays they come back
Da din tine ţîntirime	But from you, cemetery,
Cine mere nu mai zine.	They who go return no more.

Today, while a sizable portion of the village population works elsewhere (or "goes into the country") during much of the year, they almost always return for holidays. Those who remain behind know that these workers will return occasionally and that, in the interim, they will correspond. Death disrupts this pattern. The cemetery is the depot from which people leave but never return.

Nu te păzi cu drumu	Don't hurry on this road.
Ştiu că nu mei la lucru.	I know you aren't going to work;
Nu mei la gostat în ţară	You aren't going to the state farm elsewhere
S-aşteptăm că să zii-iară.	For us to wait for you to return again.
Ştiu că nu mei la gostate	I know you aren't going to the state farm
S-aşteptăm să-mni trimeţi carte.	For us to wait for you to send a card.
Că te duci a putrezî	For you are going to rot
Şî-napoi nu-i mai zini.	And you will never return again.

The language of death focuses on passage and the processing of the body. The preceding texts describe the cemetery as a medium of passage. But it is also a place of residence. Like the village of the living, that of the dead is composed of "houses." Each individual has his or her own house:

Groapa-i casa omului	The grave is man's house
Şî tătă averea lui.	And all his property.

Again, the worlds of the living and the dead are similar, but differ in fundamental ways. The houses of the dead are located under the earth rather than above ground. The words for grave are *mormînt* (hence, a funeral is an *înmormîntare*) or *groapă* (hole in the ground). The grave is a simple home, unlike homes of the living, which are a measure of social status and economic resources and the locus of social interaction among family and friends. The content and style of a house reflect a process of reconstruction of values and of self for its inhabitants. Death causes a radical deconstruction of self and of "life style." In the village of the dead, all "homes" are identical. (This does not refer to the memorials erected for the dead by the living; these perpetuate social differentiation through superficial adornment of gravesites.) No one has more or less than anyone else, regardless of former status.

Strînge omu ca furnica	A man gathers like an ant.
Cînd moare n-are nimnica.	When he dies, he has nothing:

Patru scînduri într-un cui	Four boards and a hook,
C-atîta-i averea lui.	For that's all of his property.
Tu ——— cît ai lucrat	You, ———, how much you worked:
Tăte aici le-ai lăsat.	All of it you left here.

The life process of society is predicated on material production. Thus people work hard during their lifetime, but death reduces their acquisitions to the boards that constitute the walls of their "house." Nothing else can be taken.

The homes of the dead are architecturally uniform. As with any new home, relatives and friends come to see the new "houses." They are never pleased.

Am zinit să-ţi văd casa	I have come to see your house
Să văd plăce-mni-a ori ba.	To see if it pleases me or not.
Fără uşă şi fereastă	Without door or window,
A si tare-ntunecoasă.	It will be terribly dark.
Că mîndră casă ai avut	You had a lovely house,
Ş-aceia nu ţi-o plăcut	And that one didn't please you,
Ş-ai făcut alta de lut.	So you made another of clay.
Fără uşi fără feresti	Without door or windows,
Cu nime să nu grăieşti.	You will not speak with anyone.

Houses serve as cultural loci for social exchange. Their doors and windows can encourage or discourage interaction, welcoming or preventing conversation, courtship, and general sociability. At night, for instance, doors and windows are locked, and when the body of the deceased is removed from the house, the doors and windows are shut to prevent the deceased's return among the living. In the world of the dead, however, there are no windows or doors to be opened or closed. Social interaction ceases. Communication, the fundamental feature of human culture, is impossible. The "conversation" upon which life is based ends.[16] The living are completely shut out from the intimate world of the dead. The forms of communication between the living and the dead—laments, gifts of pomană, and dreams—are mediated, and they are constituted and made meaningful only by the living. Lamenters always implore the corpse (before the burial) to "get up and talk with me, and if not with me, then with someone else." These exhortations are without result. The living can talk *to* the dead, but they cannot talk with them. The living may visit the "homes" of the dead, but they are not invited in. The occupant is forever enclosed; visitors are forever locked out. (There are many lament verses about the locked gates.) There is no possibility of direct exchange of any sort. Death negates life in all of its essential features.

Petrecanie: The Rite of Passage

As we have seen, death is inextricably bound with passage. The physical demise of the body signals the beginning of the soul's passage from this world to that world. Simultaneous parallel rites of passage for the living and the dead effect the processes of separation and integration. In the end, the soul is separated from the body, the deceased is incorporated into the world of the dead, and the mourners are reintegrated into the world of the living. Throughout this process of passage, relations between the living and the newly deceased are transformed while relations between the living and the buried dead are reaffirmed. The terms for funeral rites acknowledge the essential element of passage involving the participation of both the living and the dead: *înmormîntare* refers to the process of burying the deceased, of putting the body into the *mormînt* (grave), from which the soul sets out on its journey and in which the body decomposes; *petrecanie,* the vernacular word for funeral customarily used in Maramureş, refers to escorting and honoring the deceased as well as to passing through the difficult period of doing so. (Petrecanie thus also has a self-reflexive meaning. In general, the intransitive verb *a petrece* means to accompany, to amuse, to celebrate, and a party is called a *petrecere*. The transitive form of the verb, however, means to suffer or endure. Thus, petrecanie encompasses both indexical meanings.)

A funeral, like a wedding, is a three-day event. The burial occurs on the third day (the third day after death was allegedly the day of Christ's resurrection). The preceding days are largely occupied with preparations. Upon the pronouncement of death, immediate kin attend to necessary tasks. Someone goes to inform the priest and to arrange for the church bells to be rung. A particular style of bell-ringing signals to the community that one of its members has passed away. If the death occurs during the middle of the night, the bells will be rung at dawn. Usually, the bells are rung three times daily, a service for which the bell-ringer is paid. Another task is to order a coffin, known as *copîrşeu* (or *sicriu*, or *sălaş*). The craftsman is alerted and makes the casket as quickly as possible. Coffins are usually made of wood; they vary in price depending on the degree of decoration (carving and paint).

Meanwhile, various activities take place within the house. As soon as life has been extinguished, candles are lit to protect the body from evil spirits and other dangers as well as to illuminate the deceased's journey to the other world. It is considered a great misfortune if someone dies "without light." This figures in the lament verses for those who die away from home, notably soldiers who have died during war.

Da aşă fratiucu mneu	So that's how it is, my brother;
N-ai avut nici copîrşeu.	You didn't even have a coffin.
Rău ne doare la inimă	Our hearts ache,
C-ai murit fără lumnină.	For you died without light,
Uă fără lumnină de său	Without a tallow candle,
Departe de satul tău.	Far away from your village.

Today, the theme of dying without light also applies to those who die away from home in the hospital; this has become more frequent and has been incorporated into the laments. In addition to lighting candles in the house, a special wax candle is made; it is the length of the deceased's body and wound into a circular shape. This candle is known as the *toiag* (the staff) or the *lumina trupului* (the body's candle) and must be kept burning until the body is buried. The toiag provides light for the deceased's journey; it is considered dangerous for the soul if this light goes out. (It used to be believed that, until the body was buried, this candle also burned the sins of the newly deceased so that he or she would go to the other world with a clean slate. See Marian 1892, 150.)

The mirrors in the house are covered as a prophylactic measure, but to what end seems to be debatable. Ieudeni gave one explanation consistently: so that the priest would not see his reflection in the mirror; the mirrors were not covered for the deceased. The priest countered that this is a confusion on the part of the lay population; there is no proscription against the priest seeing his own image. He offered another reason for this practice: so as not to see the reflection of the deceased's "ghost." It is a measure meant to protect the soul, which separates from the body upon death.[17]

The corpse, of course, must be prepared. Living individuals of the same sex as the deceased wash the body. This is the customary practice although there are many exceptions, and the rule does not always obtain for children. In general, the gender relationship supersedes the kin relationship; the individual who bathes the deceased need not be a relative. (People who have washed seven or more of the dead are believed to go directly to heaven. While almost everyone aspires to reach heaven, people are frightened by the pollution of death and the confrontation with mortality that washing a corpse entails.) After the body has been cleansed, the bath water is removed from the household. People are careful to throw this water in a corner of their property where no one will tread—"so that someone won't be like the dead, without power." It is also said that "if you wish to cause harm to someone, you sprinkle the bath water from the dead on that person; no one will be attracted—except death."[18] Related associational principles dictate the fate of the bed on which the deceased slept: the straw is removed and burnt so that no one else will sleep on it—and sleep like the dead.

The body is placed on a long wooden bench or table until the casket is delivered. Then the deceased is clothed in Sunday attire. Some people will have clothing made expressly for the burial. Usually a rosary will be laced through the hands. The toiag is fixed at the head of the bench. When the coffin arrives, it is readied. The mattress and pillow consist of shavings from the wood used to make the coffin. (People are cautioned not to use feathers, which are the normal stuffing for pillows; it is thought that in that world the dead would have to chase after the feathers and could not rest.) The bedding is covered with a linen sheet. Then the body is placed inside its new "house." Other items are furnished: a small colac (ritual bread) with one coin baked in it—to pay the gatekeeper; a small stick—to use for support during the journey to the other world; and flowers, which are added on the third day.

During the three-day funeral process, death, passage, and the transformation of identity are symbolically designated by the physical presentation not only of the corpse but of the living close kin (to the third degree) as well. All dress in black—the color of death—or in somber colors. Moreover, female relatives leave their hair unbraided; men remain unshaven; and men and boys go bareheaded. It is said that leaving hair unbraided, unshaven, or uncovered helps to prevent obstacles in the path of the deceased. Simultaneously, living kin, because they are closely related to the deceased, are temporally marked as out of culture, in a more natural body state. In this way, members of the community know that there is a death in a family. (Recall that status changes are physically marked during weddings also. The braiding of the bride's hair is a symbol of her status as married woman. The inversion of the braiding symbolism in these rites of passage is noteworthy. Braiding hair creates relations; unbraiding it aids in their severance.) Following the funeral, immediate kin resume more customary behaviors, such as braiding hair and, for men, shaving and wearing hats. Their mourning continues to be noted during the year's mourning period by the wearing of black and abstention from celebration. Only at the end of the year do the living assume their former, unmarked identities; only then is the deceased finally incorporated into the world of the dead.

The most time-consuming tasks before the day of burial are the preparation of food and drink for the mourners and of the breads for alms. As for weddings, a cook is engaged to oversee these activities. Similarly, female relatives and neighbors assist. Meals will occur on the night preceding the funeral, immediately following the burial, and on the third day and the sixth week after. The menus are partially determined by whether the days on which the meals occur are ones of fasting. The basic meal consists of a bean soup, a noodle soup, stuffed cabbage, bread, and a dessert. On "sweet days" the soup stock is made with a milk base, or chicken base; on "fasting days" it is made with water and vinegar or just water. The cabbage is stuffed with meat, oil, and a cornmeal-rice mixture on sweet days, and without the meat and oil on fasting days. The dessert is a doughnut-like pastry or a fruit compote, again in keeping with the day. All meals are accompanied by plum brandy, two glasses per person. The rationale is that people drink one cup for themselves and one for the soul of the deceased. (But "no one should get drunk; that is disgraceful at a funeral!")[19]

It is said that there is "no funeral without bread." In addition to the bread eaten at the various meals, everyone who attends a funeral must leave with a small colac for the soul of the deceased. Extras must be on hand for the unexpected visitor. Children are given rolls, or pretzel-like breads (or candies). Today, most of these breads are obtained from the bakery in the city of Sighetu Marmației. This is particularly helpful if the funeral is to be a large one (with several hundred mourners); otherwise, the cook must arrange for her helpers to bake them. Although most of the breads are procured from the bakery (meaning that the family must arrange for delivery, not necessarily an easy matter), the ritual breads for the funeral officiants and honored guests are still homebaked. These colaci are larger than those given to the mourners and are decorated with Christian symbols. Another small bread shaped with seven points (*prescură*) is also prepared for specific church representatives. Together, these breads constitute pomenile. They are generally distributed in the following manner (excluding breads for honored guests, the number of which varies with each funeral):

priest	3 colaci, 1 prescură
deacon	2 colaci, 1 prescură
sexton	1 colac, 1 prescură
gravedigger	1 colac
bell-ringer	1 colac
pallbearers	1 colac per person (for six)
candle-holders	1 colac per person (for four)
church flagbearers	1 colac per person (for three)

The breads for the church officials are presented wrapped in a woven towel; a candle is placed in the middle of the top bread (and is lit on the priest's). Only colaci are presented for the meals three days and six weeks after the burial, and they are not tied together with woven towels.

Most funeral expenses are incurred during this preparatory phase. The priest (or priests) will be paid a certain fee, as will the cook, bell-ringer, and coffin-maker. Food, drink, and candles must be purchased; the coffin and the flower wreaths must be bought; flags and rugs must be rented from the church. Additional expenses include the costs of the ritual meals for the obligatory mourning days, as well as of a gravestone or carved cross. Like a wedding, a funeral is expensive (for example, a large funeral cost one family 5,900 lei, over two months' salary); usually, family budgets take these events into consideration in their long-range plans.

During the two days preceding the burial, relatives, neighbors, and friends come to pay their respects. Women who are present

lament when the church bells ring. On the evening before the
funeral, a religious service to bless the soul of the deceased is performed in the house (*parastas*). For this, the coffin is closed (although afterward it may be reopened at the discretion of the immediate family); it is covered with a woven rug on which are placed
the body's candle, a ritual bread with a lit candle in the middle on a
plate with a spoon, an icon, a woven towel, and a cross. The priest
and deacon offer the necessary prayers. After this service, there is
a meal for the invited mourners, usually relatives and close associates of the deceased. This is the last supper that will be shared with
the deceased in the house. The following morning marks the beginning of the funeral proper.

The Funeral Day

On the day of the funeral, while pots of soup and stuffed cabbage
are being heated on wood-burning stoves, and tables made of boards
and sawhorses are being set up in the courtyard (weather permitting), mourners come to pay their last respects, quietly pray for the
deceased, and listen to the laments of the bereaved before the arrival of the priest. As dictated by tradition, women approach the
coffin and lament. Members of the immediate family may lament
continuously for several hours, if circumstances and their emotional energies permit. While lamenting, it is customary for the lamenter to repeat each line of a couplet. Each line is usually punctuated by the lamenter's sobs, which are controlled to a greater or
lesser degree, depending on her state of composure. In this section
typical laments will be presented and analyzed.

Death evokes many images and has multilayered meanings;
some lamenters in their exhausted anguish may pass the final hours
philosophizing about death. Death is active: it involves passage and
transformation. At the same time, death is objectified: it has form
in time and space. Death has gender: the noun for death (*moarte*)
is feminine. Consequently—or coincidentally—death is believed
to be a woman (as are most threatening figures in Romanian folklore; see Kligman 1981).[20] Death's gender seems to be undisputed,
but there is considerable disagreement about her appearance and
age. Some claim death is a beautiful young woman, a seductress;
others assert that she is an old hag. In any case, death is female.

De-ar arde focu moartea	May death burn in fire,
Că de ie nu poţi scăpa.	Because you can't escape her—
Că ie zine cîtilin	For she comes slowly
La tineri şî la bătrîni.	To the young and to the old.

Because death is the eternal curse of the living, it, in turn, is cursed by the living who remain powerless. "Fire burn death" or "May fire strike you" are standard curses against death, itself an agent of destruction. Fire may be either constructive or destructive. Curses call forth the destructive element. Fire can destroy the physical body, thereby cremating it. Again, since cremation is not generally practiced, it is appropriately invoked in curses. Fire, in this context, scorches the emotional being of the living. It is associated with the process of transforming the body from living to dead. Because death is conceived as a live body in its world, it becomes a legitimate recipient for curses to effect its demise—but to no avail.

Tu moarte, săcere re	You, death, evil sickle:
Rău poţi tu pă om tăie	Badly can you cut a man;
Tare fuga putreze.	Very quickly [he] putrefies.
Mult ieşti moarte-nşelătoare	You are very deceptive, death,
Cînd îi omu ca o floare	For when a man is like a flower,
Cum îl iei di pă pticioare.	How you take him off his feet,
Şî îl tomneşti la răcoare	And you put him in the cool shade
Ca să nu-l agiungă soare.	So that the sun won't reach him;
Cum îl pui cătă pămînt	How you put him in the earth
Că să nu-l mai bată vînt.	So that the wind won't blow on him.

"Death" is familiar to the living and is addressed as *tu* (you). Women bring people into and take them out of being; birth and death are part of women's work. People say that death carries a sickle with which she cuts the throats of her victims: "A dying person grabs his throat so often; there is something to it, you know." (If a death occurs in a house whose walls are being painted, then the painting must be immediately stopped; otherwise, the walls will be painted with the blood from the throat of the deceased.) Women usually work with sickles in the fields; men wield scythes. (In many locales, however, death is figured as an old woman with a scythe—an inversion. She, as trickster figure, is the Reaper.) Death, being a woman, carries a woman's instrument. With the sickle, she cuts a person down, just as she works in the fields. The analogy between culture's and nature's cycles is used to rationalize death.

Implicit in this lament verse is the relationship between death and love. Men, in talking about falling in love, often mention that there is nothing to be done against the enticing power of women. Sexuality is an important aspect of their defenselessness. Females are believed to be insatiable, as is death. (Women, however, generally disagree with this estimate of their sexual appetites.) Women and death are both trickster figures. Men joke about girls who attempt through magic charms and practices to manipulate the future and "get a man." They also jest that young men lose their freedom as a result. But men are not the only ones "tricked" by women; so are women (Kligman 1984). It is always the mother who is guilty of "selling" her daughter when she "is like a flower." (As was seen, the wedding toasts underscore this.) From an ideological point of view, women are tricksters: they "manage" the deaths of their own daughters, marriage being considered a type of death.[21] On a grander scale, a female death "manages" the deaths of everyone. In the lament, "when a man is like a flower" refers to being alive, regardless of age or sex. (In the wedding verses, this simile refers to a young, virginal female.) "Taking a man off his feet" results in inactivity and, in the extreme, death. Life requires activity. Death places the deceased in the world of the dead, sheltered from life's elements: the sun and the wind. (Recall that life takes place under the sun; death, in the earth.)

The final lines of the preceding verse hint at another side of death. Death is not simply evil. Death, like woman is said to be, is nurturing; "she" protects. Thus, death and women are innately linked through their "natures." Unlike women, however, death is part of, yet out of, culture.[22] Death, the ultimate caring female, does not differentiate. Death does not favor one over another on the basis of age, gender, class, race, or religion. Death has no pretensions. While death exemplifies female nurturance, she simultaneously exercises female license, uncontrolled and unsocialized.[23] Death, in her world, is the antithesis of women, who, in the social world of the living, are subject to control and socialization. Death does what she wants, to whom and when she pleases.

Moartea-i tare blăstămată	Death is very cursed.
O zinit la noi în casă	She came into our house;
N-am dorit-o niciodată.	We never wanted her.
Şi ie la noi o zinit	But she came to us
Batăr că nu o-am dorit.	Even though we didn't want her,
Şî în casă o întrat	And into the house she entered
Batăr că nu o-am temat.	Even though we didn't invite her.
. . . .	. . . .
Că poate vede orişicine	For anyone can see
Că la tăţi vremea ne zine.	That the time comes for everyone.
Că poate vede orişicare	For whoever can see
Că nime n-are scăpare.	That no one has an escape:
Nici sărac da nici domn mare	Neither the poor, nor the important either.
Moartea grija nu-o are.	Death doesn't care.
N-are frică de-mparaţi	She isn't afraid of kings
Nici de armată-nconjuraţi.	Defended by an army.
De bătrîni nu i ruşine	She has no shame before the elderly;
Ie şî la cel tînăr zine	She also goes to the young;
Că nu i frică de nime.	For she isn't afraid of anyone.
Numa tu moartə faci bine	Only you, death, are good
Că te duci la orişicine.	Because you go to everyone.

Death is the great social leveler, the only unprejudiced one. (Not surprisingly, this is an established cliché in Western poetry as well.) Death is the best Christian, because only death "loves" all. In so doing, death flagrantly disregards the structure of social relations among the living. Propriety and deference are foreign to her: young or old, rich or poor, powerful or weak, death does not discriminate. She follows her instincts and the rules of her world, that world which is related to, yet different from, this one.

Because the world of the dead is different from that familiar to the living, lamenters attempt to convince the deceased not to depart. Recall that, during her dressing before the church wedding, the bride is also urged not to depart; singing songs forewarning the bride about the consequences of her actions, her peers try in vain to prevent her from setting out on the road to married life. Life's passages are compared with journeys on roads. These roads are unidirectional; once begun, there is no retracing one's steps. Death is no exception.

Aiesta-i un drum mare	This is a big road
Şî-napoi n-are cărare.	And there is no path back.
Cine mere-aiesta drum	Who goes on this road
Nu zine-napoi nicicum.	Does not come back at all.
Cine mere asta cale	Who goes on this route
Înapoi cărarea n-are.	Does not have a path back.

Passage culminates in the transformations of status and identity as well as of relations between individuals and groups. Birth locates one on the path of life. Marriage establishes social identity in its most comprehensive social sense; death results in the loss of this social identity. Lamenters remind the deceased of this repeatedly, but their efforts fall on deaf ears:

Dacă de-aicea îi pleca	If from here you leave,
Urma ţi s-a astupa	Your traces will be covered up;
Numele ţi s-a uita.	Your name will be forgotten.

The change of identity is substantive, in this case, erasing it. This verse may be compared with wedding couplets shouted to a bride:

Mîne-ta atît îi lasă	You leave your mother only
Numa lacrimi tri pă masă	Three tears on the table
Urmele pă lîngă casă.	And traces by the house.
Lacrimele s-or usca	The tears will dry up
Urma ţi s-a astupa.	And your traces will be covered up.

The relation between death and marriage is common and will be more fully explored in the following chapter. Here, it is nonetheless apposite to point out another analogy between them. Marriage for a woman is perceived as setting out on a "road with thorns" to live among strangers. Some brides fare well, but most *pică în foc*, or fall into fire. Death is similarly viewed in this verse:

Sînt două drumurele	There are two roads:
Unul îi bătut cu spini	One is lined with thorns
Care duce la străini.	That leads to strangers;
Altulu i bătut cu flori	The other is lined with flowers
Care duce la surori	That leads to [one's] sisters

Şî la scumpii fraţiori.   And to [one's] dear brothers.

                                                   (Marian 1892, 459)

The road with thorns goes to hell, and marriage is generally considered such for women; the road with flowers goes to heaven. Flowers are symbols of growth and vitality in the context of familial love; they also adorn heaven. Alienation from one's family is comparable to hell—difficult, "thorny." Socially transgressive behavior in life alienates one from one's family in death; the deviant is punished in hell.[24]

As one progresses along life's roads through the life cycle, life becomes more encumbered with difficulties. The joys of youth give way to the troubles and responsibilities of marriage. Marriage means that one has begun the process of aging, which brings death closer. Social maturity (adulthood) is coupled with physical tolls. In the end, death liberates the living from life's travails. Death, like youth, is considered to be a phase free from cares and worries:

De-ar şti pruncu cînd să naşte	If a baby would know when born
Cîte rele l-or mai paşte.	How many evils await him,
N-ar mai suge ţîţă dulce	He wouldn't suck the sweet breast more,
Ce-ar muri şî-n rai s-ar duce.	But he would die and go to heaven.
Că şi ieu de-aş si ştiut	And I if I had known
Cîte am de petrecut.	What I would have to go through,
Ţîţă dulce n-aş si supt	I wouldn't have sucked the sweet breast;
Făr-aş si murit demult.	Instead I would have died long ago.

This lament emphasizes the notion of life as an arduous passage (*petrecere*) that could have been avoided through death in infancy, because it is believed that baptized children who die before first communion go directly to heaven.

The tribulations experienced by the deceased during his or her lifetime, as well as those of the lamenter, figure prominently in the "discussion" a lamenter has with the deceased as she reviews these events before the coffin is removed from the house. The funeral of the mother-in-law of the family with whom I lived poignantly illus-

trates this recounting of life's hardships.[25] The death of Mătuşa
Marie was quite an occasion. She had been an esteemed personality in the community; she had been godmother to more people
than could readily be identified. All of her godchildren, in addition
to her relatives by birth and marriage, came to honor her.[26] One of
Marie's sisters (seventy-two years of age), known throughout the
valley for her way with words, commanded the attention of the
mourners. Niţa sat by the casket, "talking" with her sister:

Uă ti-o mîncat Mări năcaz	Oh, trouble has consumed you, Mări,
Uă că nime nu poate şti	For no one can know—
Că Doamne-i greu a văduvi.	My God, it is hard to be a widow.
Uă de mine tu Mări	Oh my goodness, you Mări—
Doamne greu ţi-o putut si	My God, it was surely hard for you
Sîngură-n lume-a trăi.	To live alone in the world.
Uă sîngură şî-n sat străin	Oh, alone and in a foreign village,
Zîlele ţi-o fo de chin.	Your days were filled with torment.
Uă văduvă şî-n altu sat	Oh, a widow in another village,
Uă n-ai la cine cere un sfat	Oh, you had no one from whom to ask advice
Dacă n-ai avut bărbat.	If you didn't have a husband.

Marie had not had an easy life. As discussed in the previous chapters, when a woman marries, she is alienated from her natal family
and is said to go live among strangers (foreigners). Marie had also
married out of her natal village. Tragically, her husband died when
their children were quite young, leaving Marie a widow in a village
in which she was not a native. The verse encodes the ideology of
patrilineality. With her mother in a neighboring village and her
husband gone, from whom could she seek advice? She had no allies
in this strange environment. Convention promised hardship. Despite her undesirable situation, however, Marie's circumstances
were not as dire as they might have been. She had led a life of virtue and was highly respected. More than five hundred people attended her funeral to honor her soul with their grief.

Sitting quietly by Marie's side, her sister continued her lament before the funeral:

Uă de mine tu sorucă	Oh my goodness, you, dear sister,
Uă să si fo cu mine-n sat	If you had been with me in the village,
Doamne ieu te-aş si cătat.	My God, I would have cared for you.
Uă nu si soră cu bănat	But don't be troubled, sister,
Că Doamne bine ti-o cătat.	For, my God, she took good care of you.
Uă o noră desfatată	Oh, a generous daughter-in-law,
Ti-o cătat ca şî o fată.	She cared for you as a daughter would have.
Uă de-ai si avut o fată	Oh, if you had had a daughter,
Uă mai bine nu te-ar si cătată.	Oh, Mări, she wouldn't have cared better for you.
Uă şî cumva de ţi-o greşit	And if somehow she wronged you,
Iartă-o că ti-o doicit	Forgive her because she took care of you—
Uă cîte nopţi nu o durnit.	How many nights she didn't sleep.
Uă Mări de ti-o supărat	Oh, Mări, if she upset you,
Iartă-o că ti-o cătat.	Forgive her for she looked after you.

Marie's sister emphasized repeatedly that marriage had separated them; most of their lives they had lived in different villages. Consequently, their contact had been limited by circumstance. Had they been in the same village, Niţa would have looked after her; however, Marie's daughter-in-law, Juji, had taken care of Marie as if she had been Marie's own daughter. (The expectation is that in her old age, a mother-in-law will suffer at the hands of her daughter-in-law, especially if the mother-in-law's husband is already dead. It is considered to be a form of social retribution for the mother-in-law's previous lack of generosity toward her daughter-in-law. Although it was known that Marie's relationship with her daughter-in-law had not been without "thorns," Marie had truly been fortunate; her daughter-in-law's care was extolled by many.) Juji's behavior had been so exemplary that many lamenters called Marie's attention to that fact; they repeatedly counseled her to forgive her daughter-in-law for any wrong she might have unwittingly inflicted upon her. Juji's virtues far outweighed occasional transgressions of polite behavior. Asking forgiveness, as in this lament, is a common feature of leave-taking in all life-cycle rites; it will be further discussed below.[27]

The language of death indicating imminent transformation is replete with admonishments not to leave (*nu pleca*), not to embark (*nu porni*), not to hurry (*nu păzi*) on this road. Or it warns what will happen if the deceased departs (*dacă-i pleca*). But travel along the road of life is inevitable. Thus, the lamenter, knowing that the deceased will soon set out from the household, offers him or her—like all *drumari* (travelers)—food for the journey:

Scoală mîndră de-aicea	Get up, beauty, from here
Că ți-am făcut merindea	Because I've made you food for the road.
Să vezi place-ți-a ori ba.	See if it is to your liking.
Mîndră de nu ți-a plăcea	Beauty, if it is not to your liking,
Cu noi îi mai rămînea.	You may stay with us longer.

But all attempts to negotiate with the deceased are doomed to failure. And what is lost cannot be replaced.[28]

Vai de mine ce-am ptierdut	Oh my, what I have lost
Nu ieste-n tîrg de vîndut.	Is not for sale in the market.
Vai de mine ce-am scăpat	Oh my, what I have missed
Nu-i-în tîrg de cumpărat.	Cannot be bought in a market.
Uă oricîtă lume-ai plăti	Oh, no matter what you would pay,
Mamă-n tîrg nu poți găsi.	A mother is not to be found at the market.
Oricît în lume ai da	No matter what you'd give,
Mamă-n tîrg nu poți afla.	You can't find a mother at the market.
Uă tu te plîngi plîngei cu tine	You cry, she cries with you
Nu te spune cătă nime.	And doesn't tell anyone about it.
Tu te plîngi plînge și ie	You cry, she cries also,
Uă nimărui nu-i poveste.	Oh, and she doesn't tell anyone.

There is no way to buy back the dead. The life cycle is developmental, progressing through irreversible transformations. The transformations of self are socially substantive and often physically as well: the loss of virginity is permanent; the loss of physical life for the dead defies resurrection among the living. The transformation through putrefaction is final. Succinctly, there is no way to bargain with death.[29]

Vai tu moarte cît ţi-aş da	Oh, you, death, what I would give you
Zîle să pot cumpăra.	To be able to buy days.
Vai de mine şi de mine	Oh, my goodness,
Cum zîle nu vinde nime.	But no one sells days.

The language of death, in contrast to that of marriage, does not borrow extensively from the cultural vocabulary of bargaining (see Chapter 2; and Kligman 1984). While marriage is considered a natural event in the life cycle, it is preeminently cultural in constitution. Therefore, it is subject to human endeavor and control; its terms are negotiable. But death is a natural event (barring unforeseen interference); there is nothing nor anyone with whom to negotiate. Hence, the language of death exploits the processing of the body, because the body is materially transformed by death. The body is the vehicle through which identity and self are culturally constituted. The language of death attends to the negation of identity, the altering of physical (for the dead) and emotional (for the living) states. The deceased's remains "dry up"; names are forgotten; the body "dissolves like dew." The mourners' hearts are "burned," "fried." Their bodies "dissolve" from longing. The heart is the locus of physical life and emotional conditions. Hence, the cessation of the heart's functioning means physical death; this triggers sympathetic emotional response in the hearts of the mourners. Their hearts burn up as the body of the deceased dries up. It is a parallel process of transformation centered on separation. Death for the dead means physical separation; for the living, it requires emotional separation. Fire is the medium. In the service of culture, fire is constructive; it kindles burning love (*dragoste înfocată*) that leads to marriage, and it transforms nature's yield for culture's well-being (through cooking). In the service of death, however, fire is destructive. It destroys the physical being of the deceased and the emotional energies of the living. (Death and consumption will be discussed later in this chapter.)

Because death is considered to be a natural event in the life cycle, so nature's life cycle is a metaphor for that of humans. Lamenters will elaborate this metaphor to portray the life cycle in general and the cause of death in particular. Hence, Niţa described the demise of Mătuşa Marie in the following way:

Uă fost-ai mîndră ca o floare	Oh, you were beautiful as a flower,
Uă că te-ai toptit pă pticioare.	But your legs wilted.
Uă ş-ai fo floare din fereşti	Oh, you were a flower in the window;
Te-ai toptit de nu te vezi.	You withered so one can't even see you.
Uă fost-ai florea de sansiu	Oh, you were a carnation,
Te-ai toptit pînă la brîu.	And you melted up to your waist.
Uă şî din brîu pînă-n grumaz	And from your waist to your throat
Te-ai toptit de n-ai rămas.	You withered until nothing remained.

Approximately six months before her death, Marie suffered a stroke that initially left her legs paralyzed. Over the ensuing months, her condition worsened: her paralysis extended to her waist, and, finally, she succumbed to death. Niţa chose the image of a wilting flower to account for the stages of Marie's confinement and eventual cause of death. It is worth underlining the relationship between text and context and the dual dimensions of indexicality. Laments refer to events in the life of a community; these are generally known to the participants. Symbolic language condenses the complexity of referential detail, which simultaneously heightens the hermeneutic potential of this medium. Hence, an outsider may be able to comprehend the cosmological significance of this poetry, but the pragmatic referent remains within the domain of local knowledge. (It would be difficult to discern the specificity of Niţa's intent—and consequently the full beauty of her skill—if one was not privy to the context. Marie's body, like a flower, "wilted" slowly; she successively lost strength.)

The cause of death may be incorporated in varied ways. While lamenting for Marie, one of her goddaughters sang about her god-mother's illness:

De şăse luni ce-o zinit	For the past six months,
Tu din casă n-ai ieşit.	You did not leave the house.
N-ai ieşit din cas-afară	You did not go out from the house,
C-ai avut o mare boală.	For you had a serious illness.
Şăse luni ai stat pă pat	Six months you stayed in bed
Numa cînd ti-o înturnat.	[And moved] only when someone turned you over.
Nora bine ti-o cătat	Your daughter-in-law took good care of you;
Nu s-o clătit d-ingă pat.	She did not leave your bedside.

These lines refer to Marie's paralysis, which made it impossible for her to move about, to go outside. She was confined to her bed, dependent on others to help her change position. Again, the lamenter calls attention to Marie's daughter-in-law who took extremely good care of her. She devoted herself to Marie's needs, despite the frustrations this caused in her own life. Juji remarked, "This is what a decent person has to do."[30]

While awaiting the arrival of the priest, women will continually test the finality of death by calling on the deceased to behave like a living being. Thus, Marie's daughter-in-law tried again:

Uă de mine hăi mătu	Oh my, hey, aunt,
Uă scoală-te de-aici.	Oh, get up from here.
Scoală-te şî ti uita	Get up and look about—
Uă cine o zinit p-aicea.	Oh, who has come here.
Ţi-o zinit surorile	Your sisters have come to you;
Uă scoală grăi cu dînsele.	Get up and talk with them.
Că doară mult le-ai mai dorit	For a long time you have wanted to see them,
Şî amu nimnică nu zici.	And now you say nothing.
Uă scumpa me şî buna me	Oh, my precious and good one,
Uă rău îmi pare după ie	Oh, I feel bad about her,
Uă ca şî după mama me.	As if for my mother.
Uă bunucă hăi mătu	Oh, good one, hey, aunt,
Uă fă mătu cum i fa	Oh, auntie, do what you must,
Şî din casă nu pleca	But don't leave from this house,

Că altu nu-i înturna.	For you will not return again.
Uă cît de bine te-am cătat	Oh, I took good care of you;
Nu ştiu dipt ce te-ai supărat.	I don't know why you got angry.
Uă c-amu te duci şi ne laşi	For now you are going and leaving us—
Uă mătu cu drag te strîg	Oh, aunt, with love I call for you,
Şî Dumăta nimnic nu zici.	And you say nothing.
Uă şî de nu-i grăi cu mine	But even if you don't want to speak with me,
Uă mătuşică ai cu cine.	Oh, sweet auntie, there are others.

In this excerpt, Juji asks her mother-in-law to get up and participate in the world about her. It is as though she is helping her from
her sick bed; she informs Marie that she has visitors who are eager
to see her. These guests are Marie's sisters who have come together
to pay her a visit. Because their various marriages had separated
them, they didn't meet often. Now they have come—but Marie will
not speak with them. The inversions in the poetry mirror the inversion between life and death and the disruption of familiar social
behavior. How to make sense of Marie's actions? Her daughter-in-
law notes that she had tended to her needs, yet Marie does not
care; she is leaving them. (The complex emotions associated with
the death of a loved one are encapsulated in this fragment. The
living often suffer from guilt and wonder if they are to blame; at the
same time, they are furious with the deceased for having abandoned them.) Juji calls her lovingly, yet Marie impolitely does not
respond. No matter—if she does not choose to speak with her, she
can speak with her sisters or with any of the assembled—only that
the silence of death be broken. At various intervals, Juji, like all
lamenters, interjects formulaic appellations addressed directly to
the deceased. These epithets provide the temporary illusion that
the lamenter and the deceased are engaged in conversation.

Until it is announced that the priest is approaching, women will
often lament successively instead of simultaneously; they will listen
to each other, share the other's expressions of grief, and perhaps
appropriate it into their own discourses on death. Although there
is no rule, mourners tend to respect the emotional needs of the
closest kin of the deceased; in the presence of a close relative who
wants to lament, a woman will temporarily defer her own privi-

lege. Women who are unable to contain their desire to lament may go outside in the courtyard while others lament indoors. (At one funeral, one of the deceased's sisters circled the courtyard continuously for several hours until she was overcome with emotional exhaustion.)

During Marie's funeral, her teenage granddaughter lamented for the first time in her life. Her moving cries of sorrow, themselves an initiation into the rites of women, were protected by the shadow of her mother's skilled exclamations of grief. In this instance, the ritual occasion served as a vehicle to transmit the oral tradition from one generation to the other (moreover, from a mother who lived in the village to her daughter who resided primarily in the nearby city where she was a student). Standing by her mother's side, Marie's granddaughter mourned her loss:

Uă mămucă şî hăi ma	Oh, little mother, and, hey, ma—
Uă rău îmi pare după ie.	Oh, I feel so bad about her,
Că una mamă ni-o făcut	Because my mother bore me
Şî Dumăta ne-ai crescut.	But you raised us.
Mama s-o dus şî-o lucrat	Mama went and worked,
Vai şî cu drag ne-ai legănat.	And with love, you rocked us in the cradle.
Uă pă cînd o zinit mama	Oh, by the time mama arrived home,
Pă masă i-ai pus cina.	You had put dinner on the table for her:
Uă du-te mîndră şî-i mînca	"Go, dear, and eat
Vai că o fost mare ziua.	Because you had a long day."
Uă că bine ne-ai-învăţat	You taught us well
Uă să nu sim cu bănat.	So we wouldn't be troubled.
Uă de cîte ori am zinit	Oh, how many times we came home,
Uă mămucă ne-ai sfătuit.	Oh, sweet mother, you advised us;
Ne-ai sfătuit numa bine	You counseled us well
Uă că să nu sim de ruşine.	So that we would not be shameful.
. . . .	. . . .
Vai de mine mama me	Oh my, my mother—
Rău îmi pare după ie.	How bad I feel about her.
Doamne multe ti-o mîncat	For, God, you were eaten by troubles:

Că tata s-o dus ti-o lăsat.	For grandfather went and left you
Uă cu doi bdieţi de copilaşi	With two poor little kids
Pînă cînd i-ai învăţat	Until you raised them
Mult năcaz ti-o mai mîncat.	Hardship had taken its toll.

. . . .

| Uă mămucă şî hăi ma | Oh, sweet mother, and hey, ma, |
| Mai stai mamă nu pleca. | Stay longer, mama, don't leave. |

The granddaughter includes in her lament fundamental features of extended family organization. She addresses her grandmother as *mămucă*, the diminutive form for mama. (Grandmothers are also referred to as *mama bună* or *mama dulce*, dear or sweet mother.) The distinction is between the mother who has borne a child and she who has raised it. In this family, stricken by hard times, the grandmother took the primary responsibility for caring for the children during the day while the mother worked in the fields. This "mother" made dinner for her grandchildren and daughter-in-law; she taught them the tenets of Christian love and comportment.[31] Through her laments, the granddaughter acknowledges her indebtedness and expresses her sympathy for the harshness of her widowed grandmother's life. Like all the other lamenters, the granddaughter also begs her beloved "sweet mother" not to depart; like all other such requests, hers is denied.

Indeed, not even the advances of modern medicine have been able to fulfill such requests. Although (from a theoretical point of view) intangible malevolent forces are no longer held accountable for disease, it is also no longer evident who or what is responsible. Health care is provided by the state: medical practitioners have been delegated responsibility for the physical well-being of the state's citizens. But the discourse of scientific explanation (see Foucault 1972 and 1975; Ariès 1982, 396–406) does not readily offer a meaningful frame of reference within which to make sense of disruptive experiences such as illness or death. Science's mystification of power and knowledge occurs within a rationalized, increasingly alienated environment; it is not a mystification located within an accessible or familiar "web of meanings." Robbed at least partially of this referent, those who nonetheless seek resolution of an incomprehensible dilemma—death—reconstitute "structures of meaning" to incorporate transformed practices:

La om cînd zine vremea	When one's time comes,
Nime leac nu-i poate da.	No one can give you a remedy.
Cînd zîlele s-o gătat	When your days are up,
Nu-i doftor să aibă leac.	No doctor has a cure.

The contributions of science pertain to this-worldly pursuits; only God is omnipotent. While people cannot ultimately defy their pre-ordained destiny, the prolongation of life has transformed the nature of death (see, for example, Ariès 1982, 559–601; Mitford 1963); this process is gradually impinging on the practices of dying in Ieud as well, much to the consternation of the Ieudeni:

Scoală şi ni-i povesti	Get up and tell us
Cum o fost cu străinii.	How it was among strangers.
De cînd de-acas-ai plecat	Since you left home,
Tăt la telefon am stat	I stayed by the telephone,
Şî de tine-am întrebat.	And I asked about you.
Doftorii ni-o poruncit	The doctors sent word to us
Tu Mări că ai murit.	That you, Mări, had died.
Mni-o spus doftoriţa mnie	The female doctor told me
Nu-s leacuri să-ţi treacă ţie	There are no remedies to cure you—
Numa în pămînt subt glie.	Only in the earth under the dirt.
Uă de mine tu Mări	Oh my goodness, you, Mări,
Unde ai putut tu muri	Where you died!
În spital cu doftorii.	In the hospital with doctors.

Modern practice dictates that the ailing be treated in the hospital. If it is nothing serious, the local medical facility is adequate; however, when someone is transferred to a hospital in the nearby city or elsewhere in the country, it is known that the illness is grave. The above lament fragment refers to the death of a young woman named Marie, who died of cancer. The rising incidence of terminal ailments such as heart disease and cancer, combined with the medicalization of treatment, has introduced the phenomenon of dying alone, "without light" away from home. It conversely means that the concerned family must spend hours by the phone, desperately trying to obtain information that does not inform (provided they are able to "make a [phone] connection") in a comprehensible way. In the case of Marie, a relative pleaded with her to tell them about this new experience—dying away from home as an "everyday" event as opposed to an unusual one, such as the soldier dying at the front. The lamenter plays upon the metaphoric relation between marriage and death. Marriage results in a young woman's living "among strangers" (see Chapter 2); hospitalization often results in the patient's dying "among strangers." It is a cursed situation.[32]

And this cursed situation is thought to be perpetrated by doctors. Hence, doctors, like death, are seen as agents of destruction (when their attempts fail). Consequently, they too have become the targets of wrath.

Arde-ar doftorii din lume	May the doctors of the world burn,
Că nu ţi-o dat leacuri bune.	Because they didn't give you good remedies.
Iei ţi-o dat tăt leacuri răle	They gave you bad remedies.
Nu ţi-o trecut după iele.	You didn't get better from them.
De-ar arde poticile	Would that the pharmacies burn
Cu tăte leacurile.	With all their medicines.
Ardă şî doftorii-n iele	Let the doctors burn up in them too,
Că nu ţi-o trecut după iele.	For you didn't get well after them.
Nu ţi-o trecut tu Mări	You didn't get better, Mări,
Să mai poţi cu noi grăi.	To be able to speak with us anymore.
Uă ardă tăţi doftorii	Oh, let all doctors burn—
Cum înşală oamenii.	How they trick people,
Că pă unu doi îi scoală	For they cure one or two,
Şî pă tri patru-i omoară.	And they murder three or four!

The association between the actions of doctors and death is repeatedly stressed in this lengthy excerpt.[33] Death "cuts a man down" so that he can no longer communicate with the living; doctors administer treatments that often deprive people of this same ability. Therefore, doctors are added to the cast of trickster figures (death; priests who, with promises of happiness, marry radiant brides and "put them in a harness to die"; and mothers who "sell" their daughters). The translation of the line "For they cure one or two" also requires annotation. The sense of *curing* here is to resurrect the sick, to bring them back from the dead. Illness is considered to be a state "betwixt and between" life and death. (See Kligman 1981, 71.)

The newly deceased's state is "betwixt and between" this world and that. As the time approaches for the "traveler" to begin the journey, the emotional intensity of the mourners heightens. Before the removal of the body from the household, the event that provokes extreme anguish is the sealing of the coffin, for this act encloses the corpse in its new "house" where it shall forever remain a recluse. As nails are driven into the boards, someone may woefully note:

Copîrşeu cu tintă neagră	Coffin with black tint,
Să nu-ţi sie lumea dragă.	May life not be dear to you.
Copîrşeu tintăluit	Tinted coffin,
Cum ni-i nouă mai urît.	As it is to us, even worse.

The outer walls of the coffin immediately identify it as the abode of the dead. Black is the color of death, and the house of the dead is symbolically colored black. In practice, most coffins are not painted. Nonetheless, the color symbolism is powerfully evocative. People generally do not appreciate black as a color because of what it signifies.[34] Only over time does its effect diminish.

The immediacy of death causes excruciating suffering, although the mourning process will gradually ease the pain. Eventually, the deceased will be successfully integrated into the world of the dead. But, in this tale, that process is only about to begin. Someone announces that the priest is nearing the courtyard entrance. The lamenting from within the house rises to a crescendo. In the funeral of Mătuşa Marie, her daughter-in-law wailed in desperation:

Mătuşă popa sose	Aunt, the priest has arrived.
Nu ştiu ce-aş fa cu ie.	I don't know what I will do with her.
Uă bunucă buna me	Oh, my darling good one—
Nu ştiu unde o-aş băga	I don't know where to hide her
Să nu o ducă popa.	So that the priest won't take her.
Că de-aici dacă-i pleca	For if she leaves from here,
Altu nu-i mai înturna.	She will not return.
Şî de-aici dacă-i porni	If she starts from here,
Altu-acasă nu-i zini.	She won't come home again.

As the text indicates, the arrival of the priest means that the deceased is soon to depart from home. (Recall that in the wedding ceremony, the bride is hidden when it is known that the groom and his entourage have arrived. This initiates the seeking of the bride. In the funeral rite, however, there is no one with whom to bargain nor any place to hide.) When the priest enters the house, the women are quieted; the final prayers within the home begin. The priest will also bless the bucket of water from the well; some of this water will be added to a bowl in which a lit candle has been fixed. The priest will then take the candle and extinguish it in the blessed water; this symbolizes the extinction of life. He also sprinkles the holy water from the bucket over the assembled mourners; in the courtyard, he will similarly bless the barn and other structures such as the chicken coop and the pig shed.

Inside the house, the deacon next performs the *sfeştanie*, or the consecration of the house. This entails the etching of a cross on a wall, accompanied by appropriate prayers. This cross honoring the deceased will remain until the final mourning meal one year later; it is thought that this symbol marks the presence of the deceased's soul, which has not yet completed its journey, as well as the mourning of the household. This practice illuminates the proscription against painting the interior of a house during the year-long mourning period.

Once the house is consecrated, the coffin is removed. Usually, this task is the responsibility of six male relatives or male persons significant in the life of the deceased (such as friends or co-workers). All of these individuals must be married. It is dangerous for the unwed to serve as pallbearers; death, the seductress, will claim them for her own. The exceptions are for the funerals of elderly single women and of the unmarried dead. For the former, other unmarried women or particularly religious women act as escorts; for the latter, same-sex peers accompany the deceased to his or her "marriage." (This wedding of the dead is the subject of the following chapter.)

The casket must be removed with the corpse's feet first. This is done so that "the traveler is headed in the direction of his or her journey" and so that "he won't find his way back and return." Death is unidirectional; hence, it is necessary to start off in the right direction. (Marian [1892, 75] quotes Plinius on the structural symmetry of the life cycle: "Nature is disposed that a person enter this world head first and leave it feet first.")[35] While the priest exits the house and the pallbearers prepare to transport their heavy burden, the women resume their passionate expressions of grief. The wailing is thunderous. Yet again, lamenters implore the deceased to do anything within his or her power not to leave, because the leave-taking is a final one:

Scoală-te şi ti uita	Get up and look around;
Fă bunucă cum i fa.	Do, my dear one, whatever you can do.
Din căsucă nu pleca	Don't leave our dear house,
C-altu nu-i mai înturna.	Because you will not return again.

Despite the emotional yearnings of the living for the return of the deceased, precautions are taken to prevent that return, for only the "living dead" (who are unnatural) find their way back. Thus, as soon as the casket is beyond the threshold, the door is shut three times for good measure.

While the pallbearers maneuver their way to the yard, the women continue their plaintive exhortations. It was at this point during the funeral of Mătuşa Marie that her daughter-in-law chose to make her peace publicly with her mother-in-law. Overcome with intense emotion, she wailed:

Scoală-te şi ti uita	Get up and look about:
Că-n ocol îi lume multă.	There are many people in the courtyard.
La dumăta o zinit	They have come to you,
Că lumea tare ti-o ibdit.	For people loved you very much.
Mătuşică-amu mă iartă	Dear auntie, now forgive me,
Că mătuşă te iert şi ieu.	For, aunt, I also forgive you
De la tăt sufletul meu	With my entire soul—
Ne-a ierta şi Dumnezău.	And God will forgive us.
Poate că ţi-am mai greşit	Perhaps I offended you sometimes,
Iartă-mă la despărţit.	Please forgive me as we part.
Nu ţi-am greşit de buiacă	I didn't hurt you out of insolence,
Ţi-am greşit de supărată	But because I was terribly upset

Şî de mult năcaz mîncată.   And eaten by too many troubles.
Uă bunucă buna me   Oh, dear good one,
Că şohan nu ni-om vide.   We will never see each other
                                            again.

Nu ni-om vide niciodată   We will never see each other
Uă pînă la giudecată.   Until Judgment Day.

Just as the bride and groom ask forgiveness from their respective
families before the wedding, so the relations between the living
and the dead must be terminated with the blessings of both. If all
scores are settled, there is no reason for the living to fear retribution from the dead. As will be discussed below, since relations are
mutual between the living and the dead, the deceased also asks forgiveness from the living.

The pallbearers situate the coffin in the center of the courtyard.
In full view of the mourners, the priest, by virtue of his vestments,
announces the life-cycle stage of the beloved dead. If his robes are
white or pale blue, then the bereaved mourn the loss of a child.
Red indicates that a symbolic marriage is taking place; the deceased is of marriageable age. (The priest may also wear red robes
for an elderly virgin, or a particularly religious widow.) In most
cases, however, the priest's robes are black, the customary color of
death.

Candles have been distributed to every person present. Their
glow heightens the light of day and illuminates the path of the deceased. Members of the immediate family kneel by the coffin while
the priest recites the necessary prayers. Then he reads to the assembled the names of those who have asked that their sorrow and
blessings be publicly professed. When he has finished this lengthy
list, the deacon then sings in the name of the deceased his or her
farewell. These *verşuri* (written verses) are composed by the deacon or, in some cases, a teacher; the poetry is influenced by the
literary tradition and tends to have a moralizing character. (See
M. Pop 1976, 171–72; also Ariès 1982, 143–45; de Martino 1975,
36–72, 111–63.) This is the dead's prayer for forgiveness from
those he or she may have wronged; it represents formal leave-
taking from the community. (See Appendix C, I, II, III.)

Upon the conclusion of this service, the funeral cortège, or *prohod*, forms.[36] At its head are the priest and his attendants, as well
as those who carry the church flags and an icon. The closest of

kin position themselves directly behind the casket. The afternoon quiet is overwhelmed by the poetry of remorse sung to the melody of tears. Again, someone invokes a futile plea:

Uă Doamne măi Ştefănuc	Oh, Lord—hey, Ştefan,
Du te tu numa-nainte	You go ahead
Şî porţile le-întide.	And close the gate doors,
Şî întide portiţa	And close the little gate,
Să nu iasă mama ta.	So your mother doesn't leave.

The son of the deceased is urged to go ahead of the cortège and bar the exit by locking both the large and small gates. Any means to contain the deceased in the cultural milieu of the living is proposed, but death cannot be contained.

Others who are more resigned to the inevitability of this fated journey describe the extent of rupture.

Vai plînge masă plînge casă	Oh, the table cries, the house cries,
C-amu soruca vă lasă.	Because now [my] sister is leaving you.
Vai plîngeţi şî voi păreţi	And you, walls, you will also cry
C-amu rămîneţi săcreţi.	For now you'll remain empty.
Vai cine-o locuit în voi	Oh, who has lived in you,
Cum să duce de la noi.	How she goes from us.
Uă cine-n voi o locuit	Who lived in you
Nu-i nădejde de zinit.	Has no hope of returning.
Uă plînge mîndră livegioară	Oh, and cry, beautiful garden,
Că sorucă te-nconjoară	For, sister, [she] surrounds you.
Că de-ătîţa ai de zîle	For so many years
Uă singură fără de nime.	Oh, alone with no one.

This excerpt is also from Marie's funeral. Her sister mourns Marie's loss on behalf of the walls, the table, the courtyard; these have each had personalized, or animate, relations with Marie. This is especially meaningful since Marie had been widowed at a young age, and presumably shared her confidences with these "friends." Mourning encompasses the total environment, because it is from the total environment that the deceased breaks relations.

It is hoped that a token of the departed will remain, and herein figures a theme perhaps more familiar to us through the Anglo-Saxon ballad tradition:[37]

Cind îi ieşi din ocol	When you leave the yard,
Lasă-mni doru în ocol	Leave your longing there for me,
Să răsară-un merişor.	So an apple tree may grow.
Merişoru mere-a fa	The little tree will produce apples
Şî de-a tău dor n-om uita.	So that we will not forget you.

Apples are symbols of love. The productivity of the apple tree reproduces the regenerative cycle between death and life and symbolically denies the death of the deceased whom it commemorates. Without memorials, traces of the deceased are erased from cultural memory. It is in the interest of the living to keep the dead, and therefore themselves, eternally alive.

The funeral procession makes its way from the courtyard to the cemetery. En route, there are numerous stops during which the priest offers prayers for the soul of the dead. (This also provides an opportunity for the pallbearers to rest and readjust their grips.) Everyone must respect the priest's prerogatives; the women are restrained from wailing. The number of times that the cortège is halted, however, depends on the wishes and the purse of the deceased's family; the priest is recompensed for each prayer he performs. There is no mandatory number, but in view of the belief that prayers nourish and comfort the soul as well as reflect beneficially on the living, then the more stops the better. These pauses occur at specific locations: rivers or streams, a crossroad, or a threshold (for example, the courtyard gates; the entrance to the cemetery). These places share the characteristic of ambiguity; they are between one possibility and another. Prayers assist the dead in maneuvering safely across these obstacles. The cortège's encountering of precarious spaces en route to the cemetery metonymically represents the passage of the deceased from this world to that world. Just as the living pay the priest for prayers to facilitate passage over these points, so they place items in the coffin with which the deceased can pay the gatekeepers for passage to that world.

For the duration of the funeral, women lament simultaneously. Their words are marked by exhausted sobs; the air is filled with a cacophony of tear-filled shrieks of pain and sorrow. The laments use the themes already mentioned, with the exception of those that are particular to the ritual action. Laments pertinent to the spatial and temporal progression of the cortège itself tend to comment on concerns of all travelers, such as the weather or the time of day, or (as in the following example) on the approach to the cemetery.

Mîndră vreme ţi-ai ales	You chose beautiful weather
Uă în ceia lume de mărs.	To go to that world.
Uă nici nu plouă nici nu nînge	Oh, it neither rains nor snows,
Da la inimă ne frige.	But our hearts are scorched.
Uă nici nu nînge nici nu-i ploie	Oh, neither does it snow nor is there rain,
La inimă rău ne doare.	But our hearts ache badly.

The lamenter notes that the deceased's journey has begun on a lovely day. (In bad weather, this would be omitted.) The lines refer to both levels of indexical reference: to the cosmological (in the world of the dead, there is no weather) and to the daily experiences of the living (where the weather is—at the time of utterance—lovely). Since water (rain, snow) douses fire and cools heat, the fine weather prevents the extinguishing of their pain. Death entails parallel processes of transformation: the mourners' hearts burn as the body of the deceased dries up. But eventually, the pain of the mourner subsides and the physical manifestation of the corpse disappears. The imagery of water and burning also has another connotation: mourners are cautioned to take care that their tears not fall on the cheeks of the deceased, because it is thought that tears will sear the soul of the corpse. It is an inverse relation like that between life and death.

As the cortège slowly advances toward its destination, a lamenter, resigned to the nonnegotiability of this process, may urge that the remaining moments at least be prolonged:[38]

Roagă-te cui ti-i ruga	Beg whomever you may;
Roagă-te cătă popa	Beg the priest
Tare să nu să păza.	Not to hurry,
Uă că ziuă-i bugăt de mare	For the day is long enough.
Şi-i ave vreme a mere.	There is time to go;
Ieste vreme a sosî	There is time to arrive,
Uă şî vreme a putrezî.	Oh, and time to rot.
Tătă lume mere-n rînd	Everyone goes in order—
Numa tu fratiuc în pămînt.	Except for you, brother, in the earth.

Tătă lume mere-n paşi	Everyone goes in steps—
Uă numa tu în sălaş.	Oh, except for you, in the coffin.
Uă de mine măi fratiuc	Oh my, brother,
Cine mere-aiestă drum	Who goes on this road doesn't return,
Nu zine-napoi nicicum.	Doesn't return anyhow.
Aiesta-i un drum secret	This is a secret road;
Nu-i nădejde să te văd.	There is no hope of seeing you.
Aiesta-i un drum pustîi	This is a cursed road;
Nu-i nădejde să mai zii.	There is no hope of your coming again.

Before any major step toward the final departure, such as the removal of the corpse from the household or the burial, it is typical for a lamenter to encourage the deceased to do anything possible to postpone the inevitable. In this instance, the request is directed toward savoring the last hours. Daylight is the time of the living; night is that of the dead. There are still several hours before the deceased need arrive at the depot of the village of death; moreover, it is not necessary to hurry, because time in that world is eternal. The couplets contrasting the movements of those in the cortège (going in order, in steps) with those of the deceased (in the earth, in the coffin) simultaneously underscore the certainty of death for all: everyone is taken "in order" or "one by one" (in the words of the cross inscription at the beginning of this chapter); for the moment, it is the turn of the deceased. Again, the couplets address both the particular circumstances and broader cosmological realities, of which the disjunction between this world and that world is perhaps the most mysterious. The route conjoining them is unknown to the living; it, unlike any other passageway, is unidirectional.

All that is known about this road is that one takes it from the cemetery. As the procession nears the entry, women will begin to "converse" with the cemetery itself and the dead who are thought to gather to welcome their relative. Thus, one woman began:

Bucură-te ţintirim	Rejoice, cemetery!
Cu mîndră floare zinim	We are coming with a beautiful flower
Aici să o răsădim.	Here to plant her.
N-o răsădim să-nflorea	We don't plant her to blossom,

O-ngropăm să putredea.	But bury her to putrefy.
N-o răsădim ca să zie	We don't plant her so she may live,
Făr-aicea să rămîie.	But rather that she remain here.

This lament is another example of nature's processes providing metaphors and similes for the biological and social processes of the life cycle. Life is likened to flowers. A person, like a flower, grows, blossoms, begins to wither, and dies. Both flowers and humans grow from seeds (*sămînţă* means both plant seed and semen). Men plant seeds to encourage and control the yields of nature and the "yield" of women. (Children are central to the "sustenance" of the lineage.) Wildflowers grow in fields that may be cultivated; planted flowers grow in the garden beside the house, tended by women. Children grow up in their "mother's garden"; marriage results in a flower (the bride) being picked from a mother's garden and re-planted in the "king's" (groom's) garden to bear children (see Kligman 1984). The word for flower (*floare*) is used to refer to the deceased, who will no longer live, and to the bride, who symbolically dies after leaving her natal home. The bride is planted in her mother-in-law's house to "die"; the dead are "planted" in the cemetery, or in "death's garden."

Like all gardens, death's is surrounded by a fence. It too has a carved wooden gate for an entrance. Approaching this entryway, a lamenter will turn her attention to the inhabitants within this garden. At Mătuşa Marie's funeral, Marie's sister cried out to Marie's husband:

Uă uă măi Ştefănuc	Oh, hey, Ştefan,
Hai destide poarta larg	Open the gate,
Uă că zine cine ţi-i drag.	Because she who is dear to you is coming.
Uă că ie de mult ti-o dorit	For a long time she has longed for you;
Uă şî tîrziu ti-o mniruit.	Now, after many years, you are a couple again.
Că de mult ti-o aşteptat	She has waited for you a long time,
Uă şî tîrziu ti-o cîştigat.	And it is late that she has rejoined you.
Uă de mine tu sorucă	Oh my, you, sister—

Uǎ sorucǎ bine ti-a si	Oh, dear sister, all will be well for you,
C-amu sîngurǎ nu-i si.	For now you won't be alone,
C-amu-ai zinit la bǎrbat	For now you have come to your man,
Uǎ ai la cine cere un sfat.	You have someone from whom to seek advice.

Marie's husband had left her a widow at a young age; now, upon her death, they would finally be reunited. The relations between the living and dead are continuous; therefore, Marie would join her husband's family in the other world, and not her natal family, from which she had departed at marriage. Her sister asks Ştefan to come and welcome his wife by opening the gate for her. He is told that his wife has longed for his company for many years. (The verb *a mnirui* has a double sense: it is related to the olive oil used during rituals and also to the pejorative association of a couple being found together.) Marie's sister then comforts her, telling her that finally her travails are over: she shall be with her husband and no longer alone and struggling in this world.

Upon nearing the cemetery entrance, Marie's daughter-in-law reacted similarly. She too began to speak with her dead father-in-law, Ştefan:

Uǎ de mine hǎi unte	Oh my, you, uncle—
Uǎ ieşi numa înainte	Oh, go out ahead
Şî porţile destide.	And open the gates.
Destide porţile larg	Open the gates wide,
Cǎ zine cine ţi-i drag.	For she that is dear to you is coming.
Uǎ cǎ zine Mǎtuşa	For auntie is coming
Unteşu la dumǎta.	To you, uncle.
Şî bine vi-ţi sfǎtui	And you will catch up;
Supǎrat altu nu-i si.	You will no longer be troubled.
Nu ştiu pǎ care v-aş strîga	I don't know which of you to call,
Cǎ amîndoi-îs aicea.	For you are both here.

Juji expresses the same notions that are in Marie's sister's lament above. The spatio-temporal keying of lament content is critical and partially determines formulaic features.[39] This excerpt also extols the ideology of marriage: that it is hard alone in this world; with a partner, life is fulfilling. Marie and Ştefan did not long share that privilege in this world; now, reunited in that world, their desires will be gratified.

The symbolic inversions in Juji's laments throughout the day acknowledged the nature of consanguineal and affinal ties in a patrilineal system; they also portrayed the changes in these relations— the particulars of separation and integration. When the cortège had been about to exit from their courtyard, Juji had implored her husband, Ştefan, to go ahead and close the gates, not to let his mother leave. Arriving at the cemetery, however, she asked her father-in-law to open the gates to welcome his wife. (The parallel process of breaking relations and establishing new ones also occurs in the wedding rite.)

Once inside the gates, the priest prays for the soul of the deceased, who has just entered the village of the dead. This stop occurs in all funerals. Then the entourage proceeds to the church. The *dezlegarea mortului,* or absolving (undoing) of the deceased, will be done either in front of the church or inside it. In either location, the casket, surrounded by the grieving family, is placed on the ground; the priest reads the appropriate service. (The dezlegarea is also performed on the requisite ritual mourning days during the forthcoming year.) Immediately on conclusion of these valued prayers, the women's wailing erupts. Some are too exhausted or too hoarse to sing their pain; instead, they shout their anguish. For several, the torrents of tears have subsided, their supply having temporarily ceased. But the verbal expression of grief continues, silenced only by the demands of the priest when the casket is lowered into its grave. One woman projected her concern onto her dead brother. With her words, she attempted to soothe his anxiety about entering this new locale:

Vai de mine măi fratiuc	Oh my, hey, brother—
Nu te teme n-a si rău	Don't worry, it won't be bad,
C-amu ieşti în copîrşeu	For now you are in the coffin,
Şî-amu ai scăpat de greu.	And now you have escaped from hardship.
Nu te teme rău n-a si	Don't worry, it won't be bad:
Tu cu fraţii ti-i-ntîlni.	You will meet our brothers,
Şî bine ti-i hodini	And you will rest well,
Şî altu nu-i văduvi.	And you will no longer be a widower.

The lamenter encouraged the deceased (but, in actuality, the living) with a description of the improvements the other world offers. Secure in the coffin, he will not be subject to difficulties. Moreover, in that world, he will no longer be alone. There, he shall join his relatives and his wife, whose death had preceded his. "Life" in that world will be better. It is a statement of hope that combats the grim realities of the human condition, not the least of which is the starkness of mortality.

While the women lament, the pallbearers prepare to lower the coffin. They are assisted by skilled directives from the gravedigger and priest. The casket is suspended between two long, tightly woven cloths. The woven rug that adorned the wooden box throughout the cortège is removed. (This rug is either provided by the family or borrowed from the church's collection.) Slowly, the coffin is lowered into the ground; the "ropes" are retrieved. The level of audible anguish reaches a climax as the gravedigger arranges the final position of this new inhabitant.[40] Then the priest borrows the gravedigger's shovel and moves a bit of earth onto the coffin in the place where the corpse's head rests. He repeats this to acknowledge the four directions. All the while, he utters prayers for the soul of the deceased. The women cannot be calmed. After the priest has thrown dirt upon the casket, marking the end of the burial, everyone present does the same; it is considered a sin not to honor the deceased in this manner.

As the gravedigger finishes his task, the mourners begin to leave the cemetery. Men tend to exit more quickly than the women, who linger behind. Before and after the religious burial service, the laments of the women persist. The content reflects all of the themes that have thus far been discussed, except those that pertain to particular ritual sequences. Here, examples will be given of typical lament themes that have not yet been presented. Not surprisingly, during the burial activities, the grave and the cemetery become foci of attention. Shortly after the priest had blessed the coffin in the grave, a sister of the one deceased admonished:

Vai de mine măi fratiuc	Oh my, hey, brother—
Nu şăde aici deloc	Don't stay here at all.
Lasă copîrşeu-n foc.	Leave the coffin in fire,
C-acasă-ai durnit în pat	For at home you slept in a bed—
Da aici pă lut uscat.	But here on dry earth.

C-acasă-ai durnit pă cergă	At home you slept on a woven blanket—
Da aici te culci pă ţărnă.	But here you'll sleep on earth.
Într-o groapă cu izvor	In a grave with a spring,
Şî noi n-om pute de dor.	And we won't be able to go on from longing.
Într-o groapă cu vălcele	In a grave with little springs,
Şi noi n-om pute de jele.	And we won't be able to go on from sorrow.
Vai de mine greu ţi-a si	Oh my, it will be hard for you
Pînă cînd tu ti-i cumti.	Until you get used to it here.
Asta noapte ţi-a si gre	Tonight will be hard,
Pînă ti-i cumti cu ie.	Until you get used to it.
Cine ţi-o făcut casa?	Who has made you your lovely home?
Dumnezău sfîntu-l trăia.	May the Lord bless him,
Numa nu ţi-o pus fereste	Only he didn't put windows
Să grăieşti frate cu mine	For you, brother, to talk with me
Cînd oi trece pîngă tine.	When I pass by.

The lamenter beseeches her brother to abandon his new abode, suggesting that he leave it to be destroyed by fire. (Recall that fire is a medium of destruction commonly invoked in curses.) She compares the comforts of his former home with the lack thereof in his new one. (This comparison is also often presented to a bride, reminding her that her mother-in-law will not indulge her as her mother did.) The internal structure of these rhymes relates them to each other in pairs: in the comparison between the material conveniences of the two "houses," it is pointed out that culture's bed is more comfortable; in the grave, he will sleep on dry earth. The next couplets, however, refer to the location of this grave, which negates the idea of dry earth. "In a grave with a spring" means that this individual was buried in the cemetery surrounding the Biserică din Şes (in the flatland) and not in that of the Biserică din Deal (on the hill). The graves in the flatland are sometimes flooded, hence, the earth is anything but dry. Some laments include mention that the deceased will drown. The rhyme implies that the mourners will succumb to their excess of tears; the imagery is consistent. Finally, in this fragment, the lamenter sympathizes with her brother, recognizing that it always takes time to become familiar with a new residence. She also wonders at its construction, so different from that of her own home. (The lament cited on p. 168 is often reiterated at the grave—that she has come to see the deceased's new home, to see if it pleases her or not. The answer is decidedly negative.) The absence of windows prevents communication between the living and the dead; death precludes sociality between this world and that.

While this fact is known, it is not immediately agreeable. Lamenters will propose various possibilities to continue a social relationship. In addition to asking the deceased to tell about one matter or another or to send a card (see lament on p. 167), the bereaved may also suggest:

Fă-ţi cărarea pîn grădină	Make a path through the garden
Şî zină la noi la cina.	And come to us for dinner.
Că ieu cina oi gata	I'll make dinner,
Şî cu tăţii om cina.	And we'll all eat together.

While commensality figures prominently in the establishment and maintenance of relations between the living and the dead (discussed in the first portion of this chapter), the latter join the former at table only figuratively.[41]

Because the dead are thought to be present to welcome their new member, the living take the opportunity to engage in conversation with them. This is one of the primary forms of mediated interaction between the living and the dead. The following example is again taken from Mătuşa Marie's funeral; it was lamented by Marie's daughter-in-law:

Uă de mine hăi mătu	Oh my, hey, aunt—
Dac-acolo ti-i sosî	If you arrive there
Cu fraţii mnei ti-i-ntîlni.	And meet with my brothers,
Fraţii mnei ti-or întreba	And if my brothers ask you
Cum i rîndu p-aicea.	How things are here,
Spune-le ce-i socoti	Tell them what you think appropriate
Să să poată hodini.	So that they may rest quietly.
Spune numa lui Iulci	Only tell Iulci
De cînd de-acasă o plecat	Since she departed from home,
Coconi mnici i-o lăsat.	She left young children;
Şi ie la iei nu-o înturnat	She didn't return to them
Batăr cît o aşteptat.	No matter how long they waited.
De cînd aici o zinit	Since she came here,

Doi i s-o căsătorit	Two have married.
Ie la nuntă n-o zinit.	But she didn't attend the wedding.
Noi tare mult o-am dorit	We have missed her very much,
Şi ie de fel n-o zinit	But she has never come.
Nici o carte nu ni-o scris.	She hasn't written one postcard.
Vai de mine măi Văsî	Oh my, you Văsî—
De cînd aici ai zinit	Since you came here,
De mămucă n-ai gîndit.	You haven't thought of mother.
Că săraca mamuca	For poor dear mother,
Tot mnereu te aştepta	She continues to await you.
Că ie o gîndit aşă.	For she reckoned
Că ie pă cînd a slăbdi	That when she weakened,
De ie bine i griji	That you would take good care of her
Şi ie de năcaz n-a si.	And she wouldn't be troubled.
Ie în tine s-o bdizuit	She counted on you for that,
Şî tu Văsî ai murit.	And you, Văsî, you died.
Că fecior n-o avut altu	For she didn't have another son;
Numa tu ai fost unu.	You were the only one.
Du-te moarte şî-n alt neam	Go, death, to another family;
Nu face din noi haram.	Don't destroy us.
Că nu ştiu trece-un an ori doi	For I don't know, one or two years pass,
	And death is again upon us.
Mortiţa iara-i la noi.	This death is crazy;
Moarte asta i nebună	I don't know if one month has passed
Nu ştiu de-o trecut o lună	
De cînd o luat pă tata.	Since she took father,
Şî-o zinit la dumăta	And she has come to you—
Şî rău ni-o rupt inima.	And she has broken our heart(s) badly.
Uă de mine hăi mătu	Oh my, you, aunt—
Uă Doamne bunuca me	Oh, Lord, my dearest one—
Aici dacă-i sosî.	If you arrive here
Cu tătuca ti-i-ntîlni	And you meet with father
Şî bine vi-ţi sfătui.	And you chat with each other,
Vă luaţi amîndoi de mînă	Take each other by the hand
Ziniţi la mine la cină.	And come to me for dinner.
Şî v-oi pune după masă	And I'll seat you at the table,
Şî-om cina cu tăţi în casă	And we'll all eat together at home;
Nu ne-a si inima arsă.	Our hearts won't be burned.

This lament excerpt contributes a certain tone to the occasion. It is but one fragment of 216 lines that I recorded at the gravesite (before turning to Marie's sister). Juji tells her mother-in-law to use her judgment regarding what she shall tell Juji's siblings in the other world; they should know enough to be informed, but not too much to be disturbed. (The use of the word *brothers* reflects the patrilineal bias; the masculine term is that of encompassment.) Juji asks that Marie gently chastise her sister Iulci for not having returned to care for her children. It had been hoped that she would at least appear for the weddings of the two who had thus far married, but she had not heeded the invitation. Next Juji turns her attention to her brother Văsîle. (Her dream about him was recounted in note 11.) She rebukes him for abandoning their mother. Given the general practice of ultimogeniture (and his position as the only son), he was expected to remain in the family house and care for his parents in their old age. By dying, he shirked his responsibility. Exasperated by the harshness of circumstances, Juji interrupts her dialogue and curses death, selfishly projecting her rage onto some other family. Death had seemingly found their extended family appetizing. Approximately one month before Marie's death, Juji had mourned the loss of her own father. Thus, in her lament, she also asks her mother-in-law to come with her father to dinner. They would both be welcome. Were they to come, the living would not suffer from their "burnt" hearts; instead, they would eat a cooked meal with their loved ones.

But in actuality, it is death who is enjoying the local fare. Death in the figure of the cemetery is also conceptualized corporally as a medium for physical transformation:

Vai săracii fraţii mnei	Oh, my poor brothers—
Ţintirimu-i plin de iei.	The cemetery is full of them.
Încă nu s-o umplut bine	Still it has not filled itself well
Pînă s-a umple cu mine.	Until it will be filled with me.
Foc te bată lut cernit	May fire strike you, black clay.
Multă lume-ai îndiţît	You have swallowed many people
Şî tăt nu te vezi hrănit.	And still you are not satiated;
Încă nu te-ai umplut bine	Still you won't have filled yourself well
Pînă ti-i umple cu mine.	Until you fill yourself with me.

The cemetery is the place in which corpses are processed; "black earth" and "black clay" are formulaic expressions used interchangeably for the cemetery earth. Death is a state of being for the dead, but it is also an active being itself. It is envisaged in body terms. It possesses bodily functions; that is, it swallows and has its own "life's" needs, most notably an insatiable appetite. The cemetery is a bottomless pit with an infinitely accommodating belly: it is never full. Death in the figures of the cemetery and black earth consumes everyone at will. (Also, refer to the discussion at the beginning of this section of the chapter about the association between death and female sexuality.) The relationship between culture and nature is inverted in this instance. Whereas humans prey upon the yield of nature for their own nourishment during their lives, death devours the living to maintain her physical well-being. (Also, the metaphoric relationship between the sacrifices of the human body to the earth and of Christ to the spiritual world should be mentioned. It is recapitulated through every church service and ritual practice; honoring the soul of the deceased honors that of Christ as well.)[42]

As the earth's lips are sealed, the women who remain at the grave say their last farewells. The final interactions are as touching and respectful as they are resigned to the process of fate.

Scoală-te să te mai văd	Get up so that I may see you again,
Că ne despărțim de tăt.	For we are parting forever.
Dă mîna să ți-o sărut	Give me your hand so I may kiss it,
Că nu ni-om vide mai mult.	For we won't see each other again.

The lamenter expresses her desire to see the deceased just one last time and to pay her respects properly. Upon parting of any sort, it is customary to kiss the hand of one's elder or of someone considered to be of higher status.

Another mourner chose to say goodby in a different manner:

Vai de mine unde-i durni	Oh my, where you shall sleep
În grădină cu morții.	In the garden with the dead—
Pus-ai spate la pămînt	You put your back to the ground
Ca să nu te sufle vînt.	So that the wind wouldn't blow on you.

Pus-ai spate la răcoare	You put your back in the coolness
Ca să nu te-agiungă soare.	So that the sun wouldn't reach you.
Dacă-i aşa şi-i aşa	If it is like that,
Noapte bună de-acole.	Good-night from there.

The garden of the dead is protected from nature's elements. Again, neither time nor space, not the seasons or senses, are differentiated; there is a continuing sameness. If the deceased has taken that path, then so be it. Indeed, nothing more may be done.

The state of the dead is conceived as a type of sleep, an eternal one. For the living, nightly sleep is the condition of the living body-soul in repose. The sleep of death, however, is qualitatively and quantitatively different. There is no morning awakening. Thus, the bereaved bid farewell to the deceased, wishing them good-night forever:

| Noapte bună pă viaţă | Good-night for life, |
| Nu pînă mîni dimineaţă. | Not just until tomorrow morning. |

In the world of the dead, time no longer structures action; it is no longer passing. Nor is life.

Tăte cîte îs subt soare	All that is under the sun,
Tăte huc îs trecătoare.	The whole of it is fleeting.
În lume cît om lucra	In this world, how much we'll work;
Tăte huc îs degeaba.	All of it is for naught.
Noi în lume cît ne-am zbate	How much we struggle in this world;
Nu facem numa păcate.	We don't achieve anything but sins.

From a cosmological perspective, life is illusory, for it is temporary. Life, unlike death, is progressive and eventually reaches an end. While people work hard to construct the world around them—materially and symbolically—none of these efforts are of any real significance. The only things that seem to endure from this world to the next are sins committed here that must be accounted for there. Such is the Christian resolution of the existential dilemma of human frailty.

Another lament excerpt similarly comments on the futile struggle against mortality:

Tăt aşă gînde omu	So a man thinks
Că trăie cît i pămîntu	That he will live as long as the earth,
Şî a face ce i gîndu.	And he will accomplish what he has in mind,
Şî-a zîdi zîduri de ptiatră	And he will build walls of stone,
Şî n-a muri niciodată.	And he will never die.
Da viaţa omului	But the life of man
Îi ca floarea cîmpului.	Is like a wildflower:
Azî ieşti tînăr şî voinic	Today you are young and strong
Şî pă mîni nu ieşti nimic.	And by tomorrow you are nothing.

Occasionally, an overwrought lamenter will be restrained from tormenting herself further.[43] Others will assist her from the grave-site. As she is torn from this spot, she may shout in a choked voice:

Noapte bună pă viaţă	Good-night for life—
Nu pînă mîni dimineaţă.	Not until tomorrow morning.
Că ieu nu vă pot strîga	For I cannot call to you,
Că mă doare inima.	Because my heart aches.
Nici nu te mai pot strîga	I cannot lament any longer.
Dumnezău te hodinea.	May God grant you peace.

Most mourners leave the cemetery and go home or to the house of the deceased if they have been asked to partake of the funeral repast. But not all women disperse promptly. Some may stay to "speak" with their own dead who reside in this garden. At one funeral, as the majority of mourners disappeared into the familiar paths of the everyday, one woman made her way to her uncle's grave marker, a wooden cross. Leaning heavily on it, she unburdened her agonized feelings about her brother's disappearance during World War II:

Hai moşu ti-aş întreba	Hey, uncle, I'd ask you,
Zinit-o-aici cineva?	Has someone come here?
Uă de mine şî de mine	Oh my, oh my—
Uă de mine măi fratiuc.	Oh my, you, brother—
Nu ştiu puşcă ti-o puşcat	I don't know if you were shot with a gun

Şî-n pămînt ti-o astupat   And enclosed in the earth
De bunuc n-ai înturnat.   So that you didn't return.
Uă Dumnezău te hodinea   May God grant you peace.
Sie-ţi uşoară ţărna.   May the dirt be soft.

The death of one arouses the sorrow for all others who have departed. Hence, a funeral encourages the honoring of the village's
ancestors in the other world. Through this occasion, social relations are transformed as well as reaffirmed. When the burial itself
is finished, the chasm between this world and that reopens. The
deceased begins to accommodate to unfamiliar circumstances, and
the living begin to adjust to their new conditions. As the cemetery
gates close, a verse is quietly recollected:

Uă de mine măi bunuc   Oh my, my dear one—
Amu-ai lăsat tăte huc.   Now you have left everything,
Că ţintirimu-i îngrădit   For the cemetery is enclosed;
N-ai nădejde de zinit.   You have no hope of coming.
Îngrădit şî cu lăcată   It is enclosed and with a lock;
Şî nu-i zini niciodată.   You will never come back.

The deceased is gone forever.

But the journey of the deceased has just begun, and it will not go
well without the participation of the living. To this end, the invited
mourners return to the home of the grieving family where they will
assist at the *masa mortului* (meal of the deceased), thereby honoring the soul.[44] Generally, kin, friends, and neighbors are present.
Long wooden tables, parallel to each other, are set up in the courtyard. (If the weather does not permit this, the tables are constructed indoors; that usually necessitates several "seatings" to
accommodate everyone.) A table for honored guests—the church
representatives, members of the local intelligentsia—often links
the other rows. The ritual breads for the priest, deacon, and sexton
are put on that table, indicating their places; individual settings,
material acknowledgments of ascribed higher status, are also there.
Members of the intelligentsia do not eat from the communal serving bowls nor with wooden utensils (refer to note 19). Gradually,
the mourners take their places. In Ieud, the tables are still segregated by sex (although women of high status sit with the men).
Children are not permitted to eat at the masa mortului, just as they
are not allowed to serve as pallbearers.

1. The Dancing of the Flag on the evening before the wedding ceremony. Family and friends gather in the groom's house for this event. (All photographs taken in Ieud unless otherwise noted.)

2. The braiding of the bride's hair is nearing completion.

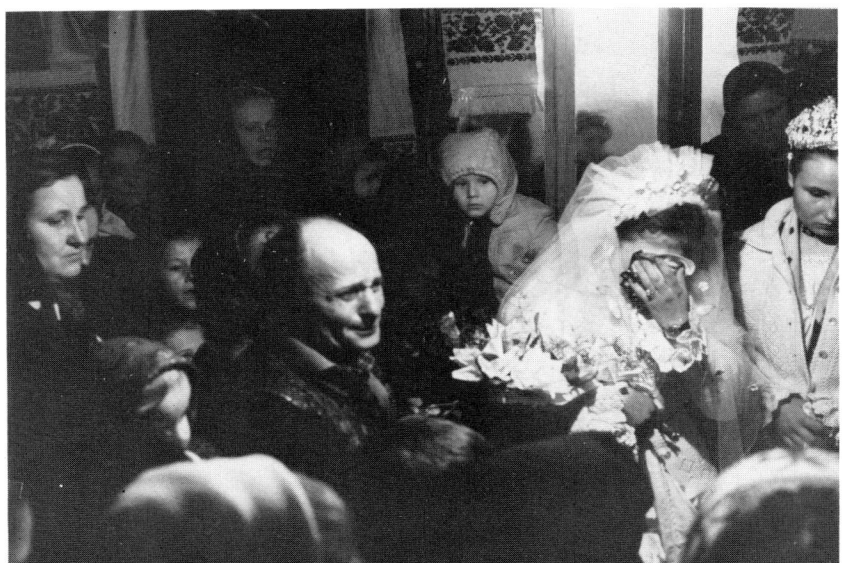

3. Before the departure for the church ceremony, the bride formally takes leave of her family. She asks their forgiveness for any difficulties 'she may have caused throughout the years and awaits their blessing. Another emotional parting has already taken place at the groom's house. (Photograph courtesy of Gavrila Chindriş.)

4. The groom takes his wedding oath during the religious consecration of his marriage. (Photograph taken in the village of Breb.)

5. In the ritual sequence known as the Asking for the Bride, the groom's godfather is first offered a young girl in response to his insistent queries. Held for all to see, she recites the only fixed text in the wedding ritual.

6. Next, the bridesmaid is presented to the godfather. She is closer to that which he is seeking, but not quite right either.

7. Finally, the bride comes forth. Following a toast, she joins her husband and their godparents at the wedding table.

8. The Song of the Hen causes the wedding guests to crowd the room. Everyone enjoys the metaphorical banter about the bride's virginity. The cook holds high in the air the decorated hen, which is adorned with bread necklaces and greenery; a cigarette is provocatively stuffed in its mouth.

9. This wedding is being celebrated in the local house of culture, which accounts for the posters and Party symbols that decorate the walls, in lieu of the woven towels and icons found in homes.

10. In the ritual sequence Coming after the Bride, the bride's family and friends have come to the groom's house with the intention of "stealing" her back. The two wedding parties dance in separate circles. The bride's entourage attempts to capture her into their number. Eventually, they succumb to their loss and merge with the groom's circle. Marriage creates the alliance of these two families, which the wedding ritual enacts and symbolizes.

11. On the day of the funeral, while awaiting the arrival of the priest, two sisters lament their deceased sibling. Engulfed in their grief, they walk back and forth in the courtyard, wailing. This picture illustrates characteristic lamenting postures.

12. The deceased has been moved from the house to the courtyard, where the final prayers before departure to the cemetery are to be offered. Because he was an important personage in the community, his funeral was celebrated by many priests in addition to the throng of mourners. (Photograph taken in Săpînţa; courtesy of M. Dăncuş.)

13. At this funeral, the deceased was placed in the coffin and the coffin closed before removal from the house. Final prayers are being said in the courtyard. (Photograph courtesy of M. Dăncuş.)

14. Mourners are seated at the table for a meal honoring the soul of the dead. Generally, men and women are segregated. (Photograph courtesy of M. Dăncuş.)

15. The black flag hanging outside the house announces the death of an unmarried person of marriageable age. The community then knows that a symbolic marriage will take place during the funeral. The black flag contrasts starkly with the wedding flag seen in Photograph 1.

16. A young bridesmaid gazes at the camera as she stands by the deceased "bride."

17. Grief and horror are reflected in the faces of the mourners when the open casket is placed in the courtyard. The "bride" was the young girl whose murder is discussed in Chapter 5. (Photograph taken in Botiza.)

18. After the casket is closed, the mother of the "bride" continues to lament painfully. (Photograph taken in Botiza.)

19. Unmarried persons are not permitted to carry the dead except in a death-wedding. Then, same-sex pall-bearers escort the deceased to the graveyard, just as they would have escorted the bride to the church for her marriage.

16. A young bridesmaid gazes at the camera as she stands by the deceased "bride."

17. Grief and horror are reflected in the faces of the mourners when the open casket is placed in the court-yard. The "bride" was the young girl whose murder is discussed in Chapter 5. (Photograph taken in Botiza.)

18. After the casket is closed, the mother of the "bride"
     continues to lament painfully.
     (Photograph taken in Botiza.)

19. Unmarried persons are not permitted to carry the
     dead except in a death-wedding. Then, same-sex pall-
     bearers escort the deceased to the graveyard, just as
     they would have escorted the bride to the church for
     her marriage.

20. If the distance is great, bachelors may carry the coffin most of the way. This was the case in the death-wedding of the murdered girl. The cortège consisted of nearly the entire village. Although difficult to discern, the black wedding flag may be seen to the right of the casket. (Photograph taken in Botiza.)

21. Members of the family of the dead "bride" are readily recognized. Her father and brother are unshaven and bareheaded. Her sister, exhausted from hours of lamenting, continues to wail as they near the cemetery entrance.

22. Following the burial of her cousin, who had been
bridesmaid at her own sister's death-wedding, this
young woman returns to her sister's grave and vents
her sorrow.

23. Her mother does the same. The grief of this mother
who has experienced life's hardships contrasts sharply
with the innocence of the infant, still oblivious to the
sorrows of life. The child's white attire is symbolic of
hope and purity. This picture encapsulates a tale of
gender and generations.

When everyone is seated, the cook and her assistants bring the food to the table. Wooden spoons are distributed, as are pieces of bread, made of either corn or white flour. Bowls filled with soup or stuffed cabbage are placed between every two or three people. The priest, seeing the meal is ready to be eaten, rises to recite the necessary prayers to bless the soul of the deceased and to dedicate the meal to it. Following the "amen" and salutations of "God rest the soul," the meal begins. Several liquor-servers offer glasses of plum brandy to each guest, two per person—one for the living and one "for the soul of the dead." As each person toasts the deceased, ritual wishes are uttered: *sie de sufletul mortului* (for the soul of the dead) or *Dumnezău s-o hodinească* (may God grant peace) or some variant thereof. The women tend to the needs of those at table. When the main courses are finished, bowls of compote are provided for dessert. The meal ends with another prayer; the priest then departs, ritual breads in hand. To reiterate, there is "no meal without breads." No one may leave the funeral repast without a bread, the ritual colac. As described earlier, the breads for the majority of mourners are small; it is critical only that they have them. Someone makes sure that the gravedigger and bell-ringer have received their due. It is a sin for anyone in the presence of the deceased (wittingly or not, which accounts for the impromptu invitations to passersby) not to be the recipient of his or her beneficence. In related fashion, the *pomana copiilor*, or alms for the children, is passed out. In particular, children of poorer families who have not necessarily participated in the funeral meal appear. This is a form of charity.[45] It glorifies the soul of the deceased; glorification of the soul is one of the primary purposes of the meal. It also reaffirms social ties among the living. Commensality nourishes the beings of this world and that world, simultaneously dissolving, creating, and reacknowledging social relations among and between the living and the dead.

Post-Funeral Mourning

The rearrangement of these relations cannot, however, be accomplished during the three days of the funeral.[46] This reorganization evolves over the year of mourning; the three-day ritual facilitates the management of the initial and most intense disruption and institutionalizes the complex processes of transformation. The ongoing cycle entails subsequent "institutionalized" (ritual) blessings, meals, and alms-giving. It should be noted that lamenting is characteristic only of the three-day funeral ritual. Because this form of communication is predicated on the dynamics of conversation, the corpse is a necessary "participant." Although the ancestors are believed to emerge at this time, their presence is dependent on that of the corpse (as vehicle). Thereafter, mediated interaction between the living and the dead is managed through dreams and through alms of food and prayers. The first such occasion occurs on the third day, when another meal is prepared. (Usually, fewer people attend this ritual repast.) Alms are again given to the priest, deacon, and sexton, although they are presented "untied" (not wrapped in the woven cloths), and the small prescure are absent. Colaci are also given to everyone present at the meal.

On the ninth day following the funeral, a special service for the soul of the deceased takes place. Nine widows gather in his or her former home. They spend the day fasting and praying; later they will sup on a meal for a day of fasting: bean soup, cabbage stuffed with rice and cornmeal, or rice alone (but not meat) and boiled fruit. The prescription that these women be widows is based on the view of widows as "purer"; they no longer experience carnal sins. (Therefore, it is also appropriate for elderly virgins to participate.) The women, kneeling in a circle around one of the deceased's shirts, say rosaries throughout the day. After they have finished their prayers and eaten their meal, they return to their homes. As they leave the house of the deceased, they are each given a colac "for the soul of the dead." The giving is reciprocal.

This practice is said to be a form of "Christian sorcery" linked to the broader category of *mătanie* (reverences) done for the living to assure love, happiness, and health.[47] The systematicity of symbolic logic is such that acts associated with the Devil, and not with goodness, work through inversion. Thus, a practitioner of the art of sorcery or a group of women will perform incantations around the designated person's shirt that is placed before them; the shirt is turned inside out to ensure the inverted (or, as it were, perverted) outcome.

For the next several weeks, mourning is a more personal matter. Individuals pray for the deceased and light candles at church as they choose; at the same time, they become slightly more accustomed to the absence of a familiar face. The public recognition of this continuing process takes place six weeks following the death.[48] For this occasion, there is a church service followed by a commemorative meal. On the designated day, the family presents the ritual breads to the church. They have paid the priest to read the dezlegarea mortului; on conclusion of the service, the family goes outside and offers two glasses of brandy and a bit of bread to those present. They also use the opportunity to invite people to honor the memory of the deceased. Shortly thereafter, a meal is served at the former home of the deceased. This is the first repast at which children are welcome. (Long ago, children were not permitted to attend any of the year-long commemorations; nowadays, everyone comes to the events from six weeks after the death on.) As at the other meals, ritual breads are bestowed on each of those partaking of the deceased's hospitality. Children do not receive the larger colaci; instead, they are given small pretzel- or doughnut-like breads. Through this meal, the deceased's supplies are refurbished.

The meal marking the final integration of the deceased into ceia lume takes place one year after death. This ritual feast is dedicated to all of the family's dead members and accordingly acknowledges the incorporation of the individual deceased among them. Again, ritual breads are given to the church officiants and to everyone at the meal. It is an important occasion for which "there must be food"—for those in this world and in that. It is a collective affair. With the conclusion of this memorial banquet, the ritual prohibitions regarding mourning for the grieving family are terminated. A parallel transformation of social relations takes place. Hence, the meal signifies not only the absorption of the deceased into that world, but also the public reintegration of the bereaved family into the daily activities of their local social world. For the family, life and death resume their more familiar places. While the scars rendered by death may never fully disappear, they nonetheless become less prominent.

The frequency of ritual markings for this process of transformation (regarding both the living and the dead) should be noted. The initial intensity of activities subsides as the "burnt" hearts of the living are soothed and the deceased progresses further on his or her journey. The cognitive relationship between time and space facilitates this parallel transformation. The increased dimensions of both time and distance contribute to the healing, or "normalizing," process. The absence gradually becomes more familiar; the pain gradually lessens. In this way, the ritual process both culturally defines grief and makes sense of mortality. It structures socially mediated images of the public self. The cycle of death-related practices culturally encodes norms of social behavior that associate the self and society. It also associates the living and the dead. The latter, although out of sight, are never completely out of mind. Their memory is honored periodically through the observances of calendar as well as through life-cycle rites.[49] Each of these occasions evokes the joys and sorrows of human experience. These joys and sorrows are thought to be shared by the living and the dead. They are most intensified during the rites of marriage and of death. It is to their conjuncture—the culminating practice of "cultural logic" and emotional force—that we now turn: the death-wedding.

Chapter Four

The Wedding of the Dead

O bunu mîndru fecior
Nu ţi-o fo vremea să mori.
Ţi-o fo vremea să te-nsori
Uă scoală-te şî te uită
Că la noi îi lume multă

C-o gîndit că facem nuntă.

Tu bine te-ai însurat
Ţi-ai luat fată de-mpărat.

Oh, good dear young man,
It was not time for you to die;
It was time for you to marry.
Oh, get up and look around,
For at our house there are many people,

Because they thought we had a wedding.

You, well you have married:
You took a daughter of the King.

Lament verse, Ieud

N-am văzut aşă o mnireasă
Să zie popa acasă

Să te cunune pă masă.
Mnireasa-i-n copîrşeu
Mnirele-i la Dumnezău.

I've never seen such a bride
That the priest comes to the house
And crowns you on the table.
Bride in a coffin;
Groom is with God.

As we have seen in the preceding chapter, funerary rites facilitate the transformation of social relations between the living and the dead and differentiate the relation between the body and the soul, distinguishing the physical manifestation of life from its post-humous immortalization. The starkness of death disrupts the temporal continuity requisite to an ontology of the individual and the collectivity through which society reassures its existence. Death flaunts herself before human production and reproduction (*herself* will be used to maintain the contextual idiom). The projection of human experience beyond itself (that is, the afterlife), however, overcomes the problem posed by a strictly materialist conception of the world. Ceia lume destines life to an eternal reality. Cos-

mologies, genealogies, and constituted histories restore "life" to
temporality, to time immemorial, so to speak.

In this chapter, we will examine the ritual practices and cosmological beliefs associated with "untimely" death—that is, the
death of an unmarried person of marriageable age. Such a death is
untimely because it occurs out of phase with the "time" for death
in the life cycle. (Sex and death have their proper "time.") As the
opening lament verse from Ieud points out:

Nu ți-o fo vremea să mori	It was not time for you to die;
Da ți-o fo vremea să te-nsori.	But it was time for you to marry.

According to H. Stahl, "To die unmarried is to die perilously, because the most important aspect of life has not been realized.
Therefore, a symbolic wedding is performed for the deceased"
(1983, 160).[1] This elaborate practice is done to placate the soul of
the dead; it is one of the many prophylactic acts said to benefit
both the living and the dead, because death is fraught with danger
for everyone involved. Especially perilous are those deaths that
pose "dangers arising from unfulfilled lives" (ibid.). Briefly, it is believed that individuals who leave behind a mortal enemy, an unre-
solved love affair, or other unfinished matters will return in the
forms of their bodies that they no longer inhabit. These "beings"
are generally known as *strigoi* (spirits, ghosts, the living dead).[2] In
the case of the deceased of marriageable age—the most pronounced
and precarious case—unless a symbolic wedding is performed during the funeral, then it is believed that this "person" will return in
search of a mate to fulfill his or her social destiny as well as frustrated sexual desires. Until the soul is satisfied, it cannot rest and
remains a menace to society. Hence, the *nunta mortului* (wedding
of the deceased, or death-wedding) quiets the turbulence caused
by the paradoxical coupling of sexuality and mortality. Sexuality
and mortality are fundamental physical and social dimensions of
the life cycle as well as of the existential crises associated with it.
They are enduring concerns of religion, politics, medicine, philosophy, jurisprudence, literature, and popular culture.[3] The seeming
obsession with this "deadly duo" attests to their ability simultaneously to attract and to repel. Desire and fear are powerful mates to
human endeavor.[4]

In Maramureş, the lives of Christ and the Virgin Mary remain motivating paradigms that curb these forces. Divine discourse has consigned sexuality to marriage, and death to ceia lume. Ritual practices (religious and secular) "familiarize" these dangers that innately threaten the foundation of the social order. Because life-cycle rites constitute a ritual system that addresses society's rules and norms for conduct, what is professed does not necessarily coincide with daily practice. "Ideology" dictates that sexual experience occur within marriage. Thus, unmarried persons of marriageable age are marked by their social status; their role is to seek a mate and to marry. (Marriage is the unmarked category.) If someone of this status dies, then two events must be accomplished: he or she must be married and must be properly buried (and the death-wedding does both). In this situation, however, the logic of the ritual system within the broader framework of cosmology privileges the social status of a person; it does not recognize the particularities of sexual experience. (Transgression is handled in the privacy of confession between parishioner and priest; the ritual consequences are felt in ceia lume.) Sexuality is acknowledged only within marriage. Hence, in some areas, "girls" (unmarried women) who have had children out of wedlock are symbolically married. They are "taken to a willow tree and married to one of its branches; or a death-wedding will take place, but the bridal crown will not be placed upon her head" (personal communication, Professor Mihai Pop, 1985). Social norms insist that the unmarried go to their graves married.[5] And it is the norms of society that are reified in ritual practices of the life cycle. Accordingly, symbolic inversion of status is also possible at the other end of the spectrum. If a widow remarries, then the horea găinii is not performed during her second wedding. This ritual sequence is about sexuality, and widows are already initiated into its secrets. Furthermore, should a widow remarry during the course of her mourning period (a transgression of ritual proscriptions), then her first marriage will be ritually "annulled." The widow goes to the cemetery dressed as a bride. There, she passes her wedding crown over her husband's grave and then gives it to a young girl of marriageable age. (Recall that the bride's crown is placed on the head of a young girl at the conclusion of a wedding.) In this manner, the widow's first marriage is symbolically undone, the price for not respecting the social norms of society. To be sure, sexuality and mortality merit social, if not individual, respect.

Thus, here we will explore the ritual relation of the conjuncture between sexuality and mortality. The nunta mortului provides a comprehensible (although not comprehensive) framework for these two provocateurs of experience. By means of the symbolic wedding of the deceased, the "otherness" of untimely death is dramatically socialized into the life cycle. This ritual creates a symbolic interface between categories ordering relations between the living and the dead, between culture and nature, and between male and female. What, if anything, may an analysis of death-weddings in an isolated Transylvanian village tell us about our own cultural practices? Perhaps it is only through the "otherness" of the "other" that our mythical fascination with sex and death may be represented.[6]

To begin an exploration of the death-wedding, it is first necessary to ponder the relationship between marriage and death. Danforth, in his moving account of Greek death rituals, puzzled: "What two occasions could be more different than the joyful celebration of life that is a wedding and the sad commemoration of death that is a funeral? What could contrast more sharply than the white dress of the bride and the black dress of the widow; the former gaining a husband, the latter losing one?" (1982, 74). The rituals of marriage and death feature the constitution and dissolution of social relations. Although (to indulge in generalization and simplification) marriage leads to biological reproduction while death leads to biological destruction, both result in forms of social reproduction. The rites of marriage and of death are related in structure and content. They emphasize successive processes of separation and incorporation. For example, in a patrilineal system, the bride takes leave of her peers and her natal family to join her husband and affines; the deceased takes leave from the living and joins relatives in ceia lume. There are parallel sequences in each rite.

Wedding	*Funeral*
the dressing of the bride	the dressing of the corpse
asking forgiveness from one's family	asking forgiveness from the living

the procession to the church	the procession to the church cemetery
gift-giving: *pominoc*	alms-giving: *pomenile*
ritual celebratory meals	ritual commemorative meals
ritual toasting of the bride and the groom	ritual toasting of the soul of the deceased

There are marked similarities; however, there are also marked differences, as the color oppositions signal: white represents life and black represents death. The relationship between marriage and death thus is paradoxical, characterized by opposition and identity, difference and likeness—all the stuff of metaphor.[7] Not surprisingly, the relationship is expressed metaphorically. "Metaphors force us to see things in a different light. . . . The power of metaphors lies in their ability to change the way we view our world" (Danforth 1982, 82). Herzfeld, also writing about Greece, stresses that the relation between marriage and death is one of structural analogy, not of identity: "Analogy provides the expressive force of tropes" (1981, 53). Marriage and death are not identical; therefore, they cannot be equated. However, they can be— and are—related.

This metaphorical association between marriage and death is not unique to Romania. Nor is the symbolic wedding of the dead. Related beliefs and practices have been recorded from almost every corner of the world.[8] For the present discussion, it is especially pertinent to mention the significance of this metaphoric relation as it pertains to Christian thought (primarily Catholic).[9] The relationship between Christ and the Church is thought to be a marriage: "Christ loved the Church as husbands their wives" (Ephesians 5:25). Paul similarly regarded it in terms of conjugal love (Feeley-Harnik 1981, 109, citing 2 Corinthians 11:1). Therefore, the Church is feminine. The soul too is feminine. According to von Hildebrand (1970, 102), the relationship between Christ and the soul is a nuptial one. (He additionally quotes C. Gay [1887]: "Whatever the position of a man in other respects, whatever the relationships which bind him to the earth, from the moment his soul is in the grace of God, it is the bride of Christ.") Warner writes that "Jesus is the bridegroom of every soul which is a member of his mystical

body [baptized]" (1959, 366). Christ as bridegroom to the soul and
to the Church is a concept established in the Song of Solomon and
in the Canticle of Canticles (ibid., 168).[10] In the death-wedding
maidens are always married to Christ, the son of God. (This is not
necessarily the case for young men, but the religious value of
divine marriage holds nonetheless.) The theological basis for this
popular allegation may be found in the practices associated with
the "consecrated virgins" (see von Hildebrand 1970, 87–142). The
"consecrated virgin is the wedded spouse of Christ in eternal
union with him. The perfect marriage on earth anticipates what
will continue to be the perfect marriage after death in heaven"
(Warner 1959, 370). The death-wedding represents the "perfect
marriage" of the deceased on earth in anticipation of a fulfilled and
peaceful "life" after death—for the dead and the living.

The *Nunta Mortului*

The unfolding of a death-wedding is the same as the unfolding of
any funeral; the ritual sequences are identical: the parastas, or pre-
funeral service, the removal of the corpse from the house and
courtyard, the cortège, the burial, the pomenile, the commemorative meals. Furthermore, the basic contents of the laments are
alike. (See Appendix D.) Therefore, rather than reiterate the detail
of the preceding chapter, the discussion about the nunta mortului
will be more thematic than schematic. The death-wedding differs
from a usual funeral in the elaboration of the association between
death and marriage, an association that is expressed metaphorically. In this regard, it is worthwhile to note Fernandez's remark
that "the complexity of expressive experience lies in the interplay
of contiguity and similarity associations" (1974, 125). Jakobson,
writing about poetry, pointed out that "where similarity is superin-
duced upon contiguity, any metonymy is slightly metaphorical and
any metaphor has a metonymical tint" (1960, 370).

In the death-wedding, the transformations through which the deceased must go involve the phenomenological actualization of the
funeral as metaphor of a wedding juxtaposed against the metonymic
realization of the funeral process. This juxtaposition is achieved by
the manipulation of symbolic codes. Thus, the deceased, who is
about to be married in death, is dressed in wedding attire; brides—

living or dead—wear white. The bridesmaid is also dressed appropriately for her role. The other participants who "celebrate" this wedding, however, are mourners; accordingly, they are dressed in black funeral clothes. Although the flagbearer carries a flag, the symbol of a wedding, it is made of the black scarves of married women, the symbols of death, instead of the brightly colored scarves of unmarried girls.[11] (Just as death is like marriage, so, it should be recalled, marriage is like death.) While the "bride" or "groom" wears a wedding crown, the mourners respect the conventions of funeral decorum; for example, the men go bareheaded. Like any bride or groom, the deceased is escorted by his or her peers to the "church" for the "marriage" ceremony, that is, to the cemetery for burial. Because these escorts are the pallbearers, this procession simultaneously represents the formal separation from the deceased's social-sexual cohort.[12] This is the only circumstance in which the unmarried (that is, those who are not sexually active, therefore, not polluted) are permitted to come in contact publicly with the dead. While friends accompany their former mate to his or her fate, their sad mission is obvious to all: the bride or groom is in a coffin carried by black-clad escorts. Music is provided by the woeful cries of women.

Throughout the death-wedding, the similarity between death and marriage is symbolically opposed through inversion. (The shining white of marriage glares against the stark black of death.) This inversion occurs both in deed and in verse. The laments are characterized predominantly by negative parallelisms—"the refutation of the metaphorical state in favor of the factual state" (Jakobson 1960, 369). Parallelism enables the relationship between meanings to be explored; negative parallelisms propose a relationship that is then contextualized through contrastive devices. In the analysis of death-wedding laments, attention will focus on the semantic level.[13] Most of the "texts" to be presented are drawn from death-weddings that I attended in Ieud, as well as in the villages of Botiza and Breb. I regret that the written word cannot convey the emotional poignancy that distinguishes these rites.[14]

Lamenters are said to communicate with the dead; therefore, their tearful words are usually directed to particular persons. Addressing someone by name implicitly assumes the participation of that person in the "conversation." The most typical forms of ad-

dress include individual names—Mări, Geo—as well as kin terms—
mama, tata, *frate, soră* (brother, sister).[15] But for a death-wedding,
another set of terms is invoked that emphasizes the deceased's social status as well as the metaphorical relation between death and
marriage. Lamenters refer to the deceased as mnireasă (bride) or
mnire (groom). And like all brides and grooms, the deceased will
be married in a "church" ceremony. The following verses are common variants on this theme.

N-am văzut aşă un mnire	I've never seen such a groom,
Măi Dumni ca şi pă tine.	Oh, Dumi, like you are—
Să zie popa acasă	That the priest comes to the house
Să te cunune pă masă.	To crown you on the table.
Mnirele stă-n copîrşeu	The groom is in a coffin;
Mnireasa-i la Dumnezău.	The bride is God's,
Cu haine albe-mbrăcată	Dressed in white clothes—
N-om vide-o niciodată.	Never shall she be seen.
N-am văzut aşă o mnireasă	I've never seen such a bride
Să zie popa acasă	That the priest comes to the house
Să te cunune pă masă.	And crowns you on the table.
Mnireasa-i-n copîrşeu	Bride in a coffin;
Mnirele-i la Dumnezău.	Groom is with God.
Druştile ti-or ntreba	The bridesmaids will ask you,
Zine mnirele ori ba?	"Is the groom coming or not?"
Mnirele-i fecior de crai	The groom is the son of the King;
Te-a duce de mînă în rai.	He'll lead you by the hand to heaven.

The lament fragments immediately identify the deceased and signal the extraordinary nature of this "wedding." In the nunta mortului, customary practice at a wedding is reversed. The priest
comes to the home of the bride or groom to perform the ceremony
instead of the couple going to him. "To crown you on the table"
refers to the Orthodox marriage service symbolized by the priest's
placing and exchanging the wedding crowns on the heads of the
couple. The "crowning" and "wedding" conducted in the sanctity
of the deceased's home (as opposed to the sanctity of God's home,
the church) is actually the performance of the last rites. The "bride"
or "groom" rests in a coffin.

As the verses indicate, the deceased's intended is usually a son or daughter of God, depending on the gender of the deceased. The husband for a dead bride is always the son of God (Lord Jesus, King of Glory), or a prince, recalling past rulers of Maramureş. (Both terms conjure images of power and divinity.) The bride is a virgin, and, like the consecrated virgins, she is "a bride of Christ."[16] Hers is a "perfect marriage." It is untainted by sin; this bride will follow in Mary's path. Therefore, the concern attributed to the bridesmaids is calmed by the response that the groom is a son of the King and will lead his bride to heaven. Heaven is pictured as a wondrous garden. Marriage results in the bride's alienation from her natal family and incorporation into that of her husband; thus, the bride will move from her mother's garden to her spouse's. In the wedding ceremonial play of Asking for the Bride, it is often said that the bride will leave her mother's garden, where she has blossomed, and be planted in the prince's, where she shall flourish. (Refer to pp. 104–5.) In the funeral rite, however, the deceased is planted in the cemetery "not to grow, but to putrefy"; the cemetery is considered to be an "enclosed garden with a lock." In the death-wedding, the dead bride is married to the son of Christ and "planted" in his garden. It is a garden to which no one has access and from which no one may return. The death-wedding, in part, secures the prevention of a return. Warner, discussing related themes in American culture, points out that "Mary is the crown of nature, the wondrous flower of the new heavenly order. . . . God is born into the world, the virgin proceeds in her blessedness—no man has intervened. She becomes a mother and remains a garden enclosed" (1959, 383). Virginity means purity. In the nunta mortului, pure symbols are related to Christian divinity: God, Christ, the Virgin Mary. For reasons that shall become apparent, this bride's marriage is considered "ideal"; it is a form of divine marriage.[17] The dead bride reproduces the immaculate virtues of Mary: virginity and motherhood.

As indicated in the first verse, a dead groom is also married to a divine being. While this is metaphorically meaningful, in Ieud such a groom is usually wed symbolically to a surrogate mortal bride. This means that an unmarried girl will serve as the deceased's bride during his death-wedding. The father of a dead "bride" observed, "A bride is 'put' only for young men; a groom is never 'put' (for girls)—only a crown."[18] If the young man had a sweetheart, then she fulfills this role; a cousin or neighbor may also volunteer. The symbolic marriage honors the soul of the deceased; but because it is not consummated, the marriage is not binding. A surrogate bride is free to marry, and, indeed, the bride at the first wedding I attended in Ieud had been the bride at a death-wedding seven weeks before her own marriage.

Another couplet indicates the unusual nature of this wedding:

N-am văzut aşă-o mnireasă	I've not seen such a bride
Să o ducă cîte şăsă.	To be carried by six.

Usually, en route to the church ceremony, the bride and groom are accompanied by their friends. At this wedding, the "bride" is conducted only by six girlfriends: her pallbearers.

Many of the laments during a death-wedding focus on the contradiction produced by untimely death. The life-cycle stage heralds marriage and arouses all the expectations associated with the celebration of a wedding:

O bunu mîndru fecior	Oh, good, dear young man,
Nu ţi-o fo vremea să mori	It was not time for you to die;
Ţi-o fo vremea să te-nsori.	It was time for you to marry.
Ţi-o fo vremea să trăieşti	It was time for you to live
Şî să te căsătoreşti.	And to wed.
Uă scoala-te şi te uită	Oh, get up and look around,
Că la noi îi lume multă	For at our house there are many people,
C-o gîndit că facem nuntă.	Because they thought we were having a wedding.
S-o strîns fete şî feciori	The girls and boys have gathered,
C-o gîndit că tu te-nsori.	Because they thought you were marrying.
Scoala-te şî îţi ale	Get up and choose
O fată pă care-i vre	A girl to your liking;
Nouă la tăţi ne-a plăcea.	That will please all of us.
Bunuc cum te-ai însurat	Dear one, how you have married—
Nici la unu nu ni-i drag	Not one of us is pleased,
Dipt ce n-ai zinit cu steag.	For you haven't come with the flag.
În loc de steag de mătasă	Instead of a silk flag,
Stau prapurii lîngă casa.	The church banners lean against the house.

| Î loc de steag împodobdit | Instead of a decorated flag, |
| Steagu negru de jelit. | A black flag of mourning. |

The functioning of negative parallelism at the semantic level is readily apparent in this lengthy excerpt.[19] The predominant emphasis of the "text" is on the wedding metaphor; however, the subtext of death is forcefully present. The lamenter states that it was not time to die, but to marry; she then describes what happens at a wedding. Here the structural analogy between wedding and funeral rites is especially obvious. Attention is called to the number of people who have come to the house. This occurs at both weddings and funerals. Moreover, when young people gather at a friend's home, it is normally to socialize. (Recall the evening şezătoare, as well as the more contemporary diversions such as listening to music or watching television.) The couplet suggests that they came to celebrate their friend's wedding, when, in reality, they mourn his death. The young man is asked to arise and choose a spouse—that would please everyone. During a wedding, the guests say that they have come to "see how the groom bargained," to lend their encouragement. This act of social approval incorporates the couple into the cohort of married people. Marriage is secularly sanctified by familial and communal endorsement. Only in the final couplets is the metaphor demystified. No one approves of this young man's marriage. There is no brightly colored flag of hope that proclaims the vitality of marriage each time the flagbearer thrusts it gaily into the air; instead, there are the church banners that create a visible bond with God as the procession solemnly makes its way to the cemetery. And there is the black wedding flag with its quiet crown of flowers that instills yet deeper sorrow because it reminds the mourners that this "flower" of a person will putrefy, not flourish.

Generally, a marriage does not take place without the approval of the respective families of the bride and groom. But death does not honor the norms of society. One mother, during the evening of the parastas, expressed her pained shock about her daughter's death in the following manner:

Uă mîndrucă şî mnireasă	Oh, little beauty and bride,
Uă a me inimă mni-i arsă.	Oh, my heart is burnt.
Uă mîndrucă te-ai măritat	Oh, little beauty, you have married;

Nimnic nu ne-ai întrebat.	You did not ask us anything
Şî nimic n-ai povestit	And you did not say
Că tu vrei să te măriţi.	That you wish to marry.

She continued:

Scoală şî ni-om sfătui	Get up and we'll chat,
C-amu-i sara cununii.	For it is the eve of your wedding.

The mother knows that her daughter's "marriage" is not negotiable; it is inevitable. Therefore, she locates her despair in the more comforting mask of metaphor. On the eve of her daughter's "wedding," she suggests that they have one last mother-daughter talk before the event that will separate them forever. Marriage, like death, severs relationships.

One of the deceased's sisters, in anticipation of the "wedding," recommended that they prepare for it:

Uă mîndrucă şî mnireasă	Oh, little beauty and bride—
Scoală mîndră hai pîn casă	Get up, beauty, around the house,
Şî noi ti-om găta mnireasă.	And we'll ready you as a bride.
Uă noi mnireasă ti-om găta	Oh, we'll ready you as a bride,
Ş-apoi te duci a giura	And then you will go take the oath
Cum mere tătă lumea.	As everyone does.
Uă noi cu drag ti-om aştepta	Oh, we will await you lovingly,
Şî ti-om pune după masă	And we'll put you at the table
C-aşă-i rîndu la mnireasă.	As befits a bride.

The lamenter alludes to the ritual dressing of the bride before her departure for the church service where she takes the marriage vows as everyone does. Again, the structural affinity is that everyone marries—and everyone dies. At a wedding, following the church service, the celebrants embark upon a series of meals. After the Asking for the Bride, she and the groom sit together at the table, recipients of their guests' well-wishes. A strigătură comments on the virtues of commensality:

Dragu mni-i de casa noastă	Our house pleases me,
Şî de cine-s după masă.	And so do those at the table.

The literal translation is "behind the table"; it refers to the nuptial couple sitting behind the table in the far corner of the room. Fochi

(1964, 516) points out that in a death-wedding, the bride or groom is not seated "behind" or "at" the table, but rather is crowned "on" the table—*să-te cunune pă masă*. Ritual meals also honor the dead, and lamenters always invite the deceased to return home to be placed "behind the table" and to share a meal with the family.

Marriage, of course, entails the reorganization of social relations; within a family, the details of this change are usually discussed and prearranged—but not in the case of a death-wedding.

Uă sorucă şî hai Ga	Oh little sister, you, Ga,
Nu m-am gîndit de aiestea.	I didn't think of this
În lume cînd am pornit	Before I went away to work.
Vai bine ne-am sfătuit.	My, we talked about everything.
Telegram-am căpătat	We received a telegram
Că îi musai de plecat.	That it was necessary to leave immediately
Să zinim pînă acasă	To come home,
Mîndrucă că ieşti mnireasă.	Little beauty, because you are a bride.

In this verse, the deceased's sister recounts how she learned of her youngest sister's "marriage." Cooperativization as it occurred in Ieud has meant that most members of this family have had to seek work as migrant laborers. They reconvene at their home on ritual occasions. Otherwise, everyone in the household leaves, except the mother and youngest daughter, Gasie (shortened to Ga). Before one such departure, the sisters "talked about everything" because they knew they would not see each other for a while. That "for a while" might be forever never entered anyone's thoughts. Ostensibly, there was no reason. But then Gasie's father and siblings received the fateful telegram urging them to return hastily. *Musai de plecat* has a double meaning: it was necessary for them to depart immediately to arrive in time for the "wedding"; death also made it necessary for Gasie to leave without delay (she would be buried in three days). I happen to have been at the post office when an utterly distraught mother arrived to send this telegram. It read simply: "*Gasie s-o făcut mnireasă*" (Gasie has made herself a bride). The grammatical construction conveyed the exact meaning. Gasie did not ask anyone's permission to marry. During a wedding, the bride's mother is blamed for her daughter's fate: "*Maica-ta ti-o făcut vînzare*" (your mother sold you). A wedding takes place with a mother's consent. A death-wedding does not.

Throughout her exhausted lamenting, Gasie's mother voiced her objections:

Ieu de noră nu te-aş da	I would not have given you as daughter-in-law,
Că tu ieşti mai pititea.	For you are younger.
Uă mîndrucă şî tu Ga	Oh, little beauty, you, Ga,
Rău m-ai putut supăra.	You have hurt me badly.
Uă pă cînd o sosît acasă	Oh, by the time they arrived home,
Gasie s-o făcut mnireasă.	Gasie had made herself a bride.
Uă tu mnireasă te-ai făcut	Oh, you made yourself a bride
Pă tăte le-ai întrecut.	You beat all of them:
Ieu mai tri fete am avut	I had three more girls,
Mîndrucă-naintea ta.	Little beauty, before you.
Ieu tăt aşă m-am gîndit	I always reasoned
Dacă am fete bugăte	Since I have many daughters
Nu le-aş da nurori pă tăte.	That I wouldn't give them all as daughters-in-law.
Că tu ieşti mai tinere	Because you are younger,
Nu te-aş si dat nurore.	I wouldn't have given you.
Tu cu mine-n casă-i sta	You would remain with me at home,
Şî ginere mni-oi lua	And I would take a son-in-law.
Sîngură nu mni-ţi lăsa.	You wouldn't leave me alone.

The mother, in the expression of her grief, alternated between self-reflection and admonishing her daughter. Encapsulated in these couplets is a commentary on the structure of social relations. The rules of marriage prescribe that daughters should marry in order of age. Two of Gasie's three older sisters were not yet married. It was not her turn; nevertheless, she beat them by marrying first, of her own accord. Moreover, this unexpected wedding confounded the family's plans. A girl who is an only child or the youngest of many is often spared separation from her family and the tribulations of living with a mother-in-law. In this circumstance, the daughter does not marry out; instead, a young man marries in as ginere. So it was to have been with Gasie; she was the one designated to keep her mother company. (In other moments, Gasie's mother addressed her own mother in ceia lume. She asked if she had taken Gasie to that world to lessen her loneliness there.)

Meanwhile, Gasie's sisters berated her for having abandoned their mother:

Noi în lume om pleca   We'll leave to go work,
D-apoi, mama, ce s-a fa?   And then, what will mother do?
Că sîngură s-a afla.   She'll be alone.

The emotional and existential conflicts that death provokes for the living are perhaps most intensified by untimely death. For Gasie's two unmarried sisters, her death temporarily heightened the contradictions they felt between their own desires to marry and their apprehensions about the consequences of marriage. These gnawing anxieties were projected onto the imagery of the death-wedding where they found eloquent expression:

Uă sorucă sora me   Oh, little sister, my sister—
Tînără se duce ie.   So young she goes.
Tu ieşti fată tinere   You are a young girl,
Şi nu te-am dat nurore.   And we didn't give you as
                                    daughter-in-law.

Nu te-am dat noră din casă   We didn't give you as a daughter-
                                    in-law from the house,
Că ieşti mai mnică mnireasă.   For you are the youngest bride.
Ia-mă sorucă cu tine   Take me, little sister, with you,
Că la fete-acolo-i bine.   For it is good for girls there.
Îi rău în lume a trăi   It's hard living in the world,
Că ieşti tăt cu străini.   For you are always with
                                    strangers,

Şi străinii-s tare răi   And strangers are very bad;
Nu-s ca şi părinţii tăi.   They're not like your parents.
Uă sorucă şi mnireasă   Oh, little sister and bride—
Tu bine te-ai măritat   You have married well,
Dup-un fecior de-mpărat.   After a son of the King's.
Iel ti-o dus la curtea lui   He has taken you to his
                                    courtyard

În fundu pămîntului.   In the bottom of the earth,
Uă unde leac de soare nu-i   Oh, where there isn't a glimmer
                                    of sunshine.

Nici nu nînge nici nu-ndeaţă   It doesn't snow, nor does it
                                    freeze,

Nici să face dimineaţă.   Nor does it become morning.
Uă bine te-ai măritat   Oh, well you have married,

Că la socri nu te-am dat.	Because we didn't give you to in-laws.
Uă bărbatu nu te-a toi	Oh, your husband won't scream at you,
Nici socrii nu te-a sfădii.	Nor will in-laws fight with you.
Da noi supărați om si	But we will be troubled
Cît pă lume-om mai trăi.	However long we live.

(Despite the repetition of couplets cited previously, I have presented this excerpt unabridged because it touchingly illustrates the "thought-feeling" process involved in the bricolage of metaphoric discourse.)[20] The opening couplets repeat the social structural point discussed above about the youngest daughter. Gasie would not have gone as noră to her husband's house had she lived. Upon her marriage, she would have assumed a new identity, however, defined by her husband's patriline. If she had died after marriage, she would have joined his family—hers acquired through marriage—in ceia lume. Kinship relations are enduring; they are reproduced in the other world.[21] But in a death-wedding the marriage is symbolic; it is not consummated, and creates no tie to a "stranger-husband's" family. Such a bride is not alienated from her natal family either in this world or that one. This conjuncture sheds light on the notion that the nunta mortului is an "ideal marriage." Normally, girls marry to live "among strangers" (who are never like family). As the strigătura warned, a husband isn't a bride's brother, and a mother-in-law isn't her mother; they will not accord her the same care.[22] Gasie's sister alludes to these "realities" in her statements about life in the other world as being good for girls. There, girls remain among loved ones. They are not subjected to "others."

The above couplets beg for a sensitivity to the particularities of context (in addition to the generalities of social structure); there are other levels of meaning subtly woven into these pained words. The lamenter herself was soon to marry and go live "among strangers," thereby making the two sisters' situations comparable. The implication, however, is that the deceased is better off.[23] She lived at home until the time of her "marriage." The lamenter, in contrast, did not have this good fortune. Through her sorrow, she also expressed consternation about the conditions forced on her. She was a regular member of the migrant work force. Although she was accompanied by family members, she still had to work away from home and live among strangers before marriage. In a sense, this situation was as alienating as marriage and tantamount to death. She and her living sisters were victims of a form of "double burden" that Gasie evaded through her "divine marriage." To be sure, there is ambiguity surrounding perceptions of "life" in that world. On the one hand, the "bride" is not alienated from her natal family; on the other, she has been taken to her husband's courtyard in the bottom of the earth (reproducing the normal pattern of social relations in which patrilocal residence is customary). In a patrilineal system, the nunta mortului avoids the hardships of marriage (especially for girls), while fulfilling the cultural ideal about it. And so a death-wedding may be thought to provide the best of both worlds.[24]

Relations between the two worlds are managed through various forms of exchange. Exchange is an essential feature of social interaction; hence, exchange is part of a lamenter's attempt to make sense of death. Marriage establishes exchange between families in this world; death, between families in this world and that. But in a death-wedding, the material components that solidify lines of exchange opened by marriage are transformed into spiritual "goods." Recall that a groom is expected to provide the house and its furniture; the bride furnishes the rest. These expectations are, however, immaterial for a death-wedding. The bride's family need not concern themselves, for example, with provision of her dowry:

Uă bine te-am măritat	We have married you well:
Puţină zestre ţi-am dat.	We gave little for your dowry—
Uă mnirele nu o poftit	The groom didn't request it—
Numa popii am plătit.	We only paid the priest.
Şî-ătîta ţi-o fo zestrea	That was all of your dowry,
Cît am plătit la popa.	What we paid the priest.
Noi nu ţi-am dat zestre multă	We didn't give you much in the way of dowry,
Numa cît îţi facem nuntă.	Only what it took to make the wedding.

The expense of weddings and funerals is of concern to all families. These events are extremely costly and require planning. For weddings, in addition to the meals, church fees, and the like, musicians must be engaged, and a dowry offered or a house built. From this perspective, a death-wedding is economical: there are rarely musicians; there is no dowry or house to worry about. (Although the coffin may be considered a house, it is considerably less expensive than a regular dwelling.) This type of wedding requires only the funds to pay for the event itself, that is, the priest, the gravedigger, the meals, the coffin, and so forth.

After the mourning period, it was hoped that one of Gasie's sisters would marry; while the celebration of a joyous event would have a certain bitter sweetness to it, it would counteract some of the pain of loss. But Gasie's premature demise did not release her extended family from the grip of tragedy. (In Chapter 3, death was accused of being enamored of a family that had experienced several losses; "she" was admonished to try another family for a while.) When I departed from Ieud, I regretted not having been able to share in that family's joy as well as their sorrow. A year and a half later, I returned for a brief visit. Shortly after my arrival, a young messenger came to the house, inviting me to a wedding at Gasie's family. My pleasure was momentary. In the excited confusion of my return, the message had been unclear. Indeed, there was a wedding, but not one that they (or I, for that matter) could enjoy. The young daughter of Gasie's eldest sister was to be "married." The deceased's mother, overcome with exhaustion, lamented:

Sorucă şi hăi Ga	Little sister, hey, Ga,
Scoală-te şi îi zini	Get up and come,
Mîndrucă pînă la noi	Dear one, to us,
Că la noi astăzî îi nuntă.	Because today we have a wedding.
Scoală-te şi îi zini	Get up and come,
Cu druşca ta îi grăi.	And talk with your bridesmaid.
Uă mîndrucă tu Mări	Oh, dear one, you, Mări,
Druşc-ai fo la mătuşă-ta.	You were your aunt's bridesmaid.
Uă mîndrucă tu Mări	Oh, dear one, you, Mări,
Tu de aici îi porni	You are starting out from here
Şi la Gasie îi sosî.	And will arrive at Gasie's.

Mări had been her aunt's honorary "bridesmaid." As is true for all close kin, Gasie was invited to her niece's marriage. The hope given by metaphor is fleeting, however; in the end, Gasie's sister— Mări's mother—knew that her own daughter would join Gasie in ceia lume. Mări's maternal grandfather (Gasie's father) sat wearily on a bench, discussing the tragedies that had befallen them: "Ioi, domnişoară, what can I tell you? You see that this time we have not 'put' a bridesmaid. How could we? It is said about weddings that the bridesmaid will be the next to marry. And now Mări has 'married.' That's tradition, and we can't have that happen again." In the wedding ritual, the bridesmaid and flagbearer are coupled; they symbolically represent the ritual reproduction of society. In practice, it is rare that this ritually constituted couple fulfills its destiny. That is not the point. Nor does it matter if Mări's grandfather really believed tradition had proved itself. The succession of events made the posited relationship at the very least compelling to think about.

Whatever the "reality," relations between the two worlds are maintained through periodic communication with the dead that a funeral makes possible. Because kinship relations are thought to be continuous, the living frequently wonder whether a dead relation has called a loved one to the other world to alleviate longing and loneliness. (Perhaps it is not only "death" herself that perpetrates death among the living. "Who can know?" a grieving woman asked, without expecting an answer.) Earlier, Gasie's mother had wondered whether her own mother had called Gasie to her. Now she was suspect of Gasie's role regarding Mări:

Nu ştiu moarte ti-o luat	I don't know if death has taken you,
Ori Gasie ti-o temat.	Or if Gasie has called you.
Ori ti-o temat Gasie la ie	Perhaps Gasie has called you to her
Să nu sie sîngure.	So she won't be alone.
Uă ti-o luat mîndră şi pă tine	Oh, she has taken you also, beauty,
Uă că la fete acolo-i bine.	Oh, because it is good for girls there.

That it is good for girls in that world is suggested as Gasie's motivation (see previous discussion on the "ideal marriage").

Mări's mother also implied that Gasie was responsible for Mări's death, that she had called her to her. But there can be no certainty in these matters; consequently, Mări's mother continued her search for a way to understand:

În scoală-te şi te uită	Get up and look around,
Că zin fetele la nuntă.	For girls are coming to the wedding.

Uă mîndrucă nunta ta	Little beauty, your wedding
Ruptu-mni-o inimioara.	Has broken my dear heart.
Nu ştiu moartea ti-o luat	I don't know if death has taken you,
Ori moaşa ta ti-o temat	Or your grandmother has called you,
Că numele iei l-ai purtat.	For you wore her name.

Mǎri had been named for a grandmother who had died. Perhaps she—and not death, as personified being, or Gasie, for whom she had been bridesmaid—had taken her. Mǎri's mother continued her "discussion" with her daughter as long as possible. She also used the opportunity to send a message to her youngest sister:

Uă mîndrucă tu Mări	Oh, little beauty, you, Mări—
Uă cînd o fo mai mîndru trai	Oh, when life was at its best,
Bunucă de şapte ai	Dear one, at seven years,
Te muţi de la noi în rai.	You have moved from us to heaven.
Mîndrucă tu Mări	Little beauty, you, Mări—
Acolo dacă-i sosî	There, if you arrive
Cu Gasie vi-ţi întîlni.	And meet with Gasie,
Spune-i tu Mări, aşe:	Tell her this, Mări:
Zie acasă de-a vre	Come home if she'd like,
Că mama-i supărăţe.	Because mama is very upset.
Că tare rău s-o supărat	She has been very upset
De cînd ie s-o măritat	Since [Gasie] married
Şî pă tine ti-o luat.	And has taken you.
Uă sorucă şî hăi Ga	Oh, little sister, you, Ga—
Nu te doare inima	Doesn't your heart pain you
Să-mni iei fata cea mai mare?	To take my eldest daughter?
O sorucă şî hăi Ga	Oh, little sister, you, Ga—
Uă asară dac-a-nsera	Oh, this evening when it gets dark,
Vă luaţi mîndră de mînă	Take [my] beauty by the hand
Şî ziniţi la noi la cină.	And come to us for dinner—
Că noi cina om găta	Because we'll make dinner
Şî pă voi v-om aştepta.	And we'll wait for you.

Mǎri was only seven years old. At that age, children are thought to go directly to heaven because they have not entered the stage of sin. Death-weddings are usually held for those of marriageable age, those who are capable of sin. Mǎri's death, however, was understood in terms of the dictates of the wedding tradition that the bridesmaid become a bride herself; therefore, she was married.[25]

How else did Mări's wedding, like all death-weddings, differ from those of the living?

Tu Mări la nunta ta	You, Mări, at your wedding,
N-aud zicînd cetera	I don't hear the violin playing—
Numa zderînd pă mă-ta.	Only your mother crying.
Bine te-ai măritat	You have married well,
Că la socri nu ti-o dat.	Because she didn't give you to in-laws,
Şî socri nu ti-or toi	And in-laws won't fight with you.
Mă-ta supărat-a si.	Your mother will be troubled.

There are no musicians at Mări's wedding. Instrumental music accompanies celebratory occasions; it is considered by Ieudeni inappropriate accompaniment at a nunta mortului.[26] Not all villages adhere to this practice. In some there are musicians; however, they walk bare-headed and play songs of sorrow.[27] The metaphor is always juxtaposed against the fact.

The only music to accompany a death-wedding in Ieud is that supplied by the women's lamenting. The mother cries, as she would at a wedding, but for different reasons. She will not later be blamed for "selling" her daughter. There is an implicit emotional inversion in the last couplet: the bride will not be troubled by her in-laws as she normally would be; instead, her mother will be the troubled one.

A last excerpt from these related death-weddings illustrates the undoing of figures of speech as a lamenter confronts the harshness of death. While Mări's casket was being lowered into the ground, final exhortations pierced the heavy air:

Doamne unde ti-or tomni	My God, where they'll put you,
Mîndră să nu poţi grăi.	Beauty, so you can't speak.
Tu Mări mîndră mnireasă	You, Mări, beautiful bride,
Ca şî-o floare din fereastă.	Like a flower in the window:
Amu vezi că-i-nflorită	First, you see that it is blossoming;
Dîntr-o dată-i veştejîtă.	All of a sudden, it has withered.
Uă mîndrucă mîndra me	Oh, little beauty, my beauty—
Faţa ta-i ca sansiu	Your face is like a carnation
Sî-a negri ca pămîntu.	And will blacken like the earth.

| Faţă ta-i ca şî spuma | Your face is like whey |
| Sî-a negri ca şî tina. | And will blacken like mud. |

The symbols of health and vitality (and therefore of marriage)—
carnations of love, and milk that is pure and nourishes—will be replaced by those of physical demise (and therefore, of death)—the
black earth that is both death's color and locale.[28]

The structural relation between marriage and death is, by now,
evident. But there are affinities with other ritual events as well.[29]
These affinities become explicit when a death-wedding coincides
with ritual celebrations associated with the calendar. These calendar celebrations are incorporated into the improvised content of
the laments that reveal the details of life in addition to those of
death. (Again, laments are temporally keyed.) Christmas and Easter are preeminently occasions to celebrate communal as well as
familial prosperity. They are also integrally entwined with the life
and death of Christ. At Christmas, secular and religiously inspired
death-resurrection plays are performed.[30] The church enacts the
sacred version of the resurrection of Christ at Easter. Both rites
are preceded by periods of abstinence, rewarded by the excesses
that ensue. Ritual feasting (inasmuch as resources permit) and social activity abound. Moreover, these holidays each mark the re-
newal of courtship endeavors, prohibited during Advent and Lent.
The "marriage season" is reinaugurated by communal dances traditionally held on the second day of Christmas and of Easter. Therefore, Dumitru's untimely death during the Christmas holidays
caused terrible anguish. He was in his early thirties, ready to be
married, but instead, he was buried on New Year's Day. (See Appendix C, II.) A sister wailed:

Uă de mine măi Dumni	Oh my, hey, Dumi—
Uă în scoală-te nu durni	Oh, get up, don't sleep!
Ţi-o zinit tăţi pretini.	All of your friends have come to you—
O zinit feciori şî fete	The bachelors and girls have come—
Şî le roagă să te ierte	And beg them to forgive you,
Şî altu să nu te-aştepte.	And not to wait for you again
Nici la gioc şî nici la nuntă	Neither at the dance nor at a wedding,

Că te duci pă vreme multă.	Because you shall be gone a long time.
Nici la nuntă nici la gioc	Not at a wedding, nor at the dance,
Că nu-i mai zini deloc.	Because you will not return at all.
Că altu nu-i mai zini	For you will not come again,
Că te duci a putrezî.	Because you are going to rot.

During the Christmas holiday period (from Christmas Eve until Epiphany), people go caroling from house to house in age groups. Children carol from the late afternoon until the early hours of the evening; teens and the unmarried begin their rounds at nine and continue until dawn; married couples and elders start out at midnight. The night is filled with the echoes of music and good cheer. At each home, the carolers sing a few songs and then are invited inside to drink and eat. "What better way to acknowledge a sense of community?" a villager remarked with a twinkle in his eye. (In general, enmities are temporarily "forgotten," although some people do avoid certain homes; in such a large village, there is always a plausible rationalization.) This visit also provides eligible bachelors and young women a not so inconspicuous opportunity to assess the "ways and means" of prospective mates. (The handiwork of available girls is displayed on the walls, beds, and tables.) After a bit, the group moves on. Needless to say, New Year's Eve at Dumitru's house was like no other New Year's Eve there. Everyone came, as expected, but their purpose was different. Normally, Dumitru would have gone on with them. Instead, he was oblivious to their presence. His sister tells him to "ask their forgiveness" for leaving them. The iertăciunea is a necessary component of weddings and funerals and serves to separate a person from former relations.[31] He would no longer join his cohort in those familiar social activities that applaud youth and vitality (the dance and weddings). Dumitru's cousin elaborated upon these themes:

Uă de mine măi Dumni	Oh my goodness, Dumi—
Azî noapte cam pă la doi	Last night around two
S-o strîns fete şi feciori	The girls and bachelors gathered
Şi o zinit Dumni la voi.	And came to your house.
Şi mîndru ti-o colindat	They serenaded you beautifully.

Tu-n casă nu i-ai temat	But you did not invite them to come in,
Nici nimnică nu le-ai dat.	And you gave them nothing.
Cum bdietu să-i temi-în casă?	But how could you invite them, poor dear?
C-amu nu mai ai viaţă.	Because now you don't have your life,
Că amu nu poţi grăi	For now you can't talk;
Astăzî pleci a putrezî.	Today you go to putrefy.
Anu-aiesta ce-o-nceput	This year that has begun,
Tu văruc îi sta în lut.	You, dear cousin, will stay in clay.
Anu-aiesta care zine	This year that is coming,
Tu văruc îi sta subt glie.	You, cousin, will stay beneath the earth.

Dumitru's friends came to honor him. They were met with silence, the antisociality of death. The intensity of grief throughout Dumitru's death-wedding was exacerbated by its convergence with the celebration of the new year (and expectations of his marriage soon thereafter). The syncretism of the otherwise differentiated emphases of marriage, death, and (re)birth in the death-wedding and the Christmas–New Year's customs was overwhelming; so was the emotional response. Under any circumstances, a nunta mortului is extraordinary; the confluence of conditions regarding Dumitru's death magnified that which was already out of the ordinary. It is often the extreme that illuminates the essence.

The death-wedding as a mode of conceptualizing and categorizing experience is deeply embedded in local culture. In 1979, a family finally received definitive confirmation of their son's death; he had not returned from World War II. (See Appendix C, III.) When he had gone off to fight, he had been a bachelor. Now that his death was certain, he had to be buried properly so that his soul could rest. Therefore, he also had to be wed. A full death-wedding took place. However, there was no body. In its stead was a young man's hat placed on a table behind which a surrogate bride, the flag-bearer, and the wedding-funeral entourage stood. In the eyes of God, this young man had taken the solemn vows of marriage and had received the holy blessing. He, and his relatives, would live peacefully.

Victims of war, dead among strangers, cause great anguish for their families.[32] Not all the wounded perish at the front, however. One young man was fortunate enough to return home, where he died soon thereafter. Dying at home was a luxury that many of his compatriots did not have. At his funeral, also a death-wedding, the following words were heard:

Uă bunuc şi măi Ioa	Oh, good one, you, Ioa—
Multe ti-o putut mînca.	Much happened to you:
Cum ai scăpat să nu mori	How you escaped without dying
Între plumbdi ca ploi din nori.	Amid a rain of bullets;
Cum ai scăpat cu viaţă	How you escaped with your life
Între plumbdi ca ploi de deaţă.	Amid a hailstorm of bullets.
C-a me inimă-i voiosă	My heart is overjoyed,
C-ai murit bunuc acasă.	Because you died, dear one, at home.
Pă tine cînd ti-om dori	When we shall long for you,
Batăr mormîntu l-om şti.	At least we'll know where your grave is.
Bugăţi mor pîn ţări străine	So many die in foreign lands:
De-a lor mormînt nu şti nime.	No one knows their graves,
Nici nu o avut sălaş	Nor was there a coffin,
Nici pînză pă obraz.	Nor a covering over the cheek.
Uă bunuc şi măi loa	Oh, dear one, you, Ioa—
Uă steag mîndru ţi-am făcut	We made you a beautiful flag,
Cum alţi feciori n-o avut.	Like other fellows didn't have.
I mîndru şî-n tri culori	It is beautiful with the tricolor,
Cum n-o avut alţi feciori.	Such as the others didn't have.

Again, the innovative use of symbols is poignant—and to the point.

As noted in the preceding chapter, one of the horrors linked to death away from loved ones is that the deceased has died "without light" to brighten the path to ceia lume and to protect him or her from potential dangers. This cruel fate is typically associated with those who have died at the front and, increasingly, with those who have died in hospitals. Another "modern" context in which death without the benefit of light occurs is murder. Until recently, murder was a relatively unknown phenomenon in Maramureş. People heard that it happened in urban areas, but not nearby ones. That is no longer the case as crime, violence, and divorce creep into local urban communities or fill the accounts of migrant workers about their experiences away from home.[33] Tales about thefts, alcoholic and sexual debaucheries, and gruesome auto or train accidents augment the customary fare of gossip. But murder is still rare in a village. Hence, a murder in a nearby village shook the sensibilities of the entire valley. The brutality of this heinous crime stretched beyond comprehension: an innocent child had been slain. Her assassin, a young man from a southern Transylvanian city, had come to Maramureş to see its much-admired beauty. He allegedly had some vague connection to the victim's family. Shortly after his arrival in the village, a streak of bad weather broke. It was the middle of summer, and every able body hastened to the fields. He offered to assist. The village was deserted. After a few days, the young man complained that he felt ill and was sent to the peasant family's home to rest. Out of generous concern, they sent their eight-year-old daughter to check on his needs and bring him some bread.[34] That was the last time they were to see her. The family returned late that evening and discovered an empty house. Their daughter was nowhere to be found; the young man was gone. They notified the police, stunned by the supposed kidnapping. It was an unsettled night. Early the next morning, the girl's mother climbed up into the attic to get corn flour out of the sack for a breakfast of mămăligă. Suddenly the family heard hysterical shrieks from the attic. The mother had found her daughter's body stuffed into the sack. Her child had been stabbed twice in the heart and across the right upper arm. It was a horrifying sight. Mări was to have celebrated her ninth birthday on the Sunday that she instead wed a son of God. This was spiritual restitution for human violence.[35]

A family tragedy had suddenly become a communal one. The village was engulfed in shock and grief. Much to my surprise, the girl had not been molested. It was a crime not easily understood, but explanations had to be supplied. Rumor had it that her attacker had attempted to set the straw bed on fire; however, it did not burn and she was "saved" from a final indignity. (At least her soul would be released through the funeral rites as opposed to burned through a criminal cremation.) The pathological was countered by the miraculous. God had prevented the destruction of the village; the houses are mostly wooden and a fire would have been catastrophic. Mări's death-wedding was attended by many hundreds of mourners, young and old. Their faces revealed the depths of horror and revulsion. Mări's mother was consumed by her grief. Her emotional exhaustion could be felt simply by looking at her. She could no longer "sing" her laments; they were shouted hoarsely as she gazed distractedly at her daughter. This "bride" was a disconcerting sight. Mări, with her fair skin and long blond hair, lay in her coffin, dressed in white and surrounded by flowers. The contrast between the symbols of life and death was disturbing. What otherwise would have been an angelic image was distorted by the discoloration of her face—visible signs of her murder.[36] The laments expressed the shock felt by everyone:

Rău mă doare inima	My heart aches badly
Tu Mări de moartea ta.	About your death, Mări.
Ai fost ca şi împuşcată	It is as though you were shot
Şi din cuţit demnicată.	And cut into tiny pieces with a knife.
Nu ti-o tăiet la o mînă	You weren't stabbed in the hand;
Ti-o tăiet drept în inimă!	He stabbed you right in the heart!
Tu Mări la moartea ta	At your death, Mări—
Nu am aprins lumnina.	I didn't light a candle.
Strajnică moarte-ai avut	You had a frightful death;
Tînără te-ai pus în lut.	You've been put in clay at a young age.

No one had lit candles to protect Mări from harm because they had not known that she was dead.

Tu Mări la nunta ta	You, Mări, at your wedding,
Gîndit-am că m-oi găta.	I thought I would dress
Cu haine şi cu mărgele	With fine clothes and beads—
Nu cu-atîta dor şi jele.	Not with so much longing and sorrow;
Şi cu struţuri de barşon	And with velvet ribbons—
Nu cu lacrimi şi cu dor.	Not with tears and longing.
Nu ti-ai măritat dup-un domn	You didn't marry a gentleman,
Da ti-o tăiet un vagabond.	But you were knifed by a vagabond.

This was, to be sure, not the wedding Mări's relatives had envisioned for her. The final couplet incorporates the extremes of modern times. On the one hand, work conditions today make it pos-

sible for a young woman to meet a "gentleman" in the city—a man
from there or someone who has adopted urban ways. (There is a
recognition of class disparity implicit in this term. Formerly, domni
were always among the privileged, although they were also looked
on with disparagement.[37] Now, anyone theoretically can become a
domn through upward mobility.) On the other hand, there is also
an increase in urban crime; rape and murder are becoming more
common. Moreover, just as domni travel from towns to villages, so
do vagabonds; they are not confined within city limits. Mări had
become a victim of the changing times.[38] Nonetheless, this heinous
wrong was "righted" through Mări's spiritual marriage to the son of
God. Her soul would rest peacefully in ceia lume. And that, of
course, is the purpose of the death-wedding.

Symbolic marriages, whether grounded in popular or in institutionalized religious beliefs about relations between the living and
the dead, find profound resonance in Romanian culture, especially
exemplified by the *Miorița*, the inspiring traditional Romanian ballad from which the following is excerpted (Fochi 1964, 772):

Iar le cea măicuță	But to that mother,
Să nu-i spui drăguță.	Don't tell her, dearest.
Că la nunta mea	For at my wedding,
A căzut o stea.	A star fell.
Soarele și luna	The sun and moon
Mi-a ținut cununa	Held my crown;
Preoți munții mari.	Priests, the large mountains;
Păsări lăutari.	Birds, the musicians.
. . . . . .	. . . . . .
Să-i spui curat	Tell her sincerely
Că m-am însurat	That I have been married
C-o fată dă crai	To a daughter of the King
P-o gură de rai.	At the mouth of heaven.

The *Miorița* is known all over Romania and has many variants.[39] It
is frequently characterized as a romantic idealization of pastoralism
(Pop and Ruxăndoiu 1976, 320–29). The *Miorița* tells of a shepherd
whose fellow shepherds plot to murder him and steal his sheep.
One of his flock, a miraculous lamb, informs the shepherd of the
designs on his life.[40] Rather than defend himself, the young shepherd resigns himself to his fate. He requests that he be buried in
his favorite place—the sheepfold (*stînă*)—and that his instruments

be placed at his head. He also asks that his death be presented to his mother as an allegorical death-wedding. She is to be told that he has married the black earth or a beautiful princess; that the sun and moon are his godparents; that birds and sheep provided the wedding music, and so forth.[41]

Symbolic marriage is the most significant feature common to the death-wedding and variants of the mioritic tradition (beyond the coincidental geographic syncretism of a Transylvanian context).[42] In a death-wedding, a dead bride or groom is married to the son or daughter of God; in the *Miorița*, a shepherd is wed to the earth. The narrative structure of these symbolic forms provides a framework within which sexuality and mortality, two of the primordial mysteries that challenge the social order, may be explored—in these instances, under the watchful eyes of God and the cosmos. The soul and sexuality "out of time and place" are of critical concern because they menace society. Therefore, each of these aesthetic representations examines the interrelations between such fundamental dualisms as life and death, male and female, and spirit and flesh. While the possibilities (and pleasures) of temptation are variously treated through narrative development, they are ultimately contained by the dictates of a patriarchal social world.[43] Thus, sexuality is heterosexual and licensed only within marriage; the finality of death is contested by the projection of life to the other world. The paradoxes of the human condition are resolved in favor of cultural control over the chaos that "nature" (human and otherwise) engenders. Desire seeks expression; culture historically suggests the means.[44] The death-wedding is one such expressive form; the *Miorița*, another.

According to Fochi (1964, 85), the shepherd in the *Miorița* often appears as a "stranger." His comments suggest that during the feudal period shepherding offered a viable alternative to the extreme hardships experienced by the landless peasants. The transhumant life style of the shepherds created a certain "margin of liberty" denied to those engaged in agricultural labor. This eventually led to a cultural esteem for pastoral life and the humanitarian qualities associated with shepherds, with a resultant idealization of the "mioritic shepherd" and the "mioritic space" (see Blaga 1969). Whether or not these interpretations are convincing, what is striking is the description of the shepherd as a stranger. Indeed, shepherds are "strangers" to the everyday happenings in a village, at least for the major part of the year. Although they are integral participants in an agricultural-pastoral exchange economy, they live much of the time in their own social world.[45] That world articulates with the practices of the village community, but it has a distinctive organization of its own. Therefore, it is fitting that the shepherd ask to be buried in the sheepfold, the "consecrated space" of his life; he is not a "stranger" there, as he would be in the village cemetery. His death will be mourned by his "family": the sheep, trees, wind, and so on. Nature's elements constitute the wedding-funeral party.

In a sense, the shepherd is like a bride who goes to live "among strangers" in a nonetheless familiar world. The shepherd "marries out" of the human order into a cosmic one. His marriage projects cultural realities onto nature, thereby "familializing" nature, transforming nature's elements into cultural affines.[46] Marriage, in general, creates affinal and ritual kin relations; marriage to the family of nature creates a type of cosmic kinship. Thus, the spiritual marriage characteristic of the death-wedding becomes, in the *Miorița*, a cosmic marriage. (Eliade [1972, 251] discusses the mioritic marriage as one whose "structure and proportions are cosmic." It is an aspect of the religious beliefs of the East European peasantry that he terms "cosmic Christianity.")[47] Both create eternal unions that contradict the finality of death.[48] In the spiritual marriage (see Scheper 1971), an eternal union between the soul and Christ is constituted. (Again, all souls, of both men and women, are considered in death to be the brides of Christ.) In the mioritic, or cosmic, marriage, an eternal union between humanity and nature is established. Marriage, in any symbolic dimension, humanizes the eternity of death by locating it (via kin obligations) in an ongoing web of human social relations.

The constitution of kinship not only keeps the dead eternally "alive" but it also keeps sexuality in marriage, thereby tempering the anxieties that untimely death, in particular, provokes. Symbolic marriages mollify the frustration caused by the nonrealization of the social condition of matrimony, as well as consequent unfulfilled sexual desire. Thus, as noted in the beginning of this chapter, the living perform these rites (or celebrate them in the ballad) to honor the soul of the deceased; the wedding is done as a

form of pomană, or alms. It is also done in part, however, as a pre-
caution to prevent the return of the dead. Recall that strigoi are
thought to molest the living unless their dissatisfactions are quieted.
On the one hand, the death-wedding is a result of love and compas-
sion for the deceased; on the other, it is also the result of fear. The
Romanian sociologist H. Stahl (1983, 165) emphasizes the importance of this fear and distinguishes between the activities associated with the giving of alms and the banishing of spirits.[49] The giving of alms incorporates the deceased among the living (and the
dead) who attend generously to his or her needs. In contrast, the
banishing of spirits involves hostile acts aimed at severing contact
between the living and the troublesome spirit, for example, by driving a stake through the heart or closing all of the body's orifices with
wax. Success in destroying an evil being returns the individual to
the fold of society and transforms perceived chaos back into order.
Symbolic weddings serve both functions simultaneously. Through
them, the dangers of death and uncontrolled sexuality are mediated to culture's benefit.

Both of these cultural texts—the death-wedding and the *Miorița*—offer a dramatic resolution to threatening circumstances—
almost beyond the control of humans. Temporarily disordered relations between the living and the dead, and between culture and
nature, as well as between the sexes, are reordered. To this end,
the nunta mortului enables the villagers to participate actively in
this process of making sense of life and death. The *Miorița* encourages an imaginative, philosophical approach to the comprehension
of paradox, notably that of sexuality and mortality united. By the
conclusion of each of these symbolic expressive forms, an "other" is
incorporated into the realm of the familiar. Culture thereby secures
its own reproduction. But does it do so eternally as these aesthetic
representations imply?

Death and Desire in a Secularized World

The past is replete with ritual practices similar to the death-wedding; salvation in one symbolic form or another from the darkness
of death is of cross-cultural magnitude. These elaborate belief systems and manifestations are, however, dying phenomena. In part,
this is because death, in many areas of the world, has been pri-

vatized. Ariès (1982, 612–13) concludes that the community "no longer thinks it necessary to defend itself against a nature which has been domesticated once and for all by the advance of technology, especially medical technology. . . . It no longer has a sufficient sense of solidarity. . . . The community in the traditional sense of the word no longer exists. It has been replaced by an enormous mass of atomized individuals." Generally, modernization has resulted in a world more concerned about material representations of the self during life than about its post-mortem spiritual comforts.[50] The gradual but certain birth of purgatory (LeGoff 1984) lessened the consequences of sin. The pursuit of scientific, "rational" knowledge brought the existence of the Devil (and later of God too) into question. Medicine has prolonged life, in some cases, beyond humane consideration—all in the name of human good. But what, then, of evil? With its traditional sources hidden, is it worthy of attention? And as Ariès asks: "If there is no more evil, what do we do about death?"[51]

Bury it, ignore its existence, or commoditize it. Progress has facilitated this process around the world. Transylvania has not been forgotten.[52] Although there is still a healthy modicum of respect for death among Romanians, nonetheless, in urban areas, the ritual honoring of the dead has already changed considerably. Funerals often end with cremation and burial of the remains (see Bellow 1982). Laments do not customarily disturb the overwhelming silence of urban cemeteries. Death-weddings are not observed in this environment; they are not part of urban cultural life. (At the same time, if the individual is buried in his or her natal village, then a symbolic marriage will be performed.) Perhaps it is poetic justice that this ritual practice, formerly known throughout much of Europe, today persists in an isolated region of Transylvania, itself most famous for an imposed legend of the living dead.[53] Yet, even in Maramureş, prompted by the encouragement of the state, secularization is increasing. The profits of seasonal labor have spawned cyclical exoduses from local villages; the desire for consumer goods has given rise to modern commodity fetishism (although it has not been fulfilled by any stretch of the imagination). Sooner or later, death-weddings will be buried in the cemetery of cultural memories there as well.

But, as the discussion in this chapter has illustrated, not all that is buried is dead. Death is the consummate vampire who thrives on the bodies and blood of humans. Death refuses to disappear, to relinquish its own "life." Death will not be controlled—ultimately. As a couplet told us:

Multă lume-ai îndiţît	Many people have you swallowed,
Şî tăt nu te vezi hrănit.	And still you are not satiated.

Death knows no limits; death's "life" is immortal.

But, for the living, there are limits. Humans are mortal. Consequently, life's fundamental dilemmas are not readily solved. Among them remain untimely death that precludes marriage and the fulfillment of sexual desire. Although the death-wedding is disappearing as a way to confront the problem of their union, the central paradox that it addresses remains. Because desire seeks expression, resolution is symbolically sought through other media. In Western culture, the reincarnation of the venerable Count Dracula in film, fiction, and theater is exemplary and attests to his immortalization. Jameson, discussing mass media, notes that "social and political anxieties and fantasies . . . must then have some effective presence in the mass cultural text in order subsequently to be 'managed' or repressed" (1979, 141). His comments pertain to the narrative "working" of cultural texts in general: "the unity of a single mechanism which gives and takes alike . . . which strategically arouses fantasy content within careful symbolic containment structures which defuse it, gratifying intolerable, unrealizable, properly imperishable desires only to the degree to which they can be laid to rest" (ibid.). Cultural texts—be they cosmologies, theologies, or art—make it possible to play with fire (a symbol of burning desire), but never beyond the limits of control. At that point, the means to extinguish it is produced. Past, present, and future—the dialectical tension between desire and death constitutes an eternally thought-provoking subject: life.

Having returned to "life," the analysis of death-weddings comes to an end. Through this rite, those who have died untimely deaths are symbolically wed. That of which they were deprived in life (sexual experience, hence, marriage) is fulfilled in death. In this way, the relationship between life and death is made meaningful. Indeed, the wedding, funeral, and death-wedding cycle of rites together form an integrated system of thought and action in which humanity, spirit, culture, and nature exist in an ordered web of relations. These life-cycle rites provide a culturally comprehensible framework through which the quest for meaning regarding the human condition may be satisfied. For this, the living, as well as the dead, are grateful.

Chapter Five

Ideology, Ritual, and Identity

The struggle between different discourses, different definitions and meanings within ideology is therefore always, at the
same time, a struggle within signification: a struggle for the
possession of the sign which extends to even the most mundane areas of everyday life.

Hebdige 1979, 19

I appreciate . . . these true works of popular art as an expression of your commitment to maintain the dress and customs of
[your] ancestors, as well as to weave them tightly with that
which is new, still basing ourselves in the traditions that our
ancestors created in the past, because only in this way will we
build a strong socialist society.

Thus, maintain the customs and dress of our great-great
forebears, so that they shall always be in our memory. I beg
that you never forget this.

Nicolae Ceauşescu, October 17, 1974,
Vişeu de Sus, Maramureş

As the preceding chapters attest, Ieudeni have heeded the advice
of their president. Ritual traditions of the life cycle and the calendar are alive and well. To this day, people wear the dress of their
ancestors: children, the middle-aged, and older on a daily basis,
and everyone on Sundays and holidays.[1] This final chapter will explore what ritual traditions and Maramureş peasant attire mean
in contemporary Romania. What effects have significant socioeconomic and political transformations had on village social organization? Why, in this peripherally located community, is there a
strong sense of local identity instead of demoralization and depopulation? Why have rituals become the primary organizing
structures through which Ieud as a community represents and reproduces itself? And, last, what are the "meanings" of these rituals

in a continually secularizing socialist state that is generally opposed
to such vestigial practices?[2] To begin to answer these questions, I
will briefly discuss the general effects of change in Romania with
Ieud as a specific referent. The task of building a socialist society
also requires the state to legitimate itself—especially for itself and
its people. This involves the creation of a national culture that
binds individuals to the state, with the state constituting its own
traditions. Therefore, I will take up the thorny issue of tradition in
a modern state. Because traditions have many meanings, it is necessary to explore the articulation of those meanings. Here, the relationship between continuity and change becomes focal; that relationship has facilitated the flourishing of tradition in Ieud. The
state's motivations and understandings are different from those of
the Ieudeni—fundamentally so. But, for the present, they are mutually self-serving.

The Effects of Change

Since World War II, Ieudeni, like others, have experienced varied
and profound changes in their lives in the interest of "building socialism." Their relations to people and property have been fundamentally altered.[3] Over the years, they have participated in such
processes as cooperativization, industrialization, diversification of
the labor force, feminization of agriculture, and expansion of educational opportunities. They have benefited from the modernization of
daily living (through electricity, refrigeration, cultural activities,
and leisure-time amenities) that has produced a consumer-oriented
society and that has visibly changed the appearance of both the
countryside and the cities. Apartment buildings, sterile complexes
that are a sign of "modernity," line urban streets, where cars, buses,
and pedestrians vie for the right of way. As mentioned in the first
chapter, villagers, by contrast, build two- and three-story villa-type
homes. Ieud now has 700 such dwellings among its total of approximately 1,260. A local official commented that people now "build
up" and forego the land for which they would otherwise have to pay
taxes. (This tax is about 40 lei per hectare, and higher for city property.) Building codes also dictate that new village homes be constructed with two stories as a minimum. Since electrification, old
and new houses are equipped with television, radio, and record

player or cassette. Small refrigerators, freezers, and gas stoves are slowly acquired. Despite gas rationing, families plan so they can purchase a car. Recall the couplets from the *horea găinii* of recent years:

Cu bani di pă o găină	With the money from a hen,
Mni-oi cumpăra o măşînă.	I'll buy myself a car—
O măşînă Dacia	A Dacia—
Cu ie să mă pot căra	So I can drive around
Cu mîndru alăturea.	With my sweetheart next to me.
C-amu mni-i dragă lumea	Because the world pleases me now,
Că nu mni-i hiie de nimnică	Because I don't need anything—
Numa de măşînă mnică.	Only a small car.

The successes, however, have been tempered by failures.[4] Recently, international concerns such as the threat of nuclear annihilation (see Appendix E), international debts, and terrorism have invaded more familiar topics of daily attention, even in remote areas of the country. While these matters are discussed, they nonetheless remain relatively abstract. The world-at-large has been incorporated into the private domain, although the geopolitical composition of that world is only vaguely comprehended.[5] Juxtaposed against these world-encompassing matters are the more mundane worries of everyday existence, increasingly wed to the interests of the state. That state has entered into the private realms of the social body: "rational alimentation" and stringent pronatalist policies have been introduced to secure the future of Ceauşescu's socialist vision.[6] Sacrifices as a result of these imposed measures may be necessary to realize Ceauşescu's dreams, but they also mean that the populace is currently struggling to "realize" the practical necessities of day-to-day living.[7] Moreover, the difficulties arising from continual food shortages and energy crises have been compounded by the weather: in 1985, a relentless summer drought followed an equally relentless winter freeze. To be sure, daily life is fraught with hardships.

Yet circumstances are not always as they appear to be. As a generic Soviet–East European joke confides: "There is nothing in the shops, but the tables are well-laden; nobody works, but the Plan has been fulfilled." What accounts for this paradox of the material markers of capital accumulation in the face of scarcity? A detailed analysis of Romanian political economy is beyond the scope of this chapter; however, insights into the resolution of the paradox shall be suggested. A national policy of *auto-provizionare*, or self-provisioning, for each region creates enormous variations (and difficulties) in production and distribution across the country. Hence, in some areas, butter or meat are available, whereas in others, they are obtainable only with a ration card. Over the years, there has been a dramatic change in the nature of urban-rural relations, which is partially the result of a policy of *sistematizare*, or systematization, that planned the reorganization of urban and rural environments (refer to Sampson 1982). Planners, in response to problems of underurbanization, have variously taken into consideration infrastructural resources of both cities and villages in their efforts to control patterns of urban in-migration and to regularize a commuter population. (Underurbanization occurs when excessive industrialization is pursued at the expense of the infrastructure; this is a common phenomenon of East European industrialization. See Konrad and Szelenyi 1976; and, for example, Cernea 1974 and 1978; Moskoff 1978; Sampson 1982; Matei and Mihăilescu 1985.)

A noteworthy inversion of customary urban-rural relations points to the relative dependence of the rural areas on urban industrial production and distribution. Staples such as oil, flour, canned goods, and bread are now generally obtained from the city, as are luxury items. Nevertheless, family production still accounts for the bulk of meat, vegetables, and dairy products.[8] Villagers (cooperative members and nonmembers) continue to raise their own chickens and pigs and to cultivate personal plots. However, this subsistence strategy is not necessarily sufficient. In recent years, the state has required supplementary quotas from the rural population to help meet the food needs of the country. (See *Scîntea*, January 17–19, 1984.) Romania's long-term neglect of agriculture coupled with an international debt partially paid through export of agricultural products have given rise to a situation that most agricultural workers view as disgraceful: Romania is an agrarian country that can no longer feed itself. Contracts with the state are mandatory for many agricultural and pastoral pursuits; for example, to have access to summer pasturage on lands that are now state-owned, sheepowners must agree to provide a certain number of pigs, as well as approximately 1 kg of sheep's wool. Some seventy eggs per year are required for each village household to receive its "rational alimentation" allocation. This has particularly burdened inhabitants of semi-cooperativized villages such as Ieud whose residents may not have the resources to fulfill their obligations to the state. Consequences for noncompliance range from fines to imprisonment.[9] As to entrepreneurial efforts, surplus (after quotas have been met) may be sold on the open market. The state, however, determines maximum prices, which frequently does not make it worthwhile for the peasant to sell produce on the open market (see Shafir 1985, 117–18).

The web of socioeconomic relations has been restructured in response to the exigencies of daily living. In most rural areas, extended kin ties still dominate rural-urban exchange relations (refer to Cole 1981; Sampson 1983). Today, these exchanges are actualized through monetary as well as "gift" currencies, which are derived from barter and second-economy relations. Hence, salaries are requisite, although not adequate, components of extended family economic organization. In cities, the character of urban-rural exchanges has also been altered; it is no longer primarily linked to extended kin relations. This is a consequence of the demographics of in-migration. Bucureşti residents, to illustrate, have established market-type as well as barter transactions with peasant entrepreneurs in villages surrounding the capital; more often than not, there is no kin tie.[10]

The situation of Ieud is typical to a certain degree (especially of peripheral locales), yet specific. A primary result of the changes of the last thirty some years is the character and composition of the work force. Ieudeni are predominantly involved in agriculture and animal husbandry. (Approximately one-fourth of the labor pool is employed in other occupations on a regular basis: forestry, construction, factory, light industry, mining, and transport.)[11] What is striking is that 90 percent of the "legitimate" work force (that is, excluding children and teenagers under sixteen as well as the elderly) are engaged to varying degrees in seasonal labor in agriculture, industry, or construction. The majority of these workers are male. Groups of Ieudeni—usually, although not exclusively, kin-based—contract their labor for payment in cash as well as in grains. As mentioned in the first chapter, the presence of kin, consanguineal or ritual, also assures the propriety of unmarried young women joining the seasonal work force. Earnings are contributed toward dowries, clothing, goods for conspicuous consumption and ritual display, and the building and furnishing of houses. Seasonal labor offers the advantage of immediate and substantial monetary gain. The best-paid jobs entail hard, back-breaking work (haying, harvesting, construction), which accounts for the predominance of male laborers performing them. Women participate in harvest work teams, but they do not work as quickly as men at the most strenuous tasks and thus cannot earn as much as men. Nonetheless, for men or women, seasonal labor is lucrative. Moroşeni have appreciated that benefit; moreover, they are accustomed to working long and hard hours. (There are innumerable stories about the disdain for them felt by groups from other regions of the country. The willingness of the Moroşeni to maximize their work time, and hence their profit, diminishes the earning power of others who do not choose to work as intensely.) Because of the potential for rapid capital increase, almost all strata of Ieudeni participate in seasonal labor.[12] Thus, during summer vacation, school teachers exchange their books and chalk for scythes and sickles.

As mentioned above, seasonal workers are paid in cash and grains. Available cash is used to acquire consumer status items and to defray necessary expenses. Grains are stored and used as necessary. While many will suffer the consequences of export and natural disasters that plagued Romania in 1985 (practically destroying the grain crop), most Ieudeni will manage comfortably. Similarly, they have wood-burning stoves, and therefore are somewhat immune to the energy crisis. While wood is expensive and Moroşeni resent the inflated cost, nonetheless, they are not shivering indoors.[13] A portion of their earnings will cover this necessary expenditure. Electricity is a problem, as it is everywhere. In response, villagers have resurrected their oil-burning lamps, which they had only recently discarded. Obtaining oil is just a bit more difficult and costly.[14] In any case, the rewards of seasonal labor enable villagers to pursue the path of conspicuous consumption. When they cannot fulfill their particular desires, it is generally because of physical limits of the body or lack of access to materials; lack of funds is not necessarily a reason. (This means that it may take longer than anticipated to build a house, for example. Cash is necessary, but not sufficient.) For some, seasonal labor has become an occupation. For others, it is temporary work that supplements wages. Although this type of labor pattern is not new to Moroşeni, its present-day scale is, and it is decidedly a result of the restructuring of property relations.[15] Whereas previously the primary bias associated with seasonal labor was one of class, it is now one of gender.

Another aspect of the restructuring of property relations has been the feminization of agriculture (see Cernea 1978) and the concomitant restructuring of village social relations. Today, the core of daily village life is women, children, and the elderly; men are generally absent from the day-to-day happenings of village life. Clearly, the practical organization of the family has been fundamentally transformed by seasonal labor (more so than by daily commuting). Women are the functional heads of households, of the gospodărie in its most encompassing sense. Just as seasonal labor is not novel to Ieudeni, neither is the running of households novel to women; it is a well-established phenomenon of wartime social organization (as it is in most other cultures). What is significant is the structural feature vis-à-vis everyday practice. Although there are men in the village, the basic composition of the local population has changed. Men are *sesonieri*, or seasonal workers.[16] Although they recognize that seasonal labor as a temporary strategy to make money is beneficial to their future hopes and plans, they are quite conscious of the resulting substantive changes in the tenor of gender relations. Many men, home for the celebration of St. Mary's Day in mid-August, commented that they did not like their removal from the daily unfolding of family life. They volunteered that now "women wear the pants in the family," and when they return home, they are the ones to be incorporated into everyday routines and their wives' decisions. A facetious couplet remarks about recent changes in gender relations:

Amu lume s-o modernizat	Now people have modernized:
Mere fata la băiet.	The girl goes to the boy.

These long periods of absence have not instigated any divorces. There is no case of formal divorce in Ieud, although there is one reluctantly acknowledged case of separation (a result of alcoholism and extreme wife-abuse). The family is still the focus of life, with marriage and children considered to be life's highest achievement. The material gains of conspicuous consumption simply embellish

that achievement. While a consumer orientation increasingly motivates socioeconomic behavior, it has not yet altered the value of the
sanctity of the family.[17]

In addition to changing gender relations, there are also changes
in generational ones. Unmarried children are now able to contribute financially to the household economy, especially through seasonal labor. Their economic power, like that of working women, has
given rise to a degree of individual autonomy heretofore nonexis-
tent in village family relations. As earning ability becomes associated with younger age and health, there is a related but inverse
emergent process: the disenfranchisement of the elderly. These
changes are captured in the following lines:

Lucră tineri din putere	Young people work as hard as they can
Să să-şi facă un leac de-avere.	To acquire some wealth.
Fac o casă cît un bloc	They make a house as big as an apartment block,
Şî bătrîni nu au loc.	But there is no room for the elders.
. . . .	. . . .
O murit bdietu tata	Poor tata has died;
Cine-a me mîni cu vaca?	Who will go with the cow tomorrow?
Noi merem în lume mare	We're going into the big world
Să cîstigăm de mîncare	To earn [money] for food
Şî hainuţe frumoşele.	And pretty clothes.
O sugniţa de o mie	A skirt for a thousand [lei],
Că să aibă şî Marie.	So that Marie has one too,
Şî năframă cu trei sute	And a scarf for three hundred—
Le-o văzut la mai multe.	She's seen many with them.

Everyone has been seduced into seeking commodities and "keeping up with the Pleşes," so to speak. But they also simultaneously
complain about the disruption of the hierarchy of patriarchal authority and the gradual demise of Christian norms and values.

Their sense that patriarchal privilege is losing to "modern times"
(a sense facilitated by effective government policies) is clearly related to the practices of everyday life. Those practices at least
partially inform the answer to the previously posed paradox of material accumulation in an economy of scarcity. They also bear inter-

estingly on the patriarchal paradox described in the first chapter, which has been seminal to understanding relations between the sexes. To reiterate, this paradox teaches that women are "in" but not "of" the patriline. Yet, today, women are responsible for the daily socioeconomic management of the family. Conversely, while men, juridically recognized as heads of household, are "of" the patriline, and indeed determinative of it, they are no longer "in" the family as integral participating members. The relationship between ethos and practice has begun to bifurcate; for the time being, the ethos persists, although it is not as related to practice.[18] The feminization of agriculture has made women nurturers for the state as well as for the family. Seasonal labor has added to their responsibilities. Women are now the practical tenders of tradition—for their families, their villages, and the state.[19] It is to this that we will now turn our attention. In so doing, we will return to the meaning of ritual and peasant attire in contemporary Romania.

Tradition

> A tradition is a pattern of understandings and evaluations that a community has worked out over time. . . . *Tradition* is not used in contrast to *reason*. Tradition is often an ongoing reasoned argument about the good of the community or institution whose identity it defines.
>
> Bellah et al. 1985, 355

Tradition is ineluctably associated with the past.[20] In contemporary Romania, the past by and large means a peasant past, and that is ideologically problematic for Marxist-Leninist regimes (Jowitt 1974; Kligman 1981; Karnoouh 1982 and 1984; Verdery 1983a, 1983b). The mythical hero of the modern state is the worker, not the peasant yearning for his own (mythologized) land in lieu of the state's. At the same time, however, rights to the past are critical to territorial claims by the state, notably with respect to Transylvania. Such rights are, at least in part, "legitimated by the historical fidelity" of the peasant (Karnoouh 1982, 105; see also Verdery 1983a). "Lineage" is therefore as important to the interests of the state as it is to Maramureş peasants.[21] In a multiethnic state, the search for "pure" cultural roots may be abetted by traditions. Whereas the bride's virginity serves as a symbol of the neam's integrity in the Maramureş wedding rite, so traditions have become symbols for the integrity of the Romanian neam. Accordingly, the state has blessed a marriage between tradition and nationalism that has reproduced its political apparatus in cultural forms.[22] (See Hobsbawm and Ranger 1983 on the significance of invented traditions.) The state uses folklore—a gloss for cultural heritage (see Lane 1981; Karnoouh 1982; Kligman 1983; Silverman 1983)—as a means to an end: the construction of a national culture that, while historically rooted in peasant traditions, is a living celebration of the present's cultural creativity. "Folklore" is viewed as a viable modality through which the specificities of a national heritage may be constituted and communicated. Folklore and traditions serve as cultural signs of difference that represent nationalist ideology and mystify the "other." Hence, "socialist culture" from the perspective of cultural ideologues attempts to articulate various levels of identity—individual, regional, national—by reifying a complex of concepts that constitute a national cultural identity construed in "familial" terms. *Patrie* (the fatherland or nation) is the symbolic family of the people.[23] Through this symbolic construction of an encompassing context, the state legitimates itself and, in the process, encourages the transformation of "peasants into Romanians," to borrow from E. Weber's title (1976).

The state's primary means of reproducing itself in cultural forms has been through the institutionalization of festivals; tourism also plays an important role in this process, although for the majority of citizens, it is the national festival system—*Cîntarea României* (The Singing of Romania)—that weds the past with the present (Kligman 1983; Giurchescu 1984; Karnoouh 1984). Honoring the past brings tradition to the stage: segments from rituals (Kligman 1981, 139–51), dances, songs, and instrumental folk music. The creativity of the present is represented by film, the plastic arts, and classical and popular music. Competitions involve "the masses" in professional and amateur categories. (See, for example, *Cîntarea României* 1981, 3.) Ceauşescu, the founder of this national cultural event, characterizes it as "the broadest framework for the intensification of cultural-educative activities, for the participation of the masses in the development of the new spiritual values of patriotism—a new form of affirming the talents, sensibilities, and creative genius of our people" (ibid., 5).

The state conscientiously develops culture as a pedagogical resource. A new cycle of socialist calendar customs has been systematized. (See Lane 1981 and Hobsbawm and Ranger 1983 for comparative purposes.) Although there have also been attempts to create new life-cycle rites, they have not met with much success. In general, local ritual practices have changed in response to material conditions of daily life and not to specific cultural council directives.[24] The state has intervened, however, in Christmas traditions (rites and carols) because these are directly associated with religion. To illustrate, in Maramureş, the now-annual Christmas–New Year's parade was intended to replace the customary seasonal practices. Masked characters that perform the Bethlehem plays in their villages participate in the Sighet parade, with the exception of the Mary, Joseph, and Jesus figures. But that has not stopped the annual reproduction of the Bethlehem plays in many villages. Instead, the parade supplements traditional practice, adding a secularized, modern component that focuses on the dramatic, aesthetic aspects of cultural creativity. The context for participation in the village is quite a different setting from that of the urban parade; the participants, active and passive, are well aware of their roles (see Kligman 1981). The modes of cultural production have changed. The parade is part of consumer culture.[25]

Here, it is important to clarify an issue of "meaning." For state ideologues, peasant traditions form a corpus of cultural artifacts. They are not viewed as constitutive of present-day social relations; rather, their "meaning-making" is attributed only a historical referentiality. In other words, peasant traditions have symbolic, but not instrumental, value vis-à-vis the ongoing experience of social actors. By confining them to reflections about the past, the state misinterprets the nature of these symbolic expressions. The new socialist traditions of cultural creativity, however, are regarded as both reflective and constitutive of socialist ideology and practice. This distinction is reflected in Ceauşescu's remarks about the festival system as well as about Maramureş traditions. Therefore, when Ceauşescu admonishes the Moroşeni to preserve their dress and traditions, his meaning does not necessarily coincide with that which is understood by the Moroşeni. For Romania's president, peasant dress and traditions are artifacts. Furthermore, Maramureş itself is a kind of cultural artifact. Maramureş is considered to be picturesque but more backward than the rest of Romania. To resolve the dilemma that backwardness poses for the state, these vestiges of the past—peasants and their lifestyles—have been redefined as dynamic testimonials of the socialist present. Moroşeni have been cast as the living guardians of a creative Romanian cultural heritage.[26] Thus, tourist information depicts the region in terms such as the following:

> Maramureş is a paradise of genuine folklore. Maramureş villages look like open-air ethnographic museums, displaying splendors of folk art.
>
> Oaş Land and Maramureş, cradles of Romanian civilization, charm the visitors with the beauty of their landscape, the richness and diversity of their peasant art and folklore, with their peasant architecture—the extraordinary richly sculptured gates characteristic of Maramureş, the houses harmoniously integrated with the landscape and the wooden churches with slender, extremely gracious spires.
>
> Also famed for the unsurpassed beauty of its villages, the Iza Valley has a special historical importance. Here, at Ieud, stands the oldest wooden church in the world (1364). It is also here that the first Romanian language school functioned, and the oldest Romanian writing was discovered— *Zbornicul de la Ieud*—for which reason historians consider the place the cradle of Romanian writing.

These advertisements represent the interests of the Ministry of Tourism. Maramureş is beautiful and does have a special historical significance. But to talk of the houses harmoniously integrated with the environment is also to deny the realities of the present; the inhabitants of this lovely region, wanting the "benefits of modernity," eagerly construct their brick or concrete two-story homes. The oldest wooden church in Romania stands in Ieud, but it is surely not the oldest in the world. There is an older one, formerly in Maramureş but now across the border in today's Ukraine. The manuscript found in Ieud has sparked heated debate among historians. It has also become the focus for another festival—a "scholarly" meeting followed by folkloric presentations—which is held in Ieud, a cradle of Romanian civilization. Maramureş, as well as Ieud, function for the national cultural heritage as spatial-temporal symbols of the nation's lineage.[27]

But what does all this mean for the Moroşeni themselves? To be sure, the significance of lineage is not lost on them. Neam is still central to social relations in Maramureş. Moroşeni are cognizant of the specialness of their dialect, its difference, and its archaisms.

They are aware of the contradiction that this fosters: their grai, or speech, marks them as "backward," but that same dialect is lauded as a testament to the history of Romanian civilization (Papahagi 1925; Vulpe 1984). It is, in any case, a distinguishing feature of their Maramureş identity. (This grai delineates the boundaries of inclusivity and exclusivity; consequently, outsiders who acquire fluency also acquire a local identity. Such has been my experience, as well as Claude Karnoouh's.)[28] The wooden churches have always been symbols of local pride, especially in Ieud. Now they are also highlights of the tourist trade and historical monuments. Newly constructed churches and houses incorporate regional stylistic features; in this manner, local identity expressed through these features is inscribed into enduring structures. These buildings represent the Moroşeni's communal self to the outside world. So do their "preserved" traditions—their rituals and dress. (See Hebdige 1979 on the meaning of style.) But for Moroşeni, their "preserved" traditions are also self-constituting and self-congratulatory. They are part of the practices of life: birth, marriage, death. Their dress signifies status and its changes; it additionally protects them from the elements, if not from the disdainful eyes of the urbanites (or the covetous eyes of the over-urbanized).

When the country's leader tells the Moroşeni to honor their traditions, they "oblige" by living their lives, their local pride glowing with state approval. In this moment, however, there is a conflation of the state's meaning of Patrie and the local meaning. The latter is used "traditionally" to condense a set of meanings within the circumscribed spatial-temporal locale, the "fatherland" of Maramureş. Official recognition of the historical richness of Maramureş' traditions as a part of the national cultural heritage legitimates the institutionalization of local cultural identity. There is a resultant tension between the family of nationhood and the local ties to kindred and tradition. The ambiguities, contradictions, and ambivalences generated by this tension consequently find expression in the lived experience of Moroşeni (for example, changes in godparenthood; Orthodox practice versus Uniate adherence; philosophical appreciation of "communism" but skepticism about its "actually existing" state). For them, that experience is ongoing; it is not understood in terms of the production of cultural artifacts for the nation's history.[29] The "museum" of life is continuously open; only death locks the door.

Which brings our discussion back to life-cycle rites. To be sure, these rites are deeply embedded in the identity of this community, as they are—differently—in the identities of all communities. Romantic views about European peasant life have been promoted by eloquent empirical accounts, but these also assign traditions to the realm of artifacts in our modern, enlightened world.[30] Rituals are believed to be conservative. As we have seen, in many respects they are. Such traditional practices are denounced because they impede the development of modernity. In defense of tradition, others decry the disruption of homogeneous communities. It is easy to argue superficially for and against these positions with respect to Ieud. On the one hand, in Ieud, located far from the pulse of modern life, it seems that the "past" is defying an overdue death. The local inhabitants are colorfully attired; women sit outside spinning wool on their distaffs—all very quaint (no matter that the wool is dyed shocking pink); there are still elaborate weddings and lament-filled funerals; Christmas, Easter, and St. Mary's Day in particular are vibrant communal celebrations. Thus, *conservative* would seem to be an apt term. But then, on the other hand, there are work schedules that cause some couples to have a one-day rather than a three-day wedding; televisions and radios disrupt the accustomed quiet; seasonal labor has radically transformed the composition of the village. Thus, the idyllic homogeneity of a tightly knit community is being destroyed by growing consumer desires and labor requirements.

But this alleged village homogeneity has never existed; there has generally been heterogeneity—of class or status, religion, and race. "Pedigreed" Ieudeni remain conscious of being *ţărani nemeşi,* or peasant nobles, and of a good lineage. Prior to World War II, Ieud was composed of Romanians, Jews, and Gypsies, all engaged in competition over resources.[31] Today, there are no longer any Jews—only Romanians and Gypsies. But there are new categories. People are members or nonmembers of the cooperative; they are *ţărani* (peasants) or *muncitori* (workers) or *şoferi* (drivers) or *intelectuali.* The significant difference between the former and the present heterogeneity is that there are more options today; there is greater mobility. Ieudeni are not formally constrained by their local social identity. They are not necessarily consigned to a particular lot in life on the basis of religion, race, or social position.[32]

In essence, life's frame of reference is no longer as restricted. Neam still matters. But it is not solely determinative. Patrie—local, regional, national—is being constantly reinterpreted; its boundaries are multiple in an everyday sense (war previously being the primary distinguishing event). It should be noted that Ieud has not experienced the consequences of sistematizare that other communities-become-industrial centers have (Sampson 1982). There are not many "outsiders" in Ieud. Non-Ieudeni generally remain outsiders; among them are teachers, engineers, and doctors who are fulfilling their training obligations. At the end of their service requirement, most of them happily relocate to cities. (Others, such as the priest and myself, are incorporated into village social relations.)

Socioeconomic change has meant, however, that many "insiders" are absent much of the year. Ieudeni now traverse the nation in search of seasonal labor. Some work in the Baragan; others, in Banat (respectively, the southeast and southwest). Still others are hired by a state enterprise for several years. Because there are limited vacation periods, the entire family may move for the duration, but not many resettle permanently. Like most Moroşeni, Ieudeni have a deeply ingrained loyalty to their natal village. It is the focal point of their identity. What facilitates the tenacity of this identification? Why has Ieud not gradually become obsolete because of decreasing population, like so many other villages in peripheral areas? (See Scheper-Hughes 1979 for a moving account of this process of obsolescence in an Irish village.) Ieud has one of the highest natality rates in the country, a result of religious conviction combined with the illegality of birth control. The demographics of Ieud's population have changed, although not in the direction of demise.[33] As is evident, the results of planned socioeconomic transformation have been varied as well as contradictory (Jowitt 1974; Chirot 1978; Verdery 1983a). To be sure, village social organization has been significantly altered. But, as Bonnell points out, "organization presupposes the existence of bases of commonality, that is, a shared identity or common sense of purpose" (1983, 441). What is the source of solidarity in the Ieud of today?

Most strikingly, as mentioned in the first chapter, the source of solidarity is the ritual system—religious and secular—that has emerged as the stable organizational locus of village social relations and identity in this otherwise much-transformed environment. The ritual cycle offers a frame of reference common to all; it is deeply embedded in local consciousness. So, in the summer of 1985 when I inquired about their experiences through the unprecedentedly harsh winter, the spontaneous response was "Oh, we were so sorry you weren't here to go Christmas caroling with us! There was a lot of snow; it was really beautiful this year." The freezing temperatures combined with energy-conserving heat reductions that were life-threatening elsewhere merited an afterthought, but not much more. For inhabitants of this region, harsh winters are not unusual. It was quite normal that their central association to the winter was that its natural beauty created a glorious setting for the holiday festivities.[34]

The church calendar broadly dictates the rhythm of activity that binds Ieudeni to one another. Seasonal laborers leave the village at the beginning of Lent to return for Easter. This cycle is repeated for Pentecost, St. Mary's Day, and Christmas (Easter and Christmas being the most compelling). Many villagers remain in residence through the cold winters, when most weddings still take place. Death of a family member supersedes all other obligations at any time. Although in practical terms, seasonal laborers live elsewhere much of the time, they do not assimilate into the life of the community in which they are working. Instead, they periodically (and eagerly) return home to Ieud where they participate in customary behaviors that reconstitute their familiar selves. Recall that the "foreigner" or "outsider" away from family and community figures prominently in conceptions about persons, social relations, life and death. Working in the Baragan or in New York City are cognitively equivalent; each is located *în străinătate,* in a foreign land, from which one comes back.[35] Thus, the ritual cycle, especially rites of the life cycle, serves to actualize fundamental features of identity. These rites reinforce cultural precepts about lineage, family, hierarchy, gender, and cosmology—precepts that are challenged by and reformulated because of change. In this respect, ritual is conservative. It speaks to a familiar identity, a familiar way of organizing and comprehending life—and death. In the face of dramatic change or "chaos" (which has recently become a popular colloquialism in Ieud), people seek refuge in the familiar, that which is "known" or believed.[36] And, ultimately, some things in life are thought to be unchanging. It is not particularly astonishing that the funeral ritual, unlike weddings, has remained virtually the same. Life is an unfolding, "noisy" story; death, in contrast, is a silent eternity. The village cemetery provides the link, locating its members in an enduring web of relations between the living and the dead, for such is the conception of neam, and so shall it remain. Thus, upon the tragic death of their six-year-old daughter, a couple now residing outside of Bucureşti returned to Ieud to bury her among her ancestors. She would not be in the midst of strangers.[37]

According to Valeri, "ritual teaches people to 'believe' in cultural principles by creating experiences in which they can be apprehended. . . . [The] 'understanding' that ritual creates is an understanding of the premises of the cultural system. But these are fundamentally implicit and unformulated; the only clear knowledge about them is that they can be 'felt'—and felt to have an effect on action and mental dispositions—in certain experiential situations" (1985, x, 344). Life-cycle rites constitute a system of beliefs and behaviors that addresses the rules and norms of society. Rules and norms are sociocultural representations that present ideal-typical prescriptions or models for thought and behavior; they are meant to be exemplary and constraining. Inasmuch as they are givens, they can be circumvented. (This is also true for the five-year plan, whose fulfillment may best be understood from the perspective of ritual.) Ritual is neither univocal nor dogmatically conservative; ritual orders experience, and in so doing, it imposes a dominant worldview on the paradoxical realities of life. Rituals are among the practices that Bellah et al. call "'practices of commitment' for they define the patterns of loyalty and obligation that keep the community alive" (1985, 154). But experience is not as neat as the social ideals valorized in ritual.

Ritual as symbolic action is part of a contradictory reality. Consequently, there is not a one-to-one correspondence between the norms and rules expounded through ritual and the particularities of everyday practices. This is readily apparent in the analysis of the wedding ritual in its contemporary context. The wedding rite extols the principles of patriarchy, which are being undermined by socioeconomic change. Women are often the functional heads of households. How may repetitive ritual insistence about, for example, the hostile mother-in-law/daughter-in-law syndrome be

reconciled with the eagerness of young village women to marry at
younger ages?[38] To review the discussion in the second chapter,
there is a noticeable disjunction between the talk about mothers-
in-law and the experiences with them. In general, most young
brides do not have to suffer their mothers-in-law for extended periods of time—nor have they ever had to do so. Because of ultimogeniture, this state of affairs has usually been the curse of the youngest son's wife. A couple generally resides with the groom's family
only until their own abode is ready. The inherent tensions in this
arrangement have traditionally prompted planning and haste.
Needless to say, there are infinite possibilities for good and bad
outcomes. But, surely, the material gains offered by seasonal labor
have done much to alleviate these problems. Many couples do not
marry unless their new house is inhabitable. Even so, the changed
relationship between the tenets of patriarchy (to which the mother-
in-law complex adheres) and contemporary practice is not reflected
in the wedding ritual. Patriarchy prevails ideologically (as it does
throughout society). The wedding rite encodes a normative system
of hierarchical social relations between and among the sexes. At an
ideational level, marriage signifies female subordination; at an experiential level, marriage entails ongoing negotiations of relations
between individuals.

While changing practices are not necessarily mirrored in popular ideology—a matter that stimulates a well-known debate—ritual practices do respond to changing material conditions in other
manifest dimensions. To examine these responses, many scholars
argue for a distinction between "rites" and "ceremonials" (for example, Binns 1979 and 1980; Lane 1981; Humphrey 1983; M. Pop,
personal communication, 1983). The gist of this distinction is that
rites emphasize relations between people and supernatural forces;
ceremonials express the nature of human social relations. In other
words, rites pertain more to the domains of religion and cosmology, the "other-worldly" concerns. Undoubtedly, these distinctions
are at best academic because there is a dialectic between them;
however, they may be heuristically viable.[39] According to this
scheme, the wedding is becoming more ceremonial while the funeral remains most associated with the defining characteristics of
rites. For the calendar customs, Christmas presents a good mixture
of rite and ceremony; Easter tends more to the former. The ar-

tificiality of these scholarly categories is revealed by the integral relationship to Christian belief. Although secularization is surely a dominant trend, it does not thoroughly dictate daily practices. Many of those are imbued with the sanctity of the relations between individuals and the cosmos regardless of a secular state and increasing veneration of material goods. Hence, in Maramureş, people continue to greet each other praising Christ (refer to p. 69). Departures are always accompanied by a blessing that God help the one who is leaving: *Dumnezău să vă ajute.* Ieudeni still precede each meal with blessings of thankfulness to the Lord. These "prayers" take the form of an individual silent offering while crossing oneself, or a jointly mumbled blessing. Women, children, and the elderly conclude each day's travails with a bedtime prayer. These incorporate "modern" requests that, for example, a grandchild succeed with university entrance exams.

Funerals are most associated with the category of rite (and the sacred) because of their essential relation with "that" world (see note 24, above). Yet, there has been an increasingly "ceremonial" or "invented tradition" emphasis in death-weddings. Hobsbawm focuses on "invented traditions" as a means to understand the changing nature of tradition(s) in local and national contexts: "invented traditions" reconcile "constant change and innovation of the modern world and the attempt to structure at least some parts of social life within it as unchanging and invariant" (see Hobsbawm and Ranger 1983, 2). In the death-wedding, this development is gender specific. Previously, only young persons of marriageable age were buried with this ritual; puberty was a determining criterion. More recently, it has been performed for young girls irrespective of biological age. As has been stressed, marriage is thought to be the crowning achievement of life. All people must marry, if not in this world, then in the next. Such were the justifications offered when I questioned why three girls, none of whom had as yet menstruated (ranging in age from six to eleven), were buried as brides. This practice is not extended, however, to prepubescent boys. That it seems to apply only to young girls supports my observation that females are today the practical bearers of tradition. It is their metaphorical (in this case, literal) "purity" that is ceremonially celebrated as a symbol of local cultural identity.

"Ceremonial" elaboration is most pronounced in weddings. In

these, the influence of the commodification of social relations is more readily evident. Before discussing various dimensions of increasing materialism, I wish to point out that the religious inviolability of marriage lingers profoundly. Law demands that all couples be married in a civil ceremony before any religious wedding; no church rite may take place if this formality has not been enacted. The civil ceremony binds the couple to the state. From the perspective of Ieudeni, however, the religious wedding binds the couple to each other and to the world at large. (This perspective is typical of other European peasants as well.) Therefore, as a local official informed me, it is common for a couple to perform their civil duty as much as one month before their religious wedding. Despite the legal recognition of their marriage, the couple will continue to live separately until their union is "crowned" in the church.[40] Although the state operates according to Marxist principles, village life continues according to traditional principles, among which religion is a guiding force.

What are some of the manifest changes in weddings? In the second chapter, I mentioned that work schedules are shortening the period of celebration to a little over one day (instead of three days). The gradual loosening of the grip of village endogamy over the choice of a marriage partner also plays a role in this shortening, because where and how a wedding will be celebrated are partially determined by the couple's places of origin. Seasonal labor, particularly of longer duration, encourages the meeting of significant others from among outsiders. (This is not yet a dominant trend, but it does occur. Most who marry out are young women; in this instance, the wedding is primarily celebrated in Ieud and is likely to be complete with all the trimmings of a peasant wedding regardless of the couple's occupational status. In this sense, the wedding becomes a more "ceremonial" representation of cultural identity.)

While the rule of local endogamy may be broken, that does not license decreased attention to matters of lineage. It is more difficult to ascertain from what type of family a potential spouse emerged when the sources of information are not at hand; nevertheless, this critical data will be acquired one way or another. Moroşeni, like all persons of lineage cultures, are deeply concerned about the issue of neam; roots are believed to affect the fruits of their intertwining. Today, occupational status may lessen family opposition to a marriage, but it is not yet believed to be sufficient cause to disregard family legacy. This is especially true for local endogamous unions. A poor young man who is from a good neam remains highly desirable, a very good match for a local woman.

Nevertheless, what are considered lacks may be enhanced by financial gains. Marriage creates economic as well as social relations. Although the economic component has been ideologically tempered in the wedding ritual as it occurs in Ieud (class and status issues having been resolved through the approval of the marriage itself), the maximization of material benefits has increasingly come into ceremonial play. This is apparent in several respects, the choice of godparents being central. Formerly, only the groom's godparents represented the couple. Over time, the bride's interests have been acknowledged by the addition of the nănaşi mnici (the "little," or bride's, godparents). And, as conspicuous consumption and ritual display enter with a vengeance the competitive status market of village life, the number of godparents on both sides has multiplied. Gossip, which always contains a kernel of truth, has it that godparents are now chosen on the basis of potential monetary, material, and influential network gains. (This is not really contrary to former practice.) The traditional hierarchical ordering of social relations that recognizes status through the establishment of ritual kin relations may, therefore, indeed be operative when the head of the collective farm, for example, is repeatedly invited to be godfather. This is a means to diminish potential conflict between the state and its citizens, as well as to structure social and status relations. Commentary on these matters informs public opinion through the ritual bargaining over the hen. The cook will acknowledge forthrightly that the godfather is salaried—no fluctuating income to worry about there. (This means that the godfather is a "good bet.") Or the godparents have only one or two children, meaning that there are ample resources to support the needs of godchildren. The cook will also account for the use of the payment she receives; her "purchases" reflect current status symbols. In the past, "the money from a hen" (symbolic brideprice) bought a pair of boots. Eight years ago it purchased a television; today it finances a car. It is also not out of the question that Ieudeni may adopt a wedding practice common to weddings elsewhere (in Maramureş and in other regions, in village as well as urban weddings): "dancing of the bride." This honor is monetarily acknowledged, resulting in considerable profits. While the collective sum is used to offset wedding expenses, there is usually enough to contribute sizeably to establishing the new household.[41]

"Modernization" is also reflected in the urban innovations that have been introduced at the levels of production and presentation. For large ritual events, villagers prefer the mass-produced breads that they may order from Sighet. This is more costly and involves arranging for transport (a difficulty now because of gas rationing); however, it does reduce the effort of preparation. At the same time, fancier cakes grace the makeshift tables. A meat salad learned from television and newspaper recipes has become standard fare for any well-laid table. (This means that in status terms it is necessary, no matter what lengths must be gone to to acquire the ingredients.) Then, there is the influence of urban style on the bride's attire. Most brides wear the traditional village dress, but, increasingly, their store-bought wedding crowns have white nylon veils attached to them. Some brides wear white evening gowns, although the wedding participants attend in village attire.

What all of this indicates is that the secularized aspects of the wedding ritual have become ceremonially more elaborated by means of increasing material expression.[42] (Karnoouh, in a recent personal communication [1985], underscored the historical process that has given rise to an inverse relation between the simplification of life-cycle rites and the expansion of their financial aspects.) This reflects the changes in socioeconomic welfare as well as in modes of production. Within this context, rituals still function to redistribute wealth and to structure important systems of reciprocal relations. They also reflect a continuous reconstruction of value, both social and economic. The ritual system provides an institutional means of "investment" through private yet (ritually) regulated exchanges. In view of the present economy of scarcity, these relations of reciprocity are and will continue to be vital to the life cycle for the foreseeable future. To be sure, rituals have "modernized" in accord with the advances of "civilization." As we have seen, there have been innovations and adaptations in the ritual system. But there have not been fundamental changes in the cultural principles that constitute that system. Commodities change more quickly than cultural beliefs. The bride may wear a city-style gown, but it will be white, the symbol (if not the actuality) of her virginity and of the neam's purity. That purity is ceremonially represented; simultaneously, it is sanctified by the defining characteristics of rites. The ritual system continues to lend cultural credence to a local and contemporary village identity.

Continuity and Change

Ritual is both conservative and sensitive to change.[43] The ritual cycle we have examined provides an institutional framework within which everyday concerns about the fundamentals of life and death as well as their existential import may be publicly represented. Therefore, the ritual cycle is a context within which the changing social, economic, and political environment may be explored. This exploration into the unfamiliar is anchored in the continuity of a familiar communal identity and set of relations that binds people to each other, to the state, and to the transcendent. Because anchors allow some movement, this continuity incorporates changes over time in that identity and set of relations. That is what an ongoing reconstruction of a system of values—material and conceptual— signifies.

The dynamic relation between continuity and change has particular bearing on certain discrete features of ritual that intensify its contemporary relevance—especially for outsiders.[44] Here, I emphasize the oral poetic tradition. As has by now become evident, poetry in the context of ritual generalizes cultural meanings. This formalized mode of expression mobilizes perceptions and values that are often not consciously recognized, thereby offering a means through which the living experience of change may be articulated and "felt." Today, public expression of individual opinion in Romania is cautious. But because poetic texts are presented as, and implicitly understood to be, objectified forms (Jakobson 1960, 371), no one can be held responsible for incriminating remarks in the context of ritual. Individuals do not express opinions; rhymed couplets do. And so a traditional couplet informs us:

Nu-i de zină a cui îi gura	He whose mouth it is, is not guilty—
C-aşă mere strîgătura.	That's only how the saying goes.

"Poetic license" permits sociopolitical commentary to enter the realm of a quasi-public discourse. The traditional authority of ritual guarantees an individual immunity from responsibility for the content of that which is uttered as "text." It is important to underscore the relationship between text and context; oral poetry in the context of ritual makes possible the symbolic manipulation of meaning. The community shares a facility with and understanding of the codes and conventions of this tradition; moreover, the texts aim at ambiguity in contextual reference, permitting a variety of interpretations within the scope of collective representations. Consequently, life-cycle rituals may be seen as a forum for the expression of general matters of concern.[45] This is not true of the calendar customs, in which "texts" are fixed by religious tradition. These rites primarily address the broader cosmological sphere within which a community exists, and its relationship to God. The life of Christ, unlike the lives of mortals, is a transcendent, unchanging referent; these ritual texts represent a sanctified, invariant version of history. There is virtually no oral innovation. Life-cycle rites, however, encompass the secular and sacred realms of existence. They represent relations between humans, as well as relations between humans and God. There is much variance; consequently, there are multiple interpretations of experience.

While this "discussion" through ritual poetry occurs in a public context, the nature of ritual language (a form of oblique discourse) denies real political efficacy. Poetic texts are held to be more expressive than instrumental in this regard. Herein lies the contradiction of this formal mode of communication: it enables criticism of the dominant order, which nonetheless appropriates the critique to itself.[46]

A lament from a relatively recent funeral serves to illustrate. During the last years, a dispute has preoccupied many Ieudeni. The problem erupted over who has the right to officiate as one of the church deacons. The factions in this argument are not publicly recognized in class terms (although there is a strong resonance) but rather are glossed in terms of Christian norms and implicit political stances.[47] Life-cycle rites have been central events in the formalization of opinions and responses throughout this dispute. It is in their practice that the "issue" about the deacon's legitimacy has been personally experienced.[48] Hence, at a funeral, a grieving niece lamented, addressing her woe to her deceased aunt:

Uă de mine hăi mătu	Oh my, hey, aunt—
Acolo dacă-i sosî	If you arrive there
Cu părinţii ti-i-ntîlni.	And you meet with my parents—
Cu părinţii şî bătrînii	With my parents and the old ones
Care au mărs a putrezî.	Who went there to putrefy—
Iei cu drag ti-or întreba	They will ask you longingly,
Gătatu-s-o biserica?	"Did they build the church?"
Spune-le că s-o gătat	Tell them that it is finished,
Aşă cum iei o disat.	Just as they dreamed it would be.
Spune-le că îi mîndră tare	Tell them it is very beautiful,
Da-i o mare supărare.	But it has created a schism.
. . . .	. . . .
Spune-le că să să adune	Tell them to gather
Şî să fac-o rugăciune.	And to pray for us.
. . . .	. . . . . .
Că poate vede oricine	For anyone can see
Că la tăţi rîndu ne zine.	That everyone's turn comes;
Că poate vede oricare	For anyone can see
Că nime n-are scăpare.	That no one escapes.

It is believed that relations between the living and the dead are continuous and that women communicate with the dead through laments; accordingly, the niece sent a message about the schism to her other dead relatives via her aunt, who would soon join them. The funeral context facilitated public expression of current events, "legitimated" through the function of ritual itself: communication with the dead. The news was embedded in the customary structure of laments.

Although this dispute is predominantly local, matters concerning the church involve a larger cast of characters. Communism brought the Orthodox church back to Ieud, Ieudeni having been Uniates since the 1700s. (Their historical memory privileges the past 275 years; it tends to repress the preceding centuries of Orthodox hegemony in this region.)[49] Many Ieudeni accept Orthodoxy as a state imposition that must be endured. Meanwhile, the state's interests seem to be rather well served by this local dispute. Although the church is tolerated by the state and often used by it, the encouragement of unity through religious solidarity is not an aim of socialist transformation. For Ieudeni, the process of "negotiating" this local crisis occurs in varied forms. Life-cycle rites serve both as occasions for provocation and as "negotiating" forums that are part of the continuing effort to redefine the collective identity of Ieudeni within the context of the socialist state.

That redefinition obviously entails a complex process. Marx and Engels wrote, "As individuals express their life, so they are. What they are, therefore, coincides with their production, both with what they produce and with how they produce" ([1932] 1970, 42). But what and how they produce has changed abruptly (relative to the temporality of history) in the last thirty-some years, as has who—I would urge, rather than "what"—they are. Most Ieudeni have been peasants. Many of them still *think* of themselves as such, even though the familiar characteristics of that identity have been radically altered. The semi-cooperativization of Ieud means that approximately half of the population still possesses its land. Yet not all the members of these families have remained peasants; many are workers. Most men, save the elderly, are peasant-workers (see Konrad and Szelenyi 1976; Bell 1984). In view of the feminization of agriculture, women are more readily categorized as peasants. Those who are cooperative members, however, are also better classified as agricultural workers. Then, there are those who have become workers out of necessity, but who understand themselves as peasants; that is the referent for a meaningful life. And there are those who consider themselves peasants because the state has cast them as the living guardians of the cultural heritage.

Clearly, several models of classification are at work, mediated through the person. For Ieudeni, history has repeatedly proved officially determined categories of and for their existence to be transient. Until 1918, for example, Moroşeni were peasants in Hungary, although not necessarily Hungarian peasants; today, they are peasant-workers (not necessarily Romanian) in Romania. They are also peasants in "open-air ethnographic museums." "There has always been change; we have to live our lives anyway," a village elder told me. That is certainly true. While this approach may assuage the traumas of change, it also mystifies the process. (Refer to Verdery 1983a, 1985.) Before the socialist state, local relations with those in power did not alter substantially, although the identities of those in power varied considerably. But with the socialist state, such as it is, fundamental transformation has affected every citizen in essential ways. Furthermore, this has been done in the name of a "self-determination" that is meant to distance the spectre of the Soviet Union from their internal affairs. What distinguishes the contemporary state from its predecessors is the degree of its power and control and the extent of its intrusiveness into daily life. The centralized state sees itself as actively engaged in "constructing the new socialist man."[50] That new socialist person has roots in the peasantry out of which the present state has emerged (see Szelenyi 1981). Hence, as already noted, the state, recognizing a certain legitimacy to peasant traditions, has taken a historical interest in peasants, as well as a contemporary one in their transformation. (See Weber 1976; Karnoouh 1982; Kligman 1983; Verdery 1983a.) One of the contradictions in this double-edged "plan" is that the state, intolerant of any forms of opposition, formally applauds the historical resistance of the peasantry to outside intentions (for example, Edroiu 1982). Those acts of resistance are celebrated moments in Romanian history. The "heroic past" has found its way into the popular culture of tourism as well. Regarding Maramureş, one may learn from tourist information that "the inhabitants of Maramureş, who gave the first voivodes of Moldavia, are hospitable and merry people, but extremely proud too. They rose more than once against those who tried to subjugate them." Ieudeni themselves are proud of their historical sense of village unity through resistance. While that unity is more fictionalized than not, the apprehension of it is significant.

Ritual as symbolic expression has the potential to assist the state in legitimating its cultural heritage, while, at the same time, allowing participants to express a certain resistance to that legitimating process. Ritual and resistance have frequently been allies through the tumult of historical change. Here, the ambiguity that Valeri (1985) discusses is critical and presupposes the dialectic between the hegemonic state and local subcultural "cultures."[51] Peasants in Ieud have unquestionably recognized the benefits that the dominant culture, the state, has brought: for example, electrification, leisure, education. They do not enthusiastically embrace all of the recent developments in their lives, however, and some of their discontent finds expression, although this ritual resistance is symbolic. (While some might characterize this local expression as "alternative culture," it is hardly "alternative" in the intentional sense that Lidtke [1985] ascribes to the socialist labor movement in Imperial Germany or that Hebdige [1979] ascribes to British working-class subcultural styles and their meanings.) Nonetheless, symbolic expressions (including ritual) facilitate oppositional "statements." For example, disgruntlement with the CAP (the cooperative) is symbolically elaborated. The cooperative stands as a dismal symbol of the state in their midst. Ieud used to be one of the wealthiest villages in Maramureş; today it is among the least prosperous. This decline is understood to be a consequence of state planning. These proud people had been free peasants; therefore, for many of them, the state has meant something quite different from what it means to villagers who were formerly serfs in other parts of Transylvania. (See, for example, H. Stahl 1980; Janos 1982, 16–30; Verdery 1983a, 72–74.) It is often implied that the state, through imposed rights of usufruct, has introduced "serfdom." That has engendered a significant transformation of their familiar, proud identity, a transformation that has not been wholeheartedly appropriated. In a very profound sense, these people are experiencing an identity crisis.

It is irresponsible, however, to push the oppositional argument too far. Although the state is indeed thought of as "other," opposition is not likely to be expressed in forms other than the symbolic. In Romania, the legitimacy of those in power has always been problematic. Historically, political culture has been characterized by a perceived distinction between state and society. Verdery recently pointed out (1983b) that the present state is carrying on a "venerable Romanian tradition": like its predecessors, it enjoys little legitimacy in the eyes of its populace. Hence, Ieudeni express their objections to the state of things symbolically.[52] The cooperative is a representative symbol of the state, not of themselves. The valorization of life-cycle rites is their symbolic response. These rites are their own; they are representative of and for themselves. In this way, the collective self of the community is distinguished from the collectivized "other" of the state.

People's subjective apprehension of their own experience through time is not necessarily that which is objectively attributed to them. Indeed, "history" as lived is often different from "history" as posited from center to periphery. To gain insight into the experience of socialist transformation (and not only its structural consequences), it is necessary to explore the local cultural categories and practices that inform the understanding of that experience (see Sahlins 1981). Ieudeni today celebrate their communal identity through their rituals, but that identity is rooted in a legacy of hierarchical social organization that is reinscribed in their ritual practices. The privileged, titled peasantry of Maramureş (nemeşi) from bygone eras is known to each and every family. Whether one is from a good or bad neam still determines marriage prospects and weighs on one's future status in the other world. The prerogatives of patriarchy remain in belief, if not consistently in practice.[53] These hierarchical principles are discordant with the egalitarian ideology of socialism. But at the same time, they are consonant with the hegemonic practices of the Orthodox church as well as the state. The church is hierarchical in spirit and in structure. The state theoretically disdains hierarchy but, as is known to all and admitted by none, practices it in its organization of power. Rituals—be they state or local—attempt to integrate contradictory principles that are inherent to the process of social change (see Lane 1981). Regardless of ideological intent, rituals structure social relations that are unequal with respect to gender or political economy. Such is the nature of power and of the processes of differentiation, or separation and incorporation.

The ritual structuring of social relations has become explicit through the detailed analysis of weddings and funerals. Life-cycle rites structure relations between the living and the dead. They also order relations between individuals and families in the social communities within which they live. Today, those relations are integrally entwined with the state. As we have seen, one strategy to lessen tensions between individuals and the state has been to transform official "others" into ritual kin, to constitute some basis of a shared identity in an experienced world. The conflation of personal with impersonal, or bureaucratic, relations (following Max Weber) is not, however, readily realizable. There is an implicit structural inequality that is not easily transcended. This inequality does not lessen the legitimacy of the attempt to appropriate the other to self; this is fundamental to human social relations—for good and for bad. It does underscore the advantage of the dominant. The state is engaged in constructing a national culture formally "shared" by its inhabitants, a system of symbols and meanings with which individuals may identify.[54] That this national culture is intentionally constructed does not mean that it is inconsequential, nor does it mean that the result is according to plan.

As Comaroff notes, "Inasmuch as collective social identity always entails some form of communal self-definition, it is necessarily predicated upon a marked opposition between 'we' and 'others'; identity, in other words, is a *relation* inscribed in culture" (1982, 4). The problem with respect to Maramureş is the need to transform the predominantly peasant population into new socialist persons while recognizing their traditions as living artifacts of the nation's cultural lineage (see Hobsbawm and Ranger 1983). Those artifacts are actually cultural expressions of the way people understand and interpret their lived experiences, and which have given rise to a regional identity for the Moroşeni that may be compared to ethnic phenomena. Their identity embodies the negotiation of relations between the traditional meaning of *patrie* and the recently formulated national *Patrie*. (Regional identity must be differentiated from the complex problem of the "coinhabiting nationalities" in Romania; class is a significant, though different, variable for both.) Comaroff, in his analysis of "ethnicity," emphasizes its inherent relational structure and argues that "ethnicity has its genesis in the asymmetric incorporation of populations into a single political economy. Consequently, the manner in which ethnic consciousness is experienced and expressed, at least initially, varies among social entities according to their relative positions in the emergent division of labor" (1982, 5). This characterization is helpful (although by no means encompassing) in illuminating the position of Moroşeni in the centralized state. Among the effects of sweeping change in Maramureş has been the creation of a substantial seasonal labor force, either of necessity or self-interest. Yet, as is especially true for Ieudeni, these migrant workers have not assimilated into the dominant cultural life of the locales where they work. I suggest that there is a direct correlation between this nonassimilation and the accentuation of the cultural expression of their identity when they return to their natal communities. The lack of "rootedness" elsewhere finds counterbalance in the representations of their roots at home. As this study has revealed, communal self-representation has found its contemporary voice primarily through the ritual system; through these ritual practices, their historical consciousness is realized.

In the Realms of Possibility

Ieud is a community in a northern corner of contemporary Transylvania. It is far away from the concerns of most fellow Romanians and inconsequential to the rest of the world, except inasmuch as it is beautiful, "traditional," and charming. Ieud and its colorfully clad inhabitants are to be "seen." The detailed analysis of the life-cycle rites of these people suggests that they should be heard as well, for they have something to say about matters that are universally consequential. Like everyone, they appreciate the joys and struggle through the sorrows of life and death. They, like so many underdeveloped peoples of the world, have been rather abruptly confronted with "modernity." Indeed, their lives' experiences are grounded in the particularities of history. But their experiences also resonate deeply with ours—our modernity has not resolved the ambiguities surrounding life, death, gender, and nature. These are issues we must all relate to in one way or another. The contradictions of the past and the present, the consequences of radical socioeconomic and political change, the construction of national cultures, and the yearning for self-determination when the national self has by and large been determined by others—these are common concerns in the developing countries of this world. But rarely do we hear the voices of those "others" as they attempt to make sense of the experienced world. This book has been an attempt to people the contemporary political economy of a Romanian village, to listen to the villagers' understanding of what life and death, and social change, are all about.

Profound transformation in all spheres of existence in Romania has necessarily caused substantive reorganization of village life. In Ieud, this isolated community in the Carpathian area, processes of obsolescence typically associated with peripherality in the modernizing world have not become entrenched. (See Pine and Bogdanowicz 1980.) Despite dramatic changes that have transformed the nature of social relations and the organization of labor, there is a strong sense of local identity. Despite the traumas of cooperativization and the reimposition of Orthodoxy, the tenacity of religious belief has brought to fruition the communal effort of Ieudeni to build a new church. This third church seems to represent the trinity of their communal soul. And their commitment to themselves as a community is today expressed and reconstituted through the elaborate ritual cycles that are extinct elsewhere in Romania.

The life-cycle rites have been the focus of this inquiry because, as effective symbolic action, they constitute a context for the analysis of cultural continuity and change. Life-cycle rituals may be viewed as synthetic expressions of the nature and dimensions of social relations and exchange. Hence, they offer a means to gain insight into the practical and meaningful concerns of daily life.[55] By objectifying experience, ritual language and action form a powerful symbolic medium through which to comprehend the social ideals of daily practice. These rites are not about daily practice per se; instead, they articulate the beliefs and practices that constitute communities and locate individuals within them. They represent the sociocentric rather than the egocentric and conjoin the past with the present. Rituals are narratives about themselves, about life and mortality, about how they "fit" into the broader scope of the universe.[56] Ritual narratives explore a community's relationship to its own history and how this history articulates with that of the state (or other bodies of authority). In essence, the system of life-cycle rites addresses fundamental features of identity—in this world and that. Rituals "naturalize" an apprehension of the experience of change. Through them, people make sense of their lives and interpret their world. These *are* the "structures of experience" that move people through the changes of the life cycle, the "passages" that cause social actors to reconstruct periodically their "social selves" within the context in which they live.

Today's context—the socialist state—has created a broader range of movements in "this world." The transformed structural foundations of daily life threaten to wither the cosmological order before that of the state. These far-reaching changes have taken place in a relatively brief time, and the state, in the process of constructing its identity, has needed to create its own traditions. To do so, the state has called upon its historical tradition-bearers—the peasants—to contribute their experience to the building of socialism.

And herein may be found a key to understanding the enigmas resulting from the theoretically unlikely combination of village tradition and socialist transformation: the complex conjuncture of religion, ritual, and the political culture of nationalism presently keeps the "peasants" of Ieud alive and well.

Will their "life" be immortalized in secular practice? Like the historical conjuncture that has maintained yet transformed this peasant way of life in Ieud (and much of Maramureş)—and extinguished or changed it elsewhere—its longevity depends on the lived experiences of Ieudeni as they interact with the structures that order those experiences. As Sahlins (1985, ix) reminds us, "If culture is as anthropologists claim a meaningful order, still, in action meanings are always at risk." In the years to come, ritual practices may no longer be seen in Ieud (to the tourists' and social scientists' disappointment). If seasonal labor remains a necessity to fulfill the desires that have become needs (that is, if it extends beyond a perceived transient phase in a family's life cycle), then the demographics of Ieud will change. Outmigration may become a cause of local depopulation. If, however, a neighboring community is finally transformed into an industrial center, bringing sistematizare to the Iza Valley, then there will be other options. If, as has recently been proposed, the elderly are consigned to villages in order to relieve urban infrastructural inadequacies, then demography will be differently altered. If the problems that have plagued urban life are resolved—which depends on Romania's position in the international political economy and on the internal policies of the state as well as of its ruler—then more young people may prefer urban lives. If transport and distribution ills are not ameliorated, then new configurations of urban-rural relations will evolve. There are many "ifs," all of which may come into play in the ongoing dialectics of experience.

The elaborate rites that have been presented in this book—the beliefs that inform them and the practices that give expression to their complexity—may indeed disappear. Such is the "logic" of development. It is also the intent of "constructing" new socialist persons. "Civilization" has gradually transformed the long-beleaguered peasant out of existence, "in his own interests." While civilization has been able to conquer many "others," it has not yet been able to conquer death, the ultimate threat to its cycles of production and reproduction. Throughout time, different voices have given the life cycle meaning in different ways. If our way often seems an attempt to deny the necessary confrontation with mortality (for example, through the hospitalization of birth and death and through the celebration of youth and the hiding of the aged), this only speaks to an emptiness of our humanistic expression and a fear of nature itself.[57] Peasants have never had the freedom to defy nature. Perhaps their experience may offer the more privileged meaningful insights about the life cycle and its mysteries.

Afterword

I have often wondered about the conjuncture that gave birth to the writing of this book. As the state mediates the transformation of peasants into workers and cultural artifacts, so I have mediated their transformation into "social texts." (On the poetics and politics of ethnography, see Clifford and Marcus 1986, and Feld 1987.) My representation of these people may differ from their own understandings of their lives. Inasmuch as intentionality and meaning are problems of communication in general, "truth" is as much a constructed fiction as it is fact. I indeed hope that I have represented their truths as they know them. In any case, I have represented them as I have understood them. Throughout my experiences with the people of Ieud, they have lent me their support and encouragement; they are eager to see this book on the shelves of the community library. It would be interesting to explore more fully the self-other dynamics of our interaction over time—an interaction that has constructed another identity for me in their world and has enabled them to incorporate a *străină*, a stranger, among them. The metaphorical significance of the "stranger" for an understanding of social relations has been emphasized throughout this study.

Concerns about history and legitimacy, of primary importance in Romania, have also been raised. While the voices and practices of peasants are being centralized and mythologized into the canons of state history and cultural performances, these "peasants" have represented another lived version to me. As M. Rosaldo emphasizes: "Culture, far more than a mere catalogue of rituals and beliefs, is instead the very stuff of which our subjectivities are created" (1984, 150). Ieudeni repeatedly welcomed me to see and "hear" the nuances of their lives that encompass the changes in their world and in their selves. They also invited me to see and hear their deaths. They are not afraid of death, even the death of a familiar way of life. But it, like all deaths, must be commemorated. Perhaps there has been a prescient recognition that "modernity" has brought with it other means of offering their respect. This book is as much in honor of the present as it is of the past. As to the future, although it is unlikely that peasants will continue to be heard and seen in the socialist state, "they" may at least be read.

Appendix A: Din Viaţa Satului
(From the Life of the Village)

Gavrila lui Birău is a peasant writer who, in addition to being recognized locally for his poetic gifts, has been awarded the national title of folk poet laureate. This poem, excerpted below, was written in 1978 and is his versified rendition of the origin legend of Ieud that was collected by P. Bilţiu-Dăncus.

Satul meu vestit şi mare tocmai ca şi
    alte sate
Plin de datini şi-obiceiuri de la moşi
    strămoşi lăsate
Se mai văd şi astăzi lucruri făcute cu
    iscusinţă
Pe cari satul le păstrează de cînd a
    luat fiinţă.

În istoria lui stau scrise toate după
    vechea modă
Dela-naintaşii noştri Bogdan şi cu
    Balcu-Vodă
Să luăm tot începutul cum se naşte
    cum provine
Cum noi sîntem şi cum fi vor cei din
    zilele de mîine.

Astăzi par'că vremea cere şi mai mult
    ca altă-dată
Să ne coborîm cu gîndul peste lumea-
    ndepărtată.
Peste negura de vremuri cari se
    pierde în uitare.
Peste ani şi ani de-a rîndul însemnaţi
    în calendare.

My renowned and large village, just
    like other villages
Full of customs and traditions from
    our ancestors.
One may still see today things skill-
    fully made
That the village has preserved since it
    came into being.

Everything in its history is written
    down in the old way,
From our forefathers Bogdan and
    Balc-Vodă.
Let's start at the beginning—how it
    began and was begotten,
How we are and how those of tomor-
    row shall be.

Today, it seems that the times de-
    mand more than before,
That we reflect upon that remote
    world
Through the mist of the ages, lost in
    oblivion
Upon years and years recorded in the
    calendar.

Simt ătîta-nviorare cînd calc pe acele
    urme
Pe care au călcat vitejii, oameni mari
    şi cu renume
Crucea cari şi azi se vede sus pe deal
    la mănăstire

Locul unde se găseşte poartă vechia
    amintire.

Căci acolo primii oameni au făcut
    două, trei case
Şi din lemn o mănăstire cari demult
    se demolase.
Cînd văd pietri din fundaţie ici şi
    'colo-mprăştiate
Parcă simt aproprierea deşi veacuri ne
    desparte.

Toate aceste se făcură pe străvechea
    temelie
Pe moşie strămoşească a Geto-dacilor
    dintîie
Care a fost ătîtea rînduri fără milă
    încercată
De popoarele străine şi de vremuri
    frămîntată.

Dar această aşezare nu era prea cu-
    ndămîna
Căci pe locurile-acele era apă prea
    puţină
Au fost nevoiţi să plece-n patru laturi
    fiecare
Căutînd izvor cu apă şi mai bună
    aşezare.

Au mers cale nu prea lungă pîn
    pădurile de brad
Unul dintre ei ajunge pe un loc mai
    ridicat
Şi de-acolo ce s-audă cînd spre marea
    lui mirare
De pe deal aude glasul unei ape
    curgătoare.

I feel inspired when I step in those
    paths
Over which great and famous men
    have stepped.
The cross that even today may be
    seen high on the hill by the
    monastery—
The place where it is located carries
    an old memory.

For there the first inhabitants of the
    village built two or three houses
And a monastery of wood that rotted
    long ago.
When I see the stones from its foun-
    dation scattered here and there,
I feel close to those times even
    though centuries separate us.

All of this was built on the old
    foundation
Of our Geto-Dacian forefathers'
    land,
Which was tested ruthlessly so
    often
By foreign peoples and tormented by
    the times.

But this settlement was not com-
    pletely satisfactory
Because in these places there was too
    little water.
They had to go searching in all four
    directions
For a source of water and a better
    settlement.

They went not a long distance
    through the fir trees;
One of them reached a higher
    point,
And from there he heard, much to his
    great surprise,
From the hill he heard the sound of
    running water.

Şi-a strigat în gura mare, "Haideţi
   mă-ă-ă-ă . . . că eu aud."

Şi la glasul lui puternic toţi tovarăşi-i
   răspund
Prin desişul de pădure cînd se mai
   apropiară
Cel ce strigă-n gura mare mai repetă a
   doua-oară.

"Eu aud izvor cu apă coalea pe sub
   deal cum sună
Hai, grăbiţi şi voi mai tare să ne
   ducem împreună."
Şi se duse toţi la vale unde au găsit
   izvorul
Şi pe-acela loc s-aşază şi-ş creează
   viitorul.

Se fac cele dintîi case în Băleşti cum i
   se spune
După numele lui Balcu om cu vază şi
   renume
Şi de-acolo peste apă se fac casă lîngă
   casă

Între două dealurele pe o-ntindere
   frumoasă.

După scurtele cuvinte pronunţate,
   "Eu aud"
Din acele vremuri satul poartă
   numele Ieud
Multe lucruri din vechime poartă
   Ieudu cu sine
Cari mereu sînt vizitate de popoarele
   străine.

Două mici bisericuţe stau de veacuri
   nemişcate
Cari ne amintesc trecutul unor vremi
   îndepărtate
Cînd cu anii se-nmulţiră oamenii în
   sat mai tare
Şi cele două biserici erau-
   neîncăpătoare.

And he shouted in a loud voice,
   "Come here, hey, because I
   hear!"
And his companions responded to his
   strong call.
Through the thick forest, as they
   approached,
The first one shouted again:

"I hear a source of water murmuring
   there at the base of the hill!
Come on, hurry, so that we may go
   together."
And they all went into the valley
   where they found the source,
And at that place they settled and
   created their future.

The first houses were raised in the
   part called Băleşti,
Named after Balc, man of fame and
   renown;
And from there on the other side of
   the water they built house after
   house
Between two small hills on a fine
   expanse of land.

From the short words pronounced: "I
   hear,"
Since then the village has been called
   Ieud.
Many vestiges of the past are to be
   found in Ieud
That foreigners come to admire.

Two little churches standing for
   centuries
Remind us of our remote
   past.
Over time, the village grew ever
   larger
So that the two churches were not big
   enough.

Au avut de gînd bătrînii alta nouă să
    clădească
Mîndră falnică să fie după moda
    românească
Din pricină că atuncia frămîntările-au
    fost grele
Hotărîrile luate au rămas fără putere.

Visul lor de altă dată de-o biserică mai
    mare
S-a-mplinit în vremea noastră după
    multă așteptare
Azi biserica cea nouă s-a ivit ca
    aurora
Și-ntr-un timp prea scurt se vede
    rodul muncii tuturora.

Pentru toți este-o mîndrie satului
    spre-nfrumsețare
Cari de noi o să rămînă pentru lumea
    viitoare
Ea e far, este lumină, peste-a secolilor
    drum
Ea ne reprezintă noul cel din vremile
    de-acum.

Toate trei se-mpart în două și ocupă
    un loc de centru
Căci în ele zugrăvit e tot trecutul și
    prezentul
Mulți vizitatori aleargă la biserici
    l-amîndouă
Și se miră cînd vizită și biserica cea-
    nouă.

Este singura pe țară după unicul ei
    plan
Și e o invenție nouă în stil maramu-
    reșan
Peste satu-ntreg se vede turla ei cea
    ridicată
Cari se-nalță cătră soare ca sub formă
    de săgeată.

The elders decided to build a new
    one,
Fine and noble in the Romanian
    style.
But because of those hard times

The plans could not then be realized.

Their past dream for a larger
    church
Has, after a long wait, been fulfilled
    in our time.
Today, the new church has emerged,
    shining like the dawn,
And in a short time the fruits of
    everyone's labor could be seen.

Source of pride for all of us, the beau-
    tification of the village,
Our legacy for the future;

The church is a bright light for the
    centuries to come
It represents that which is new in our
    times.

All three are divided in two and
    occupy a central place,
For in them are painted the entire
    past and present.
Many visitors run to both
    churches
And they are astonished when they
    visit the new church.

It is the only one in the country like
    it,
And it is a new invention in the
    Maramureș style.
Its high spire can be seen above the
    whole village
And rises toward the sun in the form
    of an arrow.

În opinci şi haine albe se mai poartă-n
    sat ţăranii
După cum odinioară purtau dacii şi
    romanii
Dumineca cu duiumul la biserică
    s-adună
Cu respect şi cu sfinţenie ţin la datina
    străbună.

. . . .

The villagers still wear sandals and
    white clothes
Like the Dacians and Romans wore in
    the remote past.
On Sunday they gather at the church
    in multitudes;
With respect and reverence they
    maintain the old custom.

. . . .

Appendix B: Satul Meu
(My Village)

This poem, also by Gavrila lui Birău, characterizes various aspects of village life.

Maramureş colţ de ţară
Vatră scumpă milenară
În care i aşăzat
Şi Ieudu al meu sat.

Maramureş, a corner of the country—
Beloved, ancient land
In which is situated
Ieud, my village.

Sat bătrîn de munţi aproape
Cu păduri, dealuri şi ape
Cu grădini cu flori frumoase
Şi familii numeroase.

An old village with mountains nearby,
With forests, hills, and rivers,
With beautiful flower gardens
And large families.

Oameni harnici ce muncesc
Pe pămîntul strămoşesc
Cînd începe primăvara
Ieudenii împlu ţara.

Hardy people who work
On the ancient land;
When spring begins
Ieudeni fill the country.

Muncesc căci munca le place
Ş-o viaţă traită-n pace
Peste munca tuturor
Rîde soarele pe-ogor.

They work because they like work
And a peaceful life.
Glancing over everyone's work,
The sun laughs on the fallow land.

Cîmpia-n cîntec tresare
Cînd spicul de grîu apare
Cîntă dealul, cîntă lunca

The fields are filled with song
When a shoot of grain appears.
The hill sings, as does the wet
    meadow;

Cîntă-n sufletul lor munca.

They sing in the spirit of their work.

Cu sapă şi coasă-n mîni
Cîntă doine din bătrîni
Îşi cîntă jalea şi dorul
Trecutul şi viitorul.

With shovel and scythe in hand,
They sing the ballads from long ago;
They sing of their sorrow and longing,
The past and the future.

Appendix C: Verşi
(The Deceased's Farewell and Prayer for Forgiveness)

The following examples of verses written on behalf of the deceased were kindly given to me by the deacon Gavrila of Ieud, to whom I express my gratitude. (Refer to p. 194, Chapter 3.) The texts are reproduced in their original form and have not been edited to conform with dialect or literary conventions, which are both influential.

I. Verşi: For Marie lui Şandri

This was written for the funeral of Marie lui Şandri, who died in 1978. She was a respected godmother to many families in Ieud. Mătuşă Marie was already bed-ridden when I joined her household.

Lume rea şi-nşelătoare	Bad and deceiving world—
Vai, mult eşti amăgitoare	Oh, you are very deceptive;
Tu multe fagăduieşti	You promise much,
Dar puţine împlineşti.	But little is fulfilled.
Văd că nu eşti desfătare	I see that you are not happiness,
Că eşti vale de-ntristare	But you are the valley of sorrow.
În astă scurtă viaţă	In this short life
Îi numai năcaz şi ceaţă.	There is trouble and darkness.
Cît lucri şi tot trudeşti	How much you work and struggle,
Pe alt an te pregăteşti	You prepare for the future,
Să-ţi fie trupul hrănit	For your body to be fed
Şi de orice rău ferit.	And spared from harm.
Tot lucri şi tot munceşti	You work and toil
Tot asuzi şi osteneşti	And sweat and tire;
Munceşti mereu zi şi noapte	You work both day and night,
Numai ca să ai de toate.	Only to have what you need.

Vezi că-ţi trece viaţa
Şi vezi că-i aici moartea
Zîlele tale să gată
Şi vezi că moartea te-aşteaptă.
Tot ce-ai strîns aici rămîne

Căci nimic nu duci cu tine
Tot ce ai de moştenit
Numai doi coţi de pămînt.
O groapă-n pămînt săpată
Asta îi averea toată
Şi haina-n care vei fi

Şi-aceea va putrezi.
Nu-i nimeni în lumea-ntreagă
Ce cu noi ar vrea să margă
Că şi cei ce ne iubesc
La mormînt ne părăsesc.
Drăgălaşă primăvară
Ai venit vesălă iară
Pentru mulţi cu voie bună
Pentru unii numai brumă.
Cînd toată lumea doreşte
Sărbătoarea ce soseşte
Dorul de mare vedere
A lui Hristos înviere.
Numai casa mea jăleşte
Plînge şi să amăgeste
Căci plec şi o las îndată

În viaţa ceialaltă.
Cît în lume am trăit
Mult năcaz mi s-o zinit
Că ieu am dus mult năcaz
De soţ tînăr-am rămas.
Am trăit tot supărată
Cu patru prunci fără tată
I-am crescut cum am putut
Pînă cînd mari i-am văzut.
Iar acuma de un timp
Puterile mi-au slăbdit
N-am căzut de tot pă pat
Slabă am fost dar am umblat.
Pruncii mei s-o năcăjit
Mult cu mine-o cheltuit
M-o purtat pe la doctori

You see that your life is passing by
And you see that death is here.
Your days are up,
And you see that death awaits you.
All that you've acquired remains here,
For you take nothing with you.
All that you have to inherit—
Two bits of earth.
A hole dug into the ground,
That is all you've got;
And the clothes in which you will be buried,
And those will putrefy.
There is no one in the whole world
That would want to go with us;
Even those that love us
Leave us at the grave.
Dear springtime,
You have come again happily,
With good will for many,
For some, only white frost.
When everyone waits
For the arrival of the holiday,
Longing for the grand sight
Of Christ's resurrection,
Only my house mourns.
It cries and suffers,
For I am going, and leaving it forthwith,
To the other world.
As long as I lived,
Many difficulties had I;
For I bore much trouble—
At a young age I was widowed.
I lived with upsets,
With four children without a father;
I raised them as best I could
Until they were grown.
But for some time now
My strength has weakened.
I wasn't completely confined to bed;
I was weak, but I wandered about.
My children worried;
They spent a lot on me.
They took me to the doctors,

Şi mi-o căutat leacuri.	Searching for a cure.
La Sighet m-o internat	In Sighet, they put me in the hospital.
Doctorii m-o vizitat	The doctors came to see me;
Doctorii m-o operat	Doctors operated on me
Şi de boală m-o scăpat.	And rid me of illness.
Iar de vreo cinci luni de zile	But for about five months
Mult năcaz a fost pe mine	I have had many ills.
O, vai, suferinţa mea	Oh, my suffering—
Nu o aibă nimenea.	No one should have it.
De-atunci a mele picioare	Since then my legs
N-o mai umblat pă cărare	Haven't wandered on the path,
Nici pe afară n-am mai fost	Nor did I go outside;
Numai cînd alţii m-o scos.	Only when others took me.
Cinci luni tot pe pat culcată	Five months in bed only
Cu dureri şi supărată	With suffering and pains,
Cu chin şi durere mare	With aches and great suffering,
Pînă ce-am avut suflare.	As long as I could breathe.
Iar joi dimineaţă tare	Early Thursday morning,
Aşa cam pe la tri oare	About three a.m.
Cînd lumea dormea mai bine	When people were sound asleep,
O venit moartea la mine.	Death came to me.
Atunci toate s-o trecut	Then everything passed;
De-atunci nu m-o mai durut	Nothing hurt any longer.
Ceasul morţii mi-o sunat	The hour of death sounded for me
Dragii mei de vă lăsat.	To leave you, my dear ones.
Dragi prunci eu vă părăsăsc	My dear children, I leave you;
Azi de voi mă despărţăsc	Today I depart from you.
Veniţi ca să vă sărut	Come so that I may kiss you,
Că nu v-oi vedea mai mult.	For I shall see you no more.
Şi tatul vost cum ştiţi bine	Your father, as you well know,
O plecat de lîngă mine	Left my side;
Iar acuma mă duc eu	And now I am going—
Rămîneţi cu Dumnezeu.	May God be with you.
O iubită nora mea	O my beloved daughter-in-law,
Iată ce durere grea	Look at this great hardship;
Azi mă despărţăsc de tine	Today I separate from you.
Dumnezeu să-ţi dăie bine.	God grant you goodness.
M-ai îngrijit ca şi pe-o mamă	You cared for me as if for your mother;
N-ai luat nimic în samă	You didn't make anything of it.
Dumnezeu să-ţi dăie bine	God grant you happiness,
Căci te-ai trudit mult cu mine.	For you have suffered much with me.
Veniţi fraţi, nepoţi, nepoate	Come brothers, nephews, and nieces,
Neamurile mele toate	All of my relatives
De-aici şi din alte sate	From here and other villages—

Rămîneţi cu sănătate.   May you remain in good health.
Rămas bun zic tuturor   Stay well, I say to you all,
Finilor şi finelor   Godsons and goddaughters;
La care ce v-am greşit   For those that I have wronged,
Mă iertaţi la despărţit.   Please forgive at the end.
  Vouă vecini şi vecine   You friends and neighbors,
  La toţi vă doresc mult bine   I wish everyone well;
  Pînă l-a două venire   Until the second coming,
  Vecinica ei Pomenire.   For eternity remembered.

II. Verşi: For Pop Dumitru

This poem was written for the death-wedding of a bachelor who had been ill for many years. The funeral took place as the New Year of 1978 began; hence the reference to it in the final verses.

O moarte rea şi amară   Oh, awful and bitter death,
Iară din cale afară   Again from the path outside,
Iară iei şi duci cu tine   Again you come and take with you
Ce-i bun de trait în lume.   Those best fit to live in this world.
  O moarte sfăşietoare   Oh, painful death,
  Groznică şi cu întristare   Horrible and with sorrow,
  Că tu ori pe unde treci   For you go anyplace;
  Tot ce afli iei, răpeşti.   All that you find you take, rape.
Moarte, moarte ce-ai lucrat?   Death, oh, death, what have you
                                        done?
Aici dacă ai întrat   Here, if you've entered,
Fecior tînăr ai luat   A young man you've taken;
Să trăiască n-ai lăsat.   You didn't let him live.
  L-ai tăiat cu a ta coasă   You cut him with your sickle.
  Moarte amară nemiloasă   Bitter and pitiless death,
  L-ai ciuntat ca pe o floare   You broke him like a flower
  Cînd o rumpe vîntul mare.   When the wind blows strongly.
Asta-i cruda morţii lege   This is death's crude law:
Căci moartea nimic n-alege   That death does not pick and choose;
Smulge, rupe şi coseşte   She uproots, tears, and mows
Tot ce încolea găsăşte.   All that she finds.
  N-are nimen ce să încrede   No one has anything to believe in,
  De-ar fi tînăr cît de verde   No matter how young and strong,
  Pentrucă a morţii săgeată   Because death's arrow
  Şi spre el este îndreptată.   Is also aimed toward him.
Aşa-i a noastră viaţă   Such is our life:
Azi stejar plin de verdeaţă   Today a healthy oak tree,
Mîine vine crudă moarte   Tomorrow comes crude death
Şi pune capăt la toate.   And puts an end to everything.

Şi eu mult am chinuit	And I suffered much,
De opt ani tot necăjit	Troubled for eight years;
De opt ani a mea viaţă	My life for eight years
A fost numai chin şi ceaţă.	Was only suffering and fog.
Traiul meu a fost un chin	My life was a trial.
Cînd vedeam tineri îmblînd	When I saw young people wandering,
Numai eu stăteam în loc	Only I stayed in place,
Că vedeam că n-am noroc.	For I saw I had no luck.
Nici o leacă liniştit.	Not a bit of peace,
Ci mereu tot necăjit	But always tormented,
Mă topeam ca şi o floare	I withered like a flower,
Şi mă uscăm pe picioare.	And my legs dried up.
Mama me s-o necăjit	My mother suffered,
Şi bine m-o sfătuit	And she advised me well
Să mă duc pe la doctori	To go to the doctors,
Da de me-ar găsi leacuri.	For perhaps they might cure me.
Ori la ce doctori m-am dus	No matter which doctor I saw,
Pentru mine leacuri nu-s	For me there were no cures;
Ori pe unde am cătat	Wherever I searched
Leacuri bune n-am aflat.	I didn't find a good cure.
Pe la Sighet şi la Cluj	In Sighet and Cluj—
Cine unde cum mi-o spus	To whom or wherever I was told—
De la Cluj la Bucureşti	From Cluj to Bucureşti,
Nu mi-i leacul să-l găsesc.	There isn't a cure to find for me.
Acolo m-o operat	There they operated on me,
Şi am crezut că am scăpat	And I thought I escaped.
Dar pe zile ce trecea	But as the days passed
Mai mari dureri îmi venea.	I had greater pain.
Şi acasă am venit	And I came home
Tot bolnav cum am pornit	Sick, just as I had left.
Vreo cinci ani acasă am stat	For about five years I stayed home;
Slab cum am fost am lucrat.	As weak as I was, I worked.
După acea m-am dus iar	After that, I went again
La Sighet tot la spital	To the hospital in Sighet.
Din nou am fost internat	Again I was hospitalized
Şi foarte bine tratat.	And well treated.
Iar de vreo trei luni de zile	But in the last three months or so,
Vai, ce rău o fost pe mine	My, how bad it has been for me.
O, vai, suferinţa mea	Oh, my, my suffering—
Nu o aibă nimenea.	No one has it.
Iar joi pe la oră trii	But Thursday around three
Mare rău mi-o putut fi	There was a terrible pain;
Atunci mi-am dat viaţa	Then I gave my life,
Atunci mi-o venit moartea.	Then death came to me.
Vai cu chin şi cu durere	Oh, with suffering and pain

Să mori cînd eşti în putere	To die when you are in your best years,
Cînd viaţă mîndră ai	When you have a good life,
Chiar trei zeci şi doi de ai.	At thirty-two years of age.
Scris mi-o fost de la început	It was written for me from the beginning
Viaţă cîtă-o am avut	How long a life I'd have
Să trăiesc cu necaz mult	To live, with much trouble,
Pînă-n ultimul minut.	Until the last minute.
Dragă mamă n-am avut	Dear mother, I didn't have the luck
Noroc să trăiesc mai mult	To live any longer,
Să fiu şi eu sănătos	For me to be healthy too,
Să ai de mine folos.	To be of use to you;
La mine satul să vie	For the village to come to me,
La nuntă şi cununie	To the wedding and crowning,
Cu voie bună să fim	To be in good spirits,
Cu toţi să ne veselim.	To celebrate with everyone.
Doar în loc de veselie	But instead of celebration,
Prohod pentru vesnicie	A funeral for eternity;
În loc să fie mireasă	In the place of a bride,
Stau praporii lîngă casă.	The church flags stand by the house.
Toate neamurile mele	All of my relatives,
Toate-s cu haine de jăle	All are in mourning clothes;
Nuntaşi-s cu cărţi deschise	The wedding guests stand with open books
Şi cu luminile aprinse.	And with lit candles.
Acum toate s-o gătat	Now everything is done,
Şi sînt gata de plecat	And I'm ready to go;
Ceasul morţii mi-o sunat	Death's hour has sounded for me,
Dragii mei de voi lăsat.	My dear ones, to leave you.
Vino, mamă mea iubită	Come, my beloved mother,
Ştiu că tu eşti cea mai tristă	I know that you are the saddest.
O vai, de inima ta	Oh, your poor heart!
Cum mai poate rezista?	How shall it continue to resist all of this?
Tata tînăr o murit	Father died young;
Eu mulţi ani tot necăjit	I have been tormented for many years.
Acuma fă ce i pute	Now, manage as you can;
Dumnezeu te-ar mînghie.	God shall comfort you.
Dragii mei, nu fiţi scîrbiţi	My dear ones, don't suffer
Şi nu vă prea necăjiţi	And don't torment yourselves too much.
Durerile m-o trecut	My pain has passed;
De joi nu m-o mai durut.	Since Thursday, it has not hurt me.
Vă mulţumesc prea ferbinte	I thank you profusely

Pentru ostenele multe
Cheltuieli nenumărate
Şi drumuri multe de toate.
  Uncheşi, mătuşi, veri şi vere
  Toate neamurile mele
  La vecini şi la vecine
  La toţi vă doresc mult bine.
Rămas bun zic tuturor
La fete şi la feciori
La care ce v-am greşit
Mă iertaţi la despărţit.
  An nou fericit vă zic
  Tuturor cu un cuvînt
  Cei care aţi ostenit

  Şi la prohod aţi venit.
Eu anul nou l-oi începe
În pămînt negru şi rece
Voi acasă îţi înturna
Şi de mine îţi uita.
  Căci de astazi niciodată
  Nu vom mai fi laolaltă
  Pînă l-a doua venire
  Vecinica lui pomenire.

For all of your efforts—
The uncounted expenses
And the many roads traveled.
  Uncles, aunts, and cousins,
  All of my family,
  My neighbors,
  I wish all of you very well.
I bid you all farewell.
The young women and men,
Whomever I have injured,
Please forgive me as we part.
  I wish you a happy New Year,
  Everyone with one word,
  Those of you that have made the
    effort
  And have come to the funeral.
I will begin this new year
In the black and cold earth;
You will go back home,
And you will forget about me.
  For from today, never
  Shall we be together
  Until the second coming;
  May He always be remembered.

III. Verşi: For Ion Văleanu

This poem was written for a young man who was killed in World War II. His death was not confirmed until 1978, however, when his family was officially notified. A death-wedding was then held.

Neştiut e omului
Moartea şi mormîntul lui
Căci nimen nu poate şti
Unde şi cînd va muri.
  Căci moartea atunci soseşte
  Cînd omul nici nu gîndeşte

  Cum trece norul sub soare
  Aşa-n grabă omul moare.
Unul moare-n casă lui
Altul moare pe drumuri
Unul moare stînd pă pat
Altul de-acasă plecat.
  Unii veselindu-să

Man is unknowing
Of his death and his grave,
For no one can know
Where and when he will die.
  For death arrives then
  When a person does not even
    expect;

  As a cloud passes under the sun,
  That quickly a person dies.
One dies at home,
Another dies on the road;
One dies at home in bed,
Another away from home;
  Some celebrating,

Alţi chinuindu-să
Unii mor plecaţi departe
Prin locuri îndepărtate.
Mulţi mor tineri şi feciori
Lîngă ei părinţii lor
Mulţi mor tineri neînsuraţi
Lîngă ei părinţi şi fraţi.

Le ţin lumină de său
Apoi le fac copîrşău
Le pun pînză pe obraz
Şi-i aşază în sălaş.
La biserică clopoţesc
Părinţi, fraţi, neamuri jălesc

A treiă zi se adună
Să-l petreacă împreună.
Preotul îl prohodeşte
Familia toată-l jăleşte
La biserică-l petrec
Şi mormîntu îl mai văd.

Dar nu-i jăle aşa mare
Pentru că şti fiecare
De ce moarte o murit
Şi cîte o suferit.
Şi nu-s aşa supăraţi
În suflet mai împăcaţi
Şi-îi mai pun din cînd în cînd
Cîte-o floare pă mormînt.
Doar mie mi s-a întimplat
Că în război am plecat
Mi s-a întimplat moartea
Departe prin Rusia.
În război care-o murit
Mult necaz o suferit
Căci o murit prin păduri
Făcuţi bucăţi de tunuri.
Mulţi o murit prin cetăţi
Prin cîte pustiă tăţi
Mulţi s-o înecat în ape
Neavînd modru să scape.
Mulţi în aer aruncaţi
Cu pămînt amestecaţi
Băgaţi de viu în pămînt
Nu să şti de ei nicicînd.

Others suffering.
Some die far away
In distant places.
Many die young, and bachelors
Beside them, their parents;
Many die young, unmarried
Beside them, their parents and
    siblings.

They hold tallow candles for them,
Then they make them a coffin.
They cover their cheek with cloth
And settle them in the casket.
At the church, the bells ring;
Parents, siblings, and relatives
    mourn.

On the third day they gather
To bury him together.
The priest prays for him;
The entire family mourns him.
They accompany him to the church,
And they see his grave from time to
    time.

But the sorrow isn't that great,
Because everyone knows
How the person died
And how much he suffered.
And they're not so upset;
They're more at peace,
And from time to time they put
A flower or two on the grave.
But to me it happened
That I left for the war;
My death happened
Far away in Russia.
Those who died in the war
Suffered much pain,
For they died in the forests,
Killed by cannon fire.
Many died in large barracks,
In emptiness everywhere.
Many drowned in water,
Without a way to escape.
Many thrown into the air,
Mixed with the earth,
Buried alive in the ground—
No one will ever know of them.

Vedeai feciori răsturnaţi
Ca brazii-în munte tăiaţi
Unii au rămas sănătoşi
S-a-ntors acasă voioşi.
 Dar eu n-am avut noroc
 Acasă să mă întorc
 C-am murit în ţări străine
 Unde n-am avut pe nime.
Clopotile n-au vestit
Moartea mea cînd am murit
Clopotile n-au sunat
Ca cînd eşti mort în sat.

N-au sunat clopotile
Să ştie neamurile
Pe mine să mă jălească
La mormînt să mă petreacă.
La mormîntul meu n-o fost
Nici un om din satul nost
Mormîntul e neştiut
Într-un loc necunoscut.
 Dragii mei fraţi şi nepoţi
 Rămas bun vă zic la toţi
 Mai ales care vă trudiţi
 Astăzi cînd mă prohodiţi.
Schimbaţi gîndurile voastre
Şi uitaţi de a mea soarte
Vă rugaţi lui Dumnezeu
Şi pentru sufletul meu.
 Faceţi cîte o rugăciune
 Şi amintiţi al meu nume
 C-am murit nespovedit
 Am murit nepregătit.
Iar voi care aţi ostenit
Şi la prohod aţi venit
Tuturor vă mulţumesc
Zile bune vă doresc.
 Că mai mult pe acest pămînt
 Nu ne-om mai vedea nicicînd
 Pînă l-a doua venire
 Vecinica lui Pomenire.

You saw young men knocked over
Like cut trees on the mountain.
Some remained healthy
And returned home jubilantly.
 But I had not the luck
 To return home,
 For I died in foreign lands
 Where I had no one.
The bells did not announce
My death when I died;
The bells did not ring
As they do when you die in the
 village.
 The bells did not ring
 So that my family would know
 To mourn for me,
 To take me to the grave.
At my grave there was
Not one man from our village;
The grave is unknown,
In an unfamiliar place.
 My dear siblings and cousins,
 Remain well, I bid you all,
 Especially those who suffer,
 Today when you bury me.
Change your thoughts
And forget about my fate.
Pray to God
For my soul also.
 Say a prayer or two
 And mention my name,
 Because I died unabsolved,
 I died unprepared.
And you that have worked so hard
And have come to the funeral,
I thank all of you,
I wish you good days.
 For again on this earth
 We will never see each other again
 Until the second coming;
 May He be eternally remembered.

Appendix D:
Death-Wedding Laments

This transcription of lamenting was recorded in October 1978 in Ieud at a death-wedding for a young girl. It is intended to offer a partial context for the lament tradition as performed. These excerpts were taped during the pre-funeral evening service, and on the day of the burial before the formation of the cortège. There is considerable repetition of verse themes, which, to a certain extent, is determined by the spatial-temporal unfolding of the death-wedding. The verses during these phases of the funeral emphasize the cause of death, the deceased's becoming a bride, readying her for the event, and the mourners' reactions to this "marriage." The repetition of particular themes by each lamenter is also a vital part of the process of grieving and of coming to terms with death.

The deceased's mother and sisters are featured. The latter generally lamented without pause (except during the priest's prayers), meaning that these examples are incomplete. It is customary for one woman to lament by the side of the deceased. While the mother or a sister was next to the coffin, the others went outside (when the casket was still in the house) and paced up and down the courtyard crying their grief; or they moved away, granting the lamenter the privilege of being close to the deceased. Other mourners gathered in the house or the courtyard, sharing the sorrow of death through the poignant expressions of the lamenters.

The death-wedding of Gasie Iusco a lui Fliţău
on October 12, 1978, in Ieud
During the Parastas

Mamă Gasiei:

Uă mîndrucă şî te scoală	Oh, and get up, little beauty,
Scoală şî ni-om sfătui	Get up and we'll talk,

C-amu-i sara a cununii.
Uă mîndrucă şî hăi Ga
Pă cînd fetele-or sosî
Uă tu ieşti gată de pornit.
Uă cînd o zinit acasă
Tu te-ai făcut mnireasă.
Tu mnireasă te-ai făcut
Pă tăte le-ai întrecut.
Uă Doamne mîndra mamii
Supărată pot ieu si
Cîte zîle le-oi trăii.
Uă mîndrucă şî hăi Ga
Uă Doamne da ce m-oi fa?
Fetele tăte-or pleca
Şi ieu sîngură m-oi afla
Uă de doru tău nu m-oi scăpa.

For now it is your wedding evening.
Oh, little beauty, you, Ga,
By the time the girls arrive,
Oh, you're ready to set off.
Oh, when they came home,
You made yourself a bride,
You made yourself a bride,
You passed by them all.
Oh, God, mother's beauty—
I shall be so upset
As long as I live.
Oh, little beauty, you, Ga,
Oh, Lord, what will I do?
All of the girls will leave,
And I'll find myself alone;
I will not escape from longing for you.

Sister 1:

.   .   .   .

Napoi cînd am zinit
Uită-te cum te-am găsit.
În scrisoare nu ne-ai spus
Uă că tu ieşti gata de dus.
Uă telegramă-am capătat
Uă să zin gata de plecat.
Tu sorucă tu Păla
Uă gată-te şî-om pleca.
Uă mîndrucă şî hăi Ga
Uă scoală-te de aicea
Şî ne poveste ceva.
Uă bine te-ai măritat
Uă puţine zestre ţi-am dat.

.   .   .   .

When we came back,
Look how we found you;
In your letter you didn't mention
That you are ready to go.
Oh, we got a telegram,
Oh, to come ready to leave.
You, sister, you, Păla;
Oh, get ready and we're off.
Oh, beautiful one, you, Ga,
Oh, get up from here
And tell us something.
Oh, well you have married,
Oh, we've given you little for a
    dowry,

Uă că mnirele nu o poftit
Uă numa popii i-am dat.
Uă şî ătîta ţi-o fo zestrea

Cît am plătit la popa.
Uă mîndră şî mărişoară
Uă bine-ai învăţat la şcoală.
Mîndrucă şî hăi Ga
Scoală-te de aicea.
Scoală şî ni-om sfătui
Că ţi-o sosît tăţi fraţii.

Oh, because the groom didn't wish it.
Oh, we only gave to the priest,
Oh, and that's all that your dowry
    was—
How much we paid the priest.
Oh, my beauty and young lady,
Oh, you did well at school.
Little beauty, you, Ga,
Get up from here,
Get up and let's talk,
For all your brothers have come to
    you.

Scoală bună şî ne spune
Cînd te-ai dus în ceia lume.
Cum ai mărs cum ai zinit
Uă şî cu cine te-ai întîlnit.
Mîndrucă şî hăi Ga
Scoală-te de aicea.
Uă mîndrucă şî mnireasă
Tînără te duci de-acasă.
N-am văzut aşă mnireasă
Să zie popa acasă
Să-te cunune pă masă.

Get up, good one, and tell us
When you went to the other world,
How you went, how you arrived,
And with whom you met.
Little beauty, you, Ga,
Get up from here.
Oh, beautiful bride,
So young you leave home.
I've not seen such a bride;
The priest comes home
And crowns you on the table.

Sister 2:

Uă bine ti-i hodini
În lume nu-i năcăjî.
Scoală bună şî ne spune
Cum îi traiu în ceia lume.

Oh, well you rest;
You won't struggle in this world.
Get up, good one, and tell us
How life is in the other world.

Sister 1:

Mîndrucă şî mnireasă
Tînără te duci de-acasă.
Scoală-te mîndră pîn casă
Şî noi ti-om găta mnireasă.
Uă noi mnireasă ti-om găta
Ş-apoi i mere a giora
Cum mere tătă lumea.
Uă mîndră mîndrucă fată
Bine ieşti tu măritată.
Nu ne-i zini niciodată
Noi om trăi supărată.
Uă mîndrucă şî mnireasă
Uă bărbatu nu ti-a toi

Little beauty and bride,
Young you leave home.
Get up, beauty, around the house
And we'll ready you as a bride.
Oh, we'll ready you as a bride
And then go to swear
Like everyone does.
Oh, beauty, dearest girl,
You are well married;
You will never come to us,
We'll live with sorrow.
Oh, little beauty and bride,
Oh, your husband won't fight with
    you,

Da noi supăraţi om si.
Vai sorucă sora me
Bine să mărită ie
Mărita-ni-om tăt aşe.
În lume cînd am plecat
Sănătosă te-am lăsat.

But we'll be upset.
Oh, little sister, my sister,
She is marrying well.
We'll all get married like that.
When we went away to work,
You were healthy.

Sister 2:

Uă sorucă şî tu Ga
Nu m-am gîndit de aiestea.

Oh, little sister, you, Ga,
I didn't think of this;

Niciodată n-am gîndit
Aşă iut de despărţit.
Uă scoală-te şî hai pîn casă
Că noi ti-om gata mnireasă.
Şî ti-i duce a giora
Cum mere tătă lumea
Şî acasă-i-ntorna.
Uă sorucă sora me
Tînără-a putrezî ie.
Faţa ta-i ca sansiu
Şî a negri ca pămîntu.
Faţa ta-i ca şî spuma
Şî a negri ca şî tina.
Uă sorucă şî tu Ga
Scoală-te şî om da mîna.
De cînd soră am sosît
Nimnic nu mni-ai povestit.
Scoală-te şî om povesti
Uă c-am sosît tăţi fraţii.
Sorucă sorucă me
Uă bine s-a hodini ie.
Uă bine s-a hodini
În lume n-a năcăjî.
Uă cîtu-i de greu a trăi
În lume cu străinii.
Că străinii-s tare răi
Nu-s ca şî părinţii tăi.
Uă sorucă sora me
Uă bine să mărită ie
Mărita-ni-om tăt aşe.
Uă sorucă şî tu Ga
Duminică pă sara.
La Măricuţa ai plecat
Noapte bună tu ai dat.
Dimineaţa o zinit
Uă tu nimnic n-ai povestit.
Uă sorucă şî tu Ga
Uă nu m-am gîndit de-aiestea.
Niciodată n-am gîndit
Cîte-om ave de-mplinit.
Mult ieşti moarte blăstămată
Uă că ai zinit la astă casă.
Ai zinit la soră-me
Ai văzut că ne tihne
Şî nime nu ne sfăde.
Uă sorucă şî tu Ilea

Never did I think
That we'd part this quickly.
Oh, get up and go around the house,
For we'll ready you as a bride
And we'll take you to swear
Like everyone,
And you'll return home.
Oh, little sister, my sister,
She will putrefy young.
Your face is like a carnation,
And it will blacken like the earth;
Your face is like whey,
And it will blacken like the mud.
Oh, little sister, you, Ga,
Get up and let's shake hands.
Since I arrived, sister,
You haven't told me anything.
Get up and we'll talk,
For all your brothers have arrived.
Little sister, my little sister,
Oh, well she will rest,
Oh, well she will rest;
She won't struggle in this world.
Oh, how hard it is to live
In the world with strangers,
Because strangers are very evil;
They aren't like your parents.
Oh, little sister, my sister,
Oh, well she is marrying;
We'd all marry like that.
Oh, little sister, you, Ga,
Sunday around evening
You went to Maricuţa's;
You said good night.
Morning came,
Oh, and you said nothing.
Oh, little sister, you, Ga,
Oh, I didn't think of this;
Never did I think
How much we'd have to go through.
You, death, are very cursed
Because you have come to this house.
You came to my sister,
You saw that we were happy,
And no one was scolding us.
Oh, little sister, you, Ilea,

Dacă Gasie-a pleca.   If Gasie has left,
Noi ce bdetucă ni-om fa?   We, what on earth shall we do?
Că noi în lume om porni   For we will go out in the world;
Uă cu cine ti sfătui?   With whom will you talk things over?
Lumea asta-i tare re   This world is very evil;
La puţine le tihne.   Only a few are happy.
Uă sorucă sora me   Oh, little sister, my sister,
Tînără putreze ie.   Young she shall putrefy.
Uă sorucă şi mnireasă   Oh, little sister and bride,
Tînără te duci de-acasă.   Young you leave home.
Tu ieşti fată tînăre   You are a young girl,
Şi noi te-am dat nurore.   And we've given you as a daughter-in-
                                       law.

Uă nu te-am dat noră din casă   Oh, we didn't give you as a daughter-
                                       in-law from the house,
Că ieşti mai mnică mnireasă.   For you are the youngest bride.
Telegramă-am căpatat.   We received a telegram.

. . . .

Mama:

Scoală-te de aici   Get up from here,
Scoală-te şi hăi pîn casă   Get up and go about the house
Şi ti-om pune după masă   And we'll put you behind the table,
C-aşă-i rîndu la mnireasă.   As befits a bride.
Uă mîndrucă şi hăi Ga   Oh, little beauty, you, Ga,
Uă spune-m tăt ce-om întreba   Tell me all that I ask you.
Ce te duci di la mama?   Why are you leaving your mother?
Uă mîndra mamii   Oh, mother's beauty,
Tăte în lume mni-or pleca   They'll all go out into the world
Şi sîngură m-oi afla.   And I'll find myself alone.
Uă de dorul tău m-oi usca   Oh, and I'll dry up from longing for
                                       you;
Pînă la tine-oi pleca.   I'll set off for you.
Uă mîndrucă şi hăi Ga   Oh, little beauty, hey, Ga,
Tăte în lume or porni   They'll all leave to work;
De dorul tău m-oi topti.   I'll wither from longing for you.
Uă mîndrucă şi mnireasă   Oh, little beauty and bride,
Tînără te duci de-acasă.   So young you leave home.
Uă mîndrucă mărişoară   Oh, little beauty, young lady,
Uă bun-ai fost şi cumnincioară   Oh, you were good and well behaved,
C-ai mărs unde te-am mînat   For you went wherever I sent you,
Uă vorbă nu mni-ai înturnat.   Oh, and you never spoke back.
Şohan nu m-ai supărat   You never upset me,
Bine m-ai ascultat.   You listened well to me.
Uă Doamne bine mni-o tihnit   Oh, God, I was happy, things were
                                       good for me;

Supărată n-am trăit.	I didn't live upset.
Uă nu m-am gîndit de-aiestea	Oh, I didn't think about this,
Niciodată n-am gîndit	Never did I think,
Uă cît-oi ave de plinit.	Oh, how much I would have to go through.
Uă Doamne mîndra mamii	Oh, Lord, mother's beauty,
Nu ştiu moartea ti-o luat	I don't know if death took you
Ori mămuca ti-o temat.	Or if dear mother called you
Să aibă şi ie o fată	So that she could have a girl also
Să nu sie supărată.	And not be upset.
Vai mămucă ce-ai lucrat?	Oh, dear mother, what have you done?
Di pă mîndra mni-ai luat	To have taken my beauty
Uă Doamne rău m-ai supărat.	Oh, Lord, you have hurt me badly.
Uă mămucă şi hăi ta	Oh, dear mother and father,
Uă rău m-aţi putut supăra	Oh, how you could hurt me so badly
Dac-aţi luat pă mîndra.	If you've taken my beauty;
Batăr am fete bugăte	Even though I have many daughters,
Tăte-or cînta-o cu sete.	All will lament her with love.
Doamne mni-o tihnit	Oh, Lord, I've enjoyed them,
Cu iele m-am sfătuit.	I've talked things over with them.
Tu de noră nu te-aş da	I would not give you away as a daughter-in-law,
Că tu ieşti mai pititea.	For you are the youngest;
Uă nu te-aş da nurorea	Oh, I wouldn't give you as a daughter-in-law.
Uă Doamne mîndruca me	Oh, Lord, my little beauty—
Rău îmi pare după ie.	I feel so bad about her.
Uă mîndrucă mărişoară	Oh, little beauty, young lady,
Bun-ai fost şi cumnincioară.	You were good and well-behaved.
Doamne mîndrele mele	Oh, Lord, my beauties,
Au mărs unde le-am mînat	They went wherever I sent them,
Vorbă nu mni-o înturnat.	They never talked back.
Doamne mîndra mamii	Oh, Lord, mother's beauty,
Şohan nu m-ai supărat.	You never angered me.
Mîndrucă şi hăi Ga	Little beauty, hey, Ga,
Pă cînd fetele-o sosît	By the time the girls arrived,
Tu ieşti gată de pornit.	You're ready to go.
Uă mîndrucă şi hăi Ga	Little beauty, you, Ga,
Rău m-ai putut supăra.	You have hurt me badly.
Uă pă cînd o sosît acasă	Oh, by the time they arrived home
Gasie s-o făcut mnireasă.	Gasie was a bride.
Uă tu mnireasă te-ai făcut	Oh, you made yourself a bride;
Uă pă tăte le-ai întrecut	Oh, you beat all of them.
Uă ieu mai tri fete-am avut.	Oh, I had three more girls,
Mîndrucă înaintea ta.	Little beauty, ahead of you.
Uă mîndrucă şi hăi Ga	Oh, little beauty, you, Ga,

Nu ştiu luat-ai tu moartea
Ori te-a temat mămuca.
Vai mamucă ce-ai lucrat?
Doamne rău m-ai supărat
Uă că pă mîndra mni-ai luat.

Mămucă şî hăi ma
Ţi-ai luat mamă o fată
Că să nu sii supărată.
Uă mîndrucă şî hăi Ga
Uă scoală şî om grăi
Uă că ţi-o sosît tăţi fraţii

Scoală şî vi-ţi sfătui.

Sister 2:

Uă sorucă şî tu Ga
Nu te duce de-aicea
Că să supără mama.
Uă că ie ce biată s-ar fa?
Noi în lume om pleca.
Cu cine s-a sfătui
Uă dacă mîndrucă nu-i si?
Uă sorucă sora me
Bine s-a hodini ie.
Ie bine s-a hodini
În lume n-a năcăjî.
Uă sorucă şî hăi Ga
Nu m-am gîndit de-aiestea.
În lume cînd am pornit
Vai bine ne-am sfătuit.
Telegramă-am căpatat
Să zinim pînă acasă
Mîndrucă că ieşti mnireasă.

Uă sorucă sora me
Tînără să duce ie.
Tu ieşti fată tînere
Şî nu te-am dat nurore.

Nu te-am dat noră din casă

Că ieşti mai mnică mnireasă.
Ia-mă sorucă cu tine
Că la fete-acolo-i bine

I don't know if you took death
Or if mother called you.
Oh, my God, what have you done?
Mother, you've hurt me badly,
Oh, because you have taken my
    beauty.

Dear mother, you, ma,
You've taken a girl, mother,
So that you won't be upset.
Oh, little beauty, you, Ga,
Oh, get up and we'll talk,
Oh, for all of your siblings have
    arrived;
Get up and you'll talk.

Oh, little sister, you, Ga,
Don't go from here
And upset mama;
Oh, for what will she do, poor thing?
We'll go away to work;
With whom will she talk,
Oh, if you, little beauty, aren't here?
Oh, little sister, my sister—
She will rest well,
She will rest well;
She won't struggle in this world.
Oh, little sister, you, Ga,
I didn't think about this
When I left to work.
Oh, we talked about everything.
We received a telegram
To come home,
Little beauty, because you are a
    bride.

Little sister, my sister—
So young she goes.
You are a young girl,
And we didn't give you as a daughter-
    in-law;

We didn't give you as a daughter-in-
    law from the house,

For you are the youngest bride.
Take me, little sister, with you,
For it is good for girls there.

I rău în lume-a trăi	It's hard living in the world,
Că ieşti tăt cu străinii.	For you are always with strangers,
Şî străinii-s tare răi	And strangers are very bad;
Nu-s ca şi părinţii tăi.	They're not like your parents.
Uă sorucă şî mnireasă	Oh, little sister and bride,
Bine te-ai măritat	You have married well,
Uă după-un fecior de-mpărat.	After a son of the King's;
Ti-o dus la curtea lui	He has taken you to his courtyard
În fundu pămîntului	In the bottom of the earth,
Uă unde leac de soare nu-i.	Oh, where there isn't a glimmer of sunshine.
Nici nînge nici îndeaţă	It doesn't snow, nor does it freeze,
Nici să face dimineaţă.	Nor does it become morning.
Uă bine te-ai măritat	Oh, well you have married,
Că la socri nu te-am dat.	Because we didn't give you to in-laws.
Uă bărbatu nu te-a toi	Oh, your husband won't scream at you,
Nici socrii nu te-or sfădii.	Nor will in-laws fight with you,
Da noi supăraţi om si	But we'll be troubled,
Cît pă lume-om mai trăi.	However long we live.
Vai de mine hăi Ga	Oh, my goodness, Ga,
Uă nu m-am gîndit de-aiestea.	Oh, I didn't think about this,
Niciodată n-am gîndit	Never did I think
Cîte avem de plinit.	How much we'd have to go through.
În lume cînd am plecat	When we left for work,
Vai cu drag ne-aţi aşteptat.	Oh, you waited for us lovingly.
Uă sorucă şî tu Ga	Oh, little sister, you, Ga,
Scoală-te şî-om povesti	Get up and we'll talk.
Cîtu-i de greu a trăi	How hard it is to live,
Uă în lume cu străinii.	Oh, in a world with strangers.

Sister 1:

Uă sorucă soră creaţă	Little sister, sister with curls,
Scurt-o fost a ta viaţă.	Your life was short;
Mîndru ţi-o fo numele	You had a beautiful name,
Scurte ţi-o fo zîlele.	Your days were few.
Cînd o fo mai mîndru trai	When life was best,
Mîndră la unsprezece ai.	Beauty, eleven years old,
Nu ştiu ce te-ai supărat	I don't know why you got angry
Uă şî de la noi ai plecat.	And left us.
Mîndrucă şî mnireasă	Little beauty and bride,
Tînără te duci de-acasă.	So young you go from home.
Bine te-am măritat	We have married you well,
Puţină zestre ţi-am dat.	We gave little for your dowry;
Uă mnirele nu-o poftit	The groom didn't ask.

Numa popii am plătit.

Şî ătîta ţi-o fo zestrea

Cît am plătit la popa.

Noi nu ţi-am dat zestre multă

Numa cît îţi facem nunta.

Uă sorucă sora me

Bine s-a hodini ie.

Şî în lume nu-i năcăjî

Scoală soră şî ţi-oi spune.

. . . .

Sister 3:

Scoală şî ni-om tîrgui

Cît i zice ţi-oi plăti.

Cît i zice ieu ţi-oi da

Scoală-te de aicea.

Uă mîndrucă şî mnireasă

Tînără te duci de-acasă

Nu ştiu mamă ce te lasă.

Uă mîndrucă şî hăi Ga

Rău mă doare inima

Şî nu te mai pot strîga.

Uă sorucă şî hăi Ga

Uă duminică pă sara.

Tu la mine ai zinit

Şî noi bine ne-am sfătuit

Şî am culcat şî am durnit.

Uă sorucă şî hăi Ga

Bunucă noaptea la tri

Ieu nu te-am putut trezî.

Ieu afară mni-am ieşit

După tata am zinit

Şî nici cu iel n-ai grăit.

Uă iute te-ai măritat

Pă nimeni n-ai întrebat.

Uă mîndrucă şî mnireasă

Tînără te duci de-acasă

Nu ştiu mama ce te lasă.

Uă mîndrucă sorore

Ce m-oi fa fără de ie?

Uă mîndruca mamii

Fără tine ce om fa?

Uă sorucă sora me

We only paid the priest,

That was all of your dowry—

What we paid the priest.

We didn't give you much in the way of
   dowry,

Only what it took to make the
   wedding.

Little sister, my sister,

Well she will rest,

And she won't struggle in the world.

Get up, sister, and I'll tell you.

. . . .

Get up and we'll bargain:

What you ask, I'll pay you;

What you ask, I'll give you;

Get up from here.

Oh, little beauty and bride,

So young you leave home;

I don't know why mama lets you.

Oh, little beauty, hey, Ga,

My heart aches

And I can't shout for you anymore.

Oh, little sister, hey, Ga,

Oh, Sunday evening

You came to my house

And we talked together,

And we went to bed and slept.

Oh, little sister, hey, Ga,

Oh, dear one, at three in the morning

I was unable to awaken you.

I went out

And came after father,

And you didn't speak with him either.

Oh, you have married early;

You didn't ask anyone.

Oh, little beauty and bride,

So young you go from home;

I don't know why mama lets you.

Oh, little beauty, my sister,

What will I do without her?

Oh, mother's little beauty,

Without you, what shall I do?

Oh, little sister, my sister,

Rău îmi pare după ie
Ca şî după mama me.
Că amu-i lumea tare re
Nu-i tihne la nimenea.
Uă sorucă şî hăi Ga
Uă am zinit bună la tine
Să văd de nu ţi-i mai bine.
Uite-te binele tău
Că ti-o pus în copîrşeu.
Uă sorucă şî hăi Ga
Uă nu ştiu aud sau n-aud
Tăt te strîg şî nu răspunzi.

Uă sorucă sora me
Ce m-oi fa fără de ie?
Fără tine ce m-oi fa?
Uă sorucă şî hăi Ga
Coconii cui i-oi lăsa?
Coconii cu cine-or si

Dacă tu nu-i mai zini?
Uă sorucă sora me
Uă bine s-a hodini ie.
Ie s-a hodini
Da noi supăraţi om si
Cîte zîle le-om trăi.
Uă sorucă şî hăi Ga
Uă tu la noi nu-i mai zini
Batăr cît de hie mni-ar si
Uă să rămîi cu coconii.
Uă mîndrucă şî mnireasă.
Tînără te duci de-acasă.
Nu ştiu mama ce te lasă.
Uă sorucă şî hăi Ga
Zi şî noaptea m-oi cînta.
Uă sorucă sora me
Ce m-oi fa fără de ie?
Că bine m-o ascultat
O mărs unde o-am mînat.
Uă mîndrucă surore
Ieu nu te mai pot cînta
Că mă doare inima.
Uă sorucă sora me
Ce m-oi fa fără de ie?

I feel so bad about her
And for my mother,
For now the world is bad;
There isn't peace for anyone.
Oh, little sister, hey, Ga,
Oh, I've come to you, dear one,
To see if you aren't better.
Look at your luck—
It has put you in a coffin.
Oh, little sister, hey, Ga,
Oh, I don't know if you hear or not;
I keep calling you, and you don't
    respond.
Oh, little sister, my sister,
What will I do without her?
Without you, what will I do?
Oh, little sister, hey, Ga,
To whom will I leave my children?
The children, with whom will they
    be,
If you don't come anymore?
Oh, little sister, my sister,
Oh, well she will rest.
She will rest,
But we will be upset
As long as we live.
Oh, little sister, hey, Ga,
Oh, you won't come to us again,
No matter how much I need you,
Oh, to stay with the children.
Oh, little beauty and bride,
So young you go from home;
I don't know why mama lets you.
Oh, little sister, hey, Ga,
Day and night I'll lament.
Little sister, my sister,
What will I do without her?
Because she obeyed me,
She went where I sent her.
Little beautiful sister,
I cannot lament for you anymore,
Because my heart aches.
Oh, little sister, my sister,
What will I do without her?

Mama:

Inima me i de ptiatră	My heart of stone,
Vai de mine şî de mine.	Oh, my goodness, and oh, my.
Uă mîndrucă şî hăi Ga	Oh, little beauty, hey, Ga,
Spune-m tăt ce ti-oi întreba	Tell me all that I ask you;
Ce te duci de la mama?	Why are you going from your mama?
Nu mă-aşă rău supăra	Don't hurt me so much
Uă pă tătă viaţa.	For the rest of my life.
Uă Doamne mîndră mamii	Oh, my God, mother's beauty,
Duminică pă sara	Sunday around evening,
Mîndrucă tu ai cinat	Little beauty, you ate
La Măricuţa ai plecat.	And went to Maricuţa's,
Şî voiosă te-ai aflat	And you were full of energy.
Noapte bună ţi-ai luat.	You said good night.
Uă Doamne mîndra mamii	Oh, Lord, mother's beauty,
Uă bine ti-i hodini	Oh, well you rest;
Da ieu supărată oi si.	But I'll suffer.
Scoală-te şî te uită	Get up and look about,
Că cum să facem nuntă.	How we are preparing for the wedding.
Doamne mîndruca mamii	Oh, Lord, mother's daughter,
Nu ştiu moarte ti-o luat	I don't know if death took you
Ori mămuca ti-o temat.	Or if mother called you.

Sister 1:

Uă drag mni-o fo cînd am fo tăte.	I liked it when we were all together.
Uă mîndrucă şî mnireasă	Little beauty and bride,
Tînără te duci de-acasă.	So young you go from home.
Uă bine te-am măritat	Oh, we have married you well.
Puţină zestre ţi-am dat.	We gave you little for a dowry;
Noi nu ţi-am dat zestre multă	We didn't give you much dowry,
Numa cît îţi facem nuntă.	Only what it took to make the wedding.
Uă mîndrucă soră creaţă	Little beauty, sister with curls,
Scurtă o fo a ta viaţă.	Your life was short,
Mîndru ţi-o fo numele	Your name was beautiful,
Scurte ţi-o fo zîlele.	Your days were few;
Cînd o fo mai mîndru trai	When life was best,
Mîndră la unsprezece ai.	Beauty, at eleven,
Bun-ai fost şî cumnincioară	You were good and well-behaved.
Mîndrucă şî hăi Ga.	Little beauty, hey, Ga,
Uă în lume cînd am plecat	Oh, when we left to work,
Sînătosă te-am lăsat.	You were healthy;
Ş-napoi cînd am zinit	And when we came back,

Uită-te cum ti-am găsît.
În scrisoare nu mni-ai spus
Că tu ieşti gată de dus.
Telegramă-am căpătat
Să sim gată de plecat.
Uă sorucă tu Păla
Gată-te şî om pleca.
Ni-o temat mama acasă
Bunucă că ieşti mnireasă.
Mîndrucă şî hăi Ga
Noi în lume om pleca
D-apoi mama ce s-a fa?
Că sîngură s-a afla.
Dacă bunuc-ai plecat.
Cu cine s-a sfătui
Dacă bunucă nu-i si?
Şî cine o-a mîngîie?
Că tu te duci nu rămîi.

Uă mîndrucă şî hăi Ga
Scoală-te şî om da mîna
Ş-apoi bună îi pleca.
Uă mîndrucă mîndra me
Bine să mărită ie
Mărita ni-om tăt aşe.
Uă de mine hăi Ga
Nu ştiu moarte ti-o luat
Ori moşica ti-o temat.
Uă mîndrucă şî mnireasă
Tînără te duci de-acasă.
Mîndrucă şî hăi Ga.

Sister 2:

Fața ta ca şî spuma
Negri-oa ca şî tina.
Uă sorucă sora me
Tînără să duce ie.
Tu ieşti fată tînăre
Nu ti-am dat nurore.

Nu ti-am dat noră din casă

Că ieşti mai mnică mnireasă.
Scoală şî om povesti
C-am sosît tăţi fraţii.

Look how we've found you.
You didn't say in your letter
That you were ready to go.
We received a telegram,
To get ready to leave.
Oh, little sister, you, Păla,
Get ready and we'll leave;
Mother called us to come home,
Dear one, because you are a bride.
Little beauty, hey, Ga,
We'll leave for work,
And then what will mama do?
She'll be alone.
Since, dear one, you've gone,
With whom will she chat
If, dear one, you aren't here?
And who will comfort her?
Because you are leaving, and won't
     stay.
Little beauty, hey, Ga,
Get up and let's shake hands
And then you'll leave.
Little beauty, my beauty,
Well she marries;
We'll all marry like that.
Oh, my, hey, Ga,
I don't know if death took you
Or if grandmother called you.
Oh, little beauty and bride,
So young you go from home,
Little beauty, hey, Ga.

Your face like whey
Will blacken like mud.
Little sister, my sister,
So young she goes.
You are a young girl;
We didn't give you as a daughter-in-
     law,
We didn't give you as a daughter-in-
     law from the house
Because you are the youngest bride.
Get up and we'll talk.
All your brothers have arrived.

Uă sorucă sora me	Oh, little sister, my sister,
Bine să mărită ie.	Well she marries.
Ie bine s-a hodini	She will rest well,
În lume n-a năcăjî.	She won't struggle in the world.
Scoală-te şi om povesti	Get up and we'll talk;
Cîtu-i de greu a trăi	How hard it is to live
În lume cu străinii.	In a world with strangers.
. . . .	. . . .
La Măricuţa ai plecat	You went to Măricuţa's
Că să stai cu coconii.	To stay with the children.
. . . .	. . . .

*During the funeral, as the casket was being taken
from the house into the courtyard:*

Sister 2:

Uă sorucă şî tu Ga	Oh, little sister, you, Ga,
Si bună şî nu pleca.	Be good and don't leave.
Uă sorucă şî hăi Ga	Oh, little sister, hey, Ga,
Oi ieşî-naintea ta	I'll go ahead of you
Că da-de ti-oi întorna.	In case you turn back,
Uă de ti-oi putea opri	Oh, so that I can stop you,
Şî de-acasă nu îi porni.	And you won't go from home.
Uă mîndrucă şî mnireasă	Oh, little beauty and bride,
Ca şî-o floare din fereastă	Like a flower in the window,
Tînără te duci de-acasă.	Young you go from home.
Uă mîndrucă mîndra me	Little beauty, my beauty,
Tînără a putrezî ie.	Young she putrefies;
Faţă ta ca sansiu	Your face like a carnation
Negri-oa ca pămîntu.	Will blacken like the earth.
Uă sorucă şî hăi Ga.	Oh, little sister, hey, Ga.
. . . .	. . . .

At the grave:

Mama:

Uă mîndrucă şî hăi Ga	Oh, little beauty, hey, Ga,
Ieu mă duc la casa ta.	I'm going to your house
Că mă doare inima	Because my heart aches,
Că ai zinit lîngă mama.	For you've come near your mother.
Uă Doamne mămucă me	Oh, God, my little mother,
În scoală-te şi îi vide.	Get up and you'll see;
Că şî nepoata sose	Because your granddaughter has arrived,
Şî ti-i sfătui cu ie.	And you'll chat with her.

Uă mămucă şî hăi ta
Rău m-aţi putut supăra
Că mni-aţi luat pă mîndra.
Uă Doamne mîndra mamii
Nu ştiu moartea ti-o luat
Ori mămuca ti-o temat.
Ti-o temat mama la ie
Să nu sie sîngure.
Să aibă şî ie o fată
Să nu sie supărată.
Uă mîndrucă şî hăi Ga
Spune-mi ce ti-oi întreba
Ce te duci de la mama?
Tu de noră nu te-aş da.

Uă Doamne mîndra mamii
Ieu tăt aşă m-am gîndit:
Dac-am fete bugăte
Nu le-aş da nurori pă tăte.

Că tu ieşti mai tînere
Nu te-as si dat nurore.
Tu cu mine în casă-i sta
Şî ginere mni-oi lua
Sîngură nu mni-ţi lăsa.
Uă mîndrucă şî hăi Ga
Şi ieu cu tine-aş pleca
Sîngură nu te-aş lasa
Că mă doare inima.
Uă Doamne mîndruca me
Duce-m-aş şi ieu cu ie.
Nu o-aş lasa sîngure
Dacă-i aşă tînăre
Să sie supărată.
Uă mîndrucă şî hăi Ga
Asară daca-nsera
Hai acasă cu mama.
Că ieu cina oi găta
Şî laolaltă om cina
Nu ne-a dure inima.
De-aş şti mîndră că-i zini
Cu cină m-aş pregăti
Şî-nainte aş ieşi.
Doamne bine mni-ar tihni
Supărată n-aş trăi.
Da aşă îs tăt supărată

Oh, mother dear and father,
Badly you've been able to hurt me
Because you've taken my beauty.
Oh, Lord, mother's beauty,
I don't know if death took you
Or if mother called you.
Mama called you to her
So she wouldn't be alone,
So that she too could have a girl,
So she wouldn't be upset.
Oh, little beauty, hey, Ga,
Tell me what I ask you:
Why are you going from your mama?
I wouldn't give you as a daughter-in-
    law.

Oh, Lord, mother's beauty,
I always reasoned,
Since I have girls enough
I wouldn't give them all as daughters-
    in-law.

Because you are younger
I wouldn't have given you;
You would remain with me at home,
And I would take a son-in-law.
You wouldn't leave me alone.
Oh, little beauty, hey, Ga,
And I'll go with you,
I won't leave you alone,
Because my heart aches.
Oh, Lord, my little beauty,
I'd go with her;
I wouldn't leave her alone,
Since she is so young,
To be upset.
Oh, little beauty, hey, Ga,
In the evening when it gets dark,
Come home with mama
Because I'll make dinner
And we'll eat dinner together,
And our hearts won't ache.
If I know, beauty, that you'll come,
I'll prepare dinner
And I'll come out to greet you—
Oh God, it would please me well.
I won't live with suffering.
But as it is, I'm only suffering

Şî voiosă niciodată.	And never in good spirits.
Noapte bună mîndra me	Good night, my beauty,
Văd bine că-i rămîne.	I see that you'll stay here.
Ieu oi si supărată	I'll be upset
Cîte zîle oi ave	As many days as I have
Dacă te-ai dus tînăre.	If you've left so young.
Uă mîndrucă floare creaţă	Oh, little beauty, curly flower,
Scurtă-o fo a ta viaţă.	Your life was short,
Mîndru ţi-o fo numele	Your name was beautiful,
Scurte ţi-o fo zîlele.	Your days were few
Cînd o fo mai mîndru trai	When life was best,
Mîndră la douăsprezece ai.	Beauty, at twelve.
Noapte bună zic amu	I'll say good night now,
C-apoi n-oi zice altu.	Then I won't say it again—
Noapte bună pă viaţă	Good night for life,
Nu pînă mîni dimineaţă.	Not just until tomorrow morning.

Appendix E: Vrem Pace
(We Want Peace)

This poem by Gavrila lui Birău expresses the sentiments of this Transylvanian villager about nuclear war. It also echoes the political stance of Romania.

De război întreaga lume
Este greu amenințată
Ce-n istorie așa ceva
N-a mai existat vreodată.

By war, the entire world
Is dangerously threatened;
In history, such a thing
Has never existed.

Nori întunecosi încearcă
Iar bătrîna Europă
Care prevestesc furtuna
Și o mare catastrofă.

Darkened clouds put to the test
Again old Europe;
They forewarn of the storm
And a great catastrophe.

Astazi cînd sîntem în viață
Și vedem zile senine
Ne-ntrebăm în gîndul nostru
Oare ce va mai fi mîine?

Today, while we are alive
And see quiet days,
We ask in our thoughts:
And what shall be tomorrow?

Cînd cei tari se înarmeaza
Și-ar vrea lumea s-o cuprindă

When the strong arm themselves,
And they would like to control the
world,

Moartea își arată colții
Focul gata-i să se aprindă.

Death shows its teeth;
The fire is ready to be lit.

Porumbelul păcii strigă
Către orice stat și țară
Jos războiul și din lume
Dușmănia să dispară.

The peace dove shouts
Toward each state and country,
Down with war,
And may hatred disappear from the
world.

Către voi conducătorii
Stîlpi ai marilor puteri

Toward you leaders,
Pillars of the great powers,

Strigă să-ncetaţi furia
Şi să-ncepeţi negocieri.

Înarmărilor nebune
Să se pună odată frîu.
Şi să faceţi tratative
Pînă nu-i prea tîrziu.

Căci în mîna voastră este
Viaţa omenirii-ntregi
Şi cîndva o să răspundeţi
De orice fărădelegi.

Sîntem împotriva unui
Nou război distrugător
Şi lozinca noastra-i PACEA
Care spune tutoror:

"Pace vrem şi pentru pace
Vom lupta fără-ncetare
Pînă pacea va ajunge
Peste tot biruitoare."

It shouts to you to slow down the fury
And to begin negotiations.

These crazy armaments—
Put a stop to them already,
And arrive at agreements
Before it is too late.

For in your hands
Is the life of all humanity,
And somehow you shall respond
For any fateful transgression.

We are against any
New destructive war,
And our slogan is PEACE
That everyone heralds:

"We want peace and for peace
We shall fight without rest
Until peace arrives
And is victorious everywhere."

Notes

Introduction

1. For works in English about the historical figure Vlad Ţepeş, see the popular works by Florescu and McNally (1972; 1973), as well as Stoicescu 1978. Also note the 1987 study in French by Cazacu. Wolf 1975, Florescu and McNally 1972, and Twitchell 1981 include notes on popular productions of Dracula in literature, theater, and film. Bram Stoker, Dracula's authorial progenitor, knew of the Transylvanian prince's macabre if nonetheless heroic deeds. It is not my intention to examine the confluence of circumstances that contributed to the birth of the West's revered count.

2. I wish to thank Robert and Rebecca Tracy for calling to my attention this detail from Browning's "The Pied Piper of Hamelin" (1931, 1130).

> And I must not omit to say
> That in Transylvania there's a tribe
> Of alien people who ascribe
> The outlandish ways and dress
> On which their neighbours lay such stress,
> To their fathers and mothers having risen
> Out of some subterraneous prison
> Into which they were trepanned
> Long time ago in a mighty band
> Out of Hamelin town in Brunswick land,
> But how or why, they don't understand.

In a discussion during my 1985 summer visit, I was intrigued to learn from a representative from the Ministry of Tourism in Bucureşti that the legend of the Pied Piper is known and used by certain Saxon Germans living in Transylvania (e.g., Covasna, Măreşti) as an origin legend.

3. Craft (1984) and Twitchell (1981, 125), among others, present interesting although different analyses of the sublimated sexuality of Stoker's novel. For Craft, it is a tale of homoerotic desire submerged by Victorian standards that required

the reification of heterosexuality. Twitchell invokes the psychoanalytic Oedipus interpretation.

Regarding science, Craft (1984, 126) provocatively suggests that Van Helsing as representative of the scientific community "polished teeth into hypodermic needles, a cultural refinement that masks violation as healing." Van Helsing himself referred to his medical tools as "the ghastly paraphernalia of our beneficial trade," thereby alluding to the "troubled relationship between paternalism and violence. The medical profession licenses the power to penetrate, devises a delicate instrumentation and defines the canons of procedure, while the religious tradition, with its insistent idealization of women, encodes a restriction on the mobility of desire (who penetrates, and whom) and then licenses a tremendous punishment for the violation of the code."

4. See, for example, the works of Foucault (1972; 1975; 1978).

5. Apropos the computer game *Transylvania:* "It's no wonder that *Transylvania* received the Electronic Games Magazine Award for outstanding visual effects" (*Microtimes*, April 1985). "Transylvania" as a concept inspires the mind's creative potential.

6. I have been somewhat astonished by the response Transylvania evokes. Most Americans do not know that Transylvania exists. The most typical queries are "You mean there really is a place called Transylvania? Where?" It is a sad commentary on the current state of knowledge that a simple answer to those questions does not edify. Many people have no sense of the location of Hungary or Romania, knowing only that these countries are "communist." Furthermore, many Americans are surprised at the suggestion that Romanians do not hold this particular configuration of vampire beliefs. An article derived from, as opposed to being based on, a lecture I presented appeared in the *San Francisco Chronicle* in 1985 and prompted months of radio talk-show interviews. No vampires in Romania? Romanian tourist representatives, who had at one time chosen to profit from this cultural capital, commented on the same reaction from American travelers. The Romanians have other related beliefs and beings, but the count as such is unknown to the indigenous population (except through tourism). Their "count" was the aforementioned Vlad Țepeș.

7. I do not pretend to be a specialist on vampire lore, although I am familiar with much of the literature. In addition to the references cited in note 1 above, see also Twitchell 1981 and Craft 1984.

8. Apparently, throughout the Inquisition vampire trials were ecclesiastical matters rather than secular, following the dictates of the *Malleus Maleficarum* (*Witch Hammer*). "The Malleus Maleficarum, first printed in 1486, was co-authored by two Dominicans, Jakob Sprengler and Prior Heinrich Kratmer. This book, probably the single most important work on demonology ever written, was the outgrowth of the Papal Bull of 1484 in which Innocent VIII called for a procedure for witchcraft trials" (Twitchell 1981, 15). The priest as exorcist is well known in both religious practice and twentieth-century popular culture. I recommend Twitchell's introduction (1981, 3–38). In general, his work is an intriguing source for anyone interested in the vampire cult. It offers interesting analyses of familiar literary texts.

9. See, for example, Pascu 1944; Seton-Watson 1963; Hobsbawm 1972; Verdery 1983a; Giurescu n.d. An extensive bibliography has been generated about the history of Transylvania as well as about the dispute between Hungary and Romania.

Dracula also figures into debates over Transylvania's social history. I thank Steve Sampson for calling to my attention a recent RFE (Radio Free Europe) report (April 23, 1986): "Who's Afraid of Dracula?" Paunescu, a poet and journalist demoted from Party favor, recently produced a xenophobic commentary in *Contemporanul* defending Romania's history against Western attempts to degrade it. "It is not the first time that strange interests have merged behind so-called works of art from abroad in order to tarnish and discredit the national history of the Romanians. Sometimes an attack on a people's history can be even more serious than an attack on the current politics of that people. . . . The Dracula film, along with the corpus of Dracula literature, are only one page in a vast output of political pornography directed by our enemies against us." This article has apparently spawned ongoing discussion. Although an analogy between Ceauşescu and Vlad Ţepeş may be tempting, it is ill founded. In this case, Western art and Romanian politics need to be distinguished from each other.

It should be mentioned that most American anthropologists have only coincidentally done fieldwork in Transylvania. See, for example, Cole 1976; Marrant 1977; Beck 1979; Kideckel 1979; Ratner 1980; Sampson 1980, 1982; MacArthur 1981; Freedman 1984; Randall 1983; and Verdery 1983a. All except Cole, Sampson, and Verdery are unpublished dissertations. This list is meant to be suggestive and not exhaustive.

10. "Historical Maramureş" was diminished in size by the 1920 treaty that delivered part of this land to the aegis of the Soviet Union. The inhabitants of Romanian Maramureş refer to the villages across the river as those *peste Tiza*. Relatives are granted, at least in theory, visitation rights every two years. Riding the train from Sighetu Marmaţiei to Bucureşti reveals that the Soviet side of the Tiza is highly illuminated. This particular border in Romania is not guarded as evidently as the Yugoslav-Hungarian area through which Romanians attempt to leave illegally for the West. For the reader interested in a summary of Maramureş history, I recommend Marrant (1977, 75–109) in particular.

11. In a pertinent report entitled "Changes in Rural Mentality" (*Amfiteatru* [February 1981]: 18), A. Mihu notes that the prewar slogan of farmers, "We want land," no longer obtains. Since collectivization, the farmer now prefers to be an "absent symbolic owner." A joke also makes this point: "What is a Romanian peasant? He is the person who stands in the fields and gives instructions to students, the military, and intellectuals who work the land."

12. It is not my intent to provide a bibliography relevant to these concerns. For studies on Romania sensitive to these issues, see, for example, Chirot 1976a; H. Stahl 1980; Verdery 1983a; and Shafir 1985.

13. The literature on peasants is enormous and well beyond the scope of this introduction to survey. See, for example, Wolf 1966; Berger 1972; Hobsbawm 1973; Meillasoux 1973; Braudel 1979; Shanin 1979; Randall 1983; Verdery 1983a; and Bell 1984.

14. Definitionally, peasants already do not exist. However, the semantic force

of this label (as category) is still operative in Maramureş, as will be discussed in the following chapters.

15. Feher et al. (1983, 39) note in more categorical terms the "survival" of former "national stereotypes, prejudices, and forms of behavior" in contemporary socialist states: "In the provinces especially one feels as if the phenomena of modernization have changed only the outward surface of existence. The nature of human relations with all their degrading personal dependencies and brutal inequalities, the basic types of life style and life practices have remained essentially unchanged. It is not a question of a lack of some ideal socialist form of life . . . but the disturbing factor of the grotesque apeing by which the middle strata of the new apparatus of power attempt to reproduce the values and forms of behaviour of their pre-Revolutionary—mostly gentry—predecessors, and that of its social inverse: the traditional unquestioning and unhesitating popular respect of authority. . . . These social systems have proved to be in an important sense deeply conservative."

16. Also see, for example, Nicolae Ceauşescu (*România Literară* 27, 1981): "The RCP [Romanian Communist Party] and the Romanian state act in such fashion that all the cultural and educational means society has at its disposal will be used for the molding of a genuinely new man inspired by the revolutionary conception of our Party." Inasmuch as no such "new man" has as yet emerged, there seems to be a discrepancy between ideology and its implementation.

For an extended discussion of the significance of culture in socialist Romania, see especially Tănase and Gheorghe 1984. On socialist state building, see Ferge 1979; Konrad and Szelenyi 1979.

17. Szelenyi (1982, 320) summarizes a vision of this "new socialist man": "If someone were to analyse carefully the ideal type of socialist man—a test still to be done—he would find striking similarities with the values and tastes of the highbrow upper middle class of any advanced industrial society. Socialist man should read books, listen to music, be dressed like, and behave with his children as doctrinaire left-wing academics do. If a semiskilled factory laborer in Prague does not match this ideal, then he should be ashamed of himself. . . . One cannot be proud of being a worker or peasant: the cultural image is a homogeneous one, and conflicting or competing values simply do not exist. There is only a single hierarchy of values." For discussion of the "new socialist man" in the Soviet literature, refer, for example, to Brown 1984, 101, n. 116. For a psychological approach to this phenomenon, see Heiliger 1980.

18. Maramureş has a particular identity in the nation's historical lineage. Peasants as a category constitute a generalized group on whom ideologues "rely." Again, peasants are problematic because of their class and property associations yet significant because of the relation between territorial presence and historical legitimacy. The regime's rhetoric is typified in the following public news statement: "A remarkable contribution to all the victories won by our socialist system has been made by the peasantry—the class which over the centuries defended at the cost of its own blood the ancestors' land, the national language and being, the homeland's independence. Under the new historical circumstances, in alliance

with the working class, the peasantry acts firmly for the implementation of the Party's socialist agrarian policies. . . while making a valuable contribution to the whole work of building the multilaterally developed socialist society" (*Romanian News*, February 26, 1982, 6).

19. This difference is reflected in the work of others who have done their research in Romania; see especially Verdery 1983a. Our discussions often seem as though we have lived in different countries. Marriage and funeral rites occur throughout Romania, but their elaboration through oral poetry and ceremonial sequences has disappeared or been significantly diminished.

20. The literature on ritual and symbolism is immense. See, notably, Van Gennep 1960; Durkheim 1965; Peacock 1968; V. Turner 1969; Geertz 1973, 1983; Ortner 1973, 1978; Munn 1974; T. Turner 1977; Todorov 1982; Valeri 1985. There are many studies of specific rituals (e.g., healing, funerary, carnival) in specific locales; it is simply beyond the scope of this endeavor to provide a bibliography.

21. Lane (1981, 24–34) discusses the relevance of the normative approach to ritual and its controlling function as utilized in Soviet society. This perspective is pertinent to the realization of the "new socialist man" and explains the rationale behind planned cultural management. Van Gennep was the first to underscore the significance of transitions and their "management"; his contributions are seminal in the study of ritual. See Van Gennep 1960; V. Turner 1969; and especially T. Turner 1977.

22. Rituals represent ideological systems. It is not novel that political powers make use of rituals and symbols. The relationship between ideology and practice has inspired considerable debate among Marxist scholars. Most Romanians today, assessing the empirical ramifications of this relationship, would scoff at intellectual arguments: there, the relationship is perceived as thoroughly mystified. The discrepancy between the idealized relations presented in ritualized political rhetoric and those existing in reality is too great.

23. There is an extensive Romanian literature on magic practices. I do not present it here, but relevant references will be noted throughout this book and may also be found in the notes of my study on *Căluş* (1981).

24. On emotion and ritual, see, for example, Durkheim 1965 (4–111, especially); Munn 1974; T. Turner 1977.

25. As we will see in the chapter on funeral rites, families are not supposed to grieve excessively over the loss of a young child; with God's blessing, there will be other children. An inscription on a child's wooden cross in the unusual Cimitirul Vesel (Merry Cemetery) in Săpînţa, Maramureş, reads:

Tată mamă mă jălesc	Tata, mama, they mourn for me
Şi la mine se gîndesc.	And think about me.
În lume cînd m-am născut	When I was born into this world,
Mare voie aţi avut.	You had great joy.
Dar voia vi s-a schimbat	But your joy changed
Dacă eu am reposat.	When I died.
Voi părinţi nu mă jaliţi	You, parents, don't mourn for me.
Altu copil pregătiţi.	Have another child.

The child admonishes his parents to get on with their lives. On the Merry Cemetery, see Simion 1972.

26. Abortion (except under extenuating circumstances) and contraception are illegal in Romania. Both generation and urban or rural residence are significant in determining attitudes regarding abortion and contraception. It would be safe to venture that most young people, urban and rural residents, would appreciate access to contraceptives. The strict ban has, as usual, made illegal abortion, "rhythm," and abstention the primary forms of contraception.

27. It was Herder in the eighteenth century who first developed the notion of poetry as the expression of a people's soul. Recently, Czeslaw Milosz stated: "At moments of cataclysm and upheaval, poetry becomes popular as the expression of the people's hope, aspirations, and identity. In such moments, poetry is the most expressive voice of freedom . . . there are some very down to earth reasons. In the Europe occupied by the Nazis, poetry was the most handy instrument of moral resistance because you could copy a poem and pass it from hand to hand. Prose was too long and difficult for this purpose. So there are various reasons, historical and practical" (1986, 34). See Lampland 1981 for an account of the poetry of 1956 in Hungary. It is pertinent to mention the humanist contributions of the literature of dissent and protest through which "the concerns of the Eastern half of European culture are voiced," notably the "failure of regimes to realize the human potential of socialism" (Hoffman and Kitromildes 1981, 172).

28. What Clark has written about the Soviet novel pertains to the RCP's explicitly didactic use of poetry to "popularize ideology, to disseminate it in a form both attractive and accessible to the masses" (1981, 44). For a comparative example of the political use of songs, see Lidtke 1982 regarding Nazi Germany; this work, as well as his 1985 book, contain valuable references.

29. When I receive correspondence from friends in the village, these letters invariably contain poems or are themselves composed in poetic form.

30. Karnoouh (1983a, 39–45) criticizes the Romanian reference to this poetry as "popular poetry." He notes that the category of *poesie populara* imposes an intellectual juxtaposition with a category linked to the poetry of the intelligentsia (making it possible to compare them in these terms), and, of great importance, removes this vital poetic production from its essential context. Karnoouh's point is well taken and informs my usage of *poetry* or of *couplets* throughout this work.

There is an extensive literature on "popular poetry" in Romania, consisting by and large of regional or village typological collections. Maramureş is well represented in this corpus. See, for example, Ţiplea 1906; Bud 1908; Papahagi 1925; Ştefănescu 1968; D. Pop 1971; Bartók (1923) 1975; Doniga 1980; Şter 1980. As a corrective to these decontextualized works, I highly recommend Karnoouh (1983a).

31. See Mukařovský 1979, as well as Needham 1972 and Burke 1966.

32. The ritual discourse of both men and women is discussed in Karnoouh's monograph (1983a). His provocative and insightful analysis is based on years of field research in another area of historical Maramureş and therefore is highly relevant to my work. It should also be of interest to anyone interested in ritual and discourse.

33. It is convenient to attribute restraint to the presence of a foreigner. In over sixty hours of verses recorded in situ, however, I find it implausible to suggest that my presence caused avoidance, especially given the considerable amount of alcohol consumed at ritual events, with its resultant weakening of self-censorship. Nonetheless, the political function of criticism was implicitly acknowledged by the authorities who demanded to check my tapes before I left the country. They were concerned that inadmissible matters had been recorded, but these suspicions were not borne out.

34. The point here, following Lakoff and Johnson (1980), is that metaphor and metonym are not simply linguistic devices: they "are part of the ordinary, everyday way we think and act as well as talk" (37). The literature on metaphor and metonym is interdisciplinary and will be cited throughout the chapters on weddings and funerals. In a sense, the analysis of Romanian ritual is an analysis of the metaphors by which the people live. On metaphor and ritual, see especially Fernandez 1974 and Tambiah 1979.

35. The local usage is highly informed by Party polemics about the nature of historical development. Unfortunately, this is a matter for another discussion. On culture and civilization, see especially Elias 1978.

36. The formal analysis of the poetry in conjunction with contextual analysis is beyond the scope of this work. This omission will create limitations for some, but including such analysis would foster limitations for others. Concerning the focus on the semantics of meaning, see especially Friedrich 1979b. From the recent Romanian scholarship, see Coteanu and Wald 1981.

37. This research was postdoctoral work. My doctoral research was also done in Romania (see Kligman 1981). Both were supported by the International Research and Exchanges Board (IREX). It is unquestionable that familiarity and experience enable researchers to better manage the frustrations that arise because of bureaucratic constraints. The current political-intellectual climate is discouraging at best, however, and research by "newcomers" has nearly ceased.

38. Generally, most researchers come to Romania under the aegis of IREX or the Department of Education Fulbright grants. For additional discussion of the problems arising from fieldwork in Romania, see also Verdery 1983a.

39. The complexity of this symbolic duel is well exemplified in the case of Romania. America, particularly under the Reagan administration, has an interest in demonstrating the failure of communism and the abuse of human rights. Yet this same administration, until recently, continued to grant Romania most-favored-nation (MFN) status. Romania does have a relatively independent foreign policy. It does have relations with Israel. And it continues to voice its disdain of the Soviet Union. But to reward Romania with a privileged position in the Eastern bloc through MFN status is to applaud ideology and neglect practice. Romania is today one of the most repressive regimes in the bloc; its policies violate the human dignity of all its citizens, not only Jews, Hungarians, and other minorities. The applause granted Ceauşescu (for whatever reasons) speaks to the superficiality of current American foreign policy in this domain. (If the situation in Romania is the price of relative "independence" from the Soviets—which is a rather superficial

view—it is surely not a state of affairs to which the other Eastern bloc countries aspire.)

40. The official noted that although this endeavor had been an error, it was not alterable. Before my arrival, people had been warned about responding to inquiries regarding politics, history, cooperativization, and so forth.

41. This requirement applies primarily to foreigners from the West and Third World countries, the former being more "dangerous" as contaminating elements. The recent debate about the continuation of MFN status for Romania was cause for an anti-American campaign in 1985. Colleagues and friends of almost a decade were noticeably more frightened to meet than before. The paranoia generated by fear of reprisal is less pervasive in villages, where it is simply easier to keep an eye on the whereabouts of any nonlocal person.

42. I was unable to surmount this difficulty during my first research sojourn in Romania in 1975–76. Needless to say, this restriction had serious consequences for my research (better, of course, than imposing serious consequences on hospitable Romanians). I had almost no difficulty in arranging housing during my postdoctoral research, however, a situation having more to do with the region than with my more advanced professional status. Researchers pursuing projects in rural areas may be encouraged to reside in the city closest to the site of research. But this is impractical, in terms of both methodology and inconvenience. Transportation difficulties such as gas rationing and reduced or unreliable bus schedules make commuting from an urban residence unacceptable; suggestion of this arrangement may be seen as a banal tactic to prohibit research without jeopardizing the formal exchange agreement.

43. See Verdery 1983a, and Kideckel and Sampson 1984, for other discussions of fieldwork in Romania. Bureaucratic oversights made it impossible for me to utilize the Academy library in Bucureşti in the summers of 1983 and 1985. By the time matters were straightened out, I was already headed north to the village. Usually, obtaining authorization to work in the library is a relatively simple process. Attempts to avoid this problem again in 1985 were unfortunately to no avail.

44. The details of this scenario are illuminating vis-à-vis the confluence of center-periphery relations and the interpretation of authority, the residual difficulties of class turmoil, and the uninvited presence of a foreigner sanctioned by the state. An enduring concern and respect for those who shared their lives with me does not permit explicit elaboration. My travails at that time formed but a small part of a series of local grievances against the village mayor, who was subsequently removed from office. (A letter written by village residents to the editors of the Party magazine, *Munca de Partid,* in 1983 made the mayor's case public.)

Had I been able to utilize the data I wanted, I would have been authorized to look at pre-1962 statistics. The year 1962 marked the end of the cooperativization drives. Access to pre-1962 data would have revealed information about property and kin relations and their transformation. I was unable to reconstruct this information accurately through intensive interviewing because people were simply frightened. Interestingly, when my permission to use these records inadvertently surfaced, another local authority attempted to avoid a scandal with higher authorities by arranging for certain statistics (household composition, education, occupation) to be hastily hand-copied by a selected team just before my departure. I was not surprised to find that certain key households (i.e., those of former landholders) were omitted.

45. The "long shadow" was a delicate euphemism meant to include members of *securitatea* (the secret police, who were more prevalent in the regional city of Sighetu Marmaţiei) and local informers. It is now often said that one can no longer even trust one's mother.

46. The RCP's Council on Culture has assigned folklore and tradition to the same status they have had in American anthropology and history until recently, thereby disavowing the dynamic nature of folklore and its importance in the study of culture. For "corrective" studies, see, for example, Weber 1975; Glassie 1975, 1982; Thompson 1979; Kligman 1981; Hobsbawm and Ranger 1983.

47. I did not intend to study ritual per se; this had been the focus of my first study, and I had hoped to work on sorcery during my postdoctoral research. Unfortunately, the sorceress with whom I had established relations died shortly after my arrival in Maramureş, and it was not possible to pursue this project. And the significance of ritual in the village to which I had been sent was too evident to avoid.

48. The first month of my fieldwork was spent in another village in Maramureş that had been recommended by Bucureşti authorities. It proved to be a poor choice. This village is isolated with a population of less than one thousand; hence, it seemed "manageable." However, the village is somewhat unusual because of the prominence of religious sect practitioners, which meant, among other things, that ritual activity was curtailed, making the small population a disadvantage in this case. More important, these sects are discouraged or illegal. They are also supported to a large extent by American groups, and it thus did not seem an auspicious situation for me. Furthermore, I was quite distressed by the anti-Semitic remarks that crept into discussion all too frequently for my taste. After consultation with local scholars, I requested to change villages. Local authorities decided they should determine where I would be located since they, not the Bucureşti ethnographers, knew the region best.

49. Usually, the house was occupied by women: myself, the mother-in-law, and my hostess. Her husband and children lived in the nearby city of Sighet where they worked or attended school. The husband commuted on a weekly basis; the children, when they could. The entire extended family assembled for holidays.

50. My arrival in the first village in which I resided illustrates this point. Because it was the dead of winter and the ground was snow-covered, I and a local ethnographer had to walk. As we approached the last hill, the children standing watch at the village edge sighted us and shrieked with enthusiasm, "Here comes the American!" My own reaction was one of simultaneous embarrassment and amusement. As we entered the village, residents lined the path and stared at me. My colleague conducted me to the village representatives; I walked on, looking to neither left nor right, but with eyes cast shyly downward.

The relationship between the researcher and the researched, and the nature of ethnographic writing, has become a topic of intense anthropological interest.

51. If the weather did not permit me to escape into solitude by hiking in the

inviting surroundings, I could think quietly and completely alone in the church bell tower. No one ever discovered this private space. The greatest difficulty with my room was that it was not the most convenient for a light sleeper. I frequently worked late into the night because that was the only quiet time; the village was asleep. But family members began their day between 4 and 5 A.M. Inevitably, women running errands, delivering milk, or whatever would catch up on the daily gossip—all before 7 A.M. (This gossip was often about me: What does she eat? Does she really drink the double-distilled brandy?) They are accustomed to speaking in loud voices, and I was plagued by too little sleep as a consequence. We eventually negotiated that gossip would go on outside the house before 7, and occasionally this worked.

52. This situation would have been further complicated had they realized that my family was Jewish. They did not, a deception to which I consciously contributed after much deliberation and consultation. This will be discussed in greater detail in the first and last chapters.

53. Having gained fluency in the dialect, I experienced similar difficulties in addressing my hosts. We lived together in the same household; we spoke intimately about life's happenings. My cultural upbringing suggested that the terms of address should be familiar. However, in that context, these terms were too jarring. If I had to be "miss," I found myself feeling more comfortable using the less formal term *dumăta* with adults, or the standard "uncle" and "aunt."

Chapter One

1. I wish to thank the retired priest, Ion Marcu, for having permitted me to copy the notes of P. Bilţiu-Dăncuş. Bilţiu-Dăncuş, a teacher from Ieud, was committed to the collection of the folklore of his village. He submitted this legend to N. Densuşianu in 1893 as a response to a questionnaire inquiry. For a recent poetic rendition of this legend, see Appendix A.

2. For the sake of clarity, I have taken the liberty to refer to Ieud as a village; however, in formal terms, it is a *comuna*. A comuna is an administrative-economic unit consisting of one or more villages. Because Ieud is large with four cantons associated with it (Grbovo, Monastire, Gură Ieudului, and Plopşor), it is formally designated a comuna. Most of Ieud's inhabitants, however, still speak about "our village."

3. The Hungarian kings Charles Robert and Ludwig I granted diplomas to certain nemeşi in recognition of services rendered. The diplomas guaranteed rights and privileges to these families. For further discussion, see, in particular, Mihaly 1934; Popa 1970.

4. The Orthodox church in Romania purportedly dates from the Middle Ages. In the 1700s, however, the Austro-Hungarian empire introduced the Greek-Catholic or Uniate church into Transylvania. Some general works on religion in Romania are Puşcariu 1900; Ionescu 1905; Iorga 1908; Staniloiae 1939; Hitchins 1983. On Maramureş, see, for example, I. Bîrlea 1909; Reli 1938. See also Sanders 1982. Some Ieudeni assert that claims of Orthodoxy in the area are the result of the current regime's propaganda. Historical memory seems to supersede

historical record. The official change from Greek Catholicism to Orthodoxy was fraught with strife in Ieud, as elsewhere. Priests who were not willing to switch and chose to fight were arrested. Today, Ieudeni will immediately respond that they are Orthodox; however, this response is more pro forma than deeply felt, and it serves to differentiate between public-private, insider-outsider, official-personal. This may be viewed as a sort of religious disemia, following Herzfeld's suggestive formulation (1982, 205–13).

5. Ieud's impoverishment is reflected in a strigătură collected in another village in the region:

Vai săracu Ieudu	Oh, poor Ieud
Cum o fo și cum-i amu.	How it was, and how it is now.

6. Church records from 1977 show 5,693 souls, or 2,384 male adults, 2,307 female adults, and 1,002 children. It is not clear at what age children are no longer classified as such for the purpose of church records (although seven is the age at which children are believed to become capable of sin). This figure is the number of "souls" in the church, which may include persons residing outside of Ieud and exclude persons who live in Ieud but do not belong to the church. For example, teachers who are assigned to Ieud and live there but go home to celebrate holidays are not represented in this total. Unfortunately, I did not have access to other local records. The population of Ieud, according to 1979 estimates, was between five thousand and six thousand, hence the approximate figure. As of 1985, local authorities suggested that the population was about 4,800, taking into account 150 families that have moved permanently from Ieud. In any case, Ieud is a large village.

7. This division is necessary from a practical point of view. Each house is supposed to be blessed by the priest on Bobotează, January 6, the day Christ was believed to have been baptized. Following the church service, the icon of Christ is taken to the river and symbolically baptized. At this time, individual households also give their annual contributions to the church. Because Ieud is so large, it is impossible for the priest to cover the entire village. If another priest from a smaller village is unable to assist, then the deacon and sexton perform this service for the half of the village they administer. Because of Ieud's size, the collection takes much time and must be begun before January 6. (Not all villages are as religiously homogeneous as Ieud. People who do not belong to the church [Baptists, Adventists, etc.] do not receive the priest in their homes or pay annual dues.) Recently, a dispute over a deacon's right to continue his calling has divided the village and wreaked havoc on these annual activities. During the height of tension, Ieudeni who disagreed with the priest's position have refused to receive him. This matter will be briefly discussed in the concluding chapter. Since the time of my extended field stay, a younger priest has become the official church representative for this community.

8. This link between land and group is basic to the conception of collective farms: communal land and groups of people owning and using it. The two forms of communal land ownership are the *gospodărie agricola de stat* (state farms) and

the *gospodărie agricola colectiva* (collective farms). See Cernea 1974b; Kideckel 1979.

9. Karnoouh, in his discussion of *statut* (1980, 84–85), which is synonymous with gospodărie in Ieud (formerly *statămînt*), mentions that until the end of World War I, the statut of a nemeş was inviolable. It virtually constituted a mini-state. Even the Austro-Hungarian authorities could not claim rights over someone who was under the nemeş' protection (on his land).

10. These small fences make it possible to go from one house to another without always having to go the long way around. One is considered an "insider" when one knows the village well enough to use these shortcuts.

11. Corn is used for the preparation of *mămăligă*, a cornmeal mush similar to the Italian polenta. In Maramureş, mămăligă is called *tocană* or *coleşă*. Before bread was made with white flour, peasants used to make a corn bread, *pită de mălai*. Of the grains, rye (*săcară*) and oats (*ovăs*) figure prominently in ritual practices as symbols of fertility, fecundity, and social intercourse. *Grîu ales,* or chosen wheat, symbolizes high status.

12. The following strigătura illustrates the personal bonds between man and house:

De m-ar şti fereastă spune	If the window could,
Cu multe m-ar da la lume.	For many reasons it would tell on me.
Şî fereastă i zinovată	And the window is guilty;
Nu mă spune niciodată.	It doesn't ever tell on me!

The implication is that the window is witness to the man's infelicitous behavior, but the window keeps this information to itself.

13. *Roots* is appropriate. A family branch is known as *ziţă* in Maramureş dialect. *Ziţă* also refers to a category of plants with strong roots. See also Karnoouh 1980, 84. If something or someone is *de ziţă*, he or she or it is of or from superior quality.

14. Jowitt's emphasis (1978, 6–21) on Weber's distinction between status and class is apposite. He stresses that "the major institutions of a peasant country have a status, not class, character." Class society is distinguished by the emergence of individuals and the nuclear family as the fundamental unit of social action as opposed to the corporate group (such as familial and neighbor associations).

15. Accordingly, marriage to a high-ranking Party official from a weak family remains less desirable than marriage to a worker from a good family.

16. Although marrying up or down occasionally occurs, interracial marriage between Ieud's Romanians and settled Gypsies is practically unheard of and would be considered scandalous. (There are no surviving Jews, nor are there any Hungarians; there is one Ruthenian who married in.)

17. In addition to Hammel's fine book on godparenthood in Yugoslavia (1968), see, for example, Mintz and Wolf 1950 and Flandrin 1976 on Europe. For discussion of other types of patron-client relations, see Gellner and Waterbury 1977.

18. Dowry expectations have been modified in response to changing socio-economic conditions. Previously a bride was expected to provide one or two heavy

woven blankets, four sheets, three or four pillows and cases (woven or embroidered), and three or four rugs (that she had woven). She was to bring ten to
twelve icons of various kinds as well as decorative plates to be hung on the walls.
For these, she had to have made an equal number of woven or embroidered towels
to drape around them. For the kitchen, she was to bring pots, plates, bowls, table-
cloths, and water buckets. Wash basins—one for the clothes and one for the children—and a wooden basin to feed the pigs were also needed. Daughters of gazde
might also add one or two oxen, pigs, twenty or more sheep, a cow, trunks, and a
wagon. Land for cultivation of oats, wheat, potatoes, corn, and hay was desirable.
Today, land is no longer requisite because many people do not have any. If possible, a cow, three or four sheep, a pig, grain, and flour are given. Household
items are still necessary, as well as money. In the city, household necessities now
include furniture: a table and four chairs, a sofa, a bed, a glass-fronted cupboard, a
kitchen table, a gas stove, a freezer.

Traditionally, if the groom married into the bride's family, he was expected to
bring one or two horses and a wagon and his own set of sheets and a woven blanket
(in the event the couple argued); if he had no sisters, he was also given a rug,
eiderdown, icons, and so on.

19. The meaning of gospodărie varies within Maramureş. Karnoouh's discussion of statut (1980) is the equivalent of statămînt in Ieud, and more colloquially,
gospodărie (see also note 9, above). The census does not apply the traditional spatial and land-use distinctions to gospodărie; in the census each head of household
is a head of a gospodărie, regardless of living and productive arrangements. Local
reckoning differs. In Ieud, a son and his family may be said to *stau ditilin* (live
apart) if they live in a separate household either on or off the family property.
Ditilin and gospodărie coincide only if residence, property, and productive management are all separate.

20. Of these 71, 67 apply to Romanians; 4 are Gypsy family names. (Jewish
names are no longer relevant.) These 71 are "traditional" names, thus excluding
the priest who is not from Ieud as well as others who are temporarily situated
there. I arrived at a total of 71 by comparing orally recounted names with names
from the cooperative-farm member lists (which are incomplete, however).

21. Silverstein's article (1981b) on naming sets presents a highly suggestive
analysis of personal names as pragmatic and metapragmatic entities. The metapragmatic content of Maramureş spoken names or nicknames makes it possible to
locate ego with respect to place in line of descent, status, and familial and communal interaction. The link between name and identity is also manipulated as a
means to "trick" illness or acts of sorcery. The name of the individual is changed so
that the agent of distress cannot identify him or her. This is referred to as the
"name death" of an individual. See Golopenţia-Eretescu 1972, 154–55.

In a discussion about childbirth practices, an elderly woman captured the relationship of women's names to patrilineal and state authority. When she was young,
she had been known as X, wife of Y. Then one day, she was given her written
name, and she had had a difficult time adjusting to it. As we discussed the current
requirement that women give birth at medical facilities rather than at home or in
the fields, she remarked, "But it's better for these arrested women, easier." To this

aged grandmother, the state, by using official names to keep records of childbirth and other once-private matters, has "arrested" its citizens.

22. See Musset (1981, 168–69) for further discussion of naming systems, especially possessive and genitive forms. Also, it should be noted that regional variations prevail. Although Musset states that the genitive form of the mother's name is never used in Moiseni, it is found in Ieud. Also see Golopenţia-Eretescu 1972.

23. The so-called mother-in-law syndrome is characteristic of southeastern Europe. See, for example, Sanders 1949; Halpern 1956; Friedl 1962; Erlich 1966; Hammel 1968; Simić 1969. Lamphere points out that this syndrome is exacerbated when "domestic and political spheres are highly differentiated and when authority is hierarchical and in the hands of male members" (1974, 104), as is the case in patricentered peasant families.

24. If the couple moves immediately to the city, she also avoids direct conflict with her mother-in-law.

25. All brides are nore; grooms, ginere. Both terms are overdetermined with respect to living arrangements. In these cases, they serve not only to classify affinal relations but also to condense a set of meanings encompassing notions of self, space, household, authority.

26. Because women inherit partible land, all women are desirable to some degree. Hence, even the simplest, the least adept, and the ugliest marry:

Sărăcile moine lungi	Poor long rows of fallow land
Cum mărită mute-n dungi.	How simple girls marry.
Sărăcile moine late	Poor wide rows of fallow land
Cum mărită mute-umflate.	How stupid girls marry.

This verse plays on the relationship between fallow land waiting to be cultivated and girls ready to be married and become pregnant. Land may be further divided (hence, poor rows or pieces) to marry off a daughter who is otherwise unattractive.

27. One woman in her mid-twenties, still unmarried, was horrified to learn that someone had been sent to awaken me to see the moş in a tree outside her window. She brought it inside and refused to allow anyone else to see it. The public ridicule typical of these rites is similar to the French charivari.

28. Costs for a large wedding were the following (collected 1979):

Musicians	4,000 lei
Drink: brandy, beer, etc.	5,000 lei
Items for food preparation (flour, oil, etc.)	2,000 lei
Pigs	3,000 lei
Chickens	0 (donated)
Total	14,000 lei (approximately $1,780)

The groom's family obtained 200 kg white flour, 20 kg sugar, 20 kg oil, 10 kg butter, 150 kg pork, 50 kg sour cabbage, 20 packets of pepper, 20 kg rice, 2 kg salt, 20 kg corn mixture for stuffed cabbage, and 20 chickens.

29. See also Barth (1979, 281–89) for a discussion of the *Nachbarschaften*

among the Romanian Saxon communities. Musset (1981, 23) notes that in urban life, closer ties exist between neighbors than between family members who live apart. She also notes that kin and neighbor relations are often confounded, because brothers, in the interest of property, may be neighbors.

30. I have included a discussion on the groups of young men who carol together. During the Christmas holidays, young men visit the homes of eligible girls in particular. Like the horă and şezătoare, this occasion is important for courtship. For more detailed discussion, see O. Bîrlea 1969 and Brătulescu 1981. For further discussion of the Sunday horă and şezătoare in the neighboring region of Oaş, see Musset 1981, 39–44; and Freedman 1983. Also see Bot 1969.

31. This is a recapitulation of the general scheme of the ritual division of labor: men—public calendar customs; women—private life cycle. See Kligman 1981, 136.

32. Love charms are worked on New Year's Eve as well. On that night, girls, especially, perform various charms to ascertain if they will marry and to what sort of man. The most famous love magic involves the plant *mătrăgună*, a variety of belladonna. Girls go to the forest and honor the plant with wine and cakes. They sing to it, praise it, and make this request of it:

Mătrăgună doamnă bună	Belladonna, good lady,
Mărită-mă-n astă lună.	Marry me in this month.
De nu-n asta, în cealaltă	If not in this one, then in the next,
Şi mă mărită odată.	Only marry me off.
Că de nu mni-i mărita	For if you don't get me married
Ieu horincă nu ţi-oi da.	I won't give you brandy
Nici prăjituri nu ţi-oi da . . .	Nor cakes . . .

The point is to be married. For a discussion of the "cult of mătrăgună," see Eliade 1972. An accomplished sorceress related to me before her death that women also used this plant for evil purposes. In this case, they beat the plant in the forest, stamp on it, and argue with it. Upon their arrival home, they place the plant in the outhouse rather than on the household icons. Evil requires the inversion of goodness.

33. Killing for blood is obviously significant in the construction of the vampire cult; satisfaction of a vampire's thirst exhausts the life supply of the human vessel from which the vampire drinks. Twitchell (1981, 14) noted the "serendipitous syncretism" of the "ecclesiastical and folk concern with blood, for in the late Middle Ages the vampire story received its greatest support from the church as a way of explaining the last of the sacraments, the Eucharist. This, the most difficult of the sacraments to understand, depended on the almost inexplicable process of transubstantiation, yet it could be described in terms of the older vampire myth. For just as the devil drank the sinner's blood and partook of his spirit, so now the righteous man might drink the wine and partake of Christ's holiness. It was a simple and straightforward way to explain this complex sacrament, and, of course, it put the fear of the devil quite literally into the sinner, as it put the salvation of Christ into the righteous."

In the novel *Dracula*, once Lucy was released from the clutches of sin, she was able to rest eternally as Arthur's symbolic spouse. For him, the sharing of their blood through the transfusions given to keep her alive, posthumously "consecrated" their marriage. This may be likened to the relationship between Christ and his believers that is constituted through transubstantiation. Arthur and Lucy's union was a symbolic one and was secured only after her actual death when her soul was finally at peace and ready to receive the sacrament of matrimony. The transfusions of blood were not able to save her life, which was then under the influence of the Devil.

34. The following verse comments on the sexual lust of females:

Săracile fetele	Poor girls,
Gură dulce place-le.	A sweet mouth [a French kiss] pleases them.
De le-ai dat tătă gura	If you give your whole mouth,
Şohan nu s-ar sătura.	They'll never be satiated.

35. Women contribute to the perpetuation of their own status. They believe that they are inherently evil. As mentioned previously, wife-beating is rather common. Women do not generally relish the experience, but they rarely question whether they deserve such treatment, unless their husbands are alcoholics.

36. This brings to mind a couplet that I first heard from a woman:

Nu-s bună de făptură	I'm not good on looks
Da-s al dracului de gura.	But my tongue is like the Devil's.

Women are commonly thought to be evil-tongued and not necessarily truthful. Women are allegedly the source of all rumors—and trouble.

37. Karnoouh's discussion (1983a) of the ritual language of men and women in the wedding rites of Maramureş is insightful. His analysis of the "ontology of desire" is particularly worthwhile.

38. The "civilizing process" analyzed by Elias (1978) acquired a different scope harnessed to the ideology of development. The paradigm of the threatening "other" that must be subdued is a potent force that motivates much of contemporary political discourse. History has not consistently lessened the vehemence with which "otherness" is regarded.

39. The following is an excerpt of a taped conversation between two men in Ieud about to take their wives home from the sărbătoarea nepoatelor (1979):

"Mine—how many times she said that she wouldn't receive me in the house. Well, I told her that she didn't make the house. I told her that I'd still drink a glass or so when I come, so what?"

"And it's a waste of time for her to lock the door, for I'll enter anyway. We're men."

"I wear the hat. If I don't, then I'll give it to her. And she didn't want to take it; I gave it to her twice. If it doesn't suit . . ."

"You, woman, do you want me to give you my hat to wear?"

(wife) "No, you wear it."

"See, she doesn't want it. Because she can't. Our heads wouldn't be cold, but you can't direct things like we men."

"Your mind is a little bit weaker."

(wife) "And our mouths aren't bigger than yours!"
"You're worse at work."

The tensions in gender relations (authority, division of labor) are self-evident—and perhaps made more explicit by *horincă*, or Romanian plum brandy.

40. The pollution-purity distinction between menstruation and lactation is well illustrated by Gypsy *marihme* practices. These further extend to body values: the upper body is cleaner than the lower, which is polluted (especially women's). Clothes worn on the upper body and those worn on the lower must be washed in separate basins. See Sutherland 1977.

41. This custom is still prevalent in Maramureş. It is not, to my knowledge, practiced in other parts of Transylvania. It occurs to a lesser extent in Sighetu Marmaţiei, although it is common there upon entering homes. Party members use it without hesitation when addressing villagers they meet in the city. It is as much a convention as it is a sign of respect.

42. I must confess that I did not inquire about the mode of greeting between Jews and Christians, in part because there is a lack of religious differentiation today, and in part because, being a Jew "incognito," I found discussion of the Jews somewhat difficult. Romanian colleagues who have also worked in the area agree, however, that greetings were probably based on times of the day.

The anti-Semitism of Transylvania does not require elaboration; Papahagi (1925, xvi) recorded the following joke:

"Who did you meet in the road, Ioa?"
"Just a man and a Jew."

My choice to remain incognito was a difficult one for many reasons. It was clear that being "out of the closet" would have complicated my ability to work. An esteemed colleague, a Jew who spent many years in prison, asked if I was interested in research and understanding the human condition, or in being a martyr. At the time, his question, contextualized by his life experience, resolved my conflict. My experience in the field has, in any case, enabled me to comprehend more intimately the meaning of anti-Semitism. Nonetheless, I remain sensitive to the ethical issues involved (secrecy in a society overrun by secret police and informers; secrecy about and distortion of self). I have often thought that I should discuss this matter with those people with whom I have close relationships. Practical experience, however, has consistently extinguished this intention. Recently, having heard repeatedly that the Jews brought communism to Romania, a matter that is not currently well-regarded, I again decided it was not appropriate to raise this "detail." I am not a religious Jew—and the religious is the only aspect that is revered. Sentiments about the Jews were, and continue to be, ambivalent. They had been admired for their religious behavior but hated for their mercantile interests and practices. I was amused by a comment of a local member of the intelligentsia, who claimed that the oil crisis was caused by the "Arabs who are real Jews."

43. Reinstitution of Orthodoxy in Ieud was met with resistance and is recalled with bitterness. Most Ieudeni privately consider themselves to be Greek-Catholics but do not choose to risk the consequences. Also, the Greek-Catholic origin of the

practice is not commonly known. Hence, it would be incorrect to say, for example, that people in the cities do not use it because it is Greek-Catholic and not Orthodox.

44. In this work, I will focus on life-cycle customs. I have discussed the relationship between life-cycle and calendar customs in my previous work on the calendar custom Căluş (1981). For Romanian calendar customs, also see Marian 1898; Pamfile 1914; Vulpesco 1927; Brătulescu 1981.

Chapter Two

1. Cartojan writes that "the peasant wedding is in the patriarchal village life, a true drama" (1974, 274). He points out that each "principal phase of the wedding is underlined by orations." His cursory discussion of the wedding reveals an emphasis on male dominance: the groom's march to the bride's house and his assistants' metaphoric mission to "pick" (escort) the "flower from heaven" (bride) from her mother's garden to "plant in the King's garden" (groom's house) so that by the year's end she will flourish (bear children). The scenario is one of symbolic appropriation and male power.

2. The interested reader should consult Marian 1890, Meiţoiu 1969, and Şeuleanu 1985 for fuller, though not necessarily systematic, descriptions of the wedding ritual. Musset 1981 and Karnoouh 1983a are also recommended.

3. The texts are drawn from transcriptions of four complete weddings as well as sequences from ten others in Ieud and one in Breb. Unless otherwise stated, the texts are from fieldwork.

4. It is not my intent to analyze the broader category of lyric poetry to which strigături belong. Pop and Ruxăndoiu (1976, 180) argue that weddings have become more spectacle-oriented over time and some of the ritual orations have been "contaminated" by lyric songs of separation. For a discussion of ritual poetry, see also Pop and Ruxăndoiu 1976.

5. During the course of fieldwork, I collected several thousand couplets of shouts, songs, and laments. The reader is referred to the forthcoming work by Karnoouh, as well as the collections of shouts, songs, and poetry from Maramureş such as Bud 1908; Papahagi 1925; I. Bîrlea 1968; Bartók 1975; Doniga 1980; and Şter 1980.

6. Marriage, like everything, has its price. If unusual circumstances, such as the groom's departure for military service, require that the three-week period be shortened, the groom may pay a certain price to the church to compensate for bending the rules.

7. Today most girls and women wear aprons of wool and mixed fibers. For the ritual handshake, however, only woolen aprons are worn, even if they must be borrowed. Regarding wool and prosperity, men and women of marriageable age play a game on New Year's Eve to foretell traits of their future spouse. A series of plates cover various symbolic objects; it is said that the person who overturns a plate and finds a clump of wool will marry someone prosperous.

8. Most marriages still occur in the winter when villagers are not as occupied with work in the fields (see Kligman 1981, 111), but this trend is changing in response to changing modes of production and occupations.

9. The bride's trousseau is prepared by young girls over the years before their weddings at work bees, at home, and with friends to pass the time.

10. The *cusutul steagului* has been considered an occasion for mourning, or *doliu*. In the nineteenth century, the groom was "lamented" with sad songs as he separated from his bachelor friends. Similarly, while girls made the bride's crown, they sang sad, nostalgic songs, all of this with tears streaming down their faces. When ready, each girl placed the crown on her head before it was settled on the head of the bride. Then they danced happily around her (see Dăncuş and Katz 1973, 122).

11. Going to the bride's house may mean walking only a few houses, or it may require traveling as much as one and one-half kilometers in the dark on snow and ice-covered paths. This "path" is walked many times during the unfolding of the wedding. The time needed to come and go is calculated so that people do not become too impatient waiting for things to proceed.

12. The braiding of the bride's hair is indeed somewhat of an ordeal; however, nowhere is it as intricate as in Ţară Oaşului. For a discussion of this procedure, see Musset 1981, 107. Musset (ibid., 109) points out that the hairstyle and bridal crown are a symbol of the bride's virginity. Hence, young women who have lost their virginity or women who are remarrying (after divorce or widowhood) do not wear the hairstyle or crown.

13. See Bogatyrev 1971 and Pop-Câmpeanu 1979 on the functions of costume to mark status changes.

14. The mother of a bride who smiled at me as I arrived to observe her ritual dressing immediately assured me that her daughter would cry as all brides do. "Don't worry, if she doesn't cry, I've got onions," she said. The utility of onions was noted by Marian (1890, 381): "If, by chance, tears were not forthcoming, only then would an old woman or a married woman come with an onion . . . so that she would not remain with dry eyes." Ceremonial crying speaks to ritual's concern with social sentiments rather than individual feelings (Radcliffe-Brown 1964).

15. This brings to mind another verse about romance destroying family ties for girls:

Fost-am patru surorele	We were four sisters
Ca şî patru floricele	Like four flowers
Şî ne-am despărţit cu jele.	And we separated with sadness.
Nu ne-a despărţit jalea	Sadness didn't separate us
Fără ni-o despărţit badea.	Except a sweetheart separated us.

16. M. Pop (1976, 152) states that, formerly, a bride who married against her will had the right to lament her fate in public during her wedding; this is no longer practiced. Wedding lamentations are famous among the neighboring Slavic populations. See, for example, Sokolov 1950, 213–14; Krimska-Ivanova 1981; Ivanova and Živkov 1981, 330–38, 359–63, 369–95. There are many pertinent works on this subject for Yugoslavia, Bulgaria, Central Eastern Europe, and the Soviet Union. (The bibliography in Krimska-Ivanova is useful for the Soviet Union and Bulgaria. Also see Grossman 1980.)

17. Long ago the groom's dressing included his ritual shaving. This event,

being the first shaving for the groom, often marked transition to male maturity. (Couples married quite young.) See also Kligman 1981, 92, for related mention of this custom.

18. The reader might refer to Marian (1890, 435–36), Leibman (1972, 135–36), and Musset (1981, 118–19) for other brief descriptions of the Crowning. It is beyond the scope of this work to describe this Orthodox rite in detail.

19. Valeri's remark about marriage prestations among the Huaulu of Eastern Indonesia is relevant: "In effect, this system of prestations creates a situation in which every marriage implies other marriages (ideally all other marriages) and expresses—at the asymmetrical level of exchange and in the symmetric form of the ritual—the interrelationship of all marriages in a system of global reciprocity or mutuality" (1980, 189).

20. The hunting theme is characteristic of wedding poetry as well as the allegorical *colinde*, or Christmas carols (Pop and Ruxăndoiu 1976, 185–86; Eliade 1980, 15–17; Brătulescu 1981). Hunting is a male pursuit and is used to establish sovereign rights; it is central to marriage in a patriarchal society.

21. This scenario is reminiscent of the Cinderella tale, when the prince and his party go in search of the woman whose foot will fit the shoe. In the ritual play, the groom (the king or prince) goes in search of the first white flower (the virgin bride). There are the customary trials that he must undergo to find his flower. See O. Bîrlea (1976, 315–23) on *probele pețirii* (trials). Lampland (1977, 65–67) describes a similar custom in the Hungarian wedding ritual.

22. Silverstein has noted the metapragmatic and metasemantic character of formal oratory as being inherent features. Recall that the formal church ceremony has already occurred. The ritual enacts the marriage, moving participants through complex changes of status and roles. Silverstein (1981a) points out that such performances "give structure to the relations among the participants in them because they literally are metaforms of the ordinary."

23. Until more recent times (post–World War II), the proof of virginity was, and still is in many areas of the world, bloodstains on the sheets. Blood was essential; whose was less important and more difficult to verify. Many a chicken honored brides in this manner.

24. The Song of the Hen is symbolically related to the bride's dance, or *jocul mniresii*, which is now done only among Gypsy families in Ieud, although it is still popular in many other areas in Romania. It used to be done in Ieud in poorer families as a way to defray costs and endow the couple with limited resources. During the jocul mniresii the bride dances with anyone who wishes to pay for the privilege. In the end, the groom "buys" his bride back; he has the last dance.

25. There are several couplets applauding the gift of being *bună de gură*—in its positive sense:

Nu-s frumoasă de făptură	I'm not great with my looks,
Da-s a dracului de gură.	But I've a devil of a mouth.
La omuțu bun de gură	The person quick of tongue,
Nu-i mai trebe băutură.	He doesn't need drink.

26. One village elder stated that long ago, the nănaş tested the bride to see if she was a virgin. The godfather supposedly slept with her. Blood on her under-skirt or the sheets attested to her virginity; otherwise, the groom had the right to cancel the wedding. My informant also said, however, he did not believe such a test was really done because it would have been a sin. But an elderly woman ar-gued that sins may be compensated for. She knew a verse from a region nearby that addressed this point:

Naşule ţi-ar si păcat	Godfather, it would be a sin
Să te culci cu sina-n pat.	To sleep with your goddaughter in bed.
Da nănaşu-are parale	But the godfather has money
Şi a plăti sălindare.	And he'll pay for a few services.

27. This text was collected in 1980 from a woman from the comună Săliştea de Sus. She was visiting relatives in Ieud. Ieudeni do not shout the more porno-graphic strigături, although they are common throughout the rest of Maramureş. Ieud is the most tenaciously religious and traditional; these strigături are consid-ered *murdare,* or dirty. But this has not always been the case. The folklorist G. Dăncuş collected ribald poetry in Ieud before World War II, of which the fol-lowing are examples:

Rău mă doare, rău mă doare	It hurts me badly, it hurts me badly,
Cînd mă fute, bine-m pare.	When he fucks me, I feel good.

Să trăia bărbatu mneu	Long life to my husband:
C-are pula ca un zmeu.	He has a penis like a dragon.
Cînd văd că bărbatu zine	When I see that my husband is coming,
Gîndesc că m-a fute bine.	I assume that he'll fuck me well.

28. Socioeconomic change in Romania has produced (thus far) a situation simi-lar to that of capitalist modes of production. The conservative role of the house-wife within the family is pertinent. Landes (1977–78, 406) points out that "the family teaches workers to sell their labor power for the sake of consumption which they come to understand as leisure time. It teaches that leisure, not productive activity, gives meaning to life."

29. It used to be a custom that the beak was sandwiched in bread and pre-sented to the ceteraş. The sexual symbolism is obvious. The nănaş would ask if the beak was from a *cioară* (crow) or *gongoi* (first male to take the female bird). People claimed that the practice was dropped when the *ţigani* (Gypsies) became sensitive about the derogatory innuendo; cioară was often used as an ethnic slur for Gyp-sies. (Most musicians are Gypsies.)

Lampland (1977, 72) describes the "Rooster Song," which accompanies the di-viding of the bird during the Hungarian wedding rite. The sexual emphasis is similarly blatant.

30. Wife-beating is a common problem, as the following verse indicates:

Că nu-i bărbat aşă de bun	There is not a man so good
Să nu-ţi dăie cîte-un pumn.	That he won't give you a few fists.
Nu-i bărbat aşă de drag	There isn't a man so dear

Să nu te tragă de cap.   Not to pull you by the head.
Că bărbatu nu ți-i frate   For your man isn't your brother;
Să gîndești că nu te-a bate.   Don't think he won't beat you.

31. The wearing of the scarf is deeply ingrained. During a year of living in close quarters, I rarely saw my gazdă without her scarf, even when we were alone in the house. Women do not sleep with their scarves on, but they put them on as soon as they arise.

32. A thorough discussion of city weddings is beyond the scope of this inquiry. Briefly, in Sighetu Marmației, the bride is escorted to the town hall or the church by her family and friends. She is frequently dressed in a white gown. After the service, the marriage is celebrated with an all-night party at a restaurant or hall that has been rented for the occasion. Food, drink, music, and dancing are plentiful.

Many people who live in the city return to their villages to have a peasant wedding; it is their heritage and locates them within the social fabric of identity. If the bride and groom hail from different regions, then the church ceremony, the first ritual meal, and the Song of the Hen take place in the village of the bride. The Asking for the Bride is omitted. Then they depart for the groom's home to continue the wedding there. Consideration is given to distance regarding the time of departure.

Chapter Three

1. The anthropological literature on death continues to pay particular homage to the works by Warner 1959; Hertz 1960; Van Gennep 1960; Goody 1962; Hubert and Mauss 1964; and Durkheim 1965. Recent and representative works on this topic include Huntington and Metcalf 1979; Thomas 1980; Weiner 1980; Humphreys and King 1981; Bloch and Parry 1982; and Danforth 1982.

2. The philosophical and existential problems evoked by death are not easily laid to rest by Marxist-Leninist ideology, although the Soviets have made serious attempts to rectify this situation. See Lane 1981, 82–88, 236. High-level Party members in Romania generally refrain from contact with the church. Nevertheless, high-ranking members have been buried with the blessings of the priest. Bellow's description (1982, 207–15) of an urban funeral is less fictional than one might assume.

3. In this chapter, I am discussing the beliefs and practices associated with death as they pertain to Ieud specifically, and to Maramureș generally. Although the belief system there is largely generalizable for all of Romania (because of the influence of Christianity), the ritual practices vary considerably. In the south of Romania, the metaphor of marriage manifests itself differently through the ritual of the death tree, and there are professional funeral singers and specific songs for the *zorii*, or three spirits of dawn (the fates). For a presentation and analysis of funeral rites in Oltenia, see J. Bernabé 1980. It is useful for comparative purposes.

4. For further discussion of the European lament traditions, see, for example,

de Martino 1975, 1–235 on the Euro-Mediterranean tradition (164–94 are about Romania); Alexiou 1974, Caravelli 1980, and Danforth 1982 on the Greek tradition; and Kaufman 1981 on Bulgarian laments.

5. For a cursory discussion of ritual redundancy, see Tambiah 1979, 134–41. That repetition is a structural feature of ritual presents problems for my attempt to convey a sense of both the cognitive and the affective components of the ritual experience. The written medium is inadequate; it necessarily reduces the sensory complexity of ritual, which is a multimedia form. In fact, there is a structural contradiction implicit in using the literary form to represent that of ritual. Redundancy in the former is a stylistic sin; in the latter, it is a virtue. Because one singer may repeat a theme several times during the lengthy ritual proceedings, I have tried to compromise in this attempt to represent in literary form the poignant ritual tradition. Throughout the discussion of the ritual sequences, lament excerpts are presented, but their order of presentation in many cases is rather arbitrary, determined to a great extent by the narrative structure of the medium in which I am working. I am fully aware of (and frustrated by) the limitations of this method. Verses that are specific to a ritual sequence are indicated as such.

6. See also, for example, Burks 1949, Jakobson 1971, and Silverstein 1976.

7. Another messenger associated with death is a bird. Birds, however, do not figure in the lament tradition. Laments function as direct reflexive media of communication between the living and the dead. Birds are messengers in ballads about death. In them, the bird is a figurative representative of the soul. (Again, it is thought that the soul "hovers" over the door during the funeral.) Also, birds as messengers from that world can tell the living only what they already know. "That world" is an environment constructed by the poet's imagination, and so it will remain.

8. Mihai Pop, paraphrasing Maxim Gorky, notes that "due to their improvisational character and the elements from real life, laments are precious social documents in which the oppressed peasants may express during the tragic moments of a funeral all of their hardships and suffering . . . not only about family life but about the entire village, about work and the conditions of their life" (1976, 171).

9. Not everyone agrees with the general prescription that death of the elderly does not merit deep pain and suffering. En route to the cemetery in Săliştea de Sus, several women in their fifties lamented for their seventy-eight-year-old deceased uncle:

Vai de mine măi unte	Oh my goodness, hey, uncle,
Aşă zice lumea-n sat	So people in the village say:
Moară-un bătrîn nu-i păcat.	An old person dies, it's not a sin.
Cine zice rău greşă	But who says so, errs greatly,
Un părinte mult plăte.	For a parent is much valued.
Numa acela ce-i cuminte	Only a mature person
Şti cît plăte un părinte.	Knows just how valuable a parent is.
Uă ai cui te jelui	Oh, you have someone who will comfort you,
Şî lumea-n sat nu te-a şti.	And people in the village won't know.

| Ai la cine cere-un sfat | You have someone from whom to ask advice, |
| Şî nu te şti lumea-n sat. | And everyone in the village won't know. |

Parental love is a rare gift. A parent may be counted on in all delicate or difficult matters: joys, sorrows, uncertainties, confidences. Unlike anyone else, a parent may be trusted; hence, his or her loss is virtually irremediable. (Here, the importance of blood relations is implicit. In theory, parents are more reliable than wives or husbands; in practice, of course, this depends on experience.)

10. Traube (1983), in an eloquent elaboration of Mauss's work *The Gift* (1967), emphasizes aspects of his concluding argument, pointing out that "exchange may be seen as culture's substitute for the two anti-social extremes of isolation and stagnation, on the one hand, war and destruction on the other." The relevance for the present discussion is evident: the cosmology of death partially negates both the isolating and the destructive components of death. In an illuminating discussion of gift exchange and advertising, Traube notes that advertising plays on the "cultural construction of the self" as "other," "as a stranger whom each of us must find and get to know, learn to respect and appreciate. And one creates a relationship with this stranger-self how else, but by gift-giving, by offering the material tokens of respect and care to the unknown guest hidden within."

11. On one occasion when someone had come to tell a dream, Juji, my gazdă, was prompted to tell me a dream she had had when her brother died. The dream had affected her deeply. I reproduce it here because of its symbolic consistency and as an intriguing example for those interested in dream analysis. The symbolic syncretism is well articulated:

"My brother Văsîle died when he was 37—of hepatitis. I was terribly upset; we were very close. Two weeks after his funeral, I had a dream in which I thought my son Văsîle also died. He, like my brother, is the middle child. I was so upset. So I buried my child; we had the funeral. I lamented:

'Vai de mine măi Văsî	'Oh, my Văsî[le],
Măi Văsî ce-ai făcut tu	Oh, Văsî, what have you done,
De mni-o luat pruncuţu?	That my child was taken?
Nu-i bugăt c-ai murit tu	Isn't it enough that you have died,
Da şî ai luat pruncuţu?'	But you've taken my child too?'

I lamented that en route to the cemetery. I knew I buried Văsîle. After a week, I came home and there was my child at the table; he was sitting on the bench. 'Oh, my beautiful Văsîlică, you died; how did you revive?' I kissed him and said, 'Did you meet your Uncle Văsîle?' He said: 'I met him.' 'And your Uncle Gavrila?' 'No, but many others came to me who I don't know but who claimed to be my ancestors.' 'Well, how are people there? Like here?' 'No, but they're people too.' 'But, Văsî, what do they eat? Is there food?' 'They have all kinds of things; the tables are full.' 'How did you get there? Who took you?' He didn't answer that. 'Well, how was it going?' 'Oh, Mom, through darkness but you can see.' 'Vai, were you told to tell how it is there?' 'No.' He didn't answer questions about life there. I woke up around 4 A.M. I couldn't sleep."

The dream is consistent with beliefs about the relations between the living and the dead as seen throughout this chapter. It is worth mentioning that Juji is esteemed for her skill with oral poetry; however, it is not surprising that a lament is embedded in the dream structure.

People are quite interested in dreams. Dream books circulate underground among the young and the old. There is a stock of symbols that signify certain consequences. People frequently came to me to inquire about the meaning of their dreams. The static understanding of dream symbols supports the universalist approach to dream interpretation (Jungian) rather than Freudian tendencies. For example, dreaming about the removal of teeth means there will be a death in the family; dreaming about an airplane signals that a letter will arrive. Of course, the inconsistencies in any discussion about this stock of symbols reveal the limitations inherent in this type of dream interpretation. People often conclude such a discussion with statements such as "Dreams are all upside-down; they're not true."

12. For an interesting discussion of "time, space and life," see Feuerbach 1980, 48–107. Succinctly, he notes that "you exist only in space and time; you begin in them, but you also end in them; they are boundaries of your being. As an individual, you cannot exist outside of time and space; therefore, you exist only in this spatiotemporal life. For, second, as a being existing in space and time . . . in this unity of temporality and spatiality, you are ensouled and corporeal—in other words, a living individual. Body and soul in unity constitute your life" (ibid., 47–48). See also Fabian 1983, especially the conclusions (143–82).

13. "Life is not determined by consciousness, but consciousness by life" (Marx and Engels [1932] 1970, 47). Marx and Engels further expound on the relationships between consciousness, language, and society: "Language is as old as consciousness, language is practical consciousness that exists also for other men . . .; language, like consciousness, only arises from the need, the necessity, of intercourse with other men" (51). See also Vološinov 1973.

14. Cremation is common in cities, although it is not popular. See Bellow's description (1982, 207–15) of an urban funeral. I am unable to provide commentary about how the fate of the soul is understood in such instances. Since urban funerals often involve a certain degree of religious content, cremation may not be explained simply in terms of a growing godless state. Generally, however, Party members are cremated. As one individual facetiously remarked, even the Devil, a construct of Christianity, would not be cremated!

15. The past tense is used here, because although a small community of Jews still remains in Sighetu Marmației (the locale of Eli Wiesel's youth), none are to be found in Ieud. For most Moroșeni, Jews exist only in history.

16. As R. Williams writes (1977, 24): "Verbal language is then distinctively human; indeed constitutively human. . . . Language is then, positively, a distinctive human opening of and opening to the world: not a distinguishable or instrumental but a constitutive faculty." It distinguishes the world of the living from that of the dead.

17. See L. Wolf (1975, 27) on the folklore of mirrors. He also points out the popular association between mirrors and Dracula. Dracula, who is betwixt the living and the dead, does not see his reflection in the mirror. He has no soul.

18. Water is associated with life as well as with death. Recall that the first bath water of a baby girl is thrown over patches of flowers so that she will have many suitors; that of a boy is thrown only over one flower patch so that he will acquire the heart he desires. See Kligman 1984, 175.

19. Two experiences left distinct impressions on me at the time of my field-work and underscored the entrenchment of hierarchical relations. I participated in the preparation of the funeral meals, partly to become integrated into the life of the community. Many women work collectively during this situation, and I was correct in assuming that my presence would quickly become known. I joined the group of women making stuffed cabbage; I noticed that another group was also making *haluşte*, or *curechi umpluţi*, as they are known there. The contents were not the same. One woman explained that the other group was making a filling that did not contain the cornmeal-rice mixture, but only meat and rice. These "deli-cacies" were for the domni attending the funeral: members of the intelligentsia such as the priest and teachers from the city. These individuals also ate from indi-vidual plates and with aluminum forks and spoons rather than from the shared bowls of food and wooden spoons of the "commoners" (i.e., peasants). Similarly, two types of bread are served: a cornflour bread and a white bread. A woman who was serving was chastised by the domni for serving me the cornflour bread. It was an insult to my status, no matter that I preferred it.

20. The conceptualization of death as female is popular in urban, intellectual environments as well. Regarding the unfortunate death of the Jewish playwright and novelist Mihail Sebastian, Geo Bogza (reporter and poet) wrote: "He passed exactly through the place in which death was not lying in wait—as she had for millions of people—but was just happening by. She too was so tired, that after the carpet bombings, after thousands of tanks, she bore the appearance of a simple truck. Under its wheels, he, who'd had the false fortune of escaping from all the dangers and horrors of war, encountered her." I am indebted to Irina Livezeanu who thoughtfully sent a copy of her article (1984, 297) in which this quote appears in a footnote. Her collegial gesture, although unrelated to the discussion at hand, was unknowingly timely.

21. The mother is not the only person accused of being a trickster:

Că popa-i tare înşelător	For the priest is a trickster
Că te-ntreabă de tre ori.	Because he asks you three times
Ş-apoi te pune să giuri	And then he makes you swear
Şi te bagi-n giug să mori.	And puts you in a harness to die.

During the wedding service, the priest asks the bride and groom, respectively, if each takes the other as her or his wedded spouse—three times. Then their vows and fates are sealed.

22. The relationships between death and nature and between women and cul-ture are, therefore, similar yet radically different. Whereas women are in, but not of, the patriline and whereas death is part of, yet out of, culture, death inverts the order of relations. Death avoids the patrilineal paradox. As will be seen in the next chapter, young women of marriageable age who die unwed escape the tribu-lations of patriarchy. They are "saved" by death and not sold by their mothers.

23. Eliade points out the relationship between Earth-Mother and the Goddess of Death: "When the Earth becomes a goddess of Death, it is simply because she is felt to be the universal womb, the inexhaustible source of all creation. . . . The frightening aspect of the Earth-Mother, as the Goddess of Death, is explained by the cosmic necessity of sacrifice, which alone makes possible the passage from one mode of being to another and also ensures uninterrupted circulation of life" (quoted in Beane and Doty 1976, 249).

24. Another verse plays with the same metaphoric relations between flowers, marriage-death, and heaven, and between thorns, marriage-death, and hell:

Câte flori sunt pe pămînt	How many flowers are on this earth,
Toate merg la jurămînt.	All of them go to [their] judgment.
Numa floarea soarelui	Only the flower of the sun
Şede-n poarta raiului.	Stays at heaven's gate
Face loc sufletului	And makes room for the soul
Şi hodină trupului.	And rest for the body.
D-apoi florea spinului	But the flower of thorns,
Şede-n poartă iadului.	Stays at the gates of hell.

See Burada 1882, 109. This was collected in Moldavia. The meaning of flowers going to their judgment is double: all flowers (girls) go to be married, and flowers (everyone) die. The phrase *a mere la jurămînt* means that someone is going to take their wedding vows.

25. I have used Marie's funeral to weave a narrative thread throughout this discussion. Examples not specifically noted as taken from her funeral are drawn from the extensive corpus of data collected during my fieldwork. Although it would be possible to introduce several different "stories" into this chapter, I felt this might have introduced more confusion into a ritual that is already characterized by redundancy.

26. In similar fashion, when a midwife died, all of her female "godchildren" came to mourn her loss. She had brought their children into the world. The following lament verses are illustrative:

Vai moşică şi odor	Oh, dear grandmother, my dear one,
De şepte ori m-ai sculat	You raised me seven times
Moşică di pă al mneu pat	From my bed.
Cu mînă m-ai rădicat.	You lifted me with your hand,
Pă obraz mni-ai netezît	You wiped my cheek,
Din gură mîndru-ai grăit	You calmed me with your words,
Inima mni-ai întîrit.	And gave me courage.
O zinit să te jălească	They've come to mourn you
Moşică să-ţi mulţumească.	And to thank you, dear grandmother-midwife,
	Because you helped them a great deal.
Că mult bine le-ai făcut	Even though you weren't salaried,
Batăr sălar n-ai avut.	You came for a week,
Cu săptămîna ai umblat	Dear midwife, to their beds.
Moşică la ele la pat	You took such good care of them,
Cît de bine le-ai cătat.	My God, you cared for them well.
Doamne bine le-ai doicit	

Coconii i-ai ciupăit.
Nu ai stat la dispensar
N-ai fost moaşă cu sălar.
N-ai fost moaşă cu liceu
Cu dar de la Dumnezău.
Da amu să să adune
Şî să-ţi fac o rugăciune
Să te primea în ceia lume.

You bathed the babies;
You weren't at the medical dispensary;
You were not a midwife with a salary;
You were not a licensed midwife;
You had a gift from God.
But now they gather
To pray for you
That you be received in the other world.

This midwife was beloved by the women she had served throughout her lifetime. She had learned her skills from her own mother. The state later imposed restrictions on those without formal training, preventing them from practicing. Her goddaughters honored her annually, however, as well as at her funeral.

27. During the wedding ritual, in addition to the formal leave-taking of the couple from their respective parents, women offer toasts to the mother-in-law reminding everyone of the structural difficulties of the mother-in-law/daughter-in-law relationship. Accordingly, these strigături ask for leniency:

De ţi-a greşi cîteodată
O sărută şî o iartă.

If she wrongs you from time to time,
Kiss her and forgive her.

Note the similarities of this couplet and the lament. Here, a married woman reminds her peers about the potential behavior of her daughter-in-law using the future tense; in the lament, the deceased's sister reminds her about the daughter-in-law's actual behavior. The tenses are opposites, as are the life-cycle circumstances.

28. Niţa's skillful use of metaphor and poetic devices moved everyone, including myself, to tears. Her words intensified yet assuaged our grief. Niţa sang her sorrow in the old style, using a more ornamentally complex melody than is heard today. The themes that Niţa voiced—that life cannot be bought back, that parents are precious—are typical, although her manner of expressing them was considered unusual: "She knows how like no one else." Refer to note 9, above, for a related text.

29. See Kubler-Ross 1969 on the stages of death and dying. The futility of denial eventually gives way to acceptance. This process is evident in the laments also. The verses work through the grieving process, moving from denial to resigned acceptance.

30. Because I lived in the household during the final weeks of Marie's life, I can attest to the veracity of these claims about Juji's treatment of her mother-in-law. In fact, because of her mother-in-law's condition and the demands it placed on Juji, she had been reluctant to take on the responsibility of having a foreigner in her house. She feared that I would be as helpless as her mother-in-law. Because of the law forbidding foreigners to reside in the homes of Romanians, I was not engaged in the negotiations over place of residence, which was managed through local authorities.

31. Later in the day, Juji similarly expressed her gratitude to her mother-in-law:

Uă buna me şî scumpa me
Rău îmi pare după ie.

Oh, good one and dear one—
How bad I feel about her:

Şî de coconi mni-ai cătat
Şî bine i-ai învăţat.
Că ieu numai i-am făcut
Şî dumnăta i-ai crescut.
Că ieu m-am dus ş-am lucrat
Şî Doamne bine i-ai cătat.

Pentru ce i-ai legănat
Nici o plată nu ţi-am dat.
Pentru ce i-ai ciupăit
Nimnică nu ţi-am plătit.
Batăr că ieu te-am cătat
Tăt nu ţi-am împrumutat.

And you cared for my children,
And you taught them well;
For I only bore them,
And you brought them up;
Because I went and worked;
And, Lord, you took such good care of
them.
For having rocked them,
I didn't pay you anything.
For having bathed them,
I paid you nothing.
Although I took care of you,
It was not enough to compensate.

Not only does Juji pay her respects, but she explains, in part, her generous care of her mother-in-law. Despite the often uneasy relations between these two women, Juji's strong sense of reciprocal obligations, especially between the living and the dead, overrode whatever resentment she may have felt. This was the least she could do to repay her mother-in-law for having assisted her in her time of need.

32. This is another use of the theme of înstrăinare, or estrangement. The most common is that which refers to the consequences of patrilineality and patrilocal residence for women. See Buga 1967 for a more thorough treatment of this theme in Romanian poetry.

33. Feuerbach (1980, 1) also draws on the relationship between death and doctors:

He is the best doctor on earth
None of his cures have yet failed;
And no matter how sick you become,
He completely heals nature.

I can only speculate that the masculine identity of the doctor reflects the tendency in the West for medicine to be a male profession.

34. Married women generally wear black as the predominant color. It may be argued that once married, women are in a perpetual condition of self-mourning because marriage is considered to be a type of symbolic death.

Coffins are made of wood; some may be decorated with painted symbols or elaborately carved. These are the prerogatives of status, but, in general, people are buried in plain caskets. What tends to vary is the type of wood; those with greater resources may use a more durable one. This assuages the status considerations of the living, but it obviously has no bearing on the comfort of the deceased. Some women will cry:

Să-ţi fac copîrşeu de-aramă
Că ne-ai fost tare bună mamă.

Să-ţi fac copîrşeu de-argint
Să nu te bag în pămînt.

Let's make you a copper coffin,
Because you were a very good mother to
us.
Let's make you a silver coffin,
So I don't put you in the ground.

The first couplet acknowledges the value of this individual, in this case, a mother. She deserves a fine coffin of metal. Nobility—people of "value"—were thought to have been buried in ornate caskets. The second couplet underscores the durability of silver. Such a casket, unlike a wooden one, will prevent the corpse from eventually rotting in the dirt.

35. The Latin is *Ritu naturae capite hominem gigni mos est, pedibus efferi.*

36. The word *prohod* is Slavic, probably derived from Ruthenian. *Prohoditi* means to go; *prohodeti*, to escort. The funeral cortège accomplishes both: the deceased goes from the community of this world (the courtyard) to the community of that world (the cemetery) and is escorted to the grave by family and friends.

37. See F. Child (1962, 481, 491) under the headings "graves, lovers, plants and trees from," and "plants from graves." This theme usually involves the intertwining of plants or branches to symbolize the endurance of earthly love in spite of death's intrusion.

38. Wedding poetry also uses the theme of postponing the inevitable departure. The following verse, which again points to the association between marriage and death, is cited in Buga (1967, 82).

Sus în stîlpu vraniţii	Above, by the porch post
Şade mama mniresii.	Rests the bride's mother.
Să roagă sfîntului soare	She begs the sun
Să ţie ziua mai mare	To make the day longer,
C-are-o fiică ducătoare.	Because she has a daughter going
Păste munţi la alte curţi	Over the mountains to other courtyards,
La părinţi necunoscuţi.	To unfamiliar parents.

39. Niţa, Marie's sister, lamented in related fashion at her elder brother's funeral the following summer. As they approached the cemetery in Sǎliştea de Sus, she began to "converse" with their brother who resided there already:

Uă de mine măi Mitrucă	Oh my, hey, Mitrucă—
Uă destide poarta larg	Open the gate wide,
Uă că zine cine ţi-i drag.	For someone dear to you is coming.
Uă că şî Văsîle o zinit	For Văsîle has come,
Că o ştiut că ţi-i urît.	For he knew you felt lonely.
Uă scoală-te fă tu bine	Oh, arise, please do this;
Ţîpă pînza di pă tine	Throw your shroud off
Şî te uită cine zine.	And see who is coming.

40. Marian (1892, 359) reported an interesting practice that occurred during the funeral of a twin sibling. The living sibling had the right to make a "brother of the cross" (akin to a blood brother or sister). The chosen individual had to be born in the same month, although not necessarily of the same sex. After the deceased twin's casket was lowered into the ground, the living one climbed into the grave. The blood brother or sister pulled the living twin out; they then took a ritual bread, broke it, and kissed to seal their ritual kin relation. Marriage between a brother and sister of this sort was prohibited. See also Kligman 1981, 176, n. 31.

41. In Juji's dream, her deceased son came back for dinner (see note 11, above). Those familiar with Paradjanov's film *Shadows of Our Forgotten Ancestors*

will recall the various occasions when the dead lover is thought to have returned for dinner or to visit. The theme of that film is the theme of this book. The mystical, dreamlike qualities of the movie noted by film critics present in another medium the cosmological system explicated in these pages.

42. Danforth (1982, 99–106) presents a related phenomenon in rural Greece. His discussion focuses on the metaphor of the human body as food mediating between life and death. He points out the parallel association between human life and plant life, as well as the inverted relations of consumption between nature and culture.

The sacrifice of human life to mother earth or to the gods is a familiar theme, but it is well beyond the scope of this work to include representative references; the classic work is Hubert and Mauss 1964. Preying upon the other for sustenance is, of course, the basis of the Dracula tale. Vampires maintain their nocturnal health by imbibing the life force of a living individual. By drinking the blood of others, their own system "flows," enabling them to "live" in death. These beings are truly "betwixt and between" this world and that. As we have seen, the disjunction between these two worlds is thought to be complete; that which survives in both is necessarily the source of fear and promulgator of things evil. To combat these forces of evil, a system of charms, incantations, and other ritual practices exists. (For example, in the Banat region, it was said that the body of a *strigoi*, or ghost, would be reburied face down with garlic in its mouth. Others claim the head was severed so that it could not eat the hearts of the living. These are variations on the driving of a stake through the heart of the suspect being.) Some of these practices are associated with Christian thought and action—such as the handwritten *Cartea de Desfăcut* that circulates quietly—and others are not. See, for example, Marian 1893; Gorovei 1931; Muşlea and Bîrlea 1970, 163–74, 462–93, 515–18; Rosetti 1975; O. Bîrlea 1976, 152–62, 382–88; Kligman 1981. For a recent study on the symbolic system of witchcraft among French peasants, I recommend Favret-Saada 1980. See also A. Strathern (1982) for an exploration of the related themes of witchcraft, greed, cannibalism, and death.

43. The more stunning reports of self-flagellation or self-mutilation that decorate the anthropological record (see, for example, Durkheim 1965, 431–64) are not apposite here. Women may attempt to fling themselves into or upon the grave and will entreat the deceased to take them along or allow them to act as substitutes.

44. Various interpretations have been offered about the meaning of funeral banquets. Some suggest that this is a form of necrophilia, a symbolic eating of the deceased. The earth ingests the dead, but in this manner, so do the living. See, for example, de Martino 1975, 225–29. Fajans (1985), offering a different interpretation, has noted among the Baining that certain mourners ingest taro soaked with the bodily fluids of the corpse as a means to reaffirm the natural ties between the deceased and the living relatives; meanwhile, social ties are broken through the observance of other food taboos. The symbolic sharing of the deceased's death through a ritual meal is also reminiscent of the Christian partaking of Christ's blood.

45. Ariès (1981, 167–68) discusses charity for the poor as part of the funeral. He also points out that "the quantity of alms and contributions that it represented

not only attested to the generosity and wealth of the deceased but also interceded in his favor before the court of heaven. The gathering of the poor at his funeral was his last act of charity." The poor take advantage of this opportunity on all ritual alms-giving days such as All Souls' Day or Easter. On Easter, in another village, itinerant Gypsies arrived before the holiday. On Easter Sunday, villagers brought their bags filled with bread, eggs, meat, and drink to the church to be blessed by the priest. Upon conclusion of the service, the Gypsy women, young children in tow, moved from person to person. Their outstretched aprons were soon filled with samples of food. While many villagers resent this practice, seeing it as manipulative, they are at a loss to protest it, for such is the will of God.

46. R. Rosaldo (1984) emphasizes this point: "Rituals can thus serve as the vehicles for processes that occur both before and after the period of their performance. Funeral rituals, for example, do not contain the entire process of mourning. It is mistaken to collapse the two because neither ritual nor mourning either fully encapsulates or fully explains the other." Despite academic analytic penchants to the contrary, his point is well taken by this author.

47. See Vancea de Buteasa's book of prayers (1893). With respect to this broader category, women diligently inquired before my departures about the exact dates of my travels. Prayers were offered that I would have a safe flight.

48. The reckoning of the specific days when the post-funeral meals occur is not precise. Some calculate the third day as the day after the funeral (the fourth day from death), and the sixth week accordingly. The intervals, however, reflect those that affected Christ; hence, six weeks is an approximation of forty days. The services held for the sixth week's and the year's observances are a variant of the Parastas, which takes place on the evening before the burial. The service is a shorter version of the full funeral benedictions. Generally, people refer to the post-burial services as the "unbinding of the dead," because that is the process that is occurring.

Some people mentioned that the sixth-week memorial (instead of a funeral) is observed for those who have committed suicide but not for unbaptized children. Marian (1892, 355) noted that a sixth-week ritual observance took place for someone who had died away from home. "The custom was to make a pole dressed with a man's shirt or a woman's blouse, if the person was a male or female, and then do a funeral service as for someone dead, that is perform the entire ritual, and then bury the pole in the ground." I will present a related tale in the following chapter.

49. Although the dead are said to be present on all ritual days, All Souls' Day on November 1 (All Saints' Day in the liturgical calendar) is specifically in their honor. In Ieud on this day, each family goes to the cemetery. Those members that go each take a candle that is implanted on the grave. Someone will tidy the grave and decorate it with flowers. The women bring ritual breads and a candle to the church where they await the priest. He is presented with a paper on which are written the names of the family's dead. (A 10-lei note is included with each list.) After the service for the dead, the priest calls out the names from every piece of paper. Then the dezlegarea is recited for all of the village dead. Everyone then gathers in the cemetery. The candles are lit so that the graveyard is illuminated and the darkness of the night is brightened. All Souls' Day is still commemorated

in cities, notably those with Hungarian inhabitants. Due to the size of the cemeteries and the number of candles ablaze, it is quite a striking display. Moreover, in some locales, funeral meals will be laid out upon the grave and eaten "with the dead." Or musicians may be engaged to serenade the dead.

Chapter Four

1. The centrality of marriage was discussed in Chapter 2. The symbolic wedding characteristic of southern Transylvania and of Oltenia differs from that in Maramureș. In the former, the most important element is the Song of the Tree, the tree being the symbol of the wedding flag. See, for example, M. Pop 1976, 161–65; Bernabé 1980.

2. The terminology for such creatures is extensive. See, for example, Kligman 1981, chapter 2; Senn 1982, for Romanian sources. Karnoouh (1983a, 85, 106) writes that the term *strigoi* is etymologically related to that for the shouted couplets, *strigături*. The Latin root *striga* refers to a witch or vampire. (In Italian, witches are *strege*.) Although I am unfamiliar with a conscious association between the terms, his analysis is compelling. Karnoouh's discussion also elaborates on the relationship between women and the Devil.

Some people are fated to become strigoi, such as those born with a caul, or tail (although corrective ritual intervention on the behalf of such people is believed to be efficacious); others suffer the consequences of errors that have occurred during their funerals, for example, a cat crossed over or under the corpse or not all of the pomenile were offered. But the greatest danger surrounds those with unfulfilled lives. Of course, here we encounter the vampire theme of the living dead. It constitutes the central core of Stoker's novel. (The word *vampire* is not common to Romanian lore, however. For discussions about the vampire in neighboring areas, see, for example, du Boulay [1982] on Greece and Georgieva [1983, 153–83] on Bulgaria.) Wolf's book (1975) includes a listing of vampire films. The Soviet filmmaker Paradjanov's masterpiece, *Shadows of Our Forgotten Ancestors*, elaborates upon the themes of unfulfilled love and the return to the living. The film is ethnographically rich. In the end, Ivan receives the "kiss of death" from his deceased lover. The imagery is fitting: her bloodless limbs reach out to grasp him to her world; his coloring then matches hers and that of the surrounding birch forest. The souls of the dead are thought to reside there (as well as in other places, such as water). Ivan's funeral (in the original version) includes a wake in which the relationship between mortality and sexuality is vividly represented. A related and similarly well-known theme is that of the "grateful dead" (see Gerould 1908). This theme is also based upon beliefs about the sacred obligations of burial and respect for the dead, adherence to which produces souls who are at rest and, hence, grateful.

3. The compelling yet contradictory "marriage" between sexuality and death has given birth to such children as psychoanalysis, existentialism, fatalism, religion—as well as to Woody Allen, the Grateful Dead, and the capitalist veneration of Count Dracula (for profit and entertainment). I leave it to the reader to continue the list of creative offspring.

4. This calls to mind a line in Coleridge's "The Pain of Sleep": "desire with loathing strangely mixed." Craft, in his recent and recommended article "'Kiss Me With Those Red Lips': Gender and Inversion in Bram Stoker's *Dracula*" (1984), discusses the ambivalent relationship between desire and fear with respect to vampirism. His sensitive analysis insists on a reading of the homoerotic elements in this tale (in addition to the general sexual "anxiety of late Victorian culture").

5. Clearly, not all people marry. For those beyond childbearing age, symbolic weddings are not performed; instead, the deceased is honored as a servant of God. For women, there is also the affiliated status of "consecrated virgin."

6. Wolf (1975, xviii) in writing about the attraction to Dracula, "a figure who confronts us with primordial mysteries: death, blood, and love," states that Stoker "makes us understand in our own experience why the vampire is said to be invisible in the mirror. He is there, but we fail to recognize him since our own faces get in the way." Indeed, the "self" (other than the critical self) necessarily fails to recognize its self; instead, it projects onto the "other" that which it prefers not to see. And so commences our mystified discourse of the self and other.

7. See, in particular, Herzfeld 1981; Danforth 1982, 71–115; and du Boulay 1982. The literature on metaphor is extensive. Classical discussions may be found in, for example, Jakobson 1960, 1966, 1968; Black 1962; and Richards [1936] 1964. For more recent works, refer to Fernandez 1974; Ricoeur 1977; de Man 1978; Sacks 1978; Ortony 1979; and M. Johnson 1981. I wish to thank Chana Kronfeld for her bibliographic assistance. Also see Kronfeld 1983.

8. Representative references for Romania include especially Muşlea 1972; Fochi 1964 (491–530, for a comparative survey of the ethnographic literature); H. Stahl 1983. For Greece: Herzfeld 1981; Danforth 1982. For China: Martin 1985; E. Johnson 1985. For Africa: Lévy-Bruhl 1963, 395–96.

Lest the reader assume that the relation between marriage and death is only typical of more "exotic" cultures, I cite the following verse, similar to those of the Romanian ballad, the *Mioriţa*, from French folklore (Fochi 1964, 80, n. 40):

Ne dites pas à ma mère que je me suis noyé.	Don't tell my mother that I have drowned.
Mais dites-lui plûtot que je me suis marié	But tell her instead that I have married
Avec la plus belle fille, qu'il y eut dans la cité.	The most beautiful girl that there is in the city.

Fochi (1964) is one of the most comprehensive sources for comparative materials, notably European and Slavic. Segalen (1983, 28) also includes numerous sayings on this topic, for example, from Gascony: "Quand on se marie, à mort il faut penser" (When marrying, think of dying).

9. For more explicit discussion of this topic, see, for example, Warner 1959; von Hildebrand 1970; Scheper 1971; Maltz 1978; Feeley-Harnik 1981.

10. Warner (1959, 368–69) notes the following passages from the Canticle of Canticles: "He brought me to the banqueting house, and his banner over me was

love" (Ch. 2); "My beloved is mine, and I am his: he feedeth among the lilies" (Ch. 2); "Thou hast ravished my heart, my sister, my spouse, thou hast ravished my heart" (Ch. 4).

11. In a cautionary comment following Fernandez's article on metaphor (1974, 139) Maltz notes "the importance of using multiple metaphors to place a single subject in two different domains at once as a means of transcending the characteristics of any single domain." The black flag would seem to be exemplary.

12. For the funerals of women who have never married or especially pious widows, women (usually postmenopausal), and not men as is typically the case, may serve as pallbearers in fulfillment of the deceased's last wishes. Again, separation from the social-sexual cohort is marked. In these cases, the deceased is like a girl, not engaged in sexual relations, and therefore is escorted by her cohort, women.

13. The analysis of the formal features of the ritual poetry is beyond the possibilities of this book. That is not intended to underplay the significance of the form-content relationship; it is seminal, and in a sense, it is assumed throughout this work. Regarding parallelism, in addition to Jakobson (e.g., 1960, 1966, 1968), see also Fox 1977. On metaphor in Maramureş folklore, refer to Brătulescu 1963.

14. I am fully cognizant of the subjective quality of this statement. I do not wish to diminish the poignancy of the laments at "normal" funerals. Death rites are emotionally exhausting under the best of circumstances. Local views, however, hold that the death of an unmarried person of marriageable age is the most difficult to bear. That is borne out in the funeral rite as a total phenomenon. The oral-visual interplay of metaphor and metonym is overwhelming. While I was also moved to tears by the imagery evoked in laments at funerals other than death-weddings, it was more difficult to maintain affective distance in the presence of a dead young woman dressed as a bride. Participation at these events became an appreciated lesson in the "poetics" of death. (I was, until that time, only accustomed to the more alienated practices typical of our "advanced" civilization.) During the course of my extended fieldwork, I attended five death-weddings. I will recount their particularities as we progress through this discussion.

15. Many of these appellations are preceded by the familiar form of the pronoun *you*. This decreases the distance between the living and the dead. As seen in the preceding chapter, death herself is frequently addressed in this manner: "Tu, moartea" (You, death).

16. Refer to the previous discussion on the relationship between Christ and the soul, and more specifically, on that between virgins and Christ. Von Hildebrand (1970, 89) includes the following pertinent excerpt from St. Athanasius' *Apologia ad Imp. Constantium:* "Jesus Christ, the Son of God, our Lord and Redeemer, has given us in virginity a pattern of angelic holiness, wherefore the Church has always called maidens adorned with this virtue brides of Christ."

17. On divine marriage, see, for example, Dumézil 1979. A related form of the divine marriage is typified by the "cosmic marriage" in the *Miorita* (the shepherd is married to the divine forces of nature).

18. Presumably, the marriage of girls to the son of Christ has its basis in Chris-

tian tradition; however, this analytic point has never been offered by a Ieudan spontaneously. At the time, I was not versed in the tradition and did not press the matter.

19. Brăiloiu (1938, 56) recorded similar verses across the mountains in nearby Ţara Oaşului:

Cetirile îz clopotile	Violins from the church bells,
Şi stiagu îz prapurile	And the flag from the church banners.
A ta nuntă-i mohorîtă	Your wedding is darkened sorrow;
La tătă lumea-i urîtă	To everyone it is ugly.
A tău steagu-i supăratu	Your flag is anguish,
Că nu-i roşu şi cu alb	For it is not red and white
Nouă să ne fie dragu.	That is dear to us.

Similar verses may be found in other collections of oral poetry, such as Marian 1892; Papahagi 1925; I. Bîrlea 1968.

20. I have consistently referred to the couplets presented as "fragments" or "excerpts" regardless of length. Lamenters continue until they are required to refrain because of ritual law (for example, the priest is reciting prayers) or exhaustion. During the course of this "wedding," I recorded one of Gasie's sisters for one and a half hours without respite. I could have done the same for another of her sisters. See Appendix D. Grief may be consuming. For some women, it is manifest in their trancelike wailing; others are too overwrought to lament in this manner. Gasie's mother had a heart condition; family members sensitively restrained her impulse to wail inconsolably. The totality of the ritual experience is exhausting. As the women say, lamenting eases the pain.

21. Even if a young man marries in as ginere, his wife is still defined with respect to him and will nonetheless join his family in that world.

22. Chapter 2 is replete with couplets about the hardships of married life for women. In the lament excerpt, it is stated that in-laws won't fight with her. Compare that with, for example:

Să ai pe unde a-nturna	To have a way to return
Cînd socra ta te-a certa.	When your mother-in-law will scold you.
Să ai pe unde-a zini	To have a way to come
Cînd socra-ta te-a sfădi.	When your mother-in-law argues with you.

These couplets caution a young bride that her mother will be there to comfort her occasionally when she cannot take the abuses of married life. Of course, unlike marriage in which there is at least in theory a "road back," there is no such path from death.

23. This brings to mind the wedding shout:

Decît măritată rău	Rather than married badly,
I mai bine în copîrşeu	It is better in a coffin,
O fată pă trăiul tău.	A girl with your own life.

Death offers a certain autonomy that a bad marriage denies through the exacerbation of submission.

24. Danforth's point is important: "The perspective of the bride is adopted because it is from this perspective (in a society where residence after marriage is patrilocal) that the analogy between death and marriage is clearest" (1982, 75).

25. There is a violation of logical consistency "evident" in the above lament examples. Clearly, while it is believed that Mări will go to heaven because she is seven, it is not certain. Nor is it certain that Gasie is involved in her death. But even scientific debate falls short of absolute certainty in the face of death (witness the dilemma of legal death). What this analysis of a conceptual system may lack in logical consistency is accounted for in the consistency of symbolic logic.

Regarding marriage, there are unusual marriages within the range of "normal" marriages. For these cases, medical and/or church dispensation must be sought. Refer to Chapter 1.

26. Brăiloiu (1938, 34) includes a verse on the same theme:

N'ireasa-i în temet'eu	The bride is in the cemetery;
N'irele la tată-său	The groom at his father's.
N'ireasa-i pusă-n sălaş	The bride is (put) in a coffin;
Nuntă fără ceteraş.	The wedding without violinist.

(The words for cemetery and coffin may be heard occasionally in Maramureş, but less frequently than *ţintirim* or *copîrşeu*.)

27. In Breb, in addition to violinists, several young men accompanied the procession intermittently blowing the *trîmdiţa*, a long alpine horn, which is also played for other occasions. The horns were not within view of the mourners, however. Their players followed a parallel route. The sounds were like echoes from the other world, beckoning the dead. (For those familiar with the film *Shadows of Our Forgotten Ancestors*, similar horn-playing occurs.) During the wedding procession to the church, the musicians play dirgelike melodies to elaborate the marriage-as-death theme. This solemnity is momentary, however, giving way to the triumphant post-ceremony music.

There were indeed reports of wakes at death-weddings in the distant past at which the sexuality-mortality relation was made quite explicit. The deceased was laid out in the midst of a room in which a party was in full swing—honoring the dead. The death was balanced by the potential of courtship. (Again, a dramatization of this occurs in the uncut version of Paradjanov's film mentioned above.)

28. These couplets were used at Gasie's funeral as well. Another sister cried a variant:

Faţa ta ca bujoru	Your face like a peony,
Cum s-a face ca lutu.	How it will become like the earth's clay.
Faţa ta ca viola	Your face like a violet,
Cum s-a face ca tina.	How it will become like mud.

29. In the discussion of marriage and death and the reproduction of cycles, birth takes on its own significance. With each marriage and death, there is a new

"birth." As stated in the introduction, however, birth is not as marked ritually as are the other events. In view of the concerns of this book, birth has not figured prominently in the discussions. It is perhaps always an absent presence.

The structural relations between rites, be they of the calendar or of life cycles, were first treated systematically by Van Gennep 1960. See also T. Turner 1977.

30. The death-resurrection plays are performed in the village. The Bethlehem play now takes place in front of the church; it has acquired a distinctly folk-theatrical tone. It as well as the other Christmas festivities are discouraged by the Party. The secular death-resurrection plays are linked with nature's cycle of death and rebirth. They usually involve a shepherd, a goat, and a Gypsy. (The Romanian folklore literature is filled with accounts and studies on this topic. For brief overviews, see M. Pop 1976, 33–84; Kligman 1981, 134–38.) The masked characters go from home to home, as is typical of mumming customs.

31. The following iertăciunea is taken from Marian 1892, 259. I have chosen to include it because of the range of experience incorporated—nature, kinship, food:

Ie-ți Marie ziuă bună	Take your leave, Marie,
Dela soare, dela nori	From the sun, from the clouds,
Dela a tale surori.	From your sisters,
Dela struțu de busuocu	From the basil sprigs,
Dela feciori, dela jocu.	From the fellows, and the dance,
Dela fete din uliță	From the girls on the path.
Ie-ți Marie ziuă bună	Take your leave, Marie,
Dela păhăruțu cu miere	From the little glass of sweetened brandy
Dela feciori, dela bere.	From the bachelors, from the drinking party.

32. The notion of "dying in the service of the motherland" is important to the process of coming to terms with this type of death. The ballads about the ravages of war are extremely moving; so are the letters—in verse—sent home from the front. One ballad includes a discussion between a dying soldier and the forest, which is often the confidant of humans. As with a mother, one may confide in her with certainty. The soldier asks the forest to hide the truth from his mother. (In the *Miorița*, the sheep are asked to tell the young shepherd's mother that he has married. In the war ballad, the soldier dies an unsung hero.)

Codrule orice-i vedea	Forest, whatever you see
În tine cît oi şedea	As long as I stay within you,
Nu spune la mama mea.	Don't tell my mother.
De mi-i vedea moartă-n tine	If you see me dead,
Spune maicii că mi-e bine.	Tell my mother that I am well.
De mi-i vedea c-am murit	If you see that I have died,
Spune că nu m-ai întilnit.	Tell her that you haven't met me.
Lasă-mi frunze de-nvelit	Let your leaves be bedding,
Crengile d-acoperit.	Branches to cover (me).
Ziua vîntu şi-a sufla	In the day, the wind will blow;
Noaptea frunze şi-a pica.	At night, leaves will fall.
Pă mine m-or astupa	They will cover me over
Şi nimen nu m-a afla.	And no one will find me.

33. During the course of my extended fieldwork, a neighbor suffered a grisly death at the hands of "hooligans." He was known to have been a decent man who had worked hard to earn money to support his family. He had been expected home for the holidays, but his actual return was shocking. He had been knifed repeatedly.

34. At this point in the recounting of this tale of horror, I was acutely aware of the confrontation of two cultures. While I was listening, I was also reacting in distinct, culturally determined ways. The murder evoked stereotypic responses in me, based on my Chicago background. My initial thought was that no one in their right mind would send a young girl alone to a deserted village with a relatively unknown young man in the house. Jumbled images from the different forms of violence in Bellow's *The Dean's December* (1982) emerged. But I was in Maramureş, not Chicago. There was no referent for my practical paranoia. It had been perfectly normal, a gesture of *omenie* (human decency) tragically exploited. For me, it was sickening.

35. No one seemed to question why God had not prevented this horrific murder to begin with. Such was her fate. Also, in view of the stabbing, it seemed curious that there had been no blood on the floor that would have led her family to her. The physician claimed that occasionally, depending on the position in which the knife pierces the heart, there may be no blood. There still should have been blood from the shoulder wound, however.

36. This was the one time that I found photographing the dead almost unbearable. The family asked that I take the photographs, and it seemed the least I could do. But it was profoundly upsetting. The room was small, crowded, and hot. Mǎri's playmates gazed at her with cupped hands covering their mouths. As I looked down upon this scene of despair, I had the sense that the room was about to spin.

37. Karnoouh (1983a, 125) discusses a similar linguistic denotation of changing economic circumstances. The word *bocotan* refers to the nouveau riche who have acquired their means as a result of the machinations of seasonal labor. Its usage distinguishes the new rich from the old, *gazde*, who have wealth as well as status in the lineage hierarchy.

38. An incident during the death-wedding also pointed to the changes wrought by modern times. In the middle of this funeral, a car filled with Japanese tourists drove into the village. Since Moroşeni intuitively step aside to let "gentlemen" and foreigners pass, the tourists were soon standing near the flower-bedecked coffin, which had already been removed from the house. The lid was not nailed shut until the procession formed. The mourners did not pay much attention to the newcomers, and vice versa. Within minutes, the tourists lined up in a row and pulled out their cameras. They took pictures for the next five minutes and then filed back to their car. They did not bother to go on to the old wooden church. This episode, for me, dramatized the stereotype of the tourist as well as the objectification of the "other."

Mǎri's murderer was caught in the train station of a southern city. He was dressed as a woman. My understanding at the time was that the accused should have been tried in the village. I have been unable to learn about the conclusion of this case.

39. See, in particular, Fochi 1964, 491–552. For variants from Maramureş, refer to Rîpă 1972; generally the *Miorița* is sung as a Christmas carol, "Trei păcurărei."

The *Miorița* has inspired much scholarly interpretation. Recently, political analysts have suggested that one "cause" of the seeming passivity of the Romanian population may be the fatalistic Weltanschauung implicit in the *Miorița*. As Shafir (1985, 405) notes: "According to Blaga [a Transylvanian philosopher who coined the notion of the "mioritic space"; see Blaga 1969, 119–31], the Romanian's is a mystical existence of reunion with nature and its contemplation, which involves disregarding or ignoring history's temporal dimensions, but remaining conscious of one's own spiritual eternity." I do not choose to engage in this type of "philosophizing"; Blaga's (as well as Eliade's) interpretations about the ballad have been critiqued by H. Stahl (1983). I do not include the *Miorița* because of its alleged contributions to understanding Romanian political culture; my interest is the wedding allegory.

Muşlea (1972, 34) claims that the ethnographic basis for the "wedding of the dead" theme that has absorbed scholars of the *Miorița* was first brought to the attention of the scholarly world by the literary writer M. Bibescu in 1923. She wrote: "The funeral of young men and girls takes all the wedding ceremony's rituals because young people who die at the age when a person seeks a husband or wife are considered to have fallen in love with death." This view has been opposed by the ethnographically minded, the school of thought to which I subscribe. Brăiloiu ([1946] 1973), among others such as H. Stahl, argues that "the simulated marriage persuades the soul that its terrestrial career has been fulfilled." In essence, the *Miorița* does not express "voluntary renouncement" nor "the adoration of death" but, rather, the defense of life itself.

40. Lambs are generally thought to be sacred; it is said that they played with Christ when he was a child. Shepherds, who have a subculture of their own, pass the long nights at the higher pastures telling each other tales. The miraculous lamb is a primary actor in this folklore. The relationship between the shepherd and the miraculous lamb is a very special one in which sexuality is highly sublimated (as is true for the ritual and literary forms). Again, the themes of purity and pollution color the discussions. Many of these tales (at least, of the ones recounted to me) present a version of the fall of man. In essence, the shepherd who prospers with the assistance of the lamb begins to have more interaction with the social world of the village. Eventually, he brings his sweetheart to the sheepfold. The lamb perceives this as a fundamental betrayal and banishes the shepherd. In the course of their argument, the shepherd utters a curse that leaves the lamb impregnated. The element of immaculate conception is obvious. The next tale in this cycle (one leading to another throughout the evening) tells about the life of the lamb's son. See also Densuşianu 1966 for poetry on pastoral life.

41. Recall that Gasie's death was similarly announced to her siblings: the telegram informed them that she had married. This is a conventional form.

42. The death-wedding and the *Miorița* share Transylvania as a setting, but they are not confined to these areas. In other words, Transylvania may be consequential, but it is not causal.

It should be noted that symbolic marriage constitutes an important aspect of the literary work *Dracula*. Arthur is eventually wed to Lucy, as are, in a perverse sense, Dracula's prey with him. Dracula's unions, through the appropriation of affinal prerogatives and the expropriation of blood, distort consanguineal relations. His "family," as he refers to his cadre of victims, disregards all sacred taboos; incest and murder are nightly affairs. This is a spiritual marriage of a very different kind from that under discussion; it is cursed rather than blessed. Ultimately, it cannot be allowed to endure. Also, Dracula's world inverts the conventional order of social relations. In this respect, the novel is similar to ritual, and Dracula may be seen as a literary figure related to folk culture's trickster and clown figures. (See Kligman 1981, chapter 4, for a discussion of inversion in Romanian ritual.) As is typical of ritual inversion, Dracula enables taboo topics to be thought of although not actualized.

43. For example, in the Song of the Hen, sexuality is "played with." This ritual sequence is about sexuality, and, safeguarded within the frame of ritual, its intimate secrets may be aired jestingly. Although the titillation of the sexual joke is much appreciated, there is considerable relief that everyday sexual norms about marital fidelity prevail. The ritual pushes the boundaries but does not sanction their transgression.

44. The tension between desire and control has found expression in the relationship between the sacred and the profane, the id and the superego, the individual and society. The Ten Commandments are an example of a mediating text.

45. Shepherds have their own stock of magic practices, which differ from the customary ones. Their magic is specifically aimed at the needs of the sheepfold and the shepherds.

46. Danforth (1982, 81) cites a Greek variant that embellishes this theme:

You, young shepherds, you unfortunate young men,
Tomorrow you will go back to our village, to our desolate homeland.
. . . .
Don't tell them that I have been killed.
    Don't tell them that I am dead.
Just tell them that I have married and taken a good wife.
I have taken the tombstone as my mother-in-law, the black earth as my wife,
And I have the little pebbles as brothers- and sisters-in-law.

Danforth calls attention to the nature of affinal relations in his analysis of this excerpt: "The weight of the tombstone suggests the oppressive nature of one's relationship with one's mother-in-law, who in Greek folk songs is invariably portrayed as a 'wicked' relative. The blackness of the earth anticipates the black dress the man's wife will put on as a result of his marriage to the earth. There is an implicit contrast between this black dress and the white dress she would have worn at her marriage. Finally, the pebbles that become the man's brothers-in-law and sisters-in-law are part of the natural world. Thus the passage of the deceased from home and family to the grave, from a social or cultural state to a natural one, is equated with the passage from one's home and family of origin to the home of one's affines."

47. Eliade (1972, 251) writes: "In the *Miorița* the whole universe is trans-figured. We are taken into a liturgical cosmos, in which Mysteries (in the religious sense of the term) are brought to fulfillment. . . . One of the characteristics of the peasant Christianity of the Romanians and of eastern Europe is the presence of many religious elements that are 'pagan,' archaic, sometimes scarcely Chris-tianized. It is a new religious creation, peculiar to the southeast of Europe, which we have termed 'cosmic Christianity' because, on the one hand, it projects the Christological mystery upon the whole of Nature and, on the other, neglects the historical elements of Christianity, only to dwell, instead, on the liturgical dimen-sion of man's existence in the world." Elsewhere he defines this cosmic Christian-ity as "dominated by a nostalgia for nature sanctified by the presence of Jesus" (in H. Stahl 1983, 170). Eliade's notion of "cosmic Christianity" seems suggestive from a hermeneutic point of view. However, I concur with Stahl's general criti-cisms of Eliade's (and Blaga's) interpretations. Eliade, like Blaga and others, con-structs his own vision of the peasant community that extensive fieldwork cannot corroborate. See H. Stahl 1983, 154–75.

48. Pop and Ruxăndoiu (1976, 329) also discuss the aspect of eternity. They note the contradiction between the fact of human mortality and the "sentiment and knowledge of infinity." Eternity mediates this contradiction that is the eternal tragedy of the human order. They state that the mioritic shepherd becomes eter-nal through the act of marriage. H. Stahl (1983, 166) refers to the transformational relation between the death-wedding and the cosmic marriage of the *Miorița*. The latter becomes a symbolization of a symbolic representation (the death-wedding). In the mioritic marriage, elements of nature substitute for the ritual roles per-formed by living people in the death-wedding; for example, the sun and moon serve as godparents. Stahl rhapsodizes that "this symbolization of the basic sym-bols elevates the general level of the verses to that of highly developed and en-chanting poetry."

49. Stahl (1983, 162–67) notes that he and Brăiloiu ([1946] 1973) essentially agree in their analyses of the *Miorița* and its fundamental relation to the eth-nographic material. He prefers, however, to stress the fear that motivates these practices, whereas Brăiloiu emphasizes alms-giving. The disagreement, if it may be termed so, seems academic. Both are "causal" features, and their relationship to each other is dynamic. Stahl's criticism of Eliade is, in my opinion, merited, although its tone is perhaps too strident. Eliade (1972, 250) states: "In the rural world, fear of ghosts does not seem to play the central role that Brăiloiu gives it. More probably, in Romania as elsewhere in eastern Europe, fear of ghosts and vampires is rather the result of an occasional crisis, of a panic that quickly spreads to the entire collectivity as the result of unusual calamities—epidemics, for ex-ample, or scourges of cosmic or historic proportions." With due respect to Eliade's enormous erudition, I must point out that this statement is simply unfounded (as the content of this book as well as the superb works of the Romanian sociological

school demonstrate). The belief in menacing spirits is still extant. Fear of the "living dead" is clearly related to the vampire lore associated with Dracula.

50. These statements are necessarily overgeneralized and do not respect the canon of cultural relativism that would argue that this is not true among the "*x*." The broad strokes of a historical brush, however, erase the particularities of experiences. Scientific rationalism, technologization, commercialization—these are not primarily concerned with the soul and its salvation. (To the contrary, many would argue that they have contributed to the corruption of the soul.) Progress has little room for death. But pretending that death does not exist does not eradicate it. Accordingly, confronted with the otherness of death, people often become "religious" despite years of denying belief or practice. Crisis in the contemporary world prompts consideration of death and its meaning. One need only think about the significance of the hospice movement for those afflicted with terminal cancer.

51. Ariès (1982, 614) summarizes the degeneration of death: "The death of the patient in the hospital, covered with tubes, is becoming a popular image, more terrifying than the *transi* or skeleton of macabre rhetoric. . . . The belief in evil was necessary to the taming of death; the disappearance of the belief has restored death to its savage state." The paradoxical coupling of sexuality and mortality tragically finds manifest (as opposed to symbolic) expression today among the victims of AIDS. The conservative and fundamentalist arguments vehemently account for AIDS as a violation of heterosexual practices. The transgression of God's will results in the divine punishment of death.

52. Perhaps it was political humor that, until recently, allowed the Romanian tourist trade to capitalize on Western fantasies and "decadence"; the Count's trail could be traced with a few indigenous cultural extras added to the tour package that invited visitors to "Dracula's land." Romanian tourism, however, does not take full advantage of the opportunity to exploit the fantasies of foreigners. In 1985 the Bureau of Tourism informed me that a group of sixty Americans was arriving to spend Halloween in Transylvania. They had not yet figured out exactly what they would do with these tourists; Halloween is not celebrated there.

53. I am unaware of the practice of the death-wedding elsewhere in contemporary Romania.

Chapter Five

1. More specifically, children as well as pubescent girls wear the customary attire daily, as do almost all women. Men tend to wear mass-produced shirts and pants. However, they always sport the local woolen or leather vest. Through the depths of winter, they may also wear the warm woolen "peasant" pants, just as they don the cool *gati*, or culotte-type pants, during the summer. Again, almost everyone dresses in village attire on nonwork days, celebrating themselves as Ieudeni. This practice is typical throughout all of Maramureş. Those who live in the cities of Baia Mare, Sighet, and Vişeu are accustomed to the mix of dress styles in their midst. Family members from the village visit relatives in the city or go to the market. Frequently, when city dwellers go to the village on the weekend, they

too dress in traditional dress. This is especially true of the younger generations, but less so of intellectuals.

2. It is beyond the interests of this work to critique the issue of whether or not Romania is a socialist state. Ceauşescu presents it as such, and Romania's citizens understand it to be socialist. It is their meaning, and not that of academic Marxist debates or state ideological treatises, that is pertinent to this study. See Burawoy 1987 for an account of Hungarian workers' "understanding" of socialism, as well as Haraszti 1978 and Kenedi 1982.

3. Clearly, the war created profound changes in their lives. The pace of change in the postwar period in Romania, however, is unprecedented.

4. See Jowitt 1974; also Georgescu 1985 and Shafir 1985. For further documentation about worsening socioeconomic conditions in Romania concomitant with Ceauşescu's hegemonic personality cult as well as the effects of the Western economic crisis, consult additionally the 1985 reports of Radio Free Europe and the indices of international newspapers for articles such as "Romanian Energy Shortage: Darkness at Noon," *Wall Street Journal*, April 10, 1985; "Romania Clings to Cult of Ceauşescu as the Nation Fast Slides into Decay," *Wall Street Journal*, January 27, 1986; "Birth and Death in Romania," *New York Review of Books*, October 23, 1986.

5. It is an interesting experience to discuss international issues at length. How may one demystify the mythical idealization of the United States, for example, when many who speak authoritatively of it have little idea of its location? Television may occasionally allow a glimpse, positive or negative, into some aspect of American life, but there is no corresponding spatial or temporal appreciation. This is not to suggest that there can be. As Romania becomes more xenophobic, the role of Radio Free Europe as an information mediator between East and West has intensified. Both sources of commentary are ideologically problematic, and both contribute variously to "mythological" apprehensions. I should mention that Radio Free Europe does provide access to current events otherwise unobtainable; it is a valuable service, despite my personal reservations about the tone of its reporting.

6. Rational, or scientific, alimentation came into public being in July 1982. In essence, it encouraged the reformulation of diet; height-and-weight charts relative to caloric intakes were published. The populace has not been very receptive, viewing this as yet another attempt to rationalize inadequate production and distribution, on the one hand, and to disguise the privileged access of the elite to scarce commodities, on the other. The discrepancy between the official and the popular understanding of this issue is revealed in its semantics. What is "rational alimentation" for the exponents of policy is "rations" for the people. A local Party official quickly corrected my colloquial reference when I inquired about the "rationing" situation. Presently, oil, rice, flour, and sugar are obtained through a ration-card system, one that is remembered from the fifties, the Stalinist postwar period. See also Georgescu 1985, 18–19. Verdery muses about the semantics of historical representation and political policy in a provocative conference paper entitled "History as Fetish and Food as Symbol: The Collective Construction of Nationalist Culture in Romania" (1983b).

The pronatalist campaign began vigorously in 1984. See, for example, *Scînteia,* March 3, 8, and 9, 1984. Also see McIntyre 1975; Moskoff 1980; and particularly, Nydon 1984.

7. Food and heat supplies are primary concerns; electricity and hot water are also significant problems, particularly in cities. As Verdery notes elsewhere, the population "is now beginning to wonder if Romania is not being industrialized at the expense of, rather than for the benefit of, the masses." This same concern, however, pertained to the turmoils of the industrialization of Western Europe in the nineteenth century.

8. Flour and oil are among the "rationed" goods; butter is a frequent addition to that list, especially in rural areas. In the summer of 1985, there simply was no butter in rural areas (although Bucureşti did not suffer from this problem). There are no longer any operating flour mills in Ieud; hence, the dependency on non-village production. (Mills were expropriated and left idle.) As part of the centralization of production, flour and bread are produced in state enterprises. Bread is delivered to the village and is "rationed" more often than not. Long lines may be joined in the middle of the village. My inquiry as to why women do not bake their own bread (as they had done as recently as two years ago) was greeted with incredulous responses: "We'd be delighted to, and how will we make the Christmas and Easter breads next year? Domnişoara, there isn't any yeast!" The statement about family production providing the bulk of meat, vegetables, and dairy products is a relative one. Recent laws about slaughtering animals have exacerbated the meat problem to a certain extent, but they have simultaneously encouraged innovations in urban-rural exchange relations as well as those of the second economy, neither of which are mutually exclusive. This applies to vegetables and dairy products as well.

9. These practices are reminiscent of Stalinist tactics formerly used to break the landed peasantry. It is typical for villagers to note bitterly that there seems to be an attempt to break everyone. It is also common to hear a peasant lament the disappearance of what seemed to be a structural feature of being a peasant: "Who has ever heard of a peasant cursing his animals? But I just can't keep them any longer." Owners are required to maintain cows that have calved for two years (for milk); calves must be kept for six months, even though this may strap the family's resources. Many attempt to evade registration of their animals. Hence, these peasants often consider themselves to be the present-day beasts of burden. It should be recalled that these peasants were not serfs, which makes their view about their circumstances comprehensible.

10. It would be interesting to ascertain the class differentiation involved in this phenomenon. For these transactions, "shoppers" must have access to a car. This, in turn, requires a calculation about gas quantities. "Carpools" tend to pool their resources for this purpose. Networking is critical to understanding the paradox of access to resources in an economy of scarcity. These networks extend the length and width of the country. It is not surprising that people involved in transport are among the important people to know.

11. All statistics are approximate figures that emerged through discussions with the local officials; I was not granted access to records.

12. A recent text that has circulated through Maramureş comments about socioeconomic change:

A făcut partidul bine	The Party did good,
Şî cel gazdă-i ca şî mine.	For that landowner is now like me.
N-are cară şî nici boi	He doesn't have a wagon nor oxen,
Nici botei mari de oi.	Nor large herds of sheep,
N-are brînză de vîndut	Nor cheese to sell,
Nici lapte de-ntrecut.	Nor milk to exchange.
Amu tătă lume vede	Now everyone sees
Şi iel poartă salopete.	That even he wears a work coat,
Şi iel mere-n lumea mare	And he goes around the country
Să cîştigă de mîncare.	To earn his food.

The state is ideologically committed to the elimination of social and class discrepancies and to the equal distribution of material goods, and it has done much toward these ends. Semi-cooperativization rid the village of landowners. Individuals now work for the state instead of at the behest of privileged persons. Furthermore, those persons are no different from anyone else; they too must sport the worker's blue coat, symbol of the industrializing worker state. They also join the seasonal labor force, to which the last lines refer. (This is a fragment of a 139-line text. It is not possible to present it or an analysis of its ambivalent commentary.)

13. The forests are nationalized; hence, "free" access to wood has been curtailed. Prices are controlled by the state.

14. Most Ieudeni do not yet have running water; hence, the lack of hot water that aggravates apartment living is not a concern (except for the "intellectuals" who live in the two small apartment buildings in Ieud).

15. This type of labor was generally associated with class position, and usually involved either the poor, or the wealthy who may have periodically travelled to sell herds. Today, the majority of the local population participates in seasonal labor.

16. The categorization of someone as a seasonal worker has had an interesting effect regarding my own status in Ieud. Over the years, I have taken on the identity of a symbolic Ieudeancă for many of Ieud's inhabitants. While some families have moved definitively from the village, I have continued to return periodically. Hence, during my fieldtrip this past summer (1985), I too was labeled a *sesonieră*. Like so many other Ieudeni, I come and go. While my periods of absence are considerably longer, it is expected that I shall return. This speaks to a fundamental change in my own identity with respect to the villagers' acceptance of me. Their concern about my identity is related to their own experience of the transformation of identity. It is a central issue of their lives.

It is beyond the possibilities of this work to discuss the comparative material on the consequences of the European *gastarbeiter* phenomenon. There are indeed similarities, although Romanians are not permitted to work outside of the country except under special conditions.

17. The yuppie life style is a long way off in Romania, and even further from

the far reaches of Maramureş. This commitment to the family is well suited to Romania's current pronatalist policies. The motivation is different from that of the state, however: Ieudeni are opposed to abortion on religious grounds.

18. This bifurcation may be thought of in terms of the mind-body split that contributes to the dissolution of an integrated cosmology. Also, the noncorrespondence between ethos and practice is noted frequently by Romanians with respect to ideology or policies and material conditions. See, for example, Georgescu 1985.

19. Bellah et al. (1985, 86) notes an observation of Tocqueville on the role of religion in nineteenth-century America that is relevant to the role of Romanian women as the bearers of tradition: "Religion, he says, 'does direct mores, and by regulating domestic life it helps to regulate the state.'" Ritual and religion are bound to each other in Ieud. Women are their most active keepers.

20. The literature about tradition is immense; it is both subject and object of interdisciplinary inquiry. I have no intention here of taking up the complexities of tradition as discussed in the literature. The curious might start with Shils 1981. Most assuredly, Hobsbawm and Ranger (1983) must also be included in reading about tradition.

21. Scholars often evaluate ideology in terms of political religion, for example, Lane 1981. Here I wish to encourage a "political anthropology" of Marxist-Leninist states as well. See, for example, Jowitt 1985. Such an approach is necessary to understand present-day Romanian politics and has given rise to concepts such as party familialization (Jowitt 1978) and dynastic socialism (Georgescu 1985) among non-anthropologists. These concerns are expressed more jokingly as well: Romanian socialism is "socialism in one family." PCR, the acronym for the Partidul Communist Român, is also that for Petrescu, Ceauşescu şi rudele (Petrescu, Ceauşescu, and kin); Petrescu is the family name of Elena Ceauşescu. The symbolic equivalence between the formal acronym and its unofficial sibling refers to the holding of important political positions by family members. Marriage, as we have seen, creates relations. In this case, the corporate families involved have benefited from a good match (perceived from a traditional peasant point of view).

22. The literature on Romanian nationalism is flourishing. Consult (in English) Hitchins 1983, 1985; Verdery 1983a, 1983b. Of the recent Romanian literature, see, for example, Edroiu et al. 1982 and S. Ştefănescu 1984. Romanian nationalism is an object of wrath for Hungarian as well as Romanian emigré groups, although their reasons differ. From scholarly and nonscholarly vantages, Romanian nationalism is a "hot" topic. I cannot here address the contradictions involved in the policies regarding the coinhabiting nations (ethnic groups) and the construction of a "pure" lineage. While folkloric presentations are meant to represent this cultural purity, they nonetheless must incorporate the coinhabiting others that contribute to the Romanian nation.

23. This notion is conceived in patrilineal terms. It is consistent with the present "ruling family" style of leadership, perhaps taken too literally in practice.

24. In Chapter 3, it was seen that the state did not concern itself with death rituals, but that urban wedding rites were quickly becoming secularized. For example, in 1972, Ceauşescu's father was buried according to the Orthodox rite in his village of origin. (The Bishop of Rîmnic and Argeş was assisted by thirteen

priests.) Villagers and Central Committee members attended. The commemorative meals acknowledged the different constituencies: one for city guests and another, a traditional one, for local mourners.

25. I do not mean to imply that the village performance is not nowadays viewed as a spectacle. In part, it is. But asserting that it is essentially dramatic is to oversimplify the influence of religious belief. The play is one manifestation of a complex of events that together constitute the commemoration of Christ. As we have seen, commemorative acts are respected.

26. The importance of Maramureş for national legitimacy is not a phenomenon unique to the socialist state; Maramureş has frequently played a similar role in the Transylvanian territorial problem. See, for example, Morariu 1944; I. Ştefănescu 1968; as well as Marrant 1977, 96–104.

27. The emphasis on Geto-Dacian origins that has pervaded scholarship in the last decade is also noted in a tourist brochure: "Maramureş is one of the most interesting counties in Romania. The origin of its name is probably Daco-Roman, although some researchers suggest a much older derivation. Anyhow, the history of Maramureş goes a long way back and holds a special place in the history of the Romanian people as a whole."

28. Although the Maramureş grai is abstractly praised for its historical significance to the identity of the Romanian people, it is regarded in practice as an indicator of backwardness: "the Moroşeni should learn to speak proper Romanian." At the same time, the fluency of a foreigner such as myself evokes different responses, as those who speak English or French, languages of civilization, cannot be backward (especially if they are professors). Hence, intellectuals are charmed, express admiration—and expect that "proper speech" will follow a demonstration of anthropological-linguistic acumen. (I had agreed to be interviewed during my first year of fieldwork in Maramureş. Having been put off by the unwarranted elitism of the journalist, I chose to respond to his questions in dialect. A British lecturer later told me that his students mentioned an interview they had heard; they were appalled that a foreign professor spoke like a peasant!) Others respond with confusion. Signs and their significations are jumbled: the style of clothing indicates a Western identity, but the language suggests someone altogether different. Usually, I am asked how long ago I left the homeland, or if I am a Hungarian.

29. To perceive oneself as a cultural artifact is to deny one's self. For the state, peasants who continue to identify themselves as such do not exist. What the state intends is akin to other "living museums" around the world. The distortion lies in the consideration of a region as a museum: museums close at specified hours and the actors in them return to their lives; Moroşeni, however, are social actors in the state of Romania. They are not museum pieces.

30. The battle between fantasy and manifest practice finds expression in many forms. The "return to the basics" ethos contributes to a mystification of the peasant that denies the harshness of subordination, a structural feature of peasant existence. The issue of "artifacts" and their meaning has become a central debate in museology and the sociology of art. What does it mean to divest other cultures of their ritual objects and transform them into art objects? What does this say about

the processes of development, imperialism, and so on? And why is it necessary to diminish the significance of ritual in modern life?

31. When the Jews were deported, their exodus was considered a loss for village identity. This is evident today when Ieudeni talk about the Jewish cemetery and occasional visits from survivors. This does not diminish the propensity for an archaic anti-Semitism. Jews were disliked for their dealings, the classic feature of the stereotype. At the same time, they were greatly respected for their knowledge and piety, both of which have always been highly valued by Ieudeni. The stereotype still thrives today, despite there being no more Jews in Ieud. Many blame the Jews for the contemporary constraints on resources (an old theme associated with Jews); it was the Jews who first brought communism to Romania. The following verses illustrate the varied character of anti-Semitism:

În grădină la vecinu	In my neighbor's courtyard,
Este un nuc	There is a walnut tree,
Şî în nuc, cînta un cuc	And in the walnut tree, there sings a cuckoo:
Ciubuc, ciubuc, ciubuc.	A bribe, a bribe, a bribe.

The Jews were referred to as *jidani*, a popular and also pejorative term—but it was part of their local identity. In 1944, the Jews became *ivrei*, the official racial term, and their relationship to the world about them changed radically.

Mai de mult ieram jidani	Before, we were *jidani*,
Şî-aveam cai şî aveam bani.	And we had horses and money.
Dar de cînd sîntem ivrei	But since we are *ivrei*,
Nici i casă, nici îs lei	There is no house nor money.
Afară cîntă o cuculie:	Outside, a little cuckoo sings:
Puşcărie, puşcărie.	Prison, prison.

Those prisons were concentration camps.

Castigation of the Jews for being "dealers" may be seen partially as a case of projecting oneself onto the other. Romanians, not only Jews, are infamous for their dealings. A *şmecher* (a cunning person, swindler) is envied, if with derogatory ambivalence, for an ability to get ahead, to avoid being had, in short, for being clever. Today, *şmecherie* is blamed for widespread corruption.

32. I do not mean to imply that democratic socialism reigns. It is difficult for young people from peripheral areas to pass the entrance exams for medicine, law, and other professions or to have the influence necessary to manage. There is structural inequality throughout the system. But, at the same time, young people can try. There is a degree of choice that was formerly unknown. And village women did not normally leave the village for extended periods unless they married out.

33. Not having been given access to local records, I am only able to generalize about the demographics of Ieud from discussions with local officials. The estimated yearly birth rate is 120–140. The mortality figure was presented as 1 to 2 in 1,000 (which seems lower than the number of funerals would indicate). Of some

1,800 families, 150 have moved from the village. But, as will be seen, because of family, ties with Ieud are not severed.

34. By the time I arrived in Ieud, I had heard countless stories about the winter's hardships. Those tales had personalized the gruesome reports in the Western press. Therefore, I was not quite prepared for the answer to my conditioned query. But, in the context of Ieud, the answer made perfect sense, especially since Ieudeni know that my research focused on ritual (a factor that should not be discounted in this exchange). They have wood-burning stoves. That the winter was a bit colder did not change things in any essential way. Blackouts were a greater source of frustration. Nothing parallels Ieudeni's disdain for the perceived destruction of their country's agricultural capacity. Into this equation is added a recognition of the impact of foreign debts and export. For these people, however, there is no tolerable justification for food shortages in an agrarian country.

35. Spatial understanding is locally determined. See Buga 1967. Also, recall the wedding verses about brides as strangers, and the funeral laments for those who have died at the front. See pp. 329–30 for the lament that weaves the meanings of alienation deriving from marriage and from unmarried girls' participation in the work force. The only type of alienation that is absolutely final is death. With regard to my own status, during my first years of acquaintance with Ieudeni, I was a "foreigner." At weddings, people often composed verses in my honor by manipulating that metaphor. My identity as foreigner is now more ambiguous, however; there are Foreigners and foreigners. My American identity has been tempered by my ascribed identity as a different type of seasonal laborer (see note 16).

36. The disintegration of familiar ordering structures, such as the family, has given rise to fundamentalist movements in the United States and elsewhere. The liberalism and "freedom" of the sixties and seventies has given way to the security and conservatism of Reagan's eighties.

37. Burial near Bucureşti would have been among strangers, which is seen as capitulation to major problems of the modern world: isolation and loneliness. Refer to Chapters 2 and 4 for discussion of the concept of "stranger" as well as to note 35, above. For this child to be taken to Ieud, arrangements had to be made for the transport of her coffin by train, which was managed hastily; formerly, it was illegal for a wagon carrying a dead person to travel from one region to another unless a disposition had been obtained.

38. Married women readily comment on the decreasing age for marriage. They are not enthusiastic and consistently state that there is time for "all of that" and they wish they had had more of their own youth. Also, it is village young women who choose to marry young. Those who pursue some form of training are less eager; they are also in the minority.

39. Hobsbawm's discussion of "invented traditions" is perhaps more helpful in understanding the changing nature of tradition(s) in local and national contexts (see Hobsbawm and Ranger 1983, 2). He distinguishes between "tradition," characterized by invariance, and "custom," associated with historical precedent yet permissive of change. As he notes, "'custom' cannot afford to be invariant, because even in 'traditional' societies life is not so" (ibid.). These distinctions may more readily encompass the contradictions inherent in contemporary practices

and capture the limits of "custom" as well as the processes of "invention" locally and nationally. While it might be interesting to illustrate these distinctions through an analysis, my immediate concern pertains to local practices as they occur within this spectrum of possibilities.

40. In the south of Romania, however, legally married couples may live together and raise children for many years before circumstances permit the celebration of their religious marriage, hence, wedding.

41. As mentioned in the second chapter, this practice was known in Ieud among the poor who needed the financial contribution. It is commonly practiced by the Gypsies in Ieud. Opinion finds this to be in keeping with Gypsies' interests in gain at the expense of others. The Romanians boast that marriage to them is a spiritual union not to be tainted by financial considerations. Their practices belie their stated convictions, however. It is interesting to me that Ieudeni have never mentioned financial benefit in association with the weddings of Jews. On the one hand, it never occurred to me to ask; on the other, Ieudeni say they were not present at these events. An urban Gypsy wedding in Bucureşti underscored the sanctity of marriage in Gypsy practice as well as the monetary significance of "gifting" the couple. This couple had been together for sixteen years and they were the parents of teenage children. Circumstances had not permitted them to finance a wedding any earlier. After the church ceremony, celebrants proceeded to the banquet. The "gifts" given both out of generosity and for calculated ritual and status display more than covered the wedding's cost.

42. I recommend Humphrey's chapter, "Ritual and Identity," in her book (1983) on the Siberian collective. There are, of course, comparable phenomena. She discusses the decline of the religious basis in Buryat ritual (375); it is also more pertinent there.

43. For those familiar with Hobsbawm's categories, my usage of *ritual* here is similar to his use of *custom* in traditional societies: "What it [custom] does is to give any desired change (or resistance to innovation) the sanction of precedent, social continuity and natural law as expressed in history" (1983, 2).

44. "Outsider" brings to mind Becker's classic study (1963), as well as those that it prompted about deviance and subcultures. Also, it should be reiterated that Moroşeni are themselves considered "outsiders" by the dominant culture; they are underdeveloped, "backward." This is strikingly apparent when one discusses Maramureş with urban intellectuals.

45. The issues raised here are intriguing but will have to receive attention in a future work. Also, it is necessary to point out that ritual context does not completely license free speech. While the formal features of ritual and poetry create "anonymity," individuals nonetheless live within the state, and the state's inhabitants are ever conscious of its presence. Local discourse exists in relation to dominant ones. Ultimately, the cultural hegemony of the state seems to modulate not only the content of but also the contexts for public discourse. The necessity for anonymity as well as an unwillingness to take responsibility underline a feature of Romanian political culture. Jowitt, in his discussion of system-building regimes, noted that "events do not occur, decisions are not made, and facts are not recognized as facts until they are allowed to occur or to be recognized" (1974, 1180).

46. There is a fundamental difference between the notion of the public sphere as it pertains to discussions about the relationship of the state and civil society, and the notion of the "public domain" of communication in this peasant milieu. Here, the matter of class and consciousness also seems critical.

47. A presentation and analysis of this provocative situation may perhaps find its way into a future article. At present, ethical concerns must modulate intellectual interests. For a certain period, this dispute caused serious cleavage in the community. This does not affect the basic argument of this book. There was no hindrance of ritual participation, although who was present where was affected. One noticeable consequence of this dispute was the selective greeting process that it fostered. While the traditional greetings based on the life of Christ were extended, they were done so selectively. As discussed in the first chapter, this type of greeting formerly functioned as a cultural form of anti-Semitism. At this point in time, who received greetings was determined by allegiances in this dispute.

48. Life-cycle rites are the foci of inflammatory actions because of the deacon's role in these rites. The local priest, however, determines the deacon's rights to fulfill his role. This has set the priest and one deacon in opposing camps. Because deacons have ritual relationships with families over the span of the life cycle, preventing one deacon's participation is considered an unwarranted intrusion into the personal lives of those families.

49. One villager insisted that an Old Church Slavonic text on the Orthodox church that I was reading was propaganda issued by the Communist Party in support of its interests.

50. The sexism of that phrase causes me to provide a corrective, which I will interject henceforth—"the new socialist person." The intrusiveness of the state into daily life raises questions about the conception of the "person." Through paternalistic excesses, this regime has maintained control over its children. Pronatalism distorts the boundaries of public and private, infantilizing the person. The politics of rape offers a comparable set of issues.

51. For a discussion on subcultures, see especially Hall and Jefferson 1976; Hebdige 1979. Their works inform my use of the concept.

52. While it is tempting to discuss bases of organization, the formation of a class consciousness, and so forth, these issues may perhaps best be examined in terms of the structural limitations that class generates. The accepted notion of a legacy of illegitimacy often leads to discussions about the historical passivity of the Romanians, their fatalistic Weltanschauung. Again, I do not find this an adequate explanation. There have been isolated acts of opposition, notably miners' strikes, but these have been extinguished by the repressive state apparatus.

53. Although women are managing households, not all practices from the past have ceased. Wife-beating is common; moreover, women accept it as their due—such is their understanding of gender roles through biblical teachings. Women's responsibility for the Fall is most readily noted.

54. Ceauşescu's method involves the institutionalization of cultural practices through the Cîntarea României.

55. It had not been my intention to study ritual per se; however, in view of the constraints upon fieldwork (and these are highly variable), I became deeply re-

spectful of the dynamics of symbolic communication. It is a commonplace of art and of media production and analysis; it is critical to the interpretation of *samizdat*, yet the social sciences have tended to trivialize its significance. This speaks sadly to the trivialization of the social in the social sciences and does not reflect well on the breadth of our intellectual (not to mention humanistic) vision.

Some may object that my attempt to people the political economy of Romania has been mediated through rituals which may represent these people but which are not "them." It is true that rituals offer idealized models of social relations and exchange, but life-cycle rites are significant events in and about these people's lives. Their voices, informed by the past yet heard in the present, speak for themselves. Gramsci suggested that "if it is true that every language contains the elements of a conception of the world and of a culture, it could also be true that from anyone's language one can assess the greater or lesser complexity of his conception of the world" (Hoare and Smith 1983, 325). I would add that that conception of the world is reconstituted over and over through time. In the interests of mutual respect and ethical concern, I offer these models as a meaningful mode of mediated presence.

56. The structural features of ritual as narrative have been discussed by many. Classics surely include Van Gennep 1960 and V. Turner 1969. See also T. Turner 1977. Discussions with Elizabeth Traube throughout our semester of co-teaching about anthropological approaches to narrative were highly rewarding. I wish to thank her, as well as the students in this course, for inspiration.

57. These broad generalizations are meant to suggest the parameters of the civilizing process that has brought mankind to the brink of self-destruction. Science has done much for life; it has also done much to dehumanize it. Taking up these complexities (and citing relevant bibliography such as Foucault) is beyond the possibilities of imminent closure. The burgeoning of humanistic concerns is a response to the gnawing questions of "meaning" that a culture of narcissism, for example, denies.

Glossary

The following are Romanian words that appear frequently throughout the text; brief definitions are provided. Words included in this glossary are written in their dialect form if they differ from the standard Romanian. Nouns are singular, unless otherwise noted (pl. = plural). When a word is feminized by the addition of an *ă*, it will be indicated with brackets after the masculine root. Not all dialect words used in the text or the poetry are included. The following, for example, are omitted: *cocon* (*cocoană*) is used instead of the customary *copil*(*ă*), meaning child; or *cetera* instead of *vioră*, or violin. Papahagi (1925, 213–37) provides a more comprehensive Maramureş-Romanian glossary.

Belciug	Abundance; refers to the ritual sequence during a wedding when the bride and groom take leave from their respective families; same as the *iertăciunea*
Căsătorie	Marriage
A se căsători	To marry or wed; same as *a se cununa, a se însura, a se mărita*
Ceia lume	That world; the world of the dead
Cererea mniresii	Asking for the Bride; wedding ritual sequence
Chiabur	Wealthy, landed peasant (formerly)
Cimitir	Cemetery; same as *ţintirim, temeteu*
A cînta	To play an instrument (elsewhere, this means to sing)
A se cînta	To lament
Colac	Ritual bread

Colindă	Christmas carol
Credinţă	Engagement party; same as *tomală;* also means belief
Cumnat[ă]	Brother-in-law; sister-in-law
A se cununa	To marry; same as *a se căsători, a se însura, a se mărita;* in the Orthodox wedding ceremony, to crown the bride and groom
Cunună	Wreath; wedding crown
Cuscru (cuscră)	Father (mother) of a son-in-law or daughter-in-law
A descînta	To charm; to cast a magic spell
Descîntec	Magic charm
Dezbrăcarea mniresii	Undressing of the Bride; refers to the ritual removal of the bride's crown and the placement of the married woman's scarf at the conclusion of the wedding rite
Doamne	My God; Oh, Lord
Druşcă	Bridesmaid
Dumnezău	God
Fată	Girl; unmarried young woman
Găină	Hen
Gătata mniresii	Readying the Bride; wedding ritual sequence prior to the church ceremony; same as *îmbrăcarea mniresii*
Gazdă	Master of a household; someone who is well-off; person of good lineage
Ginere	Son-in-law
Gioc	Dance
Gospodărie	Household
Groapă	Grave; same as *mormînt*
Hore	Song
Horea găinii	Song of the Hen; wedding ritual sequence that addresses the bride's virginity

A hori	To sing
Horincă	Plum brandy; same as *ţuică*, but double-distilled, or *palincă*
Iad	Hell
Iertăciunea	Leave-taking; see *belciug*
Îmbrăcarea mniresii	Dressing of the Bride; wedding ritual sequence; same as *gătata mniresii*
Înmormîntare	Funeral; same as *petrecanie*
A se însura	To marry; same as *a se căsători, a se cununa*
Jocul cununii	Dance of the Bride's Crown; wedding ritual sequence
Jocul steagului	Dance of the Groom's Flag; wedding ritual sequence
Lumină trupului	Candle for the body
A se mărita	To marry; used only in conjunction with a woman, unless the groom has married into the bride's family as *ginere*
Mîndră	Beauty (n.); sweetheart (n.); beautiful (adj.)
Mnire	Groom
Mnireasă	Bride
Moarte	Death
Moaşă	Aunt; also, midwife
Mormînt	Grave; same as *groapă*
Nănaş[ă]	Godfather; godmother; short form, *naş[ă]*, used interchangeably
Năşie	Godparenthood
Neam	Lineage; extended family including living and dead members
Nemneş	Titled petit nobility of Maramureş
Nepoată	Niece; granddaughter; midwife's goddaughters
Noră	Daughter-in-law
Nuntă	Wedding

Nunta mortului	Death-wedding
Nuntă ţăranească	Peasant wedding
Ospăţ	Meal for the in-laws one week after a wedding
Păcat	Sin
Palincă	Plum brandy; same as *horincă*
Petrecanie	Funeral; same as *mormîntare*
A peţi	To ask for a young woman's hand in marriage
Plînsul mniresii	Ritual crying of the bride
Pomană	Alms; commemoration
Pominoc	Gifts; ritual exchange between groom's and bride's families during the wedding
Prohod	Funeral cortège
Rai	Heaven
Rămas bun	Leave-taking; ritual sequence prior to departure in the wedding and funeral rites
Sălaş	Coffin; same as *sicriu*
Sărbătoarea nepoatelor	Ritual honoring of the midwife; celebration of the goddaughters
Sat	Village
Sicriu	Coffin; same as *sălaş*
Sin[ă]	Godson; goddaughter
Soacră	Mother-in-law
Socăciţă	Cook; woman who organizes the preparation and distribution of food and drink at weddings and funerals
Socru	Father-in-law
Stegar	Groom's flagbearer
Stînă	Sheepfold
Străin	Foreigner, stranger (n.); foreign (adj.)
Strigătură (pl. -i)	Shouted rhymed couplet

Strigoi	Spirit; ghost; living dead
Struț	Small bouquet of flowers adorning a bachelor's hat; symbol of courtship
Şezătoare	Sewing bee (and/or spinning, knitting, weaving, embroidering)
Temeteu	Cemetery; same as *cimitir, țintirim*
Tomală	Engagement party; same as *credință*
Țăran	Peasant
Țintirim	Cemetery; same as *cimitir, temeteu*
Țuică	Plum brandy; see also *horincă, palincă*
Zestre	Dowry

References

Alexiou, M. 1974. *The Ritual Lament in Greek Tradition*. Cambridge: Cambridge University Press.

Alterescu, S., ed. 1965. *Istoria teatrului în România*. Bucureşti: Editura Academiei Republicii Socialiste România.

Arato, A. 1981. "Civil Society vs. the State." *Telos* 47:23–47.

Ardener, B. 1975. "Belief and the Problem of Women." In *Perceiving Women*, edited by S. Ardener, 1–18. London: Malaby.

Ariès, P. 1974. *Western Attitudes Toward Death from the Middle Ages to the Present*. Baltimore: Johns Hopkins University Press.

———. 1982. *The Hour of Our Death*. New York: Knopf.

Babcock, B. 1978. *The Reversible World: Symbolic Inversion in Art and Society*. Ithaca, N.Y.: Cornell University Press.

Bălcescu, N. 1953. *Opere*. Vol. 1. Bucureşti: Editura Academiei Republicii Socialiste România.

Barth, F. 1979. *A Transylvanian Legacy*. Salt Lake City, Utah: Transylvania.

Bartók, B. [1923] 1975. *Rumanian Folk Music: Maramureş County*. Vol. 5. The Hague: Martinus Nijhoff.

Beane, W., and W. Doty. 1976. *Myths, Rites and Symbols—A Mircea Eliade Reader*. Vol. 1. New York: Harper-Colophon.

Beck, S. 1976. "The Emergence of the Peasant-Worker in a Transylvanian Mountain Community." *Dialectical Anthropology* 1:365–75.

———. 1979. "Transylvania: The Political Economy of a Frontier." Dissertation, Department of Anthropology, University of Massachusetts-Amherst.

Becker, H. 1963. *Outsiders: Studies in the Sociology of Deviance*. Glencoe, Ill.: Free Press.

Bell, P. 1984. *Peasants in Socialist Transition: Life in a Collectivized Hungarian Village*. Berkeley and Los Angeles: University of California Press.

Bellah, R., et al. 1985. *Habits of the Heart: Individualism and Commitment in American Life*. Berkeley and Los Angeles: University of California Press.

Bellow, S. 1982. *The Dean's December*. New York: Harper and Row.

Belmont, N. 1982. "The Symbolic Function of the Wedding Procession in the

Popular Rituals of Marriage." In *Ritual, Religion and the Sacred,* edited by R. Forster and O. Ranum, 1–8. Baltimore: Johns Hopkins University Press.

Benedict, R. 1972. *Rumanian Culture and Behavior.* Occasional Papers in Anthropology, no. 1. Fort Collins, Colo.: Anthropology Club and Anthropology Faculty of Colorado State University.

Benjamin, W. 1969. "The Storyteller." In *Illuminations.* Translated by H. Zohn, 83–111. New York: Schocken Books.

Benveniste, E. 1973. *Indo-European Language and Society.* Vol. 1. Translated by E. Palmer. London: Faber and Faber.

Berger, S. 1972. *Peasants Against Politics.* Cambridge: Harvard University Press.

Bernabé, J. 1980. *Le symbolisme de la mort: croyances et rites roumains.* Ghent: Cognition and Communication.

Binns, C. 1979–80. "The Changing Face of Power: Revolution and Accommodation in the Development of the Soviet Ceremonial System." Parts 1, 2. *Man* 14(4): 585–606; 15(1): 170–87.

Bîrlea, I. 1909. *Însemnări din bisericile Maramureşului.* Bucureşti: Socec.

———. 1924. *Balade, colinde şi bocete din Maramureş.* Bucureşti: Editura Casei Şcoalelor.

———. 1968. *Literatură populară din Maramureş.* Vols. 1 and 2. Bucureşti: Editura Pentru Literatură.

Bîrlea, O. 1969. "Colindatul în Transilvania." *Anuarul muzeului etnografic al Transilvaniei pe anii 1965–67,* 247–304.

———. 1976. *Mică enciclopedie a poveştilor româneşti.* Bucureşti: Editura Ştiinţifică şi Enciclopedică.

———. 1979. *Poetică folclorică.* Bucureşti: Editura Univers.

Black, M. 1962. *Models of Metaphor.* Ithaca, N.Y.: Cornell University Press.

Blaga, L. 1969. *Trilogia culturii.* Bucureşti: Editura Pentru Literatură Universală.

Blauner, R. 1966. "Death and Social Structure." *Psychiatry* 29:378–94.

Bloch, M. 1974. "Symbols, Song, Dance and Features of Articulation." *Archives européennes de sociologie* 15:55–81.

———. 1975. *Political Language and Oratory in Traditional Society.* New York: Academic Press.

Bloch, M., and J. Parry, eds. 1982. *Death and the Regeneration of Life.* Cambridge: Cambridge University Press.

Bogatyrev, P. 1971. *The Functions of Folk Costume in Moravian Slovakia.* The Hague: Mouton.

Bonnell, V. 1983. *Roots of Rebellion: Workers' Politics and Organization in St. Petersburg and Moscow, 1900–1914.* Berkeley and Los Angeles: University of California Press.

Bot, N. 1969. "Şezătoarea în zona Năsăudului." *Anuarul muzeului etnografic al Transilvaniei pe anii 1965–67,* 305–46.

Bourdieu, P. 1977. *Outline of a Theory of Practice.* Translated by R. Nice. Cambridge: Cambridge University Press.

Brăiloiu, C. 1938. *Bocete din Oaş.* Bucureşti: Socec.

———. 1944. *Poeziile soldatului Tomuţ din războiul 1914–1918.* Bucureşti: Arhiva de Folclor.

————. 1967. *Opere de Constantin Brăiloiu*. Vols. 1–5. Translated by E. Comi-şel. Bucureşti: Editura Muzicală a Uniunii Compozitorilor din Republica So-cialistă România.

————. [1946] 1973. "Sur une ballade roumaine." In *Problèmes d'éthnomusi-cologie*, 43–53. Geneva: Minkoff.

Brătulescu, M. 1963. "Metafore în folclorul din Maramureş." *Revista de folclor* 8(3–4): 94–116.

————. 1981. *Colinda Românească*. Bucureşti: Editura Minerva.

Braudel, F. 1979. *Les jeux de l'échange*. Paris: Armand Colin.

Brediceanu, T. 1957. *170 melodii populare romîneşti din Maramureş*. Bucureşti: Editura de Stat Pentru Literatură şi Artă.

Brown, A., ed. 1984. *Political Culture and Communist Studies*. Armonk, N.Y.: M. E. Sharpe.

Browning, R. 1931. "The Pied Piper of Hamelin." In *Famous Editions of English Poets*, edited by J. Beaty and J. Bowyer. New York: Richard R. Smith.

Bud, T. 1908. *Poezii populare din Maramureş*. Bucureşti: Academia Română.

Buga, M. 1967. "Originea şi evoluţia poetică a unor motive din lirica populară a înstrăinării." *Folclor literar*, 75–110.

Burada, T. 1882. *Datinele poporului român la înmormântări*. Iaşi: Tipografia Naţională.

Burawoy, M. 1987. "Painting Socialism: Ideology and Reality in the Lenin Steel Works." Paper presented to the Society for Social Research, University of Chi-cago, April 11, 1987.

Burguière, A. 1982. "The Marriage Ritual in France: Ecclesiastical Practices and Popular Practices (Sixteenth to Eighteenth Centuries)." In *Ritual, Religion and the Sacred*, edited by R. Forster and O. Ranum, 8–23. Baltimore: Johns Hopkins University Press.

Burke, K. 1966. *Language as Symbolic Action*. Chicago: University of Chicago Press.

Burks, A. 1949. "Icon, Index and Symbol." *Philosophy and Phenomenological Re-search* 9(4): 673–89.

Byrnes, R., ed. 1976. *Communal Families in the Balkans: The Zadruga*. Notre Dame, Ind.: University of Notre Dame Press.

Campbell, J. 1964. *Honor, Family and Patronage*. Oxford: Clarendon Press.

Caravelli, A. 1980. "Bridge Between Worlds: The Women's Ritual Lament as Com-municative Event." *Journal of American Folklore* 93:129–57.

Cartojan, N. 1974. *Cărţile populare în literatura românească*. Vol. 2: *Epoca influ-enţei greceşti*. Bucureşti: Editura Enciclopedică Română.

Cazacu, M. 1987. *L'histoire du prince Dracula en Europe centrale et orientale (XVe siècle). Edition critique, traduction et commentaires*. Geneva: Droz.

Ceauşescu, N. 1976. "Exposé on the Political-Ideological and Cultural-Educational Activity of Moulding the New Man, a Conscious and Dedicated Builder of the Multilaterally Developed Socialist Society and of Communism in Romania." Presented at the Congress of Political Education and Socialist Culture, Bu-cureşti, June 2.

Cernea, M. 1969. "Schîmbări ale structurii familiei țărănești în cooperativele agricole." *Revista de filozofia* 16(8):1009–22.

———. 1974a. "The Large Scale Formal Organization and the Family Primary Group." *Revue roumaine des sciences sociales: sociologie* 18:85–98.

———. 1974b. *Sociologia cooperativei agricole de producție: curs de sociologie rurală. Partea 1-a.* București: Institutul Agronomic N. Bălcescu.

———. 1976. "Cooperative Farming and Family Change in Romania." In *The Social Structure of Eastern Europe*, edited by B. Faber, 259–79. New York: Praeger.

———. 1978. "Macrosocial Change: The Feminization of Agriculture and Peasant Women's Threefold Economic Role." *Sociologia Ruralis* 18(2–3):107–24.

Child, F. 1962. *The English and Scottish Popular Ballads.* Vol. 5. New York: Cooper Square.

Chirot, D. 1976a. *Social Change in a Peripheral Society.* New York: Academic Press.

———. 1976b. "The Romanian Communal Village: An Alternative to the Zadruga." In *Communal Families in the Balkans: The Zadruga*, edited by R. Byrnes, 139–61. Notre Dame, Ind.: University of Notre Dame Press.

———. 1978. "Social Change in Communist Romania." *Social Forces* 57(2): 457–88.

Cîntarea României: Festival național al educației și culturii socialiste ediția 3-a 1979–1981. București: Consiliul Culturii și Educației Socialiste.

Clark, K. 1981. *The Soviet Novel: History as Ritual.* Chicago: University of Chicago Press.

Clifford, J., and G. Marcus, eds. 1986. *Writing Culture: The Poetics and Politics of Ethnography.* Berkeley and Los Angeles: University of California Press.

Cohen, A. 1981. *The Politics of Elite Culture: Explorations in the Dramaturgy of Power in a Modern African Society.* Berkeley and Los Angeles: University of California Press.

Cohn, B. 1980. "History and Anthropology: The State of Play." *Comparative Studies in Society and History* 22(2):198–221.

Cole, J. 1976. "Fieldwork in Romania." *Dialectical Anthropology* 1:239–49.

———. 1981. "Family, Farm and Factory: Rural Workers in Contemporary Romania." In *Romania in the 1980s*, edited by D. Nelson, 71–116. Boulder, Colo.: Westview Press.

Comaroff, J. 1975. "Talking Politics: Oratory and Authority in a Tswana Chiefdom." In *Political Language and Oratory in Traditional Society*, edited by M. Bloch, 141–62. New York: Academic Press.

———. 1980. "Introduction." In *The Meaning of Marriage Payments*, edited by J. Comaroff. New York: Academic Press.

———. 1982. "From Totemism to Ethnicity: Consciousness, Ideology and the Dialectics of Articulation." Department of Anthropology, University of Chicago, photocopy.

Costa-Foru-Andreescu, X. 1945. *Cercetarea monografică a familiei: contribuție metodologică.* București: Institutul Social Român, Institutul de Cercetări Sociale al României, şi Biblioteca de Sociologie Etică şi Politică, Seria 2, Studii şi Cercetări.

Coteanu, I., and L. Wald, eds. 1981. *Semantică şi semiotică.* Bucureşti: Editura Ştiinţifică şi Enciclopedică.

Craft, C. 1984. "Kiss Me with Those Red Lips: Gender and Inversion in Bram Stoker's *Dracula.*" *Representations* 8:107–33.

Dăncuş, M. 1973. "Contribuţii la cunoaşterea unui obicei de anul nou în Maramureş." *Anuarul muzeului etnografic al Transilvaniei pe anii 1971–73,* 489–97.

Dăncuş, M., and N. Katz. 1973. "Datini maramureşene consemnate într-o lucrare tipărită în secolol al 19-lea." In *Comunicări ştiinţifice pe teme folclorice.* Baia Mare: Comitetul Pentru Cultură şi Educaţie Socialistă al Judeţului Maramureş.

Danforth, L. 1982. *The Death Rituals of Rural Greece.* Princeton, N.J.: Princeton University Press.

Davis, N. 1975. *Society and Culture in Early Modern France.* Stanford, Calif.: Stanford University Press.

de Heusch, L. 1981. *Why Marry Her? Society and Symbolic Structures.* Cambridge: Cambridge University Press.

de Man, P. 1978. "The Epistemology of Metaphor." *Critical Inquiry* 5:13–30.

de Martino, E. [1958] 1975. *Morte e pianto rituale.* Turin: Paul Boringhieri.

Denitch, B. 1974. "Sex and Power in the Balkans." In *Women, Culture and Society,* edited by M. Rosaldo and L. Lamphere, 243–62. Stanford, Calif.: Stanford University Press.

Densuşianu, O. 1966. *Vieaţa păstorească în poezie noastră populară.* Bucureşti: Editura Pentru Literatură.

Dermer, I. 1934. *Maramureşul românesc.* Bucureşti: Cartea Românească.

Dolgin, J., D. Kemnitzer, and D. Schneider, eds. 1977. *Symbolic Anthropology: A Reader in the Study of Symbols and Meanings.* New York: Columbia University Press.

Doniga, V. 1980. *Folclor din Maramureş.* Bucureşti: Editura Minerva.

Douglas, M. 1966. *Purity and Danger.* London: Routledge and Kegan Paul.

Drăgan, I. 1973. "Aspects sociaux de l'industrialisation des zones rurales en Roumanie." *Revue roumaine des sciences sociales* 17:77–100.

du Boulay, J. 1982. "The Greek Vampire: A Study of Cyclic Symbolism in Marriage and Death." *Man* 17(2):219–38.

Dumézil, G. 1979. *Mariages Indo-Européens.* Paris: Payot.

Durkheim, E. [1910] 1965. *The Elementary Forms of the Religious Life.* New York: Free Press.

Durkheim, E., and M. Mauss. [1903] 1963. *Systems of Primitive Classification.* Translated by R. Needham. Chicago: University of Chicago Press.

Edroiu, N., A. Răduţiu, and P. Teodor. 1982. *Stat, societate, naţiune: interpretări istorice.* Cluj-Napocă: Editura Dacia.

Eliade, M. 1972. *Zalmoxis, the Vanishing God: Comparative Studies in the Religions and Folklore of Dacia and Eastern Europe.* Translated by W. Trask. Chicago: University of Chicago Press.

————. 1980. "History of Religions and 'Popular' Cultures." *History of Religions* 20(1–2):1–26.

————. 1982. *A History of Religious Ideas*. Vol. 2: *From Gautama Buddha to the Triumph of Christianity*. Translated by W. Trask. Chicago: University of Chicago Press.

Elias, N. 1978. *The Civilizing Process*. Vol. 1: *The History of Manners*. Translated by E. Jephcott. New York: Pantheon.

Erlich, V. 1966. *Family in Transition*. Princeton, N.J.: Princeton University Press.

Fabian, J. 1983. *Time and the Other: How Anthropology Makes Its Object*. New York: Columbia University Press.

Fajans, J. 1985. "They Make Themselves: Life Cycle, Domestic Cycle and Ritual Among the Baining." Dissertation, Department of Anthropology, Stanford University.

Favret-Saada, J. 1980. *Deadly Words: Witchcraft in the Bocage*. Translated by C. Cullen. Cambridge: Cambridge University Press.

Fedorova, M. 1982. "The Utilization of Female Labor in Agriculture." In *Women, Work and Family in the Soviet Union*, edited by G. Lapidus. Armonk, N.Y.: M. E. Sharpe.

Feeley-Harnik, G. 1981. *The Lord's Table: Eucharist and Passover in Early Christianity*. Philadelphia: University of Pennsylvania Press.

Feher, F., et al. 1983. *Dictatorship over Needs*. New York: St. Martin's.

Feifel, H., ed. 1959. *The Meaning of Death*. New York: McGraw-Hill.

Feld, S. 1987. "Dialogic Editing: Interpreting How Kaluli Read *Sound and Sentiment*." *Cultural Anthropology* 2(2):190–210.

Ferge, Z. 1979. *A Society in the Making: Hungarian Social and Societal Planning 1945–1975*. Armonk, N.Y.: M. E. Sharpe.

Fernandez, J. 1974. "The Mission of Metaphor in Expressive Culture." *Current Anthropology* 15(2):119–45.

Feuerbach, L. 1980. *Thoughts on Death and Immortality*. Translated by J. Massey. Berkeley and Los Angeles: University of California Press.

Filipaşcu, A. 1940. *Istoria Maramureşului*. Bucureşti: Univers.

Filitti, I. 1924. "Evoluţia claselor sociale în trecutul principatelor române." *Arhiva pentru ştiinţa şi reforma socială* 5(1–2):71–113.

Finnegan, R. 1979. *Oral Poetry*. Cambridge: Cambridge University Press.

Firescu, A. 1975. "Folclorul contemporan—obiect de cercetare sociologică." *Cîntecul popular românesc* 3:107–20.

Flandrin, J. L. 1976. *Familles: parenté, maison, sexualité dans l'ancienne société*. Paris: Hachette.

Florescu, R., and R. McNally. 1972. *In Search of Dracula*. Greenwich, Conn.: New York Graphic Society.

————. 1973. *Dracula—A Biography of Vlad the Impaler 1431–1476*. New York: Hawthorne.

Fochi, A. 1964. *Mioriţa*. Bucureşti: Editura Academiei Republicii Populare Romîne.

Fotino, S. 1977. "Între strigătură şi cîntec liric." *Revista de etnografie şi folclor* 22(1):63–75.

Fotino, S., and I. Nicolau. 1978. "Dinamica relaţiei individ-grup, repere pentru o teorie generală a ceremonialului." *Revista de etnografie şi folclor* 23(1):91–98.

Foucault, M. 1972. *The Archeology of Knowledge and the Discourse on Language*. New York: Pantheon Books.

———. 1975. *The Birth of the Clinic: An Archaeology of Medical Perception*. New York: Vintage.

———. 1978. *The History of Sexuality*. Vol. 1: *An Introduction*. New York: Random House.

Fox, J. 1977. "Roman Jakobson and the Comparative Study of Parallelism." In *Roman Jakobson: Echoes of His Scholarship*, edited by J. D. Armstrong and C. H. van Schoonweld, 59–90. Lisse, Netherlands: Peter de Ridder.

Frazer, J. 1936. *The Fear of the Dead in Primitive Religion*. London: Macmillan.

Freedman, D. 1984. "Dance as Communicative Code in Romanian Courtship and Marriage Rituals." Dissertation, Department of Anthropology, Temple University.

Freud, S. 1953. "On Mourning and Melancholia." In *Collected Papers*. Vol. 4: *Papers on Metapsychology, Papers on Applied Psycho-Analysis*, edited by E. Jones, 152–72. London: Hogarth Press.

Friedl, E. 1959. "The Role of Kinship in the Transmission of National Culture to Rural Villages in Mainland Greece." *American Anthropologist* 61:30–38.

———. 1962. *Vasilika: A Village in Modern Greece*. New York: Holt, Rinehart and Winston.

———. 1963. "Some Aspects of Dowry and Inheritance in Boetia." In *Mediterranean Countrymen: Essays in the Social Anthropology of the Mediterranean*, edited by J. Pitt-Rivers, 113–35. Paris: Mouton.

———. 1967. "The Position of Women: Appearance and Reality." *Anthropological Quarterly* 40(3):97–108.

Friedrich, P. 1979a. "Poetic Language and the Imagination: A Reformulation of the Sapir Hypothesis." Chapter 13 in *Language, Context and the Imagination*. Stanford, Calif.: Stanford University Press.

———. 1979b. "Semantic Structure and Social Structure." Chapter 3 in *Language, Context and the Imagination*. Stanford, Calif.: Stanford University Press.

Gay, C. 1887. *De la vie et des vertus chrétiennes considerées dans l'état religieux*. Vol. 2, x: *De la chasteté*. Paris: Oudin.

Geertz, C. 1973. "Ritual and Social Change: A Javanese Example." Chapter 6 in *The Interpretation of Cultures*. New York: Harper-Colophon.

———. 1983. "Centers, Kings and Charisma: Reflections on the Symbolics of Power." Reprinted in *Local Knowledge: Further Essays in Interpretive Anthropology*, Chapter 6. New York: Basic Books.

Gellner, E., and J. Waterbury. 1977. *Patrons and Clients in Mediterranean Societies*. London: Duckworth.

Georgescu, V. 1985. *Romania: 40 Years (1944–84)*. New York: Praeger.

Georgieva, I. 1983. *Bulgarska narodna mitologija*. Sofia: Nauka i Izkustvo.

Gerould, G. 1908. *The Grateful Dead*. London: David Nutt.

Ginzburg, C. 1985. *Nightbattles: Witchcraft and Agrarian Cults in the 16th and*

17th Centuries. Translated by J. Tedeschi and A. Tedeschi. New York: Penguin.

Giurchescu, A. 1984. "Romanian Folklore and State Cultural Management." Paper presented at the Joint Committee on Eastern Europe of the American Council of Learned Societies conference, Folklore and the State: Contemporary Eastern Europe, in Bellagio, Italy.

Giurescu, C. 1969. *Transylvania in the History of Romania.* London: Garstone.

Glassie, H. 1975. *All Silver and No Brass: An Irish Christmas Mumming.* Bloomington: Indiana University Press.

———. 1982. *Passing the Time in Ballymenone: Culture and History of an Ulster Community.* Philadelphia: University of Pennsylvania Press.

Golopenţia-Eretescu, S. 1972. "Clasificarea prin numuri." *Revista de etnografie şi folclor* 17(2): 145–56; 17(3): 193–212.

Goody, J. 1962. *Death, Property and the Ancestors.* Stanford, Calif.: Stanford University Press.

Gorer, G. 1965. *Death, Grief and Mourning.* Garden City, N.Y.: Doubleday.

Gorovei, A. 1931. *Descântecele românilor.* Bucureşti: Imprimeria Naţională.

Graham, L. 1982. *Romania: A Developing Socialist State.* Boulder, Colo.: Westview Press.

Graur, T. 1976. "Predici rituale în structura şi funcţia ceremonialului de nuntă tradiţională." *Anuarul muzeului etnografic al Transilvaniei,* 283–94.

Grossman, J. 1980. "Feminine Images in Old Russian Literature and Art." *California Slavic Studies* 2: 33–70.

Habenstein, R. 1968. "The Social Organization of Death." *International Encyclopedia of Social Sciences* 4: 26–28.

Hall, S., and T. Jefferson. 1976. *Resistance Through Rituals: Youth Subcultures in Post-War Britain.* London: Hutchinson.

Halpern, J. 1956. *A Serbian Village.* New York: Harper-Colophon.

Hammel, E. 1968. *Alternative Social Structures and Ritual Relations in the Balkans.* Englewood Cliffs: Prentice-Hall.

Haraszti, M. 1978. *A Worker in a Worker's State.* New York: Universe.

Harrell, B. 1981. "Lactation and Menstruation in Cultural Perspective." *American Anthropologist* 83(4): 797–823.

Hebdige, D. 1979. *Subculture: The Meaning of Style.* London: Methuen.

Heiliger, W. 1980. *Soviet and Chinese Personalities.* Lanham, Md.: University Press of America.

Hertz, R. 1960. *Death and the Right Hand.* Translated by R. and C. Needham. New York: Free Press.

Herzfeld, M. 1980. "Honour and Shame: Problems in the Comparative Analysis of Moral Systems." *Man* 15: 339–51.

———. 1981. "Performative Categories and Symbols of Passage in Rural Greece." *Journal of American Folklore* 94(371): 44–57.

———. 1982. "Disemia." In *Semiotics 1980,* edited by M. Herzfeld and M. Lenhart, 205–13. New York: Plenum.

Hildebrand, D. von. 1970. *In Defense of Purity: An Analysis of the Catholic Ideal of Purity and Virginity.* Chicago: Franciscan Herald Press.

Hitchins, K. 1969. *The Rumanian National Movement in Transylvania, 1780–1849*. Cambridge: Harvard University Press.

———. 1983. *Studies on Romanian National Consciousness*. Pelham, N.Y.: Nagaard.

———. 1985. *The Idea of Nation: The Romanians of Transylvania 1691–1849*. Bucureşti: Editura Ştiinţifică şi Enciclopedică.

Hoare, Q., and G. Smith, eds. and trans. [1971] 1983. *Selections from the Prison Notebooks of Antonio Gramsci*. New York: International.

Hobsbawm, E. 1972. "The Social Function of the Past: Some Questions." *Past and Present* 55:3–17.

———. 1973. "Peasants and Politics." *Journal of Peasant Studies* 1(1):3–22.

———. 1983. "Introduction." In *The Invention of Tradition*, edited by E. Hobsbawm and T. Ranger. Cambridge: Cambridge University Press.

Hobsbawm, E., and T. Ranger, eds. 1983. *The Invention of Tradition*. Cambridge: Cambridge University Press.

Hoffman, S., and P. Kitromildes, eds. 1981. *Culture and Society in Contemporary Europe*. London: George Allen and Unwin.

Hubert, H., and M. Mauss. 1964. *Sacrifice: Its Nature and Function*. Translated by W. D. Halls. Chicago: University of Chicago Press.

Humphrey, C. 1983. *Karl Marx Collective: Economy, Society and Religion in a Siberian Collective Farm*. Cambridge and New York: Cambridge University Press.

Humphreys, S., and H. King, eds. 1981. *Mortality and Immortality*. New York: Academic Press.

Huntington, R., and P. Metcalf. 1979. *Celebration of Death: The Anthropology of Mortuary Ritual*. Cambridge: Cambridge University Press.

Ionescu, G. 1905. *Istoria bisericii românilor din Dacia Traiană 44–678 a.d.* Vol. 1. Bucureşti: Editură Universală.

Iorga, N. 1908. *Istoria bisericii româneşti şi a vieţii religioase a românilor*. Vălenii de Munte: Neamul Românesc.

Ivanova, R., and T. Živkov, eds. 1981. *Bŭlgarska narodna poezia i proza: obredni pesni*. Sofia: Bŭlgarska Pisatel.

Jakobson, R. 1960. "Linguistics and Poetics." In *Style in Language*, edited by T. Sebeok, 350–77. Cambridge: MIT Press.

———. 1966. "Grammatical Parallelism and Its Russian Facet." *Language* 42(2):398–429.

———. 1968. "Poetry of Grammar and Grammar of Poetry." *Lingua* 21:597–609.

———. 1971. *Selected Writings*. Vol. 2: *Word and Language*. The Hague: Mouton.

———. 1980. "On Poetic Intentions and Linguistic Devices in Poetry." *Poetics Today* 2(1A):87–96.

Jameson, F. 1979. "Reification and Utopia in Mass Culture." *Social Text* 1:130–48.

Janos, A. 1982. *The Politics of Backwardness in Hungary 1825–1945*. Princeton, N.J.: Princeton University Press.

Johnson, E. 1985. "Grieving for the Dead, Grieving for the Living: Funeral Laments of Hakka Women." Paper presented at conference of the Joint Committee on Chinese Studies and American Council of Learned Societies, Ritual and the Social Significance of Death in Chinese Society, January 2–7.

Johnson, M. 1981. *Philosophical Perspectives on Metaphor.* Minneapolis: University of Minnesota Press.

Jordanova, L. 1980. "Natural Facts: A Historical Perspective on Science and Sexuality." In *Nature, Culture and Gender,* edited by C. MacCormack and M. Strathern, 42–69. Cambridge: Cambridge University Press.

Jowitt, K. 1971. *Revolutionary Breakthroughs and National Development: The Case of Romania 1944–65.* Berkeley and Los Angeles: University of California Press.

———. 1974. "An Organizational Approach to the Study of Political Culture in Marxist-Leninist Systems." *American Political Science Review* 68(3):1171–91.

———. 1978. *The Leninist Response to National Dependency.* Berkeley: Institute of International Studies.

———. 1985. "A Political Anthropology of Leninist Regimes." Department of Political Science, University of California-Berkeley, photocopy.

Karnoouh, C. 1980. "Case şi grădini: eseu asupra semnificaţiei termenului 'statut' în graiul maramureşean." *Revista de etnografie şi folclor* 25(1):77–86.

———. 1982. "National Unity in Central Europe: The State, Peasant Folklore and Mono-Ethnism." *Telos* 53:95–105.

———. 1983a. *Le rite et le discours: introduction à la lecture de la versification populaire.* Ghent: Communication and Cognition.

———. 1983b. "An Allegorical Genesis of the Political: Folklore." Paper presented at the conference of the Joint Committee on Eastern Europe and the American Council of Learned Societies, Folklore and the State: Contemporary Eastern Europe, in Bellagio, Italy.

———. 1984. "Culture and Development." *Telos* 61:71–82.

———. 1986. "Aider à naître ou faire des ancêtres: un commentaire du roumain *Moasà.*" *Ethnologies d'Europe et d'ailleurs* 35(1–2):73–84.

Károly, K. 1969. "Vechi forme de muncă agricolă în cîteva sate din jurul Clujului." *Anuarul muzeului etnografic al Transilvaniei pe anii 1965–67,* 227–45.

Kaufman, D. 1981. "Oplakvanija na pokoinitsi v Bŭlgarija." In *Obredi i obreden folklor,* 257–282. Sofia: Bŭlgarska Akademija Na Naukite.

Kenedi, J. 1982. *Do It Yourself: Hungary's Hidden Economy.* London: Pluto.

Kideckel, D. 1979. "Agricultural Cooperativism and Social Process in a Romanian Commune." Dissertation, Department of Anthropology, University of Massachusetts, Amherst.

———. 1981. "Socialism, Prestige and Alcohol Use in Rural Romania." Paper presented at Northeastern Anthropological Association meeting, March.

Kideckel, D., and S. Sampson. 1984. "Fieldwork in Romania: Political, Practical, and Ethical Aspects." In *Economy, Society, and Culture in Contemporary Romania,* edited by J. Cole, 85–102. Department of Anthropology, University of Massachusetts, Amherst.

Király, B. 1969. *Hungary in the Late Eighteenth Century.* New York: Columbia University Press.

Kligman, G. 1981. *Căluş: Symbolic Transformation in Romanian Ritual.* Chicago: University of Chicago Press.

―――. 1983. "Poetry and Politics in a Transylvanian Village." *Anthropological Quarterly* 56(2): 83–89.

―――. 1984. "The Rites of Women: Oral Poetry, Ideology and the Socialization of Peasant Women in Contemporary Romania." *Journal of American Folklore* 97(384): 167–88. (Revised and reprinted in *Women, State and Party in Eastern Europe,* edited by S. Wolchik and A. Meyer. Durham, N.C.: Duke University Press, 1985.)

Konrad, G., and I. Szelenyi. 1976. "Social Conflicts of Underurbanization: The Hungarian Case." In *Social Consequences of Modernization in Communist Societies,* edited by M. Field, 162–80. Baltimore: Johns Hopkins University Press.

―――. 1979. *The Intellectuals on the Road to Class Power.* New York: Harcourt Brace Jovanovich.

Konstantinović, V. 1973. "The Abduction of a Bride as an Ethnosociological Phenomenon and Tradition Transformation Among the Peoples of Yugoslavia in the 20th Century." Paper presented at 9th International Congress of Anthropological and Ethnological Sciences.

Krimska-Ivanova, E. 1981. "Svatbeni oplakvanija v ruskija i bŭlgarskija folklor." *Bŭlgarski folklor* 7(1): 50–62.

Kronfeld, C. 1983. "Aspects of Poetic Metaphor." Dissertation, University of California-Berkeley.

Kruglov, Ju. 1978. *Russkie svadbenye pesni.* Moscow.

Kubler-Ross, E. 1969. *On Death and Dying.* New York: Macmillan.

Lakoff, G., and M. Johnson. 1980. *Metaphors We Live By.* Chicago: University of Chicago Press.

Lampe, J. 1975. "Varieties of Unsuccessful Industrialization: The Balkan States Before 1914." *Journal of Economic History* 35: 56–85.

Lamphere, L. 1974. "Strategies, Cooperation and Conflict Among Women in Domestic Groups." In *Women, Culture and Society,* edited by M. Rosaldo and L. Lamphere, 97–112. Stanford, Calif.: Stanford University Press.

Lampland, M. 1977. "Burning Away the Dawn: A Symbolic Analysis of Hungarian Wedding Rituals." Master's thesis, College of Liberal Arts, University of Minnesota.

―――. 1981. "Paint our Flags Red and Black: The Hungarian Revolt of 1956." Master's thesis, Department of Anthropology, University of Chicago.

Landes, J. 1977–78. "Women, Labor and Family Life: A Theoretical Perspective." *Science and Society* 41(4): 386–409.

Lane, C. 1981. *The Rites of Rulers: Ritual in Industrial Society—The Soviet Case.* Cambridge: Cambridge University Press.

LeGoff, J. 1984. *The Birth of Purgatory.* Translated by A. Goldhammer. Chicago: University of Chicago Press.

Leibman, R. 1972. "Wedding Customs in the Ohrid Village of Peštani." *Makedonski folklor* 5(9–10): 125–40.

Lenghel-Izanu, P. 1939. "Alimentaţia şi îmbrăcamintea în Bărsana, Maramureş." *Sociologie românească* 4(4–6):271–75.

———. 1973. "Clăcile şi şezătorile maramureşene." In *Comunicări ştiinţifice pe teme folclorice*. Baia Mare: Comitetul Pentru Cultură şi Educaţie Socialistă al Judeţului Maramureş.

Lévi-Strauss, C. 1966. *The Savage Mind*. Chicago: University of Chicago Press.

———. 1969. *The Elementary Structures of Kinship*. Rev. ed. Boston: Beacon Press.

———. 1970. *The Raw and the Cooked: Introduction to the Science of Mythology: 1*. New York: Harper Torchbooks.

Lévy-Bruhl, L. 1963. *L'âme primitive*. Paris: Presses Universitaires de France.

Lidtke, V. 1982. "Songs and Nazis: Political Music and Social Change in Twentieth-Century Germany." In *Essays on Culture and Society in Modern Germany*, edited by D. King et al., 167–200. College Station: Texas A&M University Press.

———. 1985. *The Alternative Culture: Socialist Labor in Imperial Germany*. Oxford: Oxford University Press.

Livezeanu, I. 1984. "Excerpts from a Troubled Book: An Episode in Romanian Literature." *Cross Currents* 3:297–319.

Lockwood, W. 1974. "Bride Theft and Social Maneuverability in Western Bosnia." *Anthropological Quarterly* 47(3):253–69.

MacArthur, M. 1981. "The Politics of Identity: Transylvanian Saxons in Socialist Romania." Dissertation. Department of Anthropology, University of Massachusetts-Amherst.

MacCormack, C. 1980. "Nature, Culture and Gender: A Critique." In *Nature, Culture and Gender*, edited by C. MacCormack and M. Strathern, 1–24. Cambridge: Cambridge University Press.

MacCormack, C., and M. Strathern, eds. 1980. *Nature, Culture and Gender*. Cambridge: Cambridge University Press.

McIntyre, R. 1975. "Pronatalist Policies in Eastern Europe." *Soviet Studies* 27(3):366–80.

Maltz, D. 1978. "The Bride of Christ Is Filled with His Spirit." In *Women in Ritual and Symbolic Roles*, edited by J. Hoch-Smith and A. Spring. New York: Plenum.

Manuscrisul de la Ieud. 1977. Edited by Mirela Teodorescu and I. Ghetie. Bucureşti: Editura Academiei Republicii Socialiste România.

Marian, S. F. 1890. *Nunta la români*. Bucureşti: Editura Academiei Române.

———. 1892. *Înmormîntarea la români*. Bucureşti: Editura Academiei Române.

———. 1893. *Vrăji, farmece, şi desfaceri*. Bucureşti: Carol Gobl.

———. 1898. *Sărbătorile la români*. Bucureşti: Editura Academiei Române.

Marrant, J. 1977. "The Idea of Folk Tradition in Romania." Dissertation, Department of Anthropology, University of Oregon.

Martin, E. 1985. "Good Death, Bad Death, and Gender in Chinese Society." Paper presented at the Joint Committee on Chinese Studies and American Council of Learned Societies Conference, Ritual and the Social Significance of Death in Chinese Society, Jan. 2–7.

Marx, K. [1867] 1957. *Capital.* Vol. 1. Translated by E. Paul and C. Paul. London: Dent.

Marx, K., and F. Engels. [1932] 1970. *The German Ideology.* New York: International.

Masson, D. 1982. *Les femmes de Breb (Maramureş, Roumanie).* Études et documents balkaniques 4. Paris: Laboratoire d'anthropologie sociale.

Matei, I., and I. Mihăilescu. 1985. *Satul românesc: Studii.* Bucureşti: Editura Academiei Republicii Socialiste România.

Mauss, M. 1950. "Une catégorie de l'esprit humain: la notion de personne, celle de 'moi'." In *Sociologie et anthropologie*, 333–63. Paris: Presses Universitaires de France.

———. 1967. *The Gift: Forms and Functions of Exchange in Archaic Societies.* Translated by I. Cunnison. New York and London: W. W. Norton.

Meillasoux, C. 1973. "The Social Organization of the Peasantry." *Journal of Peasant Studies* 1(1):81–90.

Meiţoiu, I. 1969. *Spectacolul nunţilor.* Bucureşti: Comitetul de Stat Pentru Cultură şi Artă.

Mihaly, I. 1900. *Diplome maramureşene din secolul XIV–XV.* Sighet.

———. 1934. *Reflexii asupra diplomelor maramureşene din secolul XIV–XV.* Sighet: Asociaţiunei Pentru Cultura Poporului Român din Maramureş.

Milosz, C. 1986. "An Interview with Czeslaw Milosz with N. Gardels." *New York Review of Books*, February 27, 1986.

Mintz, S. 1973. "A Note on the Definition of Peasantries." *Journal of Peasant Studies* 1(1):91–106.

Mintz, S., and E. Wolf. 1950. "An Analysis of Ritual Co-Parenthood (Compadrazgo)." *Southwestern Journal of Anthropology* 6(4):341–68.

Mitford, J. 1963. *The American Way of Death.* New York: Simon and Schuster.

Morariu, T. 1944. "Emigrări maramureşene în Transilvania." *Transilvania* 75: 667–77.

Moskoff, W. 1978. "Sex Discrimination, Commuting and the Role of Women in Romanian Development." *Slavic Review* 37(3):440–56.

———. 1980. "Pronatalist Policies in Romania." *Economic Development and Cultural Change* 28(3):597–614.

Mukařovský, J. 1979. *Aesthetic Function, Norm and Value as Social Facts.* Ann Arbor: University of Michigan Press.

Munn, N. 1974. "Symbolism in a Ritual Context: Aspects of Symbolic Action." In *Handbook of Social and Cultural Anthropology*, edited by J. Honigmann, 579–612. New York: Rand McNally.

Muşlea, I. 1972. "La mort-mariage: une particularité du folklore balkanique." *Cercetări etnografice şi de folclor.* Vol. 2: *Obiceiuri şi literatură populară*, 7–36. Bucureşti: Editura Minerva.

Muşlea, I., and O. Bîrlea. 1970. *Tipologia folclorului.* Bucureşti: Editura Minerva.

Musset, D. 1981. *Le mariage à Moiseni, Roumanie.* Études et documents balkaniques 3. Paris: Laboratoire d'anthropologie sociale.

Needham, R. 1972. *Belief, Language and Experience*. Chicago: University of Chicago Press.

Nenola-Kallio, A. 1982. *Studies in Ingrian Wedding Laments*. Helsinki: Suomalainen Tiedeakatemia, Academia Scientiarum Fennica.

Nistor, F. 1977. *Poarta maramureşeană*. Bucureşti: Editura Sport-Turism.

Nydon, J. 1984. "Public Policy and Private Fertility Behavior: The Case of Pronatalist Policy in Socialist Romania." Dissertation, Department of Anthropology, University of Massachusetts-Amherst.

Ortner, S. 1973. "On Key Symbols." *American Anthropologist* 75:1338–46.

———. 1974. "Is Female to Male as Nature Is to Culture?" In *Women, Culture and Society*, edited by M. Rosaldo and L. Lamphere, 67–88. Stanford, Calif.: Stanford University Press.

———. 1978. *Sherpas Through Their Rituals*. Cambridge: Cambridge University Press.

Ortony, A. 1979. *Metaphor and Thought*. Cambridge: Cambridge University Press.

Pamfile, T. 1913. *Agricultura la români*. Bucureşti: Socec.

———. 1914. *Sărbătorile la români*. Bucureşti: Socec.

Papahagi, T. 1925. *Graiul şi folclorul Maramureşului*. Bucureşti: Academia Română.

Pascu, S. 1944. *Istorie Transilvaniei: Transilvania în lumina datelor geopolitice, istorice, şi statistice*. Blaj: Lumina.

Peacock, J. 1968. *Rites of Modernization: Symbolic and Social Aspects of the Indonesian Proletarian Drama*. Chicago: University of Chicago Press.

Pine, F., and P. Bogdanowicz. 1980. "Policy, Response and Alternative Strategy: The Process of Change in a Polish Highland Village." *Dialectical Anthropology* 7(1):67–80.

Pliny the Elder. 1981. *Naturalis Historiae Libri XXXVII*.Book 7 in vol. 2. Biblioteca Teubneriana, no. 1651. Stuttgart: B. G. Teubner.

Pop, D. 1971. *Folcloristica Maramureşului*. Bucureşti: Editura Minerva.

Pop, M. 1958. "Măştile de lemn din Bîrseşti-Topeşti, Vrancea." *Revista de folclor* 3(1):7–22.

———. 1971. "Folclorul în contemporaneitate." *Revista de etnografie şi folclor* 16(5):351–68.

———. 1976. *Obiceiuri tradiţionale româneşti*. Bucureşti: Consiliul Culturii şi Educaţiei Socialiste.

Pop, M., and P. Ruxăndoiu. 1976. *Folclor literar românesc*. Bucureşti: Editura Didactică şi Pedagogică.

Pop-Cămpeanu, D. 1979. "Les fonctions signifiantes des costumes populaires roumains." *Buletinul Bibliotecii Române* 7(11):233–78.

Popa, R. 1970. *Ţara Maramureşului în veacul XIV-lea*. Bucureşti: Editura Academiei Republicii Socialiste România.

Puşcariu, I. 1900. *Metropolia românilor ortodocşi din Ungaria şi Transilvania*. Sibiu: Tipografia Archidiecesane.

Radcliffe-Brown, A. R. 1964. *The Andaman Islanders*. New York: Free Press.

Randall, S. 1983. "The Household Estate Under Socialism: The Theory and Practice of Socialist Transformation and the Political Economy of Upland Peasant Workers in Romania." Dissertation, Department of Anthropology, University of Massachusetts-Amherst.

Ratner, M. 1980. "Educational and Occupational Selection in Contemporary Romania: A Social Anthropological Account." Dissertation, Department of Anthropology, American University.

Reli, S. 1938. *Biserica ortodoxă română din Maramureş în vremurile trecute.* Cernăuţi: Editura Mitropoliei Bucovinei.

Rheubottom, D. 1980. "Dowry and Wedding Celebrations in Yugoslav Macedonia." In *The Meaning of Marriage Payments*, edited by J. L. Comaroff, 221–48. New York: Academic Press.

Richards, I. A. [1936] 1964. *The Philosophy of Rhetoric.* Oxford: Oxford University Press.

Ricoeur, P. 1977. *The Rule of Metaphor: Multidisciplinary Studies of the Creation of Meaning in Language.* Translated by R. Czerny et al. Toronto: University of Toronto Press.

Rîpă, I. 1972. "Balada 'Miorira' in colindele maramureşene." In *Comunicări ştiinţifice pe teme folclorice 1970–71*, edited by M. Cupcea, 86–91. Baia Mare: Comitetul Pentru Cultură şi Educaţiei Socialistă al Judeţului Maramureş.

Rosaldo, M. 1984. "Toward an Anthropology of Self and Feeling." In *Culture Theory: Essays on Mind, Self and Emotion*, edited by R. Shweder and R. LeVine, 137–57. Cambridge: Cambridge University Press.

Rosaldo, R. 1984. "Grief and a Headhunter's Rage: On the Cultural Force of the Emotions." In *Text, Play and Story: The Construction and Reconstruction of Self and Society, Proceedings*, edited by E. Bruner, 178–95. Washington, D.C.: American Ethnological Society.

Rosetti, A. 1975. *Limba descîntecelor româneşti.* Bucureşti: Editura Minerva.

Ruxăndoiu, P., ed. 1967. *Folclor poetic.* Vol. 1. Bucureşti: Societatea de ştinţe istorice şi filologice din Republica Socialistă România.

Sacks, S. 1978. *On Metaphor.* Chicago: University of Chicago Press.

Sahlins, M. 1981. *Historical Metaphors and Mythical Realities.* Ann Arbor: University of Michigan Press.

———. 1985. *Islands of History.* Chicago: University of Chicago Press.

Salzmann, Z. 1981. "Naming Persons in Bigăr, A Czech-speaking Village in the Southern Romanian Banat." *Working Papers in Sociolinguistics* 89:1–32.

Sampson, S. 1980. "National Integration Through Socialist Planning: An Anthropological Study of a Romanian New Town." Dissertation, Department of Anthropology, University of Massachusetts-Amherst.

———. 1982. *The Planners and the Peasants: An Anthropological Study of Urban Development in Romania.* South Jutland, Denmark: Institute of East-West Studies.

———. 1983. "Rich Families and Poor Collectives: An Anthropological Approach to Romania's 'Second Economy.'" *Bidrag til Ostatsforskning* 11(1):34–43.

Sanders, I. 1949. *Balkan Village.* Lexington, Ky.: Greenwood Press.

———. 1982. "Church-State Relationships in Southeastern Europe." *East European Quarterly* 16(1):59–71.

Scheper, G. 1971. "The Spiritual Marriage: The Exegetic History and Literary Impact of the Song of Songs in the Middle Ages." Dissertation, Princeton University.

Scheper-Hughes, N. 1979. *Saints, Scholars and Schizophrenics: Mental Illness in Rural Ireland.* Berkeley and Los Angeles: University of California Press.

Segalen, M. 1983. *Love and Power in the Peasant Family.* Translated by S. Matthews. Chicago: University of Chicago Press.

Senn, H. 1982. *Were-Wolf and Vampire in Romania.* Boulder, Colo.: East European Monographs.

Seton-Watson, R. 1963. *A History of the Roumanians: From Roman Times to the Completion of Unity.* (n.p.): Archon Books.

Shafir, M. 1985. *Romania: Politics, Economy and Society.* Boulder, Colo.: Lynne Rienner.

Shanin, T. 1979. "Defining Peasants: Conceptualizations and De-conceptualizations Old and New in a Marxist Debate." *Peasant Studies* 8:38–60.

Shils, E. 1981. *Tradition.* Chicago: University of Chicago Press.

Silverman, C. 1983. "The Politics of Folklore in Bulgaria." *Anthropological Quarterly* 56(2):55–61.

Silverstein, M. 1976. "Shifters, Linguistic Categories and Cultural Description." In *Meaning in Anthropology,* edited by K. Basso and H. Selby, 11–55. Albuquerque: University of New Mexico Press.

———. 1979. "Language Structure and Linguistic Ideology." In *The Elements: A Parasession on Linguistic Units and Levels,* edited by P. Clyne et al. Chicago: Chicago Linguistics Society.

———. 1981a. "Metaforces of Power in Traditional Oratory." Paper presented in the Department of Anthropology, University of Chicago.

———. 1981b. "Naming Sets Among the Worora." Paper presented in the Department of Anthropology, University of Chicago.

Simić, A. 1969. "Management of the Male Image in Yugoslavia." *Anthropological Quarterly* 42(2):89–101.

———. 1973. *The Peasant Urbanites.* New York: Seminar Press.

Simion, P. 1972. *Cimitirul vesel.* Bucureşti: Editura Pentru Turism.

Slavjanskaja, O. 1887. *Opisanie russkoj krestjanskoj svad'by s tekstom i pesnjami.* Moscow.

Sokolov, Y. 1950. *Russian Folklore.* New York: Macmillan.

Stahl, H. 1939. *Nerej: un village d'une région archaïque.* Vol. 2: *Les manifestations spirituelles.* Bucureşti: Institute des Sciences Sociales de Roumanie.

———. 1980. *Traditional Roumanian Village Communities: Subjection and Capitalist Penetration.* Translated by D. Chirot and H. C. Chirot. Cambridge: Cambridge University Press.

———. 1983. *Eseuri critice.* Bucureşti: Editura Minerva.

Stahl, P. 1973. "L'organisation magique du territoire villageois roumain." *L'homme* 13(3):150–62.

———. 1979a. "L'identité: quelques exemples balkaniques." In *Études et documents balkaniques: sociétés traditionnelles balkaniques,* 144–69. Paris: Laboratoire d'anthropologie sociale.

————. 1979b. "The Rumanian Farm Household and the Village Community." In *Anthropology and Social Change in Rural Areas,* edited by B. Berdichewsky, 235–43. The Hague: Mouton.

Staniloae, D. 1939. *Ortodoxie şi romanism.* Sibiu: Tipografia Arhidieceză.

Stoicescu, N. 1978. *Vlad Ţepeş—Prince of Walachia.* Bucureşti: Editura Academiei Republicii Socialiste România.

Stoker, B. 1897. *Dracula.* London: Constable.

Strathern, A. 1982. "Witchcraft, Greed, Cannibalism and Death: Some Related Themes from the New Guinea Highlands." In *Death and the Regeneration of Life,* edited by M. Bloch and J. Parry, 111–33. Cambridge: Cambridge University Press.

Suliţeanu, G. 1952. "Viaţa cîntecului popular în comuna Ieud." *Muzica* 2:78–79.

Sutherland, A. 1977. "The Body as Symbol Among the Rom." In *The Anthropology of the Body,* edited by J. Blacking, 375–90. New York: Academic Press.

Szelenyi, I. 1981. "Urban Development and Regional Management in Eastern Europe." *Theory and Society* 10(2):169–204.

————. 1982. "The Intelligentsia in the Class Structure of State-Socialist Societies." In *Marxist Inquiries,* edited by M. Burawoy and T. Skocpol, 287–326. Chicago: University of Chicago Press.

Şeuleanu, I. 1985. *Poezia populară de nuntă.* Bucureşti: Editura Minerva.

Ştefănescu, I. 1968. *Arta veche a Maramureşului.* Bucureşti: Editura Meridiane.

Ştefănescu, Ş. 1984. *Naţiunea română.* Bucureşti: Editura Ştiinţifică şi Enciclopedică.

Şter, I. 1980. *Antologie de folclor din judeţul Maramureş.* Vol. 1: *Poezia.* Baia Mare: Asociaţia Etnografilor şi Folcloriştilor din Judeţul Maramureş.

Tambiah, S. J. 1981. "A Performative Approach to Ritual." *Proceedings of the British Academy, London,* Vol. 65 (1979). London: British Academy.

Tănase, A., and E. Gheorghe, eds. 1984. *Dimensiuni şi funcţii ale culturii în socialism.* Bucureşti: Editura Academiei Republicii Socialiste România.

Thomas, L. V. 1980. *Anthropologie de la mort.* Paris: Payot.

Thompson, E. P. 1979. "Folklore, Anthropology and Social History." In *Studies in Labor History,* Brighton, Sussex: J. L. Noyce. (Reprinted from *Indian Historical Review* 3[2]:247–66, 1978.)

Todorov, T. 1982. *Symbolism and Interpretation.* Translated by C. Porter. Ithaca, N.Y.: Cornell University Press.

Traube, E. 1983. "Marcel Mauss and the Analysis of Gift-Exchange." Lecture presented at the University of Chicago.

Tucker, R. 1978. *The Marx-Engels Reader.* 2nd ed. New York: W. W. Norton.

Turner, T. 1976. "Family Structure and Socialization." In *Explorations in General Theory in Social Science,* Vol. 1, edited by J. Loubser. New York: Free Press.

————. 1977. "Transformation, Hierarchy and Transcendence: A Reformulation of Van Gennep's Model of the Structure of Rites of Passage." In *Secular Ritual,* edited by S. Moore and B. Meyerhoff, 53–70. Amsterdam: Van Gorcum.

————. n.d. "The Social Skin." Department of Anthropology, University of Chicago, photocopy.

Turner, V. 1969. *The Ritual Process.* Chicago: Aldine Press.

Turnock, D. 1974. *An Economic Geography of Romania.* London: Bell.

Twitchell, J. 1981. *The Living Dead: A Study of the Vampire in Romantic Literature.* Durham, N.C.: Duke University Press.

Țiplea, A. 1906. *Poezii populare din Maramureş.* Bucureşti: Academiei Române.

Vajda, M. 1981. *The State and Socialism.* Translated by Allison and Busby Ltd. New York: St. Martin's.

Valeri, V. 1980. "Notes on the Meaning of Marriage Prestations among the Huaulu of Seram." In *The Flow of Life: Essays on Eastern Indonesia,* edited by J. Fox, 128–92. Cambridge: Harvard University Press.

———. 1985. *Kingship and Sacrifice: Ritual and Society in Ancient Hawaii.* Chicago: University of Chicago Press.

Vancea de Buteasa, I. 1893. *Euchologiu.* Blasiu: Seminar Archidiecesana.

Van Gennep, A. 1946. *Manuel du folklore français contemporain.* Vol. 2: *Du berceau à la tombe.* Paris: Picard.

———. 1960. *The Rites of Passage.* Translated by M. B. Vizedom and G. L. Caffee. Chicago: University of Chicago Press.

Verdery, K. 1983a. *Transylvanian Villagers: Three Centuries of Political, Economic and Ethnic Change.* Berkeley and Los Angeles: University of California Press.

———. 1983b. "History as Fetish and Food as Symbol: The Collective Construction of Nationalist Culture in Romania." Paper presented at the annual meeting of the American Anthropological Association, Chicago.

———. 1985. "The Unmaking of an Ethnic Collectivity: Transylvania's Germans." *American Ethnologist* 12(1):62–83.

Vernant, J. P. 1981. "Death in Two Faces." In *Mortality and Immortality,* edited by S. Humphreys and H. King, 285–92. New York: Academic Press.

Vološinov, V. N. 1973. *Marxism and the Philosophy of Language.* Translated by L. Matejka and T. R. Titunik. New York: Seminar Press.

Vulpe, M. 1984. "Subdialectul maramureşean." In *Tratatul de dialectologie românească,* edited by V. Rusu, 320–53. Craiova: Scrisul Românesc.

Vulpesco, M. 1927. *Les coutumes roumaines périodiques.* Paris: Librairie Emile Larose.

Wallerstein, I. 1974. *The Modern World System: Capitalist Agriculture and the Origins of the European World Economy in the 16th Century.* New York: Academic Press.

Warner, W. 1959. *The Living and the Dead: A Study of the Symbolic Life of Americans.* New Haven, Conn.: Yale University Press.

Weber, E. 1976. *Peasants into Frenchmen: The Modernization of Rural France 1870–1914.* Stanford, Calif.: Stanford University Press.

Weiner, A. 1980. "Reproduction: A Replacement for Reciprocity." *American Ethnologist* 7(1):71–84.

Williams, R. 1977. *Marxism and Literature.* Oxford: Oxford University Press.

Wolf, L. 1975. *The Annotated Dracula.* New York: Ballantine Books.

Index